Introduction to Positive Psychology

William C. Compton
Middle Tennessee State University

THOMSON
WADSWORTH

Australia • Canada • Mexico • Singapore • Spain
United Kingdom • United States

THOMSON
WADSWORTH

This book is dedicated to my wife, Barbara Whiteman, Ed.D.
Her life is a remarkable demonstration of how virtues such as compassion, empathy, and a sense of humor can create positive emotions in others—especially those who are lucky enough to know her well.

Publisher / Executive Editor: *Vicki Knight*
Editorial Assistant: *Monica Sarmiento*
Technology Project Manager: *Darin Derstine*
Marketing Manager: *Dory Schaeffer*
Marketing Assistant: *Laurel Anderson*
Advertising Project Manager: *Brian Chaffee*
Project Manager, Editorial Production: *Megan E. Hansen*
Art Director: *Vernon Boes*
Print/Media Buyer: *Lisa Claudeanos*
Permissions Editor: *Stephanie Lee*
Production Service: *Gretchen Otto, G&S Book Services*
Compositor: *G&S Book Services*
Copy Editor: *Karen Boyd*
Cover Designer: *Andy Norris*
Cover Art: *Digital Stock*
Printer: *Malloy Incorporated*

Printed in the United States of America
1 2 3 4 5 6 7 08 07 06 05 04

For more information about our products, contact us at:
Thomson Learning Academic Resource Center
1-800-423-0563
For permission to use material from this text or product, submit a request online at **http://www.thomsonrights.com.**
Any additional questions about permissions can be submitted by email to **thomsonrights@thomson.com.**

Library of Congress Control Number: 2004104480

ISBN 0-534-64453-8

Thomson Wadsworth
10 Davis Drive
Belmont, CA 94002-3098
USA

Asia
Thomson Learning
5 Shenton Way #01-01
UIC Building
Singapore 068808

Australia/New Zealand
Thomson Learning
102 Dodds Street
Southbank, Victoria 3006
Australia

Canada
Nelson
1120 Birchmount Road
Toronto, Ontario M1K 5G4
Canada

Europe/Middle East/Africa
Thomson Learning
High Holborn House
50/51 Bedford Row
London WC1R 4LR
United Kingdom

DR. H. NOICE

Brief Contents

Contents

Preface

One of the most enduring pursuits throughout the entire history of humanity has been the search for well-being, happiness, and the good life. It takes only a minor excursion into human history to realize that the answers to this question have been extraordinarily diverse: some people have pursued sensual pleasure, others have sought love and the joys of intimate relationships. Still others have worked toward the actualization of their potentials, while some have searched for the peace of contemplative spirituality. In spite of the importance of this search, the question of how to define and how to actualize these goals remains one of the most persistent puzzles even today. In spite of the many solutions offered throughout history, the question "What is happiness?" still plagues many people today. Positive psychology is the newest effort to answer that question.

Chapter 1 is an introduction to this new focus area of psychology. Positive psychology is defined in this brief introduction, certain assumptions that are common among positive psychologists are described, and a very brief history of how the Western world has defined well-being is presented. Chapter 2 reviews basic psychological research on positive emotion and intrinsic motivation. Therefore, these first two chapters present a very brief introduction to the theoretical and research contexts from which the new field of positive psychology has emerged and is evolving today.

The next four chapters cover a number of perspectives that all place a major emphasis on *positive emotional states.* Of course, in many ways most of the theories and perspectives in positive psychology place a good deal of emphasis on positive emotions. The perspectives discussed in these chapters, however, tend to define well-being or the good life in terms of a specific emotion or a cluster of emotional experiences. The perspectives discussed in this section have all, in one way or another, focused on positive emotional states as the primary way to study well-being and as one of the best indicators of the good life.

Chapter 3 reviews research in subjective well-being. Investigations into subjective well-being look at the predictors, causes, and consequences of happiness and satisfaction with life. These studies very directly try to answer the age-old question, "What is happiness?" Chapter 4 covers studies that look at leisure, play, and what makes a person feel as if he or she is having fun. In addition, it covers aspects of peak performance and optimal experiencing. Chapter 5 takes a look at the feelings of love and emotional intimacy. In the world today, the experiences of love and intimacy are one of the most frequently desired elements of the good life. The chapter covers theoretical perspectives on love, as well as some possible predictors of both marital satisfaction and marital stability. Chapter 6 reviews a number of perspectives on wellness, health, and positive coping skills. The emotional experiences that will be of interest in that chapter include a zest for life, a sense of physical vitality, and the ability to feel relaxed, contented, and free of stress. In addition, Chapter 6 will explore the influence of psychoneuroimmunology—an area that looks at how certain emotions, such as optimism and laughter, are important to immune system functioning.

The next four chapters explore research and theory that focus on the development and nurturance of *positive traits.* These perspectives all describe well-being in terms of certain consistencies in behavior that can be observed over time and over different situations. Of course, someone who is generally happy also exhibits consistency in his or her emotional responses. Perspectives in these chapters, however, all study well-being by measuring personality traits, virtues, or other behavioral consistencies rather than focusing on the measurement of specific emotions. Of course, both behavior and emotion are important to well-being. The distinction being made here between research studies is one of emphasis, not exclusion. The chapters in this section cover a fairly wide range of perspectives on well-being.

Chapter 7 looks at states of excellence, creativity, and how a sense of aesthetics can enhance an appreciation of life. Chapter 8 is a quick overview of the ways in which psychology has tried to define positive mental health. This chapter also covers some recent finding relevant to positive mental health and resilience at different points in the life span. Chapter 9 looks at how psychologists have been trying to create new styles of assessment and psychotherapy in order to help people create positive personality traits that are habits of behavior. Last, Chapter 10 looks at one of the oldest institutions for helping people bring positive traits into their lives—religion and spirituality. In sum, many of the theoretical perspectives in this section have attempted to produce models of what human beings are like when talents, strengths, virtues, and positive character traits are habits of behavior rather than occasional visitors.

Chapter 11 covers topics relevant to another major focus area of positive psychology—the development of positive institutions. When most people think of psychology, they think of the study of persons or individuals. What is often lost when focusing on individuals is the very obvious fact that people exist in groups and those groups make up families, neighborhoods, communities, and societies. Therefore, the topics covered in Chapter 11 include discussions of job satisfaction, community psychology, and the cultural factors that may impact a sense of well-being. The book ends with a final chapter on the future of positive psychology. I hope you enjoy this all-too-brief exploration of the fascinating new area of positive psychology.

Acknowledgments

I have been fascinated with how people define and pursue psychological well-being for the past thirty-five years. When I decided to pursue this interest through the discipline of psychology, I found very few psychologists who recognized the value of a career based on the study of positive psychological development. Luckily, I have managed to find a few mentors that helped to validate my interests and encouraged me to continue my studies. Thomas Roberts at Northern Illinois University, Gordon Becker at the University of Nebraska–Omaha, and Jules Seeman at George Peabody College of Vanderbilt University provided me with encouragement and role models of how psychologists can focus their careers on the study of psychological well-being.

I would also like to thank my colleagues at Middle Tennessee State University: Tom Brinthaupt, Jerden Johnson, Rick Moffett, and Greg Schmidt, who reviewed earlier drafts of the chapters or made very helpful suggestions about relevant research literature. A special thanks goes to another of my colleagues, Janet Belsky. Janet has been such an enthusiastic supporter of this book that I might have given up my efforts to get it into print were it not for her efforts. Janet, I can't thank you enough!

In addition, I would also like to thank the Committee on Non-Instruction Assignments at MTSU for granting me a sabbatical leave to begin writing this book. Later, another grant from the Faculty Research Committee at MTSU allowed me to continue work on the manuscript.

Appreciation is also extended to Jason Long, who did much of the research on Web sites related to positive psychology. Dustin Thoman provided extraordinary assistance and enthusiasm with all manner of necessary research tasks (good luck in your doctoral program Dustin—you will be a great psychologist). In addition, the efforts of CoTonya Mitchell and Karen Nunley are gratefully acknowledged. The students who have taken my Psychology of Happiness and Well-being course since 1992 also deserve thanks for their interest, questions, and enthusiasm for a positive approach to psychology. The contributions of my nephew, Dave Compton, are also gratefully acknowledged. Dave carefully reviewed much of the manuscript for grammatical and stylistic errors. Thanks, Dave! Thanks to Jessica Willard for the name index (good luck in graduate school).

For their help and careful attention to the quality of this book, I am grateful to my publisher at Wadsworth, Vicki Knight, and to the many others who worked on the production of this book.

This book is also much better than it would have been otherwise because of the valuable comments provided by several reviewers. They are James Davis at Drury University, Michael Sakuma at Dowling College, and Janice M. Vidic at University of Rio Grande, as well as other reviewers who wished to remain anonymous.

About the Author

William Compton has had a fascination with and enthusiasm for ideas about psychological well-being for over 35 years. He began his search in a somewhat unusual place for a future psychologist—as a Far Eastern Studies major at the University of Wisconsin-Madison studying Eastern religions. Seeking a more applied and practical approach to well-being, he entered psychology and received his doctorate in clinical psychology from George Peabody College of Vanderbilt University in 1987. He worked as a psychotherapist until joining the psychology faculty at Middle Tennessee State University in 1989. Soon after joining the faculty, he created a course on the psychology of well-being—at that time, one of the only courses of its kind offered in American universities. Six years later, much of the same material offered in this course would be gathered together under a new research banner called positive psychology which was created by Martin E. P. Seligman. Compton is extremely grateful to Seligman and the other founders of positive psychology for fostering a new recognition of well-being in psychology. Throughout his career as an academic psychologist, Compton has published papers that focused on various aspects of positive mental health. This is his first book.

PART

i

POSITIVE PSYCHOLOGY FOUNDATIONS

CHAPTER 1

An Introduction to Positive Psychology

> Psychology is not just the study of weakness and damage; it is also the study of strength and virtue. Treatment is not just fixing what is broken; it is nurturing what is best within us.
>
> *Martin E. P. Seligman*

Welcome to Positive Psychology!

In 1998, Martin E. P. Seligman, who was then president of the American Psychological Association, urged psychologists to remember psychology's forgotten mission: to build human strength and nurture genius. In order to remedy this omission from psychology, Seligman deliberately set out to create a new direction and new orientation for psychology. He called this new focus area **positive psychology.** Many psychologists saw his challenge to increase research on human strengths and psychological well-being as a welcome opportunity.

Definition of Positive Psychology

In the most general terms, positive psychology uses psychological theory, research, and intervention techniques to understand the positive, the adaptive, the creative, and the emotionally fulfilling elements of human behavior. In their introduction to a special issue of the *American Psychologist* on positive psychology, Kennon Sheldon and Laura King (2001) describe **positive psychology** as follows:

> What is positive psychology? It is nothing more than the scientific study of ordinary human strengths and virtues. Positive psychology revisits "the average person" with an interest in finding out what works, what's right, and what's improving. It asks, "What is the nature of the efficiently functioning human being, successfully applying evolved adaptations and learned skills? And how can psychologists explain the fact that despite all the difficulties, the majority of people manage to live lives of dignity and purpose?" . . . Positive psychology is thus an attempt to urge psychologists to adopt a more open and appreciative perspective regarding human potentials, motives, and capacities (p. 216).

Therefore, positive psychology studies what people do right and how they manage to do it. This includes what they do for themselves, for their families, and for their communities. In addition, positive psychology helps people develop those qualities that lead to greater fulfillments for themselves and for others. Sheldon, Frederickson, Rathunde, Csikszentmihalyi, and Haidt (2000) provide another prospective: they define positive psychology as "the scientific study of optimal human functioning. It aims to discover and promote factors that allow individuals, communities, and societies to thrive and flourish."

The Dimensions of Positive Psychology

The range of possible interest areas in positive psychology is quite large; however, some broad dimensions have been used to define the new area in a general way. In order to nurture talent and make life more fulfilling, positive psychology focuses on three areas of human experience (Seligman & Csikszentmihalyi, 2000) that help to define the scope and orientation of a positive psychology perspective.

1. At the subjective level, positive psychology looks at *positive subjective states* or positive emotions such as happiness, joy, satisfaction with life, relaxation, love, intimacy, and contentment. Positive subjective states also can include constructive thoughts about the self and the future, such as optimism and hope. Positive subjective states may also include feelings of energy, vitality, and confidence, or the effects of positive emotions such as laughter.
2. At the individual level, positive psychology focuses on a study of *positive individual traits,* or the more enduring and persistent behavior patterns seen in people over time. This study might include individual traits such as courage, persistence, honesty, or wisdom. That is, positive psychology includes the study of positive behaviors and traits that historically have been used to define "character strengths" or virtues. It can also include the ability to develop aesthetic sensibility or tap into creative potentials and the drive to pursue excellence.
3. Last, at the group or societal level, positive psychology focuses on the development, creation, and maintenance of *positive institutions.* In this area, positive psychology addresses issues such as the development of civic virtues, the creation of healthy families, the study of healthy work environments, and positive communities. Positive psychology may also be involved in investigations that look at how institutions can work better to support and nurture all of the citizens they impact.

Therefore, in many ways, the focus of positive psychology is the scientific study of positive human functioning and flourishing at a number of levels, such as the biological, personal, relational, institutional, cultural, and global (Seligman & Csikszentmihalyi, 2000).

The Scope of Positive Psychology

These definitions and dimensions give a general sense of positive psychology. It will be helpful to give a partial list of topics that may be studied by a positive psychologist (a complete or comprehensive list would be quite exhaustive). Evidently, people are quite good at doing things well. In fact, the ways in which a person can excel is much more extensive than has been recognized in psychology.

With that introduction, here is an A to Z list of possible topics: altruism and empathy, building enriching communities, creativity, forgiveness and compassion, the role of positive emotions in job satisfaction, the enhancement of immune system functioning, lifespan models of positive personality development, styles of psychotherapy that emphasize accomplishments and positive traits, savoring each fleeting moment of life, strengthening the virtues as way to increase authentic happiness, and the psychological benefits of Zen meditation (see Snyder & Lopez, 2002; Aspinwall & Straudinger, 2003; www.positivepsychology.org). One of positive psychology's early accomplishments was to help psychologists pay attention *to what people do right.* Once psychologists began to notice the many ways that human beings succeed in life, these neglected aspects of behavior became the focus of theory, research, and intervention strategies. At this point, it is helpful to discuss why the perspective of positive psychology is needed today. This will be followed by a discussion of related themes and assumptions that contribute to a conceptualization of the good life and to positive psychology.

Why Positive Psychology Is Needed Today

Psychology has not always focused on the adaptable, the healthy, and the positive aspects of humanity. In fact, for many years professional psychology largely ignored the study of the positive side of human behavior. Seligman (2000) noted that prior to World War II there were only three major missions in psychology: to cure mental illness, to find and nurture genius and talent, and to make normal life more fulfilling.

Early Missions of Psychology

The first early mission was to *cure mental illness.* The terrible consequences of mental illness for many people, their families, and the community demanded that psychology use the methods of science to seek solutions to this problem. Over the years, psychology and medicine have been remarkably successful. In the early 1950s, no real cures existed for the major types of mental illness. Today, there are real cures for many types of mental illness, such as panic disorder and depression, and highly effective treatments exist for others, such as schizophrenia and bipolar disorder (Seligman, 1994).

The second early mission of psychology was to *find and nurture genius and talent.* Many of the early studies in this area focused on the development of intelligence. Other researchers studied how changes in the environments of schools, the workplace, and families could help human beings to be more creative and find latent and yet untapped potentials. While considerable work has been done in terms of this mission, few studies have looked at how to nurture genius and talent. This second mission for psychology has been relatively ignored over the years.

The third early mission of psychology was to *make normal life more fulfilling.* Obviously, there is more to living a satisfied and happy life than simply getting one's immediate needs met in a reasonable amount of time. People need challenges, tasks that test their skills, opportunities for learning new ideas and developing talents, as well as the freedom to reinvent themselves throughout their lives. However, just as with the nurturing of genius, the creation of more life fulfillment was, unfortunately, largely ignored as psychology concentrated on other areas of research. For instance, while the accomplishments in finding treatments for mental illness were impressive, from a practical standpoint their achievement was to help people move from a state of negative emotionality to what might be described as a state of neutral emotionality. The question of how one moved from the neutral position to a positive place of enhanced adaptability, well-being, and happiness was not central to the direction that psychology was then taking. Much of the emphasis in positive psychology is to remedy the relative neglect of these areas. It has taken up the challenge to focus attention on how to nurture genius and talent as well as how to help people lead lives that are more fulfilling.

Importance of Positive Emotions to Both Mental and Physical Health

Positive psychology is also needed today because scientific research is revealing how important positive emotions and adaptive behaviors are to living a satisfying and productive life. For much of the twentieth century, many scientists assumed that the study of positive emotions was somewhat frivolous at best and probably unnecessary. Many assumed that psychology should focus on more pressing social problems, such as drug abuse, criminal behavior, or the treatment of serious psychological disorders like depression. This assumption is only partially correct. It is quite true that psychology does need to study serious social and psychological problems. In fact, positive psychologists do not reject the need to study and attempt to eliminate the terrible social and personal costs of these problems. Recent research, however, suggests that the study of positive emotions can actually help to fight these problems. For instance, some newer forms of psychotherapy focus on the development of positive emotions and adaptive coping strategies rather than focusing on negative emotions, internal conflicts, and anxieties formed in childhood. These forms of psychotherapy can be quite successful in helping people emerge from debilitating psychological problems (see Chapter 8).

Recent studies also support the important influence that positive emotions and adaptive behavior have on a number of positive outcomes in life. People who experience and express positive emotions more often are likely to be satisfied with their lives and have more rewarding interpersonal relationships. They are more productive and satisfied at their job, are helpful to other people, and are more likely to reach desired goals in life (Diener, Suh, Lucas, & Smith, 1999). Interestingly, people who experience and express positive emotions often are also more likely to be physically healthier, more resistant to illness, and may even live longer than others (Danner, Snowdon, & Friesen, 2001). Therefore, the study of positive emotions and adaptive behavior can offer real benefits to learning how to build more fulfilling lives, both by helping people reach their potentials and by helping to eliminate negative emotions and problematic behaviors.

Positive psychology represents another direction for psychology by focusing investigations of who we are as human beings in more positive directions. In some ways, positive psychology is an attitude that people can take to research, to other people, and to themselves. With this in mind, a person may reasonably ask, just what are the ideas and attitudes that help shape positive psychology? The next section describes a number of the basic themes and perspectives that have helped to create and shape positive psychology today.

Basic Themes and Assumptions of Positive Psychology

The Good Life

One of the major themes that define positive psychology is a focus on the elements and predictors of the *good life*. The term "good life" may be somewhat unfamiliar to many students of psychology. The only connection that some people have with this phrase comes from its popular use of the term as a reference to having extreme wealth, power, prestige, and beauty. That use of the phrase "the good life" is quite incorrect, however. In fact, the idea of the good life comes from philosophical speculations about what holds the greatest value in life or what is the nature of the highest or most important "good." When we apply this idea to human life, "the **good life**" refers to the factors that contribute most to a well-lived and fulfilling life. Nicholas Dent says, "Things that are good may also be considered from the point of view of how they will contribute to a well-spent or happy human life. The idea of a complete good is that which will wholly satisfy the complete need and destiny of humans, the *summum bonum*" (in Honderich, 1995, p. 322). Qualities that help define the good life are those that enrich our lives, make life worth living, and foster strong character. Seligman (2002a) defines the good life as "using your signature strengths every day to produce authentic happiness and abundant gratification" (p. 13).

In positive psychology, the good life has been seen as a combination of three elements: *positive connections to others, positive individual traits, and life regulation qualities.* Aspects of our behavior that contribute to forging *positive connections to others* can include the ability to love, the presence of altruistic concerns, the ability to forgive, and the presence of spiritual connections to help create a sense of deeper meaning and purpose in life. *Positive individual traits* can include, among other elements, a sense of integrity, the ability to play and be creative, and the presence of virtues such as courage and humility. Finally, *life regulation qualities* are those that allow us to regulate our day-to-day behavior in such a way that we can accomplish our goals while helping to enrich the people and institutions that we encounter along the way. These qualities include a sense of individuality or autonomy, a high degree of healthy self-control, and the presence of wisdom as a guide to behavior.

In summary, one of the distinguishing features of positive psychology is a focus on what constitutes the type of life for human beings that leads to the greatest sense of well-being, satisfaction or contentment, and the good life. In addition, positive psychology views the good life not just as an individual achievement that is removed from the social context. On the contrary, if it is to be a worthwhile definition of "the good," the good life must include relationships with other people and with the society as a whole. The definition of the good life has so far been rather broad and somewhat abstract. The rest of this book will flesh out some of the finer points and details that go into ideas about the good life.

Past Assumptions about Human Behavior

For a number of years, much research in psychology was based on the assumption that human beings are driven by base motivations such as aggression, egoistic self-interest, and the pursuit of simple pleasures. Because many psychologists began with that assumption, they inadvertently designed research studies that supported their own prior assumptions. Therefore, the older view of humanity was of a species that barely keeps its aggressive tendencies in check and manages to live in social groups more out of motivated self-interest than out of a genuine affinity for others or a true sense of community. Both Sigmund Freud and the early behaviorists believed the humans were motivated primarily by selfish drives. From that perspective, social interaction was possible only by exerting control over those baser emotions. Therefore, people were always vulnerable to eruptions of violence, greed, and selfishness. The fact that humans actually lived together in social groups was seen as a tenuous arrangement that was always just one step away from violence.

An unfortunate offshoot of this assumption was the idea that people are motivated by a "survival of the fittest" mentality. This theory of social behavior has been termed Social Darwinism. Darwin, however, never proposed this theory! It was, in fact, created by nineteenth and early twentieth century thinkers who wished to support the current social hierarchy. They sought to find in Darwin's theory a way to justify social disparities by saying that those who had more wealth and power deserved to have it because they were the "fittest" (Honderich, 1995). However, psychological theory has never subscribed to this idea, and positive psychology certainly does not either.

People Are Highly Adaptive and Desire Positive Social Relationships

A new vision of human beings has been emerging from psychological research. According to these newer perspectives, socialization and the ability to live in groups are highly adaptable traits (Buss, 2000). Newer psychological thinking views the ability to interact peaceably in social groups as a trait that would actually enhance the evolutionary advantage of the species. That is, as the human race developed, those people who could live together in groups would have an advantage over those who could not. Therefore, they would be more likely to survive and pass on their genetic material to their children.

People Can Thrive and Flourish

Positive psychology seeks to investigate what people do *correctly* in life. As in Sheldon and King (2001)'s definition, positive psychology recognizes that many people adapt and adjust to life in highly creative ways that allow them, and those they come in contact with, to feel good about life. All too often, psychological research displays a blatant bias toward assuming that people are unwitting pawns to their biology, their childhood, or their unconscious. Positive psychology takes the position that in spite of the very real difficulties of life, we must acknowledge that most people do quite well. Most people at least try to be good parents, to treat others with some degree of respect, to love those close to them, to find ways to contribute to society and the welfare of others, and to live their lives with integrity and honesty. These achievements should be celebrated rather than explained away as "nothing but" biological urges or unconscious attempts to ward off anxiety and fear.

In addition, while knowledge of how people adjust well to life's ups and downs is extremely important, in the past psychology paid less attention to how people move beyond simple adjustment to actually flourishing and thriving in the face of change. That is, some people do not just adapt to life—they adapt extraordinarily well. Some adapt so well that they serve as role models of incredible resiliency, perseverance, and fortitude. One of the goals of positive psychology is to understand how those people manage to accomplish such high levels of thriving and flourishing.

It is interesting to note that some of these ideas are even beginning to move into the offices of psychotherapists as they work with people experiencing psychological distress (see Chapter 9). For instance, Volney Gay (2001) has recently challenged the idea that the repression of negative experiences during childhood is the primary factor in the development of adult psychological distress. Gay's argument is that the anxiety, depression, and worry that go along with adult distress actually occur because people cannot recollect joy, which in turn leads to a retreat from active participation in life. Therefore, the real work of the psychotherapist is to help her or his clients reconnect with and rekindle the joy in life that has been hidden and suppressed.

Strengths and Virtues Are Central to Well-Being

Another distinguishing feature of positive psychology is that discussions of virtues and what used to be called "good character" are important to conceptualizations of the good life. Positive psychology recognizes that any discussion of what constitutes the good life must inevitably touch on virtues, values, and character development. It is not possible to discuss the dimensions of an admirable and fulfilling life without introducing discussions of virtues such as honesty, fidelity, or courage. This is not to say that positive psychologists advocate certain virtues and values simply because they personally admire them. Science cannot address in any ultimate or absolute sense what values a person *must* believe in or practice in her or his life. Science will never be able to say, for instance, that everyone *should* value happiness as the ultimate goal of life. However, a science of positive psychology does have a role in the investigation of values.

Over thirty years ago, M. Brewster Smith (1969) said that psychology cannot decide which values are "best." What psychology can do is investigate the consequences of holding certain values. For instance, psychology can use scientific methods to investigate the consequences of living a life based on the values of honesty, integrity, tolerance, and self-control. In addition, scientific methods can be applied in any cultural setting or in any society around the world to discover what values tend to enhance the quality of life for everyone in a community. Therefore, the consequences of holding certain social values can be investigated within that specific culture. In addition, scientific methods can be used to investigate the possibility that certain values are found almost universally and, therefore, may represent a common core of virtues that have grounded many cultures over time (see Chapter 8).

Persons Exist in Social Contexts

A final theme of positive psychology is the recognition that people exist in social contexts and that well-being is not just an individual pursuit. Of course, positive psychology is not alone in recognizing the importance of the social context for human behavior. What positive psychology has done is to embrace ideas about positive social environments, such as social well-being and empowerment. Many of these ideas were adopted from community psychology (see Chapter 11), but many positive psychologists have welcomed them. For instance, Corey L. M. Keyes & Shane Lopez (Keyes, 1998; Keys & Lopez, 2002) have argued that a complete classification system for mental health should include three general components: emotional well-being, psychological well-being, and social well-being.

Related to this idea is the recognition that differences may exist in how cultures conceptualize, encourage, or teach their children about the nature of happiness and the good life (see Matsumoto, 1994). In general, the search for happiness is a universal quest. Nonetheless, a fascinating variety of ideas about the specific nature of happiness exists among cultures of the world. One of the more prominent distinctions is between cultures that view happiness as an emotion that individuals achieve through their own unique efforts and those that view it as a more collective experience—a joint product of persons and their immediate family environments. (These distinctions will be covered in more detail in Chapter 11.) Positive psychology, as well as all of psychology, is beginning to explore cross-cultural comparisons that may enhance our understanding of how people throughout the world experience psychological well-being.

Assumptions about Human Emotions

The Predictors of Positive Emotions Are Unique

Another basic theme in positive psychology concerns the relationships between positive emotional states and well-being. Psychologists used to assume that, if a person could eliminate their negative emotions, then positive emotions would automatically take their place. Indeed, many people who hope to win large sums of money on the lottery are driven by this assumption. They assume that money will eliminate negative emotions such as worry and desire, and then they will be happy. In reality, while the elimination of distressful and debilitating negative emotions is a worthy goal for psychology, when it is accomplished positive emotions are not the inevitable result. After negative emotions are gone, what remains for many people might be termed a state of neutral emotionality. In order to move from a neutral position to more positive emotions, some other procedures need to be followed.

Michael Argyle (1987) illustrates this point. He noted that the probability of experiencing negative emotionality is predicted by a number of factors, such as unemployment, high stress, and low economic status. It should be quite apparent, however, that happiness and psychological well-being are not automatically achieved when a person has a job, is under normal stress levels, and is middle class. Under those circumstances, a person feels better but is not necessarily as happy as he or she could be. Just eliminating one's negative feelings does not automatically create human strengths, virtues, and the capacity to thrive and flourish. Just because someone is relatively free of anxiety, depression, and worry, they do not automatically exhibit inspiring instances of courage, self-sacrifice, honesty, and integrity. Another example comes from Christopher Peterson and his colleagues (Peterson et al., 2000 cited in Peterson & Steen, 2002). Their study of pessimism and optimism showed that optimism was reliably associated with positive mood. If someone was optimistic, then he or she tended to also experience positive moods. However, the degree of pessimism had no significant link to mood. People who tended toward pessimism could be in bad moods or fairly neutral moods. Therefore, simply decreasing a person's degree of pessimism may have no major impact on whether a person feels happy or not. It may only make them less pessimistic. To increase positive mood, a person has to increase optimism in addition to decreasing pessimism. So, while some of the predictors of positive emotionality and negative emotions are similar, they are not identical. There are unique psychological processes that help a person move from feeling negative emotions such as anxiety and depression to a position of neutral emotionality. At the same time, other equally unique psychological processes help a person move from neutral emotionality to greater happiness, life satisfaction, and joy in life. Many of these positive psychological processes will be the subjects of the chapters to follow.

All Positive Emotions Are Not the Same

Enjoyment and Pleasure At this point, some readers may ask, is positive psychology then simply a way to help people feel good all the time? Can we sum up positive psychology with the popular phrase, "If it feels good, do it!"? Many scientists are fond of saying that the basic motivating factor in behavior—human and nonhuman alike—is the desire to avoid pain and find pleasure. Could this, in fact, be the secret of a fulfilled and happy life? Is the goal of life simply to find as much pleasure and as little pain as possible? Is the highest good simply defined as pleasure? A few distinctions between the types of positive emotions may be helpful in answering these questions.

Mihayi Csikszentmihalyi (1990) said that **pleasure** can be defined as the good feeling that comes from satisfying needs and meeting expectations. These expectations can come from our biological needs for rest, food, or sex, for example. They can also come from social conditioning. This type of pleasure might come from obtaining socially desirable status symbols. While pleasurable experiences can be fun and can add some positive experiences to our life, they often do not produce any psychological growth or development. Pleasurable experiences must be continually renewed. Nonetheless, pleasure is undoubtedly important to life satisfaction.

Seligman (2002a) made a distinction between bodily pleasures and the higher pleasures. *Bodily pleasures* are based on biological needs, such as the examples given above. *Higher pleasures* are experiences that feel good but are also more cognitively complex and tend to have a more lasting effect on mood. Examples of the higher pleasures include joy, vigor, mirth, and excitement. These all involve cognitive operations as well as the stimulation of bodily pleasure. The question of real interest is how experiences are interpreted and made meaningful.

In general, the simple proposition that we behave in order to increase physiological pleasure and to avoid physiological pain is violated frequently enough that it simply cannot serve as the ultimate basis for any serious inquiry into the good life or psychological well-being (Parrott, 1993). If the good life cannot consist solely of pleasure, then what about enjoyment? How does enjoyment differ from pleasure?

Csikszentmihalyi (1990) said that **enjoyment** involves meeting expectations or fulfilling a need and then going beyond those expectations to create something new, unexpected, or even unimagined. Enjoyment has within it the sense of accomplishment and novelty. Enjoyment creates something new and expands our possibilities and potentials. Therefore, one of the tasks of positive psychology is to investigate how people create *both* pleasurable experiences *and* a deeper sense of enjoyment in life. Further, positive psychology seeks to find out how episodes of enjoyment throughout life can help to create a sense that life has been lived well.

Hedonic and Eudaimonic Well-Being

The distinction between pleasure and enjoyment is related to another major theme that is often found in positive psychology. This is the difference between hedonic and eudaimonic conceptualizations of well-being (eudaimonia can also be spelled as eudaemonia). As has been suggested, definitions of what constitutes the good life are numerous and are focused on an amazing variety of goals. In an attempt to bring some order to this variety, researchers have attempted to identify subgroupings of the ways in which people define and pursue well-being. One of these groupings that are seen frequently in positive psychology research is between hedonic and eudaimonic approaches to well-being (Ryan & Deci, 2001).

The *hedonic approach* is similar to, but not identical to, the perspective on pleasure that was discussed above. Hedonism is one of the oldest approaches to a definition of the good life, and it focuses on pleasure as the good life's basic component. Hedonism in its narrowest and most restricted form is the belief that the pursuit of well-being is fundamentally the pursuit of individual sensual pleasures. While the single-minded pursuit of pleasure is one of the oldest approaches to the good life, this form of hedonism has been seen as self-defeating and unworkable by most societies throughout history. Nearly everyone realizes that sensual pleasures are short-lived, that they result in a constant struggle to repeat them, and that when focused on exclusively they produce no lasting changes in personality and no personal growth. The hedonic approach, however, does not have to be simple self-indulgence or a "me first" attitude toward life.

The broader form of hedonism, however, includes the idea that pleasure is the basic motivating force behind most human behaviors but also recognizes that certain pleasures require positive social interactions with other people. For instance, some variations of the hedonic approach view family life or civic involvement as ways to maximize pleasure and contentment for all people involved. Applying this more "civilized" definition of **hedonic well-being** to the good life, the goal is to create high levels of happiness for oneself and for other people. This form of hedonism has been a basic assumption behind many conceptualizations of the good life throughout history and is very much alive today (see Kahneman, Diener, & Schwartz, 1999). Given this caveat, the main goal of the hedonic perspective is to increase happiness in a variety of ways. The good life is defined in terms of positive emotions such as happiness, contentment, satisfaction, or joy. This approach focuses on finding and fostering positive emotionality.

The *eudaimonic approach,* on the other hand, tends to focus on well-being as a function of fulfilling one's potential. In this case, well-being may or may not be associated with the maximization of happiness. Eudaimonic well-being is, however, most associated with the fulfilling of one's "true nature" and finding one's "true self" (Ryan & Deci, 2001). The eudaimonic approach may also be associated with living one's life in accord with the values and virtues that are the most desirable and most indicative of the highest good. The focus of this approach is on expanding potentials and cultivating personal growth. For instance, Alan Waterman (1993) referred to the eudaimonic dimension as "personal expressiveness." He found that this approach to well-being was associated with activities that allowed opportunities that help develop a person's best potentials and the realization of the true self.

Since the time of the ancient Greeks, the hedonic and the eudaimonic approaches to well-being have played a major role in defining how people think about the nature of the good life. In addition, research has supported the idea that these two conceptualizations are important in how psychology thinks about and measures well-being even today (Waterman, 1993; Compton, Smith, Cornish, & Qualls, 1996; McGregor & Little, 1998; Ryan & Deci, 2001).

Negative Emotions Are Still Important

At this point, it should be emphasized again that positive psychologists do not wish to limit the topics of study but rather to expand the topics to include aspects of human flourishing. Positive psychology does not deny that there are many problems in the world that need attention. It is also obvious that at times negative emotions can be necessary for survival. We would be far too vulnerable if we completely eliminated fear, anxiety, or skepticism from our lives. In addition, positive psychology also includes a recognition that the tragic elements in life can enrich our experience of being human (Woolfolk, 2002). There must be a reason why people throughout history have been drawn to plays, paintings, poetry, and even music that express sadness, tragedy, and defeat. It may be that in order to appreciate the positive in life we must also know something of the negative. Positive psychology does not deny that every effort should be made to help eliminate problems associated with social injustices and social inequalities.

Having recognized the place for negative emotions, however, we note that the desire to be happier and more satisfied with life is universal. People simply operate better within whatever world they live if they are more optimistic, hopeful, and can rely on solid supportive relationships. Interestingly, some of the findings from positive psychology approach universal applicability. For instance, Ed Diener (2000b), one of the preeminent researchers on well-being, said that the closest thing psychology has to a "general tonic" for well-being is to improve happiness. One of the best things a person can do to increase quality of life is to help others increase their level of happiness and life satisfaction. This applies to people at all levels of income and psychosocial adjustment.

Assumptions about the Role of Science in the Study of Well-Being

One of the most distinguishing features of positive psychology is an insistence that research must follow the standards of traditional scientific investigations. Positive psychology is certainly not the first attempt by psychologists to study well-being and the good life. From the very beginnings of psychology, some researchers have been interested in studying healthy personality development and optimal states of well-being. Many of these investigations, however, were theoretical, scholarly analyses, or in-depth case studies of individuals.

For example, in the early part of the twentieth century many investigations into psychological well-being and the nature of the good life began first as scholarly studies or as observations of clients in psychotherapy. Attempts were then made to move the results of those studies into the psychological laboratories for further experimental research or into real-life situations to help people increase well-being. Unfortunately, many attempts to move results into the laboratory were difficult or even impossible.

Viewing many of these past difficulties, a number of positive psychologists have seen a need to reverse the direction of information flow. That is, many positive psychologists hope to build an experimental knowledge base in the psychological laboratory and then move those results out into real-world arenas such as schools, clinics, and workplaces. To further this end, many of the founders of positive psychology have placed considerable emphasis on promoting and developing opportunities for experimental research on psychological well-being and the potentials we have for even greater fulfillment in life.

As mentioned, positive psychology is not the first attempt by psychologists to focus research on positive emotions, healthy adaptation, and the development of human potentials. Most recently, the humanistic school of psychology has focused on many of the same goals as positive psychology. Abraham Maslow, one of the founders of humanistic psychology, even had a chapter titled "Toward a Positive Psychology" in his seminal book, *Motivation and Personality* (1954). Even today, humanistic psychologists study what is healthy, adaptive, creative, and the full range of human potentials. Humanistic psychology and positive psychology differ in their emphases on empirical research and the application of research findings. Over the years, a number of humanistic psychologists have been actively involved in empirical styles of research (see Bohart & Greenberg, 1997; Greenberg & Rice, 1997; Cain & Seeman, 2002). However, positive psychologists have placed a much greater emphasis on the use of scientific methods to study well-being and positive adaptation (see, e.g., Strack, Argyle, & Schwartz, 1991; Kahneman, Diener, & Schwartz, 1999). In addition, much of the emphasis in humanistic psychology—particularly early humanistic psychology—was on theories of optimal personality development such as self-actualization. While positive psychology also investigates potentials for greater psychological development, it places greater emphasis on the well-being and satisfaction of the "average" person on the street (see Sheldon & King, 2001). In most studies, positive psychologists have focused on the benefits of simply being more happy and satisfied with life.

A Short History of Well-Being in the Western World

One of the more important ways to understand any field is to look at the history of how ideas in that field have developed over time. Positive psychology is the latest effort by human beings to understand the nature of happiness and well-being, but it is by no means the first attempt to solve that particular puzzle. Therefore, the next section of this chapter turns to a very brief history of how people in the Western world have answered the question, "What is happiness?" Other cultures have different histories of well-being; however, space limitations do not permit a cross-cultural review. Nevertheless, Chapter 10 presents a short section on how Eastern psychology thinks about well-being, and a brief exploration of cross-cultural ideas on well-being will be covered in Chapter 11.

The Early Hebrews

Judaism is one of the most influential factors in the development and proliferation of the Western worldview. The religion and culture of the ancient Hebrews represent one of the three pillars of knowledge that have sustained Western culture—the other two being the Greek civilization and Christianity. The ancient Hebrews developed a new social identity by developing a relationship with their personal God. For the Hebrews, many of the rules that governed their relationship to God were expressed as prohibitions. For the ancient Hebrews, the main list of prohibitions was the Ten Commandments. In general, these are prohibitions against self-centeredness, greed, and irrational anger, as well as requirements to accept the God of the ancient Hebrews as the only true God.

Philosophically, this approach to the search for happiness has been called a **divine command theory** of happiness. According to this theory, happiness is found by living in accord with the commands or rules set down by a supreme being (see Honderich, 1995). In its most basic form, this theory says that if one follows the commands, there will be rewards. In addition, if one does not follow the commands, there will be punishments. Therefore, for the Hebrew patriarchs, and later for many Christians, true happiness was related to a religious piety that was based on submission to God's supreme authority and a rejection of self-centered and simple hedonistic behaviors. The influence of this worldview on Western culture for the next 2,500 years cannot be overemphasized.

The Greeks

The second pillar that has sustained the intellectual and moral developments in the Western world was the legacy of the Greek culture. While the Jewish traditions were largely influential in the development of ethical, moral, and religious beliefs, the Greek culture would set the stage for developments in philosophy, science, art, and psychology for the next 2,500 years. In fact, in the Greek world can be found the original core of most of the significant philosophical ideas of the Western world.

The new element that was introduced into Greek society during its Golden Age was the idea that the good life and the proper path to happiness could be discovered through logic and rational analysis. That is, neither the gods nor the social traditions of the culture need be the ultimate arbitrator of individual values and goals. The general answer to the happiness question was that human beings could decide for themselves what paths most reliably lead to well-being.

Socrates

The person most responsible for the new direction in Greek intellectual life was Socrates (c. 469–399 BCE). He turned rationality to questions of human knowledge and especially to ideas on the nature of the good life or what we really need to be truly happy. In his method, Socrates affirmed the Delphic motto, "Know thyself." The search for truth must be centered on an exploration of the unchanging truths of the human psyche (Robinson, 1990). He believed that true happiness could be achieved only through self-knowledge, which would reveal wisdom and the true nature of the person's soul. Yet to know what is truly good, and not just self-indulgent or socially expected, a person must know the essence or the core of virtue—one must know "the good" or the core element of the good life. Socrates believed that once the true nature of "the good" is known, it will be automatically desired and will then motivate virtuous behavior. However, Socrates distrusted the perceptual forms of knowledge. For him, true wisdom must be found in a reality that expresses timeless and unchanging truths. Any search or well-being based on the sensory experiences or the emotions cannot reveal that truth because they are constantly changing in response to external circumstances.

Plato

Following in Socrates' footsteps was his most important student, Plato (427–347 BCE). Plato also believed that changeable sensory experiences cannot be the basis of true wisdom. Rather, true wisdom must be found in an unchanging realm that transcends the sensory world. The search for wisdom involves a passionate and difficult quest that looks beneath surface appearances and challenges preconceived notions and assumptions. The methods for this search are both reason and intuition. The person who undertakes this quest must have courage to find the truth hidden beneath both surface appearances and simple sensory experiences.

In a famous analogy, Plato compares most men and women to people who have been chained inside a cave and can look only at the back wall. As other people pass by outside the cave, the bright sun projects their shadows on to the back wall of the cave. According to Plato, those inside the cave would perceive the shadows as "reality" because they know no other reality. A philosopher, on the other hand, is someone who can loosen the chains, turn around to bear the brightness of "the sun" (i.e., true knowledge) and finally see the real truth outside the cave.

In the contemporary world, Plato's influence can be seen in any search for happiness or the good life that involves looking beyond sensory experiences toward a deeper meaning to life. This could include searching for one's "true" self, looking at unconscious motivations that keep someone from happiness, a spiritual quest for deeper meaning, as well as other internal directives in the search for well-being.

Aristotle

With Aristotle (384–322 BCE), who was Plato's student, the intellectual tradition of the West took a significantly different turn. According to Aristotle, the universal truth was to be found in an intellectual discovery of order in the world. The vehicle for this search was to be the senses, and the tools would be logic, classification, and definition. Unlike his teacher Plato, Aristotle would not use the emotions or intuition into a deeper reality in his search for higher truth and well-being. The Aristotelian ideal was based on poise and harmony and the avoidance of emotional extremes. He believed that "the emotions were to be tamed, by rigorous self-discipline, to accept the dictates of reason" (Kiefer, 1988, p. 43).

One of Aristotle's goals was to find the "golden mean" that exists between the extremes. The golden mean, a point of balance, harmony, and equilibrium, would lead to a life lived in accordance with the principle of eudaimonia (see earlier note on eudaimonia). Robinson (1990) explains **eudaimonia** as

> That condition of flourishing and completeness that constitutes true and enduring joy. . . . [E]udaimonia is not merely a set of pleasures or creature comforts or Epicurean delights. It is a life lived in a certain way, where life here refers to life-on-the-whole, not some number of moments strung together. Progress toward this end calls for the recognition that the better course of action is not the one that invariably satisfies the current desire or even an abiding desire. . . . To be wise is to strive for a condition of moral perfection or virtue (*arete*) by which the "golden mean" is found and adopted in all of the significant affairs of life (pp. 16–17).

The good life, then, is to be found in the total context of a person's life. It is not just a momentary emotional state or even one specific emotion.

While eudaimonia is usually translated as "happiness," it can also signify "truly fortunate" or "possessed of true well-being" (Telfer, 1980). The idea here is that the person who is truly happy is one who has what is *worth* desiring and *worth* having in life. Implied in this is the idea that certain goals or objectives in life may produce positive emotions, but they may not lead to eudaimonia. In many ways, it is a value or goal that exists as a possibility for the future. The search for eudaimonia should pull the person through life toward that ideal.

Aristotle also spoke of twelve basic virtues as dispositions of character that when cultivated lead a person toward a state of eudaimonia

(Schimmel, 2000): courage, liberality, pride (as self-respect), friendliness, wittiness, justice, temperance, magnificence, good temper, truthfulness, shame (or appropriate guilt for our transgressions), and honor (Aristotle, trans. 1908). These virtues were seen as examples of the golden mean between extremes. For instance, courage lies between the excesses of rashness and the deficiency of cowardice. Because these virtues are innate in every person, Aristotle's theory represents a naturalistic conception of happiness. Recognizing and cultivating our innate potentials can find happiness.

This approach to happiness has been called the **virtue theory** of happiness (see Honderich, 1995). The idea behind this theory is that the cultivation and development of certain virtues will lead a person toward the greatest well-being and, therefore, toward the good life. In contrast to the divine command theory, Aristotle did not list specific behaviors that must be avoided. He knew that whether any single behavior is a virtue or a vice depends upon the specific situation in which it occurs. Aristotle's perspective on well-being has been termed the *Aristotelian circle* because well-being, virtue, and practical wisdom are all interrelated such that each continuously influences the other (see Honderich, 1995). Today, many theories of mental health postulate a set of admirable or virtuous traits that are associated with healthy personality development. As seen earlier, positive psychology has also been partially defined as the search for human strengths and virtues.

The Epicureans

Toward the end of the fourth century BCE, the philosopher Epicurus founded the school of Epicureanism. Those drawn to **epicureanism** asserted that happiness is best achieved by withdrawing from the world of politics to cultivate a quiet existence of simple pleasures in the company of friends. Because of their focus on relaxed leisure, they were known as the "garden philosophers" (Robinson & Groves, 1998). This image of the good life and happiness as a combination of relaxation, moderated pleasure, freedom from pain or worry, and the company of cultured and civilized friends is one of the more popular ideals of happiness even today. Many perspectives view well-being in terms of intellectual stimulation, moderated pleasures, greater ability to control emotions, positive relationships, and less stress. Many people in today's world, and many psychologists, could be considered modern-day Epicureans.

The Stoics

Stoicism was founded by the philosopher Zeno concurrently with the founding of Epicureanism. The stoics distrusted human emotions because they felt that emotions inevitably lead to unhappiness. They argued that a person cannot know great joy without knowing great sorrow, so why pursue joy and pleasure? Instead, the way to find lasting peace of mind was to use reason and discipline to control the emotions. Stoicism ultimately became one of the major philosophical schools in the Roman world (Robinson & Groves, 1998). Today, there are any number of approaches to happiness that are based on stoic ideas. These approaches often focus on teaching people how to control their emotional reactions to events by using rational and analytical thinking.

Summary of the Greek Ideas on the Good Life

Only somewhat facetiously, Kiefer (1988) summarized the Greek approach to knowledge by saying, "Once its straightforward principles were grasped, anyone who could stand several hours a day of brutal self-criticism could be a philosopher" (p. 38). While one might argue with Kiefer's summary of Greek philosophy, there is no argument that the Greeks offered a democratic structure to the search for well-being that was based on self-awareness, rationality, and logic. The legacy left to Western civilization by the Greeks cannot be overestimated.

In terms of how people think about the nature of the good life, most of the current positions on how to achieve well-being and contentment were expressed by the Greeks at one time or another. In addition, the considerable variety of options available to the ancient Greeks in their search for well-being was unique in the history of the ancient world. Unfortunately, the emphasis the Greeks placed on rational analysis, the freedom to choose one's own beliefs, and the emphasis on an honest and thorough search for wisdom and truth was lost during the Middle Ages. These qualities would not again be central to the search for well-being in Western civilization until the late nineteenth century.

Early Christianity and the Middle Ages

The rise of Christianity represented one of the most significant developments in Western civilization and constitutes the third pillar of Western civilization. Christianity also transformed the meaning of religious devotion in Western society by viewing God not as an awesome and powerful God to be feared but as a loving presence who deeply cares for humanity. The way to find true happiness is found in the message and life of Jesus. The message of Jesus is one of love and compassion: people should love others as God loves the world—"love thy neighbor as thyself." Christians are encouraged to emulate the love of Jesus. Christians believe that by expressing God's love and sharing it with other people, a person can find peace, happiness, and salvation.

During the early Middle Ages (approximately AD 500 to AD 1200) the Church and the monasteries were the center of spiritual, intellectual, and often political life. Conceptions of the good life were, therefore, based on religious perspectives. By this time, the perspective of the Church was that true happiness, as opposed to secular and temporary pleasures, was delayed until after death and the resurrection into heaven. In this doctrine, the pleasures of the "flesh" and the "spirit" were rigidly separated. The official Church doctrine was that the enjoyment of even simple pleasures was a distraction from more "spiritual" concerns. Lowry's (1982) summary of the medieval conception of human nature is useful:

> In the Middle Ages, man[1] was regarded as a creature of conflict and contradictions. He had been formed in the image of his Creator, and yet he was tainted by Original Sin. He had a spiritual nature and a carnal nature, and so long as the spirit inhabited the flesh, the two were constantly at odds. . . . In short, human nature was held to be the scene of a constantly raging battle between the demands of the spirit and the demands of the flesh (p. 59).

This idea of an internal battle between the physical appetites and the more rational intellectual aspects is still quite common today. The most familiar example is Freud's theory that the irrational pleasure principle of the id must be moderated by the ego, which is driven by the reality principal.

The Virtue Theory in the Middle Ages

Given the pervasiveness of this struggle between physical and spiritual needs, Christian leaders deemed it necessary to warn people about the dangers of temporary pleasures and how they could ensnare the careless. The Church's doctrine of the *seven deadly sins* was a list of basic evils—anger, envy, sloth, pride, lust, intemperance, and greed—that destroy character and could lead to a host of other sins (Schimmel, 1997). In general, at the core of these sins are self-indulgent hedonism and narcissism.

Less well known is the list of opposite behaviors called the *four cardinal virtues* (or the *natural virtues*) and the *three theological virtues*. As might be expected, this was a list of behaviors that lead to virtuous behavior and the abandonment of sins. The four cardinal virtues are those on which all others depend. These virtues—justice, prudence, fortitude, and temperance—were derived by St. Ambrose in the fourth century from the four basic virtues of the Greeks (Bowker, 1997). The medieval scholastics added the three theological virtues: faith, hope, and charity. Again, a number of contemporary conceptualizations of psychological well-being rely on this list of core traits. The basic foundations of ethical behavior and humanitarianism in the Western world appear to be based on this list of seven positive virtues.

The Renaissance to the Age of Enlightenment

Creativity and the Rise of the "Artist"

During the Renaissance—between 1400 and 1600—people began to change their ideas of a person as an *artist.* Two related changes contributed to this transformation: the idea that artists possess a special gift and the rise of individualism. One lasting change was the elevation of artists' social status and the belief that they possessed a special gift that other people did not have. Certainly, there had been persons throughout history who were recognized as being creative in their societies. However, they were regarded as craftsmen rather than artists. Note that the concept of the creative artist involves the element of a *personal vision* that is expressed through painting, sculpture, music, or architecture. This idea of a personal vision implies a certain individuality and uniqueness to the person that was not afforded artists of the Middle Ages. The rise of individualism eventually changed the image of a person in ways that brought significant alterations to how people search for happiness (Baumeister, 1987).

The Rise of Science

By the end of the seventeenth century, a new idea of human nature was taking hold. Lowry (1982) stated, "The historical significance of the seventeenth century can scarcely be exaggerated. For it was during this century that Western intellectual life first became recognizably *modern* in mood, temper, purpose, and presupposition" [italics in original] (p. 6).

The new worldview that was advocated by these enthusiastic thinkers was based on two general ideas. The first was that rational persons could decide for themselves what was true and of ultimate value. To search for truth, a person would use a rationality based on dispassionate and objective observation of the events in the world. The keys were logic, objectivity, and *empiricism,* the belief that valid knowledge is constructed from experiences based on the five senses (Honderich, 1995; note the difference between this idea and those of Socrates and Plato). The second idea was that the "universe as a whole is one vast machine, a kind of cosmic clockwork, and that all its parts and processes are likewise governed by the inexorable laws of mechanical causation" (Lowry, 1982, p. 4). This philosophy became known as *mechanism,* and it was applied equally to events in nature and to human psychology.

The Rising Importance of the Social Environment to Well-Being

The focus on empiricism, rationalism, and mechanism created an image of human nature that appeared simple, understandable, and clear. Social reformers such as Jeremy Bentham and John Stuart Mill believed that the basic need of people to seek pleasure and avoid pain could be used to create a more stable and enlightened society. If a person wants to know if a certain behavior is right, ethical, or fosters the good life, then he or she must show that it leads to the enhancement of happiness for the greatest number of people. Around these ideas was created a philosophical system called **utilitarianism,** or the belief that actions are right if they tend to promote happiness for the greatest number of people and wrong as they do not. This principle was called the *hedonic calculus* (Viney & King, 1998). Therefore, those who believed in utilitarianism thought that happiness for all people was the ultimate aim of all human actions and should be used as the standard by which actions are evaluated as right or wrong (Hoderich, 1995). The hope and the promise for a scientific understanding of well-being, happiness, and the good life were being born.

The Rise of Democracy

By the mid eighteenth century, some people believed that the prevailing political power structure in a society could be at odds with the welfare of the individual. They believed that when these two were in conflict, the members of the society had the right to overthrow the state and put in its place a system that was more conducive to individual liberty. Thomas Jefferson made these the founding principles of a new government when he wrote in the Declaration of Independence, "We hold these truths to be self-evident, that all men are created equal, that they are endowed by their Creator with certain inalienable Rights, that among these are Life, Liberty, and the pursuit of Happiness." A form of government had been instituted for an entire country that elevated the individual to a status above that of royalty and gave to its citizens power to make decisions about their own lives that had previously resided only with a ruling elite. The pursuit of happiness was now a right as well as a personal choice. Democracy was joined with utilitarianism to create a new system of government that, in theory, would result in the greatest happiness for everyone. Now the search for happiness also involves a search for the social environments that will best promote well-being.

Romanticism and the Nineteenth Century

Emotionalism and the Romantics

In the early nineteenth century, the growth of Western individualism began to turn toward the emotional expressions that made each person unique. In fact, the word "individualism" first appeared in 1835 when Alexis de Tocqueville used it to describe the emerging American perspective. People began to believe that the best way to express their individualism was to explore their own unique emotional experience of the world. The Romantic movement captivated the intelligentsia as they explored the full range of their emotional lives from the spiritual to the mundane. At times, the *intensity* of emotions was important rather than the emotion itself. For instance, Morton Hunt (1959) noted that, "The typical romantic prided himself on the ability to fall tumultuously and passionately in love. . . . [H]owever, in place of sexuality, the romantics delighted in being demonstratively sentimental, melancholic, tempestuous, or tearful, according to the occasion" (p. 309). They felt that the ability to feel emotions intensely was important to living a full and significant life.

During this period, the focus on personal emotional expression combined with the idea that social environments can inhibit individualism. The result was the idea that a "true self" exists beneath the social masks that people wear. Today, numerous perspectives on well-being urge people to find and express their true selves.

Love in the Romantic Period

In the early seventeenth century, the Puritans began to transform the idea of love and marriage. Although they still lived in a rigidly patriarchal society, they did begin to introduce a new idea: within the family, men and women were supposed to be good companions to each other. The Puritans stressed the emotional harmony that should exist between a wife and husband. One Puritan writer said that the husband and wife "should be closer and more nearly attuned to each other than to any other people on earth" (in Hunt, 1959, p. 236).

The idea of marriage being based on affection between two people along with the unique emotional bonds that they create together was also a consequence of rising individualism. This type of marriage and love presupposed that two people voluntarily enter into an emotional, legal, and religious commitment. It required choice and a certain degree of personal autonomy from family, friends, and institutions. It also assumed that individual sentiments and emotions should be more important to the decision to marry than any other authority in the society (Taylor, 1989). Love was also now seen as the major avenue to soothe the sense of being alone in the world—another consequence of rising individualism. I. Singer (1987) said that from this point forward, "Romantic love . . . involved oneness with an alter ego, one's other self, a man or woman who would make up one's deficiencies, respond to one's deepest inclinations, and serve as possibly the only person with whom one could communicate fully . . . this would be the person one would marry, and establishing a bond that was permanent as well as ecstatically consummatory" (quoted in Hendrick & Hendrick, 1992, p. 4).

Of course, today in Western industrialized countries, people assume that love should be the only real motivation for marriage. Today, the ultimate test of whether two people should commit themselves to each other is found in the answer to a simple question, "Are you in love?" If the answer to this question is a resounding "yes," then many people assume that the two should commit to each other for the rest of their lives. Today, for many people, the search for intimacy and love is the major activity of their lives and the ultimate emotion for true happiness.

The Twentieth Century

The most significant early twentieth century development in the search for the good life came from Freud and his followers. Twentieth century behaviorists and cognitive psychologists also developed ways to enhance well-being, but they worked with ideas that had largely existed since the time of the ancient Greeks. The theory of the unconscious, although not completely new, did bring a new element into the search for well-being. Although there is a wide variety of ideas on how the unconscious affects behavior, most psychologists agree that at least some motivations for behavior are hidden from conscious awareness (Cramer & Davidson, 1998). Therefore, the search for happiness may be either helped or hindered by unconscious forces. Contemporary studies, however, have found that unconscious factors are often not as overwhelmingly significant as Freud imagined. Nevertheless, for some people their unconscious psychological forces may keep them from achieving as much happiness as they might (Vaillant, 2000).

The people in Western industrialized nations entered the twentieth century with a range of freedoms unprecedented in history. The ideals of freedom, democracy, and self-reliance allow people to choose their professions, spouses, religious beliefs, system of government, homes, and make other choices that are important to their pursuit of the good life. In fact, as citizens of democratic countries they expect to exercise those freedoms and make individual choices that affect their daily lives.

When these choices are brought to bear on the question of the good life, or happiness, people today find a veritable cornucopia of different philosophies, beliefs, theories, ideas, and pronouncements that all lay claim to the final authority. The freedom of full inquiry creates a stunning array of possible answers. In fact, the number of definitions for the good life seems to expand to fit the growing complexity of the world (Tatarkiewicz, 1976). One of the goals of positive psychology, therefore, is to bring some understanding to these various perspectives on the good life and well-being.

Positive Psychology Today

In spite of the fact that positive psychology is a very new area, its popularity appears to be growing rapidly. Seligman and others have worked extensively to provide awareness of the new area and to provide opportunities for researchers interested in the area. The January 2000 and March 2001 special issues of the *American Psychologist* (the journal of the American Psychological Association) were devoted to articles on positive psychology. The first summit on positive psychology was held in 1999 in Lincoln, Nebraska. In October 2000, the second summit on Positive Psychology was convened at the headquarters of the Gallup Organization in Washington, DC. Interest was so great that half of those who wished to attend the summit had to be turned away because of limited space. In February 2000 the first recipients of the Templeton Prize in Positive Psychology were announced. In October 2002, the First International Conference on Positive Psychology took place. So, although positive psychology is a new area in psychology, the ideas, theories, research, and motivation to study the positive side of human behavior is as old as humanity. Positive psychology appears to be well on its way to gaining a permanent place in scientific psychology. Findings from research that takes a positive psychology approach are already influencing interventions that help people enhance their strengths and develop their potentials for greater happiness and satisfaction with life.

Summary

This chapter introduced the concept of positive psychology as the scientific study of optimal human functioning. Positive psychology searches for those qualities that allow individuals, communities, and societies to thrive and flourish. It focuses on three major dimensions: positive subjective states, positive traits, and positive institutions. A number of themes or basic assumptions differentiate positive psychology from other approaches to research in psychology, including a focus on positive behavior, an emphasis on scientific investigations, and a search for the parameters and predictors of the good life. This chapter also reviewed the history of how people in the Western world have thought about happiness, well-being, and the good life. The chapter ended with an appropriately hopeful note that speculated about the future of positive psychology. Interest in this new field is growing rapidly, and positive psychology will be a thriving area in the field for many years to come.

Note

1. Throughout this book the gender-specific term "man" will be used only when it is a direct quote or when its use accurately reflects the cultural understandings of the time or place.

Learning Tools

Key Terms and Ideas

DIVINE COMMAND THEORY
ENJOYMENT
EPICUREANISM
EUDAIMONIA
GOOD LIFE
HEDONIC WELL-BEING
PLEASURE
POSITIVE PSYCHOLOGY
UTILITARIANISM
VIRTUE THEORY

Books

Snyder, C. R., & Lopez, S. J. (Eds.). (2002). *The handbook of positive psychology.* New York: Oxford University Press. An impressive collection of research articles on the wide variety of topics studied in positive psychology (professional, but can be read by interested undergraduate students).

Tarnas. R. (1991). *The passion of the Western mind: Understanding the ideas that have shaped our world view.* New York: Ballantine. A beautifully written book that makes reading about history a real pleasure (popular/professional).

Research Articles

Two special issues of the American Psychologist devoted to positive psychology that contain a number of articles on different areas of positive psychology.

Seligman, M. E. P., & Csikszentmihalyi, M. (Eds.) (2000). Happiness, excellence, and optimal human functioning [special issue]. *American Psychologist, 55*(1).

Sheldon, K. M., & King, L. (Eds.) (2001). Positive psychology [special issue] *American Psychologist, 56*(3), 216–263.

Film

Celebrating What's Right in the World. A film by *National Geographic* photojournalist Dewitt Jones that invites people to appreciate the world around us. Distributed by Star Thrower, St. Paul, MN.

On the Web

http://www.positivepsychology.org. The main Web page for positive psychology.

http://www.apa.org. The Web page for the American Psychological Association. There are links to positive psychology articles and books.

http://www.goodnewsnetwork.org. The Web site for the Good News Network, which publishes a newsletter covering good news from around the world.

Personal Explorations

Have a beautiful day: applying principles of positive psychology, by Martin E. P. Seligman. This exercise is designed to help you explore qualities of the good life that exist in your life right now. It requires no special materials or equipment. For instructions go to the following Web site http://www.positivepsychology.org/teachingresources.htm.

Some of the Personal Exploration exercises cited in this book come from the Positive Psychology Teaching Resources Web site. I am extremely grateful to Amy Fineburg and her colleagues, who have done a tremendous job of bringing positive psychology into the classroom.

CHAPTER 2

Emotions and Motivation in Positive Psychology

> The often incidental effect of experiencing a positive emotion is an increment in durable personal resources that can be drawn on later in other contexts and in other emotional states.
>
> *Barbara Fredrickson (1998)*

Chapter 1 presented a number of terms and ideas that help define positive psychology. In order to place these ideas in a broader context, it is necessary to review some basic research areas in psychology. One of the ways that positive psychology may change the entire field of psychology is by presenting new ways of looking at old problems in more established research areas in the field. In that spirit, this chapter will examine how findings relevant to positive psychology can be found in research on positive emotions and intrinsic motivation.

Positive Psychology and Emotion

The Basic Emotions

Throughout the history of psychology, some investigators have focused on the classification of basic emotions. The exact number of basic emotions varies from seven to ten depending on the theorist; however, the various lists show a fair amount of agreement (Plutchik, 1980; Ekman, 1993). It is relevant for positive psychology that all agree that emotions such as enjoyment, happiness, or joy are basic emotions. A number of these theorists also agree that interest or anticipation is also basic. So, at least a few positive emotions are basic building blocks of our emotional world. Further, the number of basic positive emotions is less than the number of the other basic emotions. (This observation will be important for a newer theory of emotion to be discussed later in this chapter.) In any case, it is obvious that the variety of emotional experiences people feel cannot be completely captured by a list of eight or ten emotions. So, then, where do all the subtle variations come from?

Most theorists agree that the basic emotions can be combined in many ways to create other, more subtle variations. For example, Robert Plutchik (1980) believes that optimism is a combination of anticipation and joy. Interestingly, he also sees the emotion of awe as a combination of surprise and fear. In other words, he suggests that a positive emotion that is often related to religious experiences can be created from a specific combination of a somewhat positive emotion—surprise—and a basic negative emotion—fear. If our emotional experiences really do combine in ways similar to this, it would suggest that any attempt to totally eliminate negative emotions from our life would have the unintended consequence of eliminating the variety and subtlety of our most profound emotional experiences.

Although there is considerable agreement on what the basic broad dimensions of negative emotions are, there is less agreement on the basic dimensions of positive emotions. In an effort to clarify the basic dimensions of positive emotion, David Watson (2002) proposed that there are three basic dimensions: (1) joviality (e.g., happiness, cheerfulness, enthusiasm), (2) assurance (e.g., confidence, daring), and (3) attentiveness (e.g., alertness, concentration, determination). Note how all three of these dimensions are involved when we are happily absorbed in an activity that we enjoy and are performing well.

Note, too, that how we experience our emotional lives is also influenced by the societies and cultures we live in (see Matsumoto, 1994). While it is true that some aspects of positive emotionality are innate, at the same time, there is considerable variation in how people express, label, and promulgate positive emotions around the world. Many of these variations will be explored further in Chapter 12.

The Evolutionary Need for Positive Emotions

So, at least a few basic emotions are innate. A question still remains, however: why do we need positive emotions? Some might argue that they are pleasurable but ultimately trivial to our survival as a species. While this argument may have swayed some scientists in the past, more contemporary evolutionary psychologists have argued that positive emotions are evolved adaptations to our environment. As we saw in Chapter 1, David Buss (2000) has argued that positive emotions may, in fact, be quite necessary to the survival of the species. He notes that human beings are social animals and need the protection and support of others in order to survive. Without the bonds of attachment, caring, and love we feel for certain people, the requirements of communal living, cooperative raising of children, and mutual defense would be impossible. Other reasons for the necessity of positive emotions will be discussed later in the chapter. For the moment, suffice it to say that there are reasonable scientific arguments that support the idea that positive emotions are absolutely necessary for human evolution, adaptation, and survival.

The Biology of Positive Emotions and Pleasure

Evidence suggests that at least some of our pleasurable responses are caused by the release of chemicals in the brain called neurotransmitters, which are the chemical messengers that relay information between nerve cells. Specifically, increased levels of the neurotransmitter dopamine have been implicated in the experience of happiness (Ashby, Isen, & Turken, 1999). Levels of some neurotransmitters may also increase under certain circumstances, which helps increase positive emotional reactions to events. In the mid-1970s, a team of Scottish researchers discovered a variety of neurotransmitters that appear to act like the brain's natural opiate system. Specifically, the *endorphins* or *encephalins* appear to increase pleasure and decrease the experience of pain. Increased levels of endorphins are a possible cause of the "runner's high" that may accompany physical exercise (Farrell, Gustafson, Morgan, & Pert, 1987). Levels of endorphins also increase as much as 200 percent during sexual intercourse (see Pert, 1997). In addition to these neurotransmitters, recent work has suggested that the brain also makes its own version of tetrahydrocannabinol, or THC, which is the active ingredient in marijuana (Fackelmann, 1993).

Given this experimental evidence that relates brain structures and biochemicals to our experience of emotion, does this mean that positive emotions such as joy or love are just patterns of neurotransmitter activity? A recent bumper sticker humorously expressed this position as "I'm not really happy, it's just a chemical imbalance!" Is this true? Is that all there is to our emotional experiences? Actually, the neurochemical processes involved in emotion are a complex integration of neurotransmitters and hormones from multiple areas of the brain and body. For human beings, at least, the experience of emotion also involves cognitive processes, such as labeling physiological responses and the interpretive meanings that we apply to those stimuli.

The Different Roles of Positive and Negative Emotions

In positive psychology, it is not very surprising that positive emotions should play a prominent role in research. However, the role of positive emotions in psychology has been overlooked for many years. As mentioned in Chapter 1, one of the barriers to the development of positive psychology was the assumption that positive and negative emotions were simply opposite and balanced ends of an emotional continuum. Therefore, if one studied the predictors of negative emotions, one automatically knew something about the predictors of positive emotions. We have seen that this assumption proved to be false.

One of the barriers to the study of positive emotions is that positive emotions are somewhat difficult to study in the laboratory. There appear to be fewer basic positive emotions than negative emotions by a ratio of one positive to every three or four negative emotions (Fredrickson, 1998).

It may be that because negative emotions alert us to possible dangers and threats, we need a variety of them to warn us against numerous potential threats. Also, positive emotions are fairly diffuse and tend to have nonspecific markers in terms of autonomic activation. For instance, relatively specific biological and neurological processes are associated with certain negative emotional responses triggered by the "fight or flight" response to unexpected danger. In fact, many negative emotions are associated with urges to act in certain ways that are called *specific action tendencies*. The response to unexpected fear can be immediate behavioral responses designed to protect us by either fighting off an attack or fleeing from the danger. Unexpectedly, this direct linkage between emotion and action does not appear to be associated with positive emotions. Even the unique facial expressions that accompany negative emotions are more easily recognizable than facial expressions that go along with positive emotions. While fear, anger, and sadness create different facial expressions, all positive emotions share the characteristics of a basic genuine smile—known as the Duchenne smile (Ekman, Friesen, & O'Sullivan, 1988). So, by an interesting twist to our biology, the negative emotions are simply easier to study in scientific laboratories.

As a result of these differences between positive and negative emotions, it is also easier for researchers to hypothesize about the usefulness of negative emotions. As mentioned, emotions such as fear, anxiety, apprehension, and anger serve an obvious function in terms of adaptation, protection, and survival of the organism. But what about positive emotions? Is their function simply to make us feel good after all of the dangers have been taken care of and the "important" emotions have done their job? In fact, many scientists believed this was so. A recent theory has begun to change that assumption. Barbara Fredrickson (1998, 2001, 2002) formulated what she called the broaden-and-build model of positive emotions. In her model, the purpose of positive emotions is quite a bit different from the purpose of the negative emotions.

The "Broaden-and-Build" Model of Positive Emotions

As mentioned, the purpose of many negative emotions is to rapidly respond to the environmental threats with specific action tendencies that will propel the organism—in this case, rapidly propel people—out of harm's way. According to Fredrickson, positive emotions help preserve the organism by providing a different service. First, they provide *nonspecific action tendencies* that can lead to adaptive behavior. How would these processes work? One of the examples that she gives is the emotion of joy. Fredrickson (1998) cites Nico Frijda (1986), who said that joy "is in part aimless, unasked-for readiness to engage in whatever interaction presents itself and [it is also] in part readiness to engage in enjoyments" (p. 304). In children, for example, the feeling of joy is associated with urges to play, to explore, to investigate, or to create. In adults, when people feel positive emotions they are more likely to interact with others, seek out new experiences, take up creative challenges, or help others in need. Think of how much more open and curious one is about the world when one feels good.

Second, positive emotions also provide the spark for changes in cognitive activity that can lead to newer and more adaptive **thought-action tendencies.** This means that people behave in specific ways because they have learned to associate certain cognitive activities or ways of thinking with certain actions. Returning to the example of children's play, when children allow themselves to be motivated by joy and happily engage in playful activities, they are simultaneously learning about their environment and about themselves. New ways of thinking about the world can emerge from play activities, and these new ways of thinking can be stored in memory and used later on. In summary, the process of play (for children or adults) begins with joy, which motivates a number of exploratory activities that result in new learning that is then stored in memory and can be used to direct future behaviors. The same processes can be seen with many other positive emotions and other behaviors beside play.

Therefore, Fredrickson's **broaden-and-build** model posits that positive emotions *broaden* our awareness and then *build* upon the resultant learning to create future emotional and intellectual resources. In Fredrickson's (1998) words,

> Not only do the positive emotions . . . share the feature of broadening an individual's momentary thought-action repertoire, but they also appear to share the feature of building the individual's personal resources. . . . Importantly these resources are more durable than the transient emotional states that led to their acquisition. By consequence, then, the often incidental effect of experiencing a positive emotion is an increment in durable personal resources that can be drawn on later in other contexts and in other emotional states (p. 307).

This quote calls attention to another aspect of Fredrickson's theory. The reference to broadening response repertoires has another meaning in addition to increasing our awareness of behavioral options. Once again, a contrast with negative emotions is helpful. One characteristic of thought-action tendencies in negative emotions is that they generally lead to a narrowing of options for thought and behavior. For instance, when we are under immediate threat or danger it is more adaptable to make a quick decision and then act to avoid the danger. It is not very helpful, for instance, to leisurely mull over your available options if you notice that your kitchen is on fire. Rather, the situation demands quick decision-making and decisive action.

With positive emotions, however, a narrowing of attention is not what is required. Positive emotions help us to broaden our available options to maximize our future resources. For instance, the emotion of love leads not just to thoughts about how to immediately express that love. It also leads to thoughts about how to express love in the future, how to share love with others, how to maximize the potential for love, and how to help other people feel love. Positive emotions such as love or joy often lead to a desire to share those feelings with others, and many people will spend considerable time trying to find ways to share their positive experiences with others. So, not only can positive emotions broaden our awareness and build up resources, but also those resources are more long lasting than the positive emotions that initiated them. As another example, think about social support and the numerous advantages it can provide for people throughout their lives. Those bonds of closeness, caring, compassion, and love are forged by allowing ourselves to act on positive emotions that compel us toward interactions with others. In turn, those bonds can act in a reciprocal fashion to increase the likelihood that we will experience more positive emotions in the form of supportive feedback from others, which, once again, leads to interactions that are more positive. That, in turn, can foster the creation and deepening of those relationships and other social attachments.

Another advantage of positive emotions, according to Fredrickson , is that they may act as antidotes to the unfortunate effects of negative emotions (Fredrickson & Levenson, 1998; Fredrickson & Joiner, 2002). Her **undoing hypothesis** states that positive emotions help both the body and the mind regain a sense of balance, flexibility, and equilibrium after the impact of negative emotions. She reviewed a number of research studies that found that positive emotions help undo the aftereffects of stress reactions in a shorter period of time. Take, for example, a group of friends who are on a backpacking trip and unexpectedly come upon a huge rattlesnake in the trail, coiled and ready to strike. They all panic and run screaming down the trail. For these hikers, the sight of the snake has stimulated the "fight or flight" response, which has created numerous changes to their biochemistry that need to be corrected now that the danger is past. Imagine further that when this group of hikers finally stops, they all realize how silly they must have looked and immediately begin to laugh hysterically at themselves. Fredrickson believes that their laughter will help to clear their bodies of the physiological and biochemical aftereffects associated with the fight or flight response. She also believes that the same effect can help to restore flexibility and openness to thinking after experiencing the narrowing of attention associated with the negative emotion of panic (further evidence for the salutary effects of positive emotions on health will be discussed in Chapter 6).

Emotional Intelligence

At this point, it should be quite obvious that emotions can serve a very useful function if used properly. The ability to use emotions wisely might be considered a type of intelligence. In fact, some researchers believe that there is such a thing as *emotional intelligence.* According to John Mayer, David Caruso, and Peter Salovey (2000), "Emotional intelligence refers to an ability to recognize the meanings of emotions and their relationships, and to reason and problem-solve on the basis of them. Emotional intelligence is involved in the capacity to perceive emotions, assimilate emotion-related feelings, understand the information of those emotions, and manage them" (p. 267). People who are high in emotional intelligence have the ability to use their emotions wisely, and they appear to have a deeper understanding of their emotional lives (Salovey, Mayer, & Caruso, 2002). In addition, emotional intelligence is associated with the ability to accurately read the emotions of other people, the practical knowledge of how to manage one's own feelings and impulses, as well as a deeper sensitivity to the emotional undercurrents that lie behind many social interactions.

Salovey and Mayer (1990) presented the original model for emotional intelligence. They proposed that five characteristics would define the idea.

1. The first is *knowing one's emotions* or the ability to recognize an emotion as it happens. People high in emotional intelligence should be able to accurately recognize exactly what they are feeling when they are feeling it. This can include the ability to accurately express the emotion as well.
2. Second is the ability to *handle interpersonal relationships* well. People high in emotional intelligence should be socially competent and good at creating and maintaining effective interpersonal relationships.
3. Third is the ability to use emotions to *motivate oneself.* This means that people high in emotional intelligence should be able to control and marshal their emotions to help them reach goals and remain focused.
4. Fourth, emotional intelligence should be related to the ability to *recognize emotions in others,* or the skill of reading what other people are feeling and being empathetic.
5. Fifth, emotional intelligence involves a good ability to *manage one's emotions.* This includes the ability to regulate one's moods, handle stress, and rebound after an emotional setback. Interestingly, high emotional intelligence may be found most often with moderate ability to regulate one's own emotions rather than with high emotional control (Salovey, Meyer, & Caruso, 2002). Too little control of emotions leads to impulsivity; however, too much control leads to repression and the inability to use information from our emotions to learn about our world and ourselves.

In summary, emotional intelligence consists of self-insight into the richness of one's emotional life, a moderate degree of self-control, empathy, and good social skills. In a later model, Mayer, Caruso, and Salovey (2000) presented the necessary skills for the development of emotional intelligence as a hierarchy of increasingly complex abilities. In a person with high emotional intelligence, the (1) ability to perceive and express emotions leads to (2) skills at assimilating emotions into cognitive representations of emotion and cognitive processing of feelings, which leads to (3) deeper understanding of the complexities of emotion as they related to the social world, which leads to (4) being able to regulate emotions more effectively. Mayer, Caruso, and Salovey (2000) also found that emotional intelligence scores increased with age and with a person's experience dealing with emotions, just as one would expect. Scores on their emotional intelligence scale also correlated positively with verbal IQ scores, a variety of empathy scales, life satisfaction, and level of perceived parental warmth as a child. Their results suggested that a large component of emotional intelligence is the degree of empathy developed over the years. Women tended to score higher on their measure of emotional intelligence than men did. Types of emotional intelligence may also be an aid to problem-solving and social interactions. For instance, Robert Sternberg (2004) has found that "practical intelligence," or the ability to adapt well to one's physical and social environment, is significantly correlated with both physical and psychological well-being.

There may also be other aspects of our emotional lives that can help us find more meaning and fulfillment in life. James Averill (2002) has proposed a theory of emotional creativity. His idea is that people can use their emotions in creative ways that foster a greater sense of meaning, vitality, and connectedness in life. That is, it may be possible to teach people how to use their emotions more wisely and more creatively. Although the research in this area is fairly new, there is little doubt that the ability to understand and use our emotions wisely and creatively is related to personal well-being.

Genetic Influences on Positive Emotions

Another biologically based perspective on emotion concerns the question of whether heredity impacts our emotional responses. It is quite obvious that some people are more cheerful and more easy-going while others are more prone to anxiety and worry. Could it be that being a cheerful person, an anxious person, or someone who always takes it all in stride is a matter of genes and not necessarily the result of learned coping skills? In fact, some researchers have proposed that average lifetime levels of emotionality are primarily inherited.

Lykken and Tellegen (1996) suggested that up to 80 percent of the long-term stability of well-being is due to heredity. Specifically, they found in their studies of twins that 40 percent of the long-term variability among people in positive emotionality, 55 percent of the variability in negative emotionality, and 48 percent of the variability in overall well-being is due to genetics (Tellegen, Lykken, Bouchard, Wilcox, & Rich, 1988). They also found that shared family environment or learning accounted for only 22 percent of positive emotionality and an extremely small 2 percent of negative emotionality. Figure 2.1 shows their findings on the heritability of emotionality.

In other words, they suggest that our families may be important to our eventual emotional lives as adults but not because of what we learn from our families, as Freud, Skinner, and others have suggested. Rather, families are important because they provide us with genetic material that largely determines our basc emotional responsiveness to the world. Therefore, they concluded that genetic makeup was far more important to the long-term quality of our emotional lives than is learned behavior or the quality of our early childhood environments.

The Happiness Set Point

Lykken and Tellegen (1996) took the results of their research and proposed the idea of a **happiness set point.** They believe that their heritability studies show most people have an average level of happiness—or a set point—that they return to after they adjust to the effects of temporary highs and lows in emotionality. Of course, very intense feelings of joy or sadness keep people off their set points for somewhat longer periods of time, but eventually everyone returns to an average or baseline level of well-being—a level set by genetics. For some people, their set points lean toward positive emotionality, and those people tend to be cheerful most of the time. For others, their set points direct them toward more negative emotionality, and they may tend to gravitate toward pessimism and anxiety more than others. Other studies have also suggested that there are genetic contributions to our basic emotional reactions to the world.

Jerome Kagan came to a similar conclusion by studying patterns of temperament in children. *Temperament* is a term used to describe our basic emotional reaction to events. Kagan found that there is considerable genetic contribution to the emotional continuum of extroversion to shyness. In his estimate, about 15 to 20 percent of children are born with a shy temperament and about 25 to 30 percent are born with an outgoing and extroverted temperament (Kagan & Snidman, 1991). This does not mean, however, that a temperamentally shy person is doomed to a lonely and anxious existence. Remember that being born with a shy temperament does not inevitably produce a person who is painfully shy in social situations. Many people who tend to be introverted, somewhat private, and hesitant to leap into social situations can

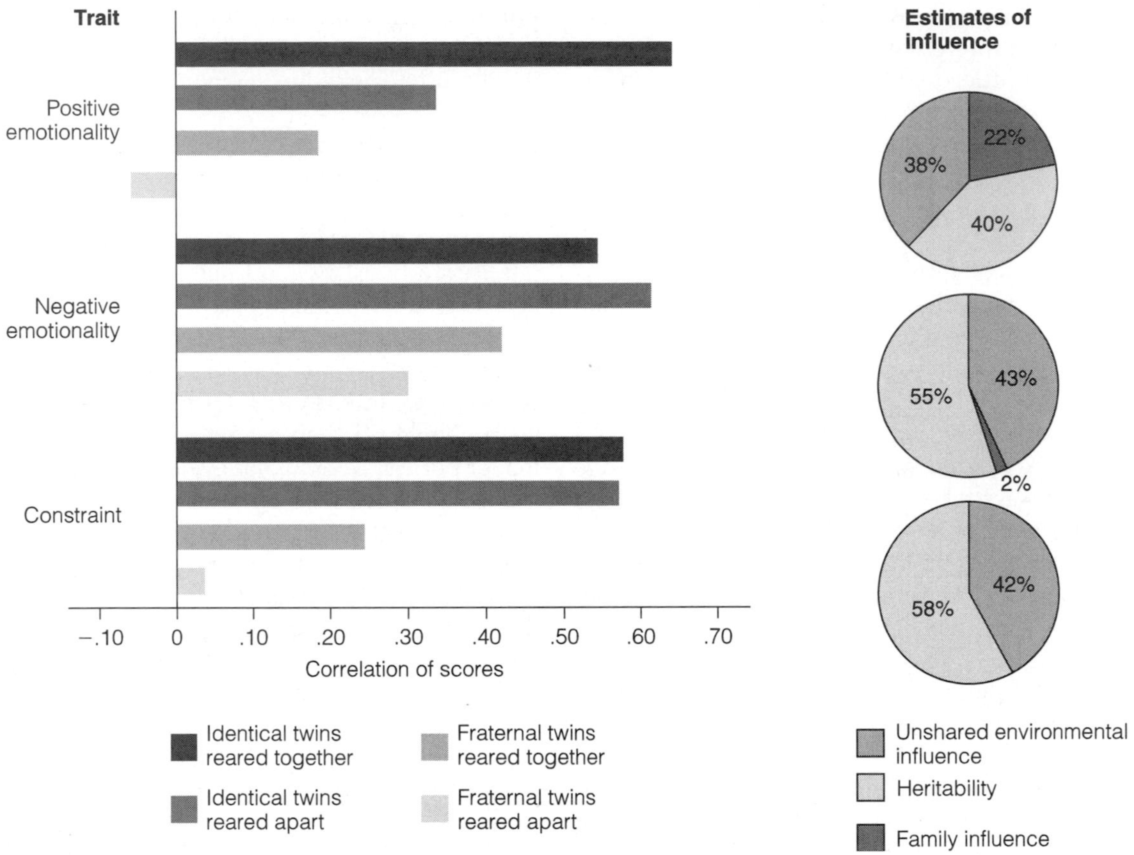

FIGURE **2.1**

Genetic Influences on Well-Being. Left: For three basic personality traits, identical twins were more similar than fraternal twins, even when twins were reared apart (Tellegen et al., 1998). Right: Estimates of heritability derived from the correlational data were relatively high; although investigators also found evidence of environmental influence, the family influence appeared to be neglible for two of the traits (ibid.).

Source: A. Tellegen, D. T. Lykken, T. J. Bouchard Jr., K. J. Wilcox, N. L. Segal, & S. Rich (1988), Personality similarity in twins reared apart and together, *Journal of Personality & Social Psychology,* 54 (6), 1031–1039 with permission. Copyright 1988 by the American Psychological Association.

also be very warm, personable, and open once they are familiar with people. The same idea applies to the happiness set point.

Can We Adjust Our Happiness Set Point?

One of the problems with the research on genes is that estimates of heritability show considerable variation across studies. The results of these studies also work better at predicting levels of emotionality over long periods of time. When looking at shorter time intervals, genes may play less of a role in self-reported well-being. While our genes certainly do not completely control our emotional lives, it is becoming more evident that the genetic contribution to our emotional makeup is more significant than we realized.

If there is a strong genetic component to long-term stability of emotionality, does this mean that we can do little to enhance a positive experience of life? On the contrary, everyone can do something to bring more happiness into his or her life. When dealing with the topic of genes and emotionality, scientists agree that genes do not completely determine the level of happiness or life satisfaction in any given person. Even David Lykken, one of the major proponents of the heritability and set point theories, has said that we can influence our level of well-being by creating environments that are more conducive to feelings of happiness and working with our genes. Lykken (2000) said,

> The basic point one must remember is that genes affect the mind largely indirectly, by influencing the kinds of experiences people have and the kinds of environments they seek out. . . . If your happiness set point is below average, that means that your genetic steersman is guiding you into situations that detract from your well-being and is tempting you to behave in ways that are counterproductive. If you let your genetic steersman have his way, then you will end up where he wants to go. But it is *your* life and, within wide limits, you can choose your own destinations instead of having them all chosen for you (p. 60, italics in original).

Therefore, factors such as the family environment that a person grows up in, education, and cultural factors do have an impact on a person's sense of happiness and well-being. We can do something about our average level of well-being.

While some debate exists over the exact contribution of genetics to long-term well-being (see Diener & Lucas, 1999), the genetic influences on dispositional positive and negative emotionality are not open to debate. The same is true for certain personality traits, such as extroversion and neuroticism, which are often associated with dispositional emotionality; significant portions of these personality traits are inherited. Nevertheless, recall that we can do things to influence our sense of well-being on a daily basis. In addition, as we will see throughout this text, self-reported happiness is not the only important gauge of psychological well-being.

Moods and Psychological Well-Being

Any discussion of emotions must eventually turn to the topic of moods. Although moods are different than emotions, psychologists do not agree on exactly how they are different. Some see moods as more or less mild forms of emotions, while others see moods and emotions as fairly distinct entities serving unique purposes. What everyone does agree on is that moods are more diffuse, more global, and more pervasive than emotions (Morris, 1999). That is, emotions are focused feelings that can appear or disappear rapidly in response to events in the environment. Moods, however, are generally fairly pervasive and maintain their general tone in spite of a number of minor changes in the environment. For instance, imagine a person who is usually in a fairly good mood. People describe her as cheerful. Today she is driving home with her children in the car and someone driving rather dangerously cuts in front of her and endangers her and her children. Understandably, she reacts with anger. An hour later, however, she has returned to her normal emotional state or her normal cheerful mood. Therefore, a person can be in a good mood for hours, days, or weeks, in spite of fluctuations in emotional states.

Another characteristic of moods is that they are partially caused by how we think about the world. Just like many emotional experiences, moods may rely on certain ways of thinking about the world and us. In the case of moods, the thought processes involved may be our expectations about potential positive or negative emotions in our future (Hewitt, 2002). From this perspective, when we are in a good mood we are probably experiencing relatively positive emotions at the moment *and* we are also expecting to experience more or less positive emotions in the future. Because expectations are personal beliefs and the future has not yet occurred, moods become dependent on personal beliefs that often cannot be verified. In other words, in many instances, moods do not depend upon "facts" (Hewitt, 2002). For instance, if our friend Robert is in a good mood most of the time because he believes that the woman of his dreams is waiting "just around the next corner," then we have no way to verify if Robert's mood is based on an accurate picture of the future. Of course, if Robert is currently in a mental hospital suffering from schizophrenic delusions, then we might more reasonably conclude that his expectations are wrong. In many instances, however, it is hard to prove that a person's mood state is wrong or unjustified. This interesting quality of moods is important to positive psychology because positive moods have a number of advantages. It may be that we do not have to wait for our expectations to be "proved" in order to reap some benefits of positive moods.

Advantages of Positive Moods

Recent studies have found that emotions and moods have a significant impact on almost any psychological process, such as memory, attention, perception, and our experience of self. In particular, being in a happy or positive mood fosters more adaptable responses to the world in a number of ways. For instance, being in a positive mood tends to increase altruism, increase the efficiency of decision-making, promote creativity, and decrease aggression (Isen, 2002). In addition, positive moods enhance the quality of interpersonal relationships and help to increase job satisfaction (Morris, 1999; Isen, 2001).

Studies have also found that mood can have an impact on memory, perception, judgment, and self-focused attention. In general, studies have found that when people are in a certain mood, it is easier for them to recall memories that are congruent with that mood (see Morris, 1999). This phenomenon is called *mood-congruent recall.* Interestingly, for positive psychology, the effect can be seen when people are in a positive mood. Being in a good mood helps to promote the recall of positive memories (Matt, Vazquez, & Campbell, 1992). This effect may be especially strong when the information to be recalled is highly relevant to the self (Sedikides, 1992). In addition, being in a good mood may also inhibit the recall of negative memories.

Influences of Moods

If moods can impact our memories, is it also true that they can influence our current perception of events? Research suggests that there are mood-congruent effects on our current perceptions and judgments, as well as on memory. We can see the effect by asking a question. Is a person more likely to go out on a first date with someone they are very attracted to when they are in a good mood or a bad mood? Obviously, most people are more likely to take the risk when they are in a good mood. Why would this be true? The effect may be simply another version of memory. That is, if we are in a good mood, then we remember previous "dates made in heaven." If we are in a bad mood, then we recall our "dates from hell." Norbert Schwarz and G. Clore (1996), however, have argued that what we consult are feelings and moods more than our memories. When we are feeling very good, we may be willing to take some action that we have previously and repeatedly failed at because our good mood helps us to ignore prior difficulties and memories of bad experiences in the past. With this in mind, you can see that the results of any decision-making based on rational risk-benefit analysis can easily be overridden by our current mood.

An interesting line of research has looked at how our moods may influence our attention to ourselves. Repeatedly, studies show being in a bad mood leads people to focus more attention on themselves (see Morris, 1999). That is, being in a bad mood makes it more likely that people will focus their attention on their own thoughts and feelings. Neuroticism is also associated with rumination or the tendency to obsessively go over a problem or situation in one's mind (Nolen-Hoeksema, 1991). So, when one's friends are in a bad mood they seem to be more self-absorbed, more preoccupied with their own issues, and even appear a little selfish.

The relationship between mood and self-attention, however, does not appear to be consistent when people are in good moods. Being in a good mood can either propel us toward self-focused attention, such as congratulating ourselves on a job well done, or it can facilitate us to direct attention away from ourselves, such as in altruism. In Chapters 4 and 10, some perspectives on well-being will be discussed that show how enhanced well-being is associated with decreased self-focused attention.

Finally, William Morris (1999) believes that a basic function of moods is to provide us with information about the adequacy of our current resources to meet current or future demands. He believes moods provide us with a continuous monitoring system that gives on-going information about how well we can cope. For instance, when most people are in a really good mood they feel as if they can take on challenges and risks. Being in a bad mood, however, leads to a drop in confidence and optimism. Note that David Watson (2002) reminds us that tendencies toward mood fluctuations are related to biological rhythms, so that many people experience drops in energy or enthusiasm at different points during the day. Given these findings, we need to be aware of the fact that not everyone will experience the same levels of positive emotions. In addition, not everyone will be able to sustain a high level of positive emotions throughout the day. Therefore, we need to remind ourselves that the goal of studying positive psychology is not simply to create high levels of positive emotionality for everyone throughout the entire day, each and every day, over the course of an entire lifetime. That goal is not possible. The challenge of creating greater well-being is far more interesting than can be expressed by that overly simplistic formula. Nonetheless, the message for a positive psychology is that positive moods help us to adapt better and help to provide us with opportunities to learn and grow. Obviously, good moods are not all that is required for greater flourishing and thriving, but they are one necessary piece of the puzzle.

Positive Psychology and Motivation

Early Theories of Motivation

If part of positive psychology involves the investigation of human flourishing and finding one's own personal best, then somehow people must be motivated to pursue those goals. This section of the chapter will look at how psychology has explained the forces that propel people toward their goals.

As might be expected, there is no simple answer to questions about what causes us to pursue certain goals. Animal models often focus on a small set of basic biological instincts. However, while certain human emotional responses, such as fear, may be innate, the behavioral responses to those emotions in humans can show considerable variation. In general, the amazing varieties of motivations behind human behavior are too complex to be explained in any satisfactory way by instinct theories. Up until the 1950s, the predominant theories of human motivation mostly assumed that people were compelled to act in order to (1) increase pleasure and decrease painful experiences, (2) get innate physiological needs met, or (3) compensate for innate drive states that were potentially threatening to the social fabric. In these perspectives, various needs produce drives or internal drive states that motivate people to reduce the needs that when satisfied will return them to a state of

homeostasis. This term refers to a state of equilibrium in which a person is not compelled to act in any specific way. In this state, no compelling need motivates behavior because needs are satisfied, and a state of equilibrium exists. The need for food, for instance, would produce a drive that motivates a person to search for food, which when found and consumed, would eliminate the need (hunger), and the person would return to homeostasis. As in this example, the needs were often given a biological origin, and a number of psychologists over the years have searched for the fundamental set of basic biological needs. But is this all we are looking for in life—just a state of quiet equilibrium and mild satisfaction?

In fact, research has found that even rats were motivated by such intangibles as novelty and curiosity (Berlyne, 1960). That is, just having their needs met was not enough for them—they needed something more in life. If this is true for rats, imagine how much more true it is human beings. Once again, the complexity of human beings proved too great to be explained by biologically based needs. There is no biological need, for instance, to be the world's greatest violinist. And yet, people are driven to achieve that goal. So while drive reduction theories of motivation each have some merit and can be used to explain behavior under certain circumstances, none of them is particularly appealing as an explanation for why some people actually thrive or do extraordinarily well in life.

Almost fifty years ago, Robert W. White (1959) argued that people can be motivated by more than just drives to fulfill physiological or "tissue" needs. White urged psychologists to consider the relevance of intrinsic motivations that propelled people toward a sense of competence—or *effectance motivations.* He said that people are also compelled to engage their immediate environments in ways that will produce effective outcomes. In his view, people are active participants in their worlds and not just reactive to events or circumstances that they confront. People are driven to engage the world in ways that will give them a sense of competence and accomplishment that goes beyond the meeting of physiological needs.

Intrinsic and Extrinsic Motivation

One of the more interesting lines of research in motivation concerns the difference between intrinsic and extrinsic motivation. **Intrinsic motivation** is operating when we are compelled to engage in some activity for its own sake, regardless of any external reward. **Extrinsic motivation** comes into play when we act to obtain some external reward, be it status, praise, money, or other incentive that comes from outside ourselves. Studies in this area grew out of research that, ironically, found decreased motivation when people were given rewards for pursuing intrinsically satisfying goals (Deci, 1975). In other words, under some circumstances, if people are motivated to engage in a certain activity simply for their own enjoyment then being rewarded for the same activity can act as a deterrent.

A study by Lepper, Greene, and Nesbitt (1973) illustrates this idea. They introduced a fun drawing activity into children's "free-play" activity time. After observing the children playing, they selected those children who appeared to find intrinsic satisfaction in drawing. Later, they placed the children in three conditions. Some children were shown a "Good Player" certificate and asked if they wished to draw in order to win the award. In other words, the children were given the opportunity to do what they liked in order get a reward. Some children simply engaged in drawing and later were unexpectedly given the "Good Player" certificate. Finally, some children simply drew, and they neither expected nor received any reward. Two weeks later the children were again allowed to engage in the drawing activity. What researchers found was that children who chose to draw in order to win the reward showed less interest in drawing. Further, when the rewards were taken away, these children simply stopped drawing pictures! It seemed almost as if the external reward destroyed the original intrinsic reasons for drawing. Children in the other two conditions showed no significant change in their interest in drawing.

This phenomena of displacing intrinsic motivations by providing extrinsic rewards has been termed *overjustification*. Later, Lepper and Greene (1978) reviewed the studies on this phenomenon. They concluded that there was "considerable evidence" that under certain conditions if a person is given a reward for doing something that they find intrinsically satisfying, the reward can "undermine that individual's subsequent intrinsic motivation to engage in the behavior" (p. 121). This does not disprove the idea that people will often work for external rewards, but it does show that external rewards are certainly not the only goals that compel people's behavior.

As an illustration of this point, imagine that someone offered to pay a person money to fall in love. Each time the person felt more affection and caring for their boyfriend or girlfriend they were given a cash reward. For most people, being given money for this very intrinsically satisfying emotional experience would "take the spark" out of love. Chapter 4 discusses research that supports the idea that activities we engage in just for fun or intrinsic satisfaction—intrinsically motivated activities—can be necessary components of well-being.

Self-Determination Theory

Some researchers view the difference between intrinsic and extrinsic motivation as extremely important for an understanding of mental health, achievement, and well-being, as well as for an understanding of basic motivation. Richard Ryan and Edward Deci (2000) state that people who are intrinsically motivated tend to show enhancements in performance, persistence, creativity, self-esteem, vitality, and general well-being when compared to people who are motivated by external rewards. They note that this difference is even found when the two groups are of equal competence performing the same task. This is an amazing list of advantages for the intrinsically motivated. In fact, Ryan and Deci (2000) go even further and state, "Perhaps no single phenomena reflects the positive potential of human nature as much as intrinsic motivation, [or] the inherent tendency to seek out novelty and challenges, to extend and exercise one's capacities, to explore, and to learn" (p. 70).

Although at first glance Ryan and Deci's statement may seem to be a bit overly enthusiastic, when the research literature is examined there is justification for their energetic endorsement of intrinsic motivation. A positive relationship has been found between being intrinsically motivated and achieving positive outcomes in numerous areas, such as health behaviors, religious participation, intimate relationships, and even political activism (Ryan & Deci, 2000).

Deci and Ryan (1985) took the research on intrinsic and extrinsic motivation and from those studies developed what they called **self-determination theory,** which postulates that certain inherent tendencies toward psychological growth, along with a core group of innate emotional needs, are the basis for self-motivation and personality integration. In self-determination theory, the three basic needs are

1. *Competence:* the need for mastery experiences that allows a person to deal effectively with her or his environment.
2. *Relatedness:* the need for mutually supportive interpersonal relationships.
3. *Autonomy:* the need to make independent decisions about areas in life that are important to the person.

Ryan and Deci (2000) state that these three needs "appear to be essential for facilitating optimal functioning of the natural propensities for growth and integration, as well as for constructive social development and personal well-being" (p. 68). That is, intrinsically motivated behavior is often an attempt to meet our innate needs for competence, relatedness, or autonomy. If those needs are met, then people show better adaptive functioning. Studies have found that the combination of high autonomy and the perception of low levels of coercive control from others is associated with better ego development, higher self-esteem, higher self-actualization scores, greater consistency of the self, more persistence in working toward goals, more satisfaction at work, and fewer experiences of boredom (see Knee & Zuckerman, 1998). Therefore, if positive psychology is partially defined as the investigation of factors that support human flourishing, then one way to measure the success of those factors might be to look at the degree to which they foster a sense of competence, contribute toward the development of positive relationships, and enhance a sense of healthy autonomy.

Cognitive Evaluation Theory

What are some of the conditions that support a self-determination theory approach to human flourishing? As a subset within self-determination theory, Deci and Ryan (1985) presented **cognitive evaluation theory** as a way to help explain social and environmental factors that lead to variations in intrinsic motivation. One of the conditions that help to enhance these needs is an activity that involves both challenges and the type of feedback that helps the person to learn. Along with this is freedom from evaluations that are demeaning and belittling. In addition, these are activities that often involve novelty or provide a sense of aesthetic value for the person. Another condition that helps meet these needs is fostering an internal locus of control, as when a person is given choices, opportunities for self-direction, and is allowed to acknowledge feelings. Further, social contexts in which a person feels somewhat secure and knows that social support is available are conducive to meeting the three needs. In contrast, conditions that hinder intrinsic motivation and the meeting of the three needs include overly critical evaluations, lack of social support, external rewards that are designed to decrease a sense of autonomy, and achievements that are not tied to freely chosen goals.

TABLE 2.1 Activities and Environments That Support or Inhibit Intrinsic Motivation

	Support intrinsic motivation
Activities that	Allow a sense of autonomy Stimulate a sense of competence Have intrinsic interest Contain novelty and stimulate curiosity Have some aesthetic value Present optimal challenges Are freely chosen Allow acknowledgment of feelings.
Environments that	Provide competence promoting feedback Involve supportive personal relationships Are safe and provide a sense of security Are free from demeaning evaluations.
	Inhibit intrinsic motivation
Activities that	Involve goals imposed by others Involve deadlines and pressures Involve tangible rewards given only on the basis of task performance
Environments that	Involve extrinsic rewards Involve pressured evaluations Involve threats or directives to perform.

Source: Ryan & Deci, 2000; Lyubormirsky, 2001.

Table 2.1 presents a summary of the conditions that foster and hinder the development and use of intrinsic motivations.

Motivation and the Pursuit of Goals

While some researchers have investigated motivation by looking at internal drive states, others have focused more on our expectations or hopes for the future. For instance, when we discuss what our hopes and dreams are for the years ahead, then we are talking about our goals. The unique goals we have for our life determine where we place our efforts and commitments. In addition, the specific character of our goals and our relationships to them at any moment in time determine our emotional state. Imagine a person who has been training for the Olympic gold medal in the marathon race for the last ten years. She is now ahead of all the other runners with only 10 yards to the finish line and the next runner at least 25 yards behind her. How would she feel? It does not take too much imagination to realize that when we attain our goals we tend to feel happier. This is especially true the more important those goals are to us. In fact, goals may be extremely important to our positive emotional state at any point in time and to our general emotional well-being.

Qualities of Goal Pursuit that Predict Greater Well-Being

Researchers who have studied goals and their relationships to well-being have found that certain types of goals are more effective in producing happiness and satisfaction than are other types (see Ryan & Deci, 2000; Lyubomirsky, 2001). In general, goals that are the result of *intrinsic motivation,* are *personally valued, realistic,* and *freely chosen* seem to be better at raising subjective well-being. The pursuit of goals that are meaningful to us is more fulfilling than chasing after goals that are imposed on us by others or that we do not value. For example, Oishi, Diener, Suh, and Lucas (1999) obtained ratings of how much satisfaction college students gained from engaging in a variety of activities. They found differences among activities such that high subjective well-being was related to activities involving both interpersonal relationships and community contributions. However, higher subjective well-being was found when the activity reflected a person's individual values. For instance, students who valued benevolence experienced higher subjective well-being when they were involved in helpful social activities or when showing other people that they cared for them.

In general, it appears that well-being is enhanced by seeking goals associated with *positive relationships and helping others,* while relatively self-centered goals decrease well-being. One example is a study by Tim Kasser and Richard Ryan (1993) that found subjective well-being was enhanced when people pursued goals that facilitated affiliation, intimacy, self-acceptance, and community involvement. Goals that are *valued by one's culture* may also be more effective in raising well-being (Cantor & Sanderson, 1999). The influence of culture can also be seen in how people view the social context of achievement. Yang (1982) distinguished two forms of achievement motivation: individually oriented and socially oriented. In Western cultures, individually oriented achievement is more common, but the socially oriented form is more common in Chinese cultures. Bond (1986) and Doi (1985) both found that high socially oriented achievement was associated with high motives for affiliation and involvement with family. In Western cultures, the affiliation and achievement motives are usually fairly independent. On the other hand, too much individually oriented achievement motivation can be hazardous to happiness. Nancy Cantor and Catherine Sanderson (1999) reported that well-being is lowered when people seek relatively self-centered goals related to physical attractiveness, fame, and wealth. In the same way, people who are too materialistic or too power-oriented tend to have lower well-being (Sirgy, 1998).

The next issue concerns approach versus avoidance goals. Approach goals motivate us to move toward something (e.g., "I want to get a Ph.D. in psychology"). Avoidance goals motivate us to avoid difficulties, dangers, or fears (e.g., "I try to avoid speaking in public because it makes me nervous"). Studies have found that *approach goals* are more likely to be associated with subjective well-being than are avoidance goals. Well-being is higher when people see themselves as moving toward something they value rather than trying to avoid something difficult or painful. Once again, however, cultural differences may be important. Studies suggest that approach goals are more central to people in individualistic cultures. People in cultures that are more socially oriented may be more concerned with avoiding failure because failure reflects on their family as well as themselves (see Diener, Oishi, & Lucas, 2003).

The rate at which people approach their valued goals is also important. *Adequate or better than adequate progress* translates into higher well-being (Hsee & Abelson, 1991). The rate of progress that a person makes toward goals or expects to make toward goals is even more important than actual achievement of the goals. Acceptable rates of progress are associated with more positive emotions. For instance, a goal such as "learn to play the piano well" is one that is never quite reached because one can always play better than one does now. For most people, satisfaction comes, in part, from learning to play better with an acceptable rate of progress.

The impact that our goals may have on our sense of happiness or life satisfaction may also depend upon how specific our goals are. In terms of specificity, Robert Emmons (1992) found that highly abstract goals may decrease immediate well-being because their abstract nature makes it hard to know when they have been achieved. For instance, if one's goal is to "be a caring and compassionate person," it is hard to know when one has treated people with enough compassion. In contrast, a goal such as "treat at least one person every day with caring, compassion, and understanding" is more concrete, and a person knows immediately if he or she has achieved it or not. On the other hand, not having any abstract or high-level long-term goals that serve to orient one's life direction is associated with lower well-being. Brian Little (1989) has called this dilemma the conflict between "magnificent obsessions and trivial pursuits." Emmons (1992) suggested that it is best to find a *balance between specific and abstract goals* by setting concrete, behavioral short-term goals that are directly linked to more abstract and meaningful longer-term goals. For example, it may be that we can work toward the goal of "ending world hunger" as long as we do it step by step.

Relationships among Goals

Another important quality of our goals concerns the relationships among our goals. The first issue here concerns the levels of congruence and conflict among our goals. In particular, greater subjective well-being is associated with *more congruence among different goals* and less internal conflict between competing goals. For instance, people who have eight or ten major goals in life that are all "very important" may end up creating conflicts among those goals because of a real lack of time to fully accomplish all their goals. Note that the contemporary wish to "have it all" in terms of career, family, self-development, community involvement, and leisure may actually exaggerate internal conflicts among goals and may lower happiness. Social adaptation and adjustment can be defined as the process that reduces conflicts among our important life goals.

Emmons (1986, 1992; Emmons & King, 1988) suggested that it is possible to group a number of smaller goals around common themes. He called this common theme in our goal pursuits our *personal strivings*—larger groupings of smaller goals that may help to facilitate bigger more abstract goals. As an example of a personal striving, Emmons listed, "Find that special someone." Note that many smaller goals such as "Be open with other people," "Take an interest in other people," and "Get out and socialize more" may all be part of this personal striving that is, in turn, related to the higher-level goal of "Find a lasting and satisfying intimate relationship." Emmons found that personal strivings are related to subjective well-being in ways similar to goals. For instance, people with high life satisfaction believe that their personal strivings are "important, valued, not likely to produce conflict, and [they] expect to be successful at them" (Emmons, 1986, p. 1064). Interestingly, Emmons (1992) also found that having meaningful and successful personal strivings is a stronger predictor of subjective well-being than personality traits.

Hope Theory

One of the most important elements in whether people are motivated to pursue their goals is the expectation or the hope that they will eventually attain those goals. In most instances, it is hard to bring much enthusiasm to the pursuit of an important but unreachable goal. Many older theories of hope and motivation were based on the idea of expectations for success in attaining goals. However, is that all there is to our hopes for the future? Is it simply the expectation that we will reach our goals?

Hope theory says that hope is actually the result of two processes: (1) pathways, or believing that one can find ways to reach desired goals; and (2) agency, or believing that one can become motivated enough to pursue those goals (Snyder, Rand, & Sigmon, 2002). Therefore, this theory says that hope about the future is the result of believing we can create both realistic plans and enough drive to reach important goals. People who are hopeful also tend to feel more positive emotions. Among a number of other positive benefits, people who are high in hope tend to anticipate greater well-being in the future, are more confident, may be able to deal with stress more successfully, are flexible enough to find alternative pathways to their goals, and tend to have higher social support (Snyder, Rand, & Sigmon, 2002).

Participation in Life

Finally, Nancy Cantor and Catherine Sanderson (1999) suggested that one of the reasons that goal pursuit is associated with well-being is because it implies that people are being active participants in life. The pursuit of goals is simply an indication that people are taking part in life; they are involved, interested, and active participants in living a full life. As in goal pursuit theories, Cantor and Sanderson believe that greater well-being is found through participation in activities that are intrinsically motivating, freely chosen, desired, and involve realistic, feasible goals. In addition, they believe that activities that increase opportunities for participation in a variety of other activities will tend to increase well-being. Of course, the types of activities people choose to be involved with will certainly change over the lifespan, by gender and according to other factors. It is not which activity people choose but the process of being involved in an active life that really matters.

Summary

This chapter reviewed topics in psychology that are relevant to positive psychology. Quite appropriately, the first topic reviewed was positive emotion. Current psychological perspectives on emotion see positive emotional experiences as biologically given, innate, and influenced by hereditary factors. However, our cognitions matter a great deal in that people can create different emotions for similar events depending on how they interpret and give meaning to the events. The positive emotions were explored through the broaden-and-build theory of positive emotions. Positive emotions may help us adapt by broadening our response options and building psychological and social resources for the future. Newer theories of motivation view people as actively involved in seeking out intrinsically satisfying experiences and engaged in a process of continuous development centered on needs for competence, relatedness, autonomy, and hopeful expectations for the future.

Learning Tools

Key Terms and Ideas

BROADEN-AND-BUILD MODEL
COGNITIVE EVALUATION THEORY
EXTRINSIC MOTIVATION

HAPPINESS SET POINT
HOMEOSTASIS
INTRINSIC MOTIVATION
SELF-DETERMINATION THEORY
THOUGHT-ACTION TENDENCIES
UNDOING HYPOTHESIS

Books

Deci, E., & Flaste, R. (1996). *Why we do what we do.* New York: Penguin. An explanation of intrinsic motivation and self-determination theory for the general public (popular).

Kahneman, D., Diener, E., & Schwartz, N. (Eds.) (1999). *Well-being: The foundations of hedonic psychology.* New York: Russell Sage. A collection of papers on positive emotions and well-being (professional, but some articles would be fine for undergraduate students).

Lykken, D. (2000). *Happiness: The nature and nurture of joy and contentment.* New York: St. Martin's Griffin. A readable exploration of well-being by a leading proponent of the genetic and heritability theories of positive emotionality (popular).

Research Articles

Buss, D. (2000). The evolution of happiness. *American Psychologist, 55*(1), 15–23. Evolutionary perspective on positive emotions.

Fredrickson, B. (1998). What good are positive emotions? *Review of General Psychology, 2,* 300–319. The first presentation of the broaden-and-build model of positive emotions.

On The Web

http://www.ukans.edu/~crsnyder. C. R. Snyder's home page with links to articles and measurement scales related to hope.

http://eqtoday.com. Information on *EQ Today,* a magazine devoted to emotional intelligence.

http://www.utne.com/azEQ.tmpl. This is a short "test" of your emotional intelligence. Note that this is just for fun—the test has not been studied scientifically. The site does offer some good information on emotional intelligence.

Personal Explorations

What things intrinsically interest you? What would you do even if you were not paid for it? Are you studying that interest area now in school? If not, why not? Remember there are no "right" answers to this question. That is, some people work at jobs that truly interest them, while others save those interests for their time outside of work.

List the things that have intrinsic interest for you—things you just love to do. Next, list how frequently you have done these things in the past month. For the exercise, double the frequency of two to three of these activities for the next two weeks. Record how you feel after the two weeks.

How would you set up a classroom for sixth-grade children so that *intrinsic* motivation would be enhanced? Just for contrast, set up the same classroom so that *extrinsic* motivation was emphasized.

PART

ii

POSITIVE EMOTIONAL STATES

CHAPTER 3

SUBJECTIVE WELL-BEING

> An increase in happiness is the closest thing psychology has to a "general tonic" for greater well-being.
>
> *Ed Diener (2000a)*

Contemporary studies that investigate the causes, predictors, and consequences of happiness and satisfaction with life are referred to as studies of *subjective well-being*. Researchers in psychology tend to index subjective well-being with scores on two major variables: happiness and satisfaction with life. When researchers ask people about their **happiness,** they are asking them to report on their *emotional* state and how they *feel* about their world and themselves. Questions about a person's **satisfaction with life** tend to address a more global *judgment* about the acceptability of his or her life. These answers are the result of a more *cognitive* process. That is, a person needs to weigh the actual outcomes in life against the alternative outcomes and make a judgment about whether he or she is satisfied with the result of that comparison. In addition, a third factor—low *neuroticism*—is sometimes added to form the basic triad of subjective well-being.[1] Recently, however, the sharp distinction between emotional and cognitive measures has been called into question (Crooker & Near, 1998). Yet, most studies have shown that these three areas should be considered as separate components of subjective well-being and need to be measured as such (Diener & Lucas, 1999). Therefore, high subjective well-being is found when people report they are feeling very happy, very satisfied with life, and when experiencing low levels of neuroticism. Research on subjective well-being became the first systematic study of happiness to focus on large groups of people and to utilize the statistical procedures and methodology of contemporary psychology.

THE MEASUREMENT OF SUBJECTIVE WELL-BEING

One of the problems that held back research on happiness was how to measure it. The major problem with the measurement of subjective well-being is the issue of who will define it. At the time of Plato and Aristotle, many people thought that philosophers or intellectuals should define it for everyone. Later, leaders of

Christianity believed that they should define happiness for everyone. In the twentieth century, a number of theories on positive mental health were proposed, but it was often hard to tell how the author's own personal preferences and values influenced those theories. So, if philosophers, religious leaders, or psychologists could not define happiness, life satisfaction, or well-being, then who could?

One solution to the problem was to use a very straightforward approach. Researchers began to allow the research participants themselves to define these terms. In this way, the real judge of how happy someone was would be "whoever lives inside a person's skin" (Myers & Diener, 1995, p. 11). Researchers reasoned that, because evaluations of happiness are subjective phenomena, they should be measured with subjective reports. Therefore, researchers would simply ask someone, "Are you happy?" or "How happy are you?" and then use their responses as valid data in their studies. Note that this particular strategy would be completely unacceptable to someone like Freud, who believed in the fallibility of conscious explanations for one's own behavior. For Freud, self-reports of being "very happy" could be the result of defense mechanisms designed to protect one's conscious awareness from unacceptable impulses. If Freud were correct, then self-reports of happiness would often differ from collateral assessments—that is, reports given by others who know the person well. Somewhat unexpectedly, however, research has found that self-reports and reports from others who know the person well often show reasonable agreement (Sandvik, Diener, & Seidlitz, 1993; Diener, 1994). Studies on subjective well-being found that people who reported higher levels of happiness and satisfaction with life also tended to behave as if they were happier and more satisfied. In addition, other people perceived these people as being happier and more satisfied. Therefore, it was acceptable to ask people about their own perceived happiness and satisfaction with their lives and then give credence to the answers they gave.

Self-Report Measures of Subjective Well-Being

A number of measurement instruments were devised for this research endeavor. Almost all of them assumed that happiness and life satisfaction could be ordered on a continuum from "very happy" to "very unhappy." The actual measurement scale might assess self-perceptions of happiness (see Fordyce, 1988). The scale might ask people to compare themselves with their peers (Lyubomirsky & Lepper, 1999), or it might ask a person to respond to a statement such as, "In most ways my life is ideal" (Diener, Emmons, Larsen, & Griffin, 1985). Or, the scale could provide a series of cartoon faces that vary from big smiles to deep frowns and ask people to choose which one expresses how they feel about their lives (Andrews & Withey, 1976). Figure 3.1 gives examples of these measurement strategies.

While the particular questions asked were slightly different, they were all based on two assumptions about the answers to those questions. First, all assumed that the amount of happiness or satisfaction that a person experienced could be translated into number scales. In this way, if a person scored a 6 on a test of happiness before marriage and an 8 on the same test after marriage, then it was scientifically justifiable to say that the person's happiness had increased after marriage. The second assumption was that if two different people both scored an 8 on the same test, then they both had approximately the same level of happiness. For instance, if one person is a millionaire living on the French Riviera and the other is a New York cab driver but they both scored an 8 on the same test of happiness, then they are about equally happy. These types of assumptions are necessary in order to do quality scientific research. If either of these assumptions had proved to be inaccurate, then the field of subjective well-being might

a

Which face comes closest to expressing how you feel about your life as a whole?

b

____ 1. In most ways my life is close to ideal.

____ 2. I am satisfied with my life.

Strongly disagree	1	2	3	4	5	6	7	Strongly agree

c

Compared to most of my peers, I consider myself:

Less happy	1	2	3	4	5	6	7	More happy

Some people are generally very happy. They enjoy life regardless of what is going on, getting the most out of everything. To what extent does this characterization describe you?

FIGURE 3.1

Measurement Scales: (a) Subjective well-being faces; (b) Satisfaction with life scale (partial); (c) Subjective happiness scale (partial)

Source: (a) Andrews & Withey (1976); (b) Diener, Emmons, Larsen, & Griffin (1985); (c) Lyubormirsky & Lepper (1999).

have quickly faded from the psychological landscape. However, studies tended to support the use of these two assumptions. Happiness and life satisfaction could be ordered along a continuum and that equivalent scores reflected roughly equivalent levels of happiness and satisfaction with life (Diener, 1984). In addition, current measurement strategies allow for at least some degree of validity in cross-cultural comparisons of subjective well-being (Diener, Oishi, & Lucas, 2003).

The Stability of Subjective Well-Being

The other question that needed to be answered was whether scores on any measure of subjective well-being represented stable aspects of psychological functioning or whether they were simply temporary reactions to life events or fluctuations in mood. If scores on a test of happiness, for instance, changed dramatically from hour to hour, day to day, or month to month, then it might be impossible to make any predictions about the causes of happiness. Luckily, research has supported the idea that a person's average level of happiness and life satisfaction is relatively stable (Costa, & McCrae, 1984, 1988; Diener, 1994). In fact, studies have found that self-ratings of life satisfaction and happiness are really quite stable for up to six years after testing (i.e., correlations in the .40 to .50 range between time 1 and time 2) (Diener & Lucas, 1999). Even more interesting are the studies of personality traits related to subjective well-being that have shown reasonable stability of those traits for up to thirty years (Costa, & McCrea, 1986). In a very creative study related to the stability of happiness, LeeAnn Harker and Dacher Keltner (2001) recently found that the amount of positive emotion expressed by women in their high school yearbook pictures—as measured by their smiles—was significantly related to their well-being thirty years later.

Although self-reports of subjective well-being appear to be quite stable over time, it may be that the stability is a result of stability in people's environments. That is, if people rated their happiness in a consistent way over time, but that stability was simply because their lives did not change all that much, then it would be the environment that was primarily responsible for their stable well-being. Once again, this is not the case. People are relatively stable in their self-reports of their own subjective well-being in spite of changes in their external circumstances (Diener & Larsen, 1984).

These measurement strategies did not completely solve all the issues. Self-reports of happiness do not show a perfect match with other indicators of well-being. In addition, a substantial amount of research has found frequent use of a number of self-enhancement strategies that allow people to distort their self-perception (discussed later in this chapter). At the same time, it is not true that people's self-reports of their own happiness and life satisfaction are completely unchangeable across different situations. Life events, moods, and other daily fluctuations do have an impact on how people evaluate their subjective well-being on a day-to-day basis. Therefore, some researchers have looked at other ways to measure well-being in addition to self-reports. These other methods have included physiological indicators, multiple measures of well-being over time, or measures of success in real world roles. Ed Diener, one of the leading researchers in this field, has proposed that studies of well-being should often include multiple indicators in order to help solve some of these problems. However, self-report measures of well-being are still the most widely used assessment tool in research studies. Although self-report measurement strategies are very general and ask people to make rather global assessments of their lives, they still provide an acceptable starting point for scientific research.

So, with these methodological hurdles overcome, the stage was set for a small explosion of research into happiness and life satisfaction. Diener (1984) noted that in 1967 there were relatively few research articles published on happiness. Fifteen years later, that number had increased dramatically by over 700. Currently, an on-line database of research on happiness contains over 5,000 articles (Veenhoven,1999)! Today, the investigation of subjective well-being is a recognized research area in psychology, and the results of these studies are being seen in many professional journals. Some of these, such as the *Journal of Happiness Studies,* are entirely devoted to research on happiness and subjective well-being.

Are Most People Happy or Unhappy?

With this small explosion of research into subjective well-being, just what did researchers find when they asked people about their happiness and life satisfaction? A quick glance at various social indices could lead one to conclude that unhappiness is rampant. News reports portray a society with rising rates of divorce, drug problems, crime, and rising sales of pop psychology books designed to fix a plethora of human miseries. Instead of reflecting this apparent pessimistic view of collective well-being, the surprise was that most people reported levels of happiness and satisfaction with their lives that were higher than expected. Surprisingly, subjective well-being studies in many Western industrialized nations routinely find that most people rate their life as "above average." David Myers (2000) reports on surveys done by the National Opinion Research Center, which have found that about 60 percent of Americans describe themselves as "pretty happy" and 30 percent say they are "very happy." Only 10 percent say they are "not too happy." Subjective well-being reports from over one million people in 45 nations have shown that the average global self-report of subjective well-being was an impressive 6.75 on a 10-point scale (see Myers & Diener, 1995;

Myers, 2000). Therefore, when studying the causes and correlates of happiness, it is not necessary to diligently search out those few individuals who are actually feeling happy.

Top-Down and Bottom-Up Theories

When studying the topic of satisfaction with life, there are have been two general approaches to the question of what is important for happiness. The first is that happiness and satisfaction depend on the sum of many smaller pleasures and happy moments (Diener, 1984). In this perspective, known as the **bottom-up theory,** well-being is a summation of the positive experiences in a person's life. It assumes that people create their self-ratings of subjective well-being by summing up a variety of external circumstances and making a judgment. The more frequent the pleasant moments, the happier a person will be. These circumstances may include the quality of one's marriage, how satisfying one's job is, or the amount of one's income. The other perspective postulates that subjective well-being is more related to a general tendency to evaluate and interpret experiences in a positive way. From this perspective, a person brings tendencies toward positivity to the situations he or she encounters in life. This approach to subjective well-being is known as the **top-down theory.** Often this approach is measured by looking at personality traits, attitudes, or the ways a person interprets experiences in life. Note that if the bottom-up perspective is correct, then efforts to improve well-being should focus on changing the environments and situations that a person experiences—better jobs, safer neighborhoods, and more income, to name just a few options. If the top-down is correct, then efforts to increase happiness should focus on changing the person's perceptions, beliefs, or personality traits.

In support of the bottom-up theory, most cross-national studies have found that people living in the more impoverished countries report lower levels of subjective well-being (Diener & Biswas-Diener, 2002). That is, external circumstances do matter. The top-down theory is supported by studies that have found that certain personality traits, attitudes, and self-perceptions are highly correlated with self-reported subjective well-being (see DeNeve & Cooper, 1998; Diener & Lucas, 1999). When Diener and Larson (1984) compared the top-down and the bottom-up approaches, they found that 52 percent of the variation in happiness scores was a result of personality and only 23 percent was due to a summary of situational events. In similar studies, other researchers have found even smaller effects of 8 to 15 percent for situational variables (see Diener, Suh, Lucas & Smith, 1999; Lyubomirsky, 2001). Therefore, while studies strongly suggested that both personality and situations are important, personality appears to be the most important factor in subjective well-being. As with most ideas, however, further analyses suggested that life is more complicated than this simple conclusion.

More recent studies have found that objective life circumstances and personality traits can interact in different ways depending upon the measure of well-being being used and the type of judgment required of the person (Headey, Veenhoven, & Wearing, 1991; Leonardi, Spazzafumo, Marcellini, & Gagliardi, 1999). For instance, whether a person is satisfied with his or her income may depend on factors such as level of achievement motivation, whether the person is a college student or a retiree, or the person's expectations for future earnings, as well as many others. On one hand, it may be that when people are asked how satisfied they are with specific aspects of life (e.g., their job or marriage), then bottom-up assessments may be more important to their answers. On the other hand, questions about broad domain (that is, "life in general") may tap into top-down processes for the answer (Diener, Oishi, & Lucas, 2003).

Predictors of Subjective Well-Being

If there is no trouble finding people who report being fairly happy (at least in many Western industrialized nations), then what might predict subjective well-being? Investigations into happiness and satisfaction with life have found a number of variables that are reliably associated with happiness and satisfaction with life. Various reviews of the literature have been completed, and a general consensus has emerged about the strongest predictors of subjective well-being. The six core variables that best predict happiness and satisfaction with life—at least in Western industrialized cultures (Argyle, 1987; Myers, 1992; Diener et al., 1999) are

1. Positive self-esteem
2. Sense of perceived control
3. Extroversion
4. Optimism
5. Positive social relationships
6. A sense of meaning and purpose to life.

In addition to these variables, remember that the third component of subjective well-being is low self-reported neuroticism. Therefore, the *resolution of inner conflicts* should be considered another predictor as well.

Self-Esteem

As might be expected, the first trait listed as being important to both happiness and life satisfaction is positive self-esteem. Campbell (1981) found that self-esteem was the most important predictor of subjective well-being. In fact, it is difficult to imagine anyone with chronically low self-esteem who feels satisfied with life. Positive self-esteem is associated with adaptive functioning in almost every area of life. Studies have found it to be associated with less delinquency, greater anger control, greater intimacy and satisfaction in relationships, more ability to care for others, and a heightened capacity for creative and productive work (Hoyle, Kernis, Leary & Baldwin, 1999). High self-esteem provides people with a number of advantages, including a sense of meaning and value. It is a helpful guide to negotiating interpersonal relationships and is a natural by-product of healthy personal growth (Ryan & Deci, 2000).

Interestingly, the strong relationship between self-esteem and happiness is not found as consistently in some countries. Specifically, in collectivist countries such as China, where autonomy and self-assertion take a back seat to family and social cohesiveness, self-esteem is a less important predictor of well-being (Diener & Suh, 2000). The relationship between conceptualizations of the self and subjective well-being will be explored further in Chapter 11.

Last, it is also possible to have self-esteem that is *too* high. A sense of self-esteem that is too high is composed of positive self-evaluations but is also somewhat fragile. The fragility comes from positive self-evaluations that are based on unrealistic self-appraisals or are vulnerable to self-reproach or self-condemnation. Roy Baumeister and his colleagues have demonstrated that under these conditions, threats to "high" self-esteem can lead to increased violence or to setting unrealistic goals that have a greater potential for failure (Baumeister, Heatherton, & Tice, 1993). In general, the development and maintenance of self-esteem is a fairly complex process that is sensitive to any number of internal and external cues (see discussion below).

Sense of Perceived Control

The sense of having personal control refers to the belief that one has some measure of control over events in life that are personally important. Indeed, without this sense, life becomes a chaotic whirlwind of random events, which most people would find to be distressing. The need for perceived control may even be an innate need (Ryan & Deci, 2000). This does not imply, however, that a person should have complete control over all events in life. A desire for that level of control is a desire for absolute power and is destructive to well-being—besides being impossible.

In the past, this particular predictor was usually measured as *locus of control* in subjective well-being studies. In research studies, locus of control is generally measured as a continuum from internal to external (Rotter, 1966). A person with a strong *internal locus of control* tends to attribute outcomes to self-directed efforts rather than to external factors or chance. For instance, an average student with an internal locus of control who gets an unexpected "A" on a chemistry test may attribute the grade to the effort put into studying for the exam. An *external locus of control* is the belief that outcomes in one's life are the result of factors outside of the person's immediate control. For instance, an average student with an external locus of control who gets an unexpected "A" on a chemistry test may attribute the grade to the unexpected good mood of the instructor. Last, sometimes a third option is added: chance. A belief in *chance* is essentially a belief that no one is in charge of outcomes. Over the past forty years, there has been a tremendous amount of research on locus of control in psychology. In general, having an internal locus of control is related to a number of positive outcomes (Lefcourt, 1981).

Recently, this predictor of subjective well-being has been slightly redefined. Many researchers now see this factor as a sense of personal control. Peterson (1999) defines *personal control* as "the individual's belief that he or she can behave in ways that maximize good outcomes and/or minimize bad outcomes" (p. 288). Further, a sense of personal control "encourages emotional, motivational, behavioral, and physiological vigor in the face of demands" (Peterson & Stunkard, 1989, p. 290). This newer and expanded vision of personal control encompasses locus of control theory, as well as other ideas in psychology, such as intrinsic motivation and empowerment. (Peterson, 1999). The basic ingredient of personal control is, of course, the belief that one can interact with the world in order to maximize good outcomes or minimize bad outcomes, or both (Peterson & Stunkard, 1989). This belief may take the form of how a person can influence events, choose among outcomes, cope with the consequences of choices, and understand and interpret the results of choices. In other words, personal control runs the whole gamut: from beliefs and expectations to making actual choices, dealing with the consequences of choices, and finding meaning as we reflect on the entire process. Personal control is also viewed as a transactional process such that it is not just a trait but also a dynamic relationship between a person and the environment. Each influences the other in complex patterns of mutual influence.

One of the curious contradictions to the significance of control as a factor in greater subjective well-being comes from religion. Very religious people may believe that God has the ultimate control over their lives. The World War II slogan "God is my co-pilot" and the saint who declares, "Not my will but thine," are examples of what appear to be an external locus of control leading to greater well-being. However, these instances may be what Rothbaum, Weisz, and Snyder (1982) called *secondary control.* With secondary control, people can gain a sense of control by associating themselves with a person, philosophy, or system that they view as more powerful than themselves. Therefore, in a somewhat paradoxical way, it is also possible to feel in control by consciously and deliberately giving up control to a more powerful force, such as God. In other words, one can gain a sense of control by knowing that it was a conscious choice to relinquish control. In spite of these complexities, having a sense of personal control is associated with subjective well-being in many different cultural contexts (Diener, Oishi, Lucas, & Smith, 2003).

Extroversion

An extroverted person is someone who is interested in things outside him- or herself, such as physical and social environments, and is oriented to the world of experiences external to self. In contrast, an introverted person is interested more in his or her own thoughts and feelings. A number of studies have found extroversion to be one of the most significant predictors of subjective well-being (Diener et al., 1999). Some studies even report correlations of .80 between extroversion and self-reported happiness (Fujita, 1991). In addition, extroversion has been shown to predict levels of happiness up to thirty years from the initial testing (Costa & McCrae, 1986). While this variable is consistently correlated with subjective well-being, it does not mean that introverted persons are doomed to depression and ennui. For instance, when Larsen and Kasimatis (1990) asked university students to report their daily moods over the course of a week, extroverts reported an average rating of approximately 2.0 on a scale that listed zero as "neutral" and 3.0 as "happy." Introverts reported an average rating of just over 1.0 for the week. So even though extroverts rated themselves as feeling happier than introverts during the week, both reported levels of happiness that were above the neutral point. Interestingly, in what might be called the weekend effect, Larsen and Kasimatis also found that levels of positive mood began to rise after Wednesdays (the "hump day") and dropped again on Sunday. It is especially important to emphasize the fact that introverts were also on average above the neutral point because extroversion is, in part, inherited.

Recent studies have also looked at exactly how extroversion may influence well-being. Researchers initially thought the sociability component of extroversion was the one most related to well-being (Bradburn, 1969). For instance, studies have found that the number of friends a person has is related to his or her well-being (Okun, Stock, Haring, & Witter, 1984). The more friends a person has, the higher his or her well-being. Therefore, researchers believed that, because more sociable people have greater opportunities for positive relations with other people and more opportunities to obtain positive feedback about themselves from others, this would translate into greater well-being. Recent studies, however, have found that extroverts did not spend more time with other people than did introverts (Pavot, Diener, & Fujita, 1990). However, extroverts seemed to be happier than introverts even when they were spending time alone (Diener, Larsen, and Emmons, 1984). If sociability is not a factor, then why are extroverts more likely to report being happier?

Some researchers have suggested that extroverts tend to report higher levels of happiness because they are born with greater sensitivity to positive rewards (Rusting & Larsen, 1998) or may also have stronger reactions to pleasant events (Larsen & Ketelaar, 1991). It may also be that extroverts may report greater well-being because they have a predisposition to experience positive emotions (Lucas, Diener, Grob, Suh, & Shao, 2000). This, in turn, leads to a greater likelihood that those events are encoded in memory as positive and later recalled as positive memories. Consistent with this idea, studies have found that happier people initially encode events in more positive ways (Seidlitz & Diener, 1993). That is, positive mood leads us to interpret events in positive ways, which are then encoded as positive memories. Later, when asked to recall the events, happier people recall positive memories. In addition, extroverts may report higher levels of happiness because they are more likely to find social situations stimulating and comfortable, and many sources of gratification come from social interactions (Moskowitz & Cote, 1995). That is, the trait of extroversion is often a better "fit" with contemporary life, which is often highly social. Finally, a positive relationship between extroversion and greater subjective well-being has also been found in cross-cultural studies (Lucas, Diener, Grob, Suh, & Shao, 2000). This finding supports the theory of genetic influences on extroversion. You may recall that another predictor of subjective well-being—neuroticism—also has a significant genetic component.

Optimism

In general, people who are more optimistic about the future report being happier and more satisfied with life (see Diener et al., 1999). In light of the other variables discussed, this makes perfect sense. A person who evaluates self in a positive way, believes that he or she is in control of important aspects of life, and is successful at social interactions would more than likely look to the future with hope and positive expectations. Optimism even appears to have an impact on perceived physical health status such that people who are more optimistic report fewer health problems (Scheier & Carver, 1985, 1992). Also, it is obvious that expectations for positive outcomes in the future not only enhance mood but also allow for better coping strategies when under stress.

Like personal control, the concept of optimism has been viewed in a number of ways (Peterson, 2000). It can be viewed as *dispositional optimism,* or the global expectation that things will turn out well in the future (Scheier & Carver, 1987, 1992). It may also be viewed as *hope,* or the belief that one's actions and perseverance will allow goals to be achieved (Snyder, 1994; see Chapter 2). Finally, optimism can be seen as an *explanatory style* or a way in which people explain the causes of events for themselves. For instance, Seligman (1990) proposed that people can learn to be more optimistic by paying attention to how they explain events in life to themselves. He refers to this process as **learned optimism.** Whatever the definition used, people who have a more positive outlook report greater levels of happiness and satisfaction with life. But are optimists just looking at the world through rose-colored glasses because they cannot stand the light of reality?

Lisa Aspinwall (see Aspinwall & Brunhart, 2000) believes this is not the case and that optimists may be the true realists. She found that optimists were more willing than pessimists to receive negative feedback about their performance, to hear bad news about their health, and to bring up difficult issues in their relationships. That is, on one hand, optimism may help people believe that they have the potential to make situations turn out well. On the other hand, it is also true that some people hold optimistic beliefs that are unrealistic or even dangerous (Weinstein, 1980).

Sandra Schneider (2001) makes the case that there is also an alternative, called **realistic optimism.** According to Schneider, realistic optimism is optimistic thinking that does not depart from reality: "Realistic optimism relies on regular reality checks to update assessments of progress, fine-tune one's understanding of potential opportunities, refine causal models of situations, and re-evaluate planned next steps. This involves attention to both environmental and social feedback about whether beliefs fall outside the range of plausible (positive) possibilities" (p. 257). Realistic optimism is an honest recognition that there may be opportunities for positive growth or learning experiences in even the most difficult of situations. Many evaluations and interpretations that we must make about the meaning of events simply cannot be based on facts and certainties. Often we do not know what the future holds for us, and we do not know what ripples may result from any single event in our life. Therefore, we often have substantial latitude for how we can interpret the meaning of life events. In fact, we even have expressions in common use that recognize these potentials. During trying times, we urge people to "see the glass as half full rather than half empty" or to "look for the silver lining behind the dark cloud." At other times, we can give others and ourselves the benefit of the doubt, look for new windows of opportunity amidst a crisis, or at least appreciate the moment with gratitude and acceptance (Schneider, 2001).

Yet, because optimism is a belief, it can be a false belief. For example, most people believe their own risks for developing cancer, heart disease, or divorce is much lower than their statistical risks for those events (Weinstein, 1980). This type of *unrealistic optimism* creates a false sense of security and a bias in risk perception that in some cases can literally be fatal. In general, optimism must be realistic in order to help foster long-term well-being (Schneider, 2001).

Positive Relationships

Another strong predictor of subjective well-being is the presence of positive social relationships (see Diener et al., 1999; Myers, 2000). As discussed in Chapter 2, the need for social interaction may be innate to human beings. The positive relationship between high subjective well-being and satisfaction with family and friends is one of the few true universally found relationships in cross-cultural studies of well-being (Diener, Oishi, & Lucas, 2003). In general, there are two related aspects to having positive social relationships: social support and emotional intimacy. Numerous studies (see, e.g., Sarason, Sarason, & Pierce, 1990) have documented the positive impact that good social support can have on well-being. The perception that one is embedded in supportive social relationships has been related to higher self-esteem, successful coping, better health, and fewer psychological problems. As we will see in Chapter 6, social support also has a positive impact on physical health status. Interestingly, one study found that when people sought out social support there were enhanced effects on subjective well-being for positive self-esteem, optimism, and perceived control (Aspinwall & Taylor, 1992). That is, the impact of the other predictors of subjective well-being was increased if people also had good social support. In a sense, good social support helped to create a rising tide that increased the effects of all the other predictors.

Emotional Intimacy

Intimate social relationships appear to provide even greater enhancements of subjective well-being. For example, one study found that intimacy, defined as relationships with spouse and family and high-quality friendships, was the strongest predictor of life satisfaction (Cummins, 1996), more so than other predictors such as material well-being, health, and leisure satisfaction. Ed Diener and Martin Seligman (2002) decided to look at the happiest 10 percent of a college student sample to see what factors differentiated them from those who were unhappy or of average happiness. The one factor that really stood out was that the happiest group had a very rich and very fulfilling social life. They spent the most time socializing, were rated the highest on positive relationships both by their own ratings and their friends', and all but one was currently involved with a romantic partner. In a study of friendship, Parlee (1979) found that the most frequently reported experience (i.e., 90 percent) women friends share is having an intimate talk. In spite of the cultural assumptions about men and emotional intimacy, having an intimate talk was the second most frequently reported (i.e., 80 percent) friendship experience for men.

Social Contact

A person might wonder whether people prefer to be with others when they are happy or when they are sad. One study asked people in which situations they would most prefer to be alone or with others (see Middlebrook, 1980) and found that people most wanted to be with others when they were very happy. In other words, feeling happy may increase social contact. Because positive social contact also appears to increase well-being, the relationships between subjective well-being and positive social relationships may be reciprocal. Further discussion of the relationships between well-being and intimate relationships will be found in Chapter 5.

A Sense of Meaning and Purpose

Having a sense of meaning and purpose in life is also an important predictor of higher subjective well-being. In subjective well-being studies, this variable has often been measured as religiosity (see Myers, 1992, 2000). A number of studies have found that people who report greater religious faith, greater importance of religion to their lives, and more frequent attendance at religious services also report greater well-being. Of course, one reason for these findings is that religion provides a sense of meaning for people. However, it is also true that religion provides social support and enhances self-esteem via a self-verification process as the person associates with others who share his or her values. Obviously, religion can also help eliminate existential anxiety and the fear of death. Note, however, that a sense of meaning and purpose in life need not be tied to religious beliefs (see McGregor & Little, 1998; Compton, 2000). For instance, studies have found that when people are actively engaged in pursuing a variety of goals that are meaningful to them, well-being is increased (Oishi, Diener, Suh, & Lucas, 1999). Those goals need not be religious in order to be meaningful (Emmons, 1992). The relationship between well-being and religion will be covered more thoroughly in Chapter 10.

Resolution of Inner Conflicts or Low Neuroticism

The fact that higher subjective well-being is associated with fewer debilitating psychological conflicts is quite obvious. Let us recall that the third major component of subjective well-being is an inverse relationship with negative emotionality and neuroticism: the less neuroticism, the higher the subjective well-being. In many ways, this predictor represents that relationship. A reference to neuroticism, however, defines subjective well-being by what it is *not.* This way of defining an area is problematic, so is there any way to define what this predictor actually describes?

Researchers have found that the less fragmentation of the self or greater integration and coherence among aspects of the self-system, the higher a person's perceived subjective well-being (Donahue, Robins, Roberts, & John, 1993). Therefore, *personality integration* may be a better description of what is meant by this predictor of subjective well-being. Personality integration implies a greater coordination between aspects of self, along with a greater tolerance for differing aspects of one's personality. Thinking in terms of greater personality integration also allows for understandable connections with higher self-esteem, greater optimism, an internal locus of control, and better social relationships. Finally, it also allows for a personality factor that may operate while people are still striving to reach their goals, and it may increase resiliency of the self. One caution, however, is that these findings may be applicable only to individualist cultures or those people that value autonomy and individualism (Suh, 1999).

FACTORS THAT INCREASE SUBJECTIVE WELL-BEING

At this point, then, there is evidence for a positive relationship between subjective well-being and the personality factors listed above. They all are important in some way. Further, evidence shows that some of those predictors by themselves can actually *cause* people to be happier and more satisfied with their lives. This is especially true of extroversion, positive relationships, a sense of meaning and purpose, and low neuroticism (Argyle, 1999; Diener & Lucas, 1999). The next question is, how do these personality factors influence subjective well-being? How is it that these variables are able to impact our lives in relatively consistent ways that increase our subjective well-being?

There is very good evidence that extroversion and neuroticism can have direct causal influences on average self-reported levels of subjective well-being. Similarly, there is good evidence that having positive social relationships and being employed can cause people to be happier. The evidence is less strong, but still compelling, that having a sense of meaning and purpose can cause people to be happier. Interestingly, the causal directions for self-esteem and optimism are less clear. That is, researchers are still not sure if being happy causes a person to have positive self-esteem and feel optimistic or whether they both actually cause greater feelings of happiness.

Should You Feel Emotions Intensely or Frequently?

Research into subjective well-being has also helped to clarify a number of smaller, although important, points about positive emotions and happiness. First, studies have investigated whether it is the *frequency* or the *intensity* of positive feelings that produces happiness. That is, are people happier if they feel mildly positive everyday or if they feel extremely happy once a month? It appears that both intensity and frequency make independent contributions to subjective well-being (Diener, Larsen, Levine, & Emmons, 1985). However, consistent feelings of general well-being have a more beneficial effect than the occasional experience of ecstasy. This is so in part because really intense emotional experiences are quite rare and would be unlikely causes of daily well-being. Novels and films about a brief but passionate romance or a sad and struggling athlete who wins the gold medal often fuel the popular imagination; in reality, a daily dose of mild positive feeling is more likely to result in long-term benefits than the infrequent big dose of positive emotion.

Research has also found that the intensity of positive and negative emotionality is correlated (Diener, Larsen, Levine, & Emmons, 1985). In other words, a person who tends to feel happiness very intensely will also tend to feel negativity very intensely. This is related to age as well. Obviously, young people tend to feel emotions more intensely than older persons, but older people often report being more satisfied with life (see Argyle, 1999). Gender may be a factor, too, in that women report feeling emotions more intensely than men.

Cognition: Is the Glass "Half Full or Half Empty"?

Cognitive theories of subjective well-being say that the causes of higher subjective well-being are the result of how people process information about themselves, others, and their environment. It is not necessarily the events of our lives that cause us happiness or unhappiness. Rather, it is how we interpret those events that really cause us to feel more positive and optimistic. This idea is, in fact, an old one that has been given new life in contemporary psychology. Shakespeare's Hamlet expressed this idea when he said, "There is nothing either good or bad, but thinking makes it so." Even earlier, Epicetus, a Roman of the first century AD, said, "Men are disturbed not by things, but by the view which they take of them." Theorists who use the cognitive model also would argue that predictors of subjective well-being, such as self-esteem, optimism, perceived control, and a sense of meaning and purpose, are all basically beliefs, expectations, or interpretations of reality. A person's freely chosen interpretations of reality are termed *construals* (Funder, 1997). Consistent patterns of positive interpretation create relatively stable ways to relating to the world. These, in turn, create personality descriptions such as "cheerful" or "optimistic." Years of research support the idea that how we *feel* is often determined by how we *think* about and interpret the events of our lives. In order to illustrate how cognitive interpretations may work to determine levels of subjective well-being, psychological perspectives on the creation of positive self-esteem will be explored. Note that similar processes often operate in the creation and maintenance of optimism, personal control, and a sense of meaning and purpose.

How Cognition Creates Positive Self-Esteem

One of the more interesting aspects of self-esteem is that it is a judgment we make about ourselves. This characteristic is called *self-reflexivity*, which means that we can take our "self" as an object in awareness and evaluate it from a second vantage point. Once we begin to evaluate our "self," we find that a comparison or standard is needed to reach a conclusion about the worth or value of the self under consideration. Research on the self has found that what we choose to compare ourselves with is intimately tied to our self-esteem, as well as to memories about our past and expectations for the future (note the similarity to the discussion of moods in Chapter 2).

Social Comparison Processes and Well-Being

If our sense of self-esteem is intimately tied to the judgments we make about ourselves, then what standards do we use to make those comparisons? Greenberg, Pyszczynski and Solomon (1986) suggest that it is social and cultural standards of behavior that provide us with both a context for comparisons and the actual standards we use to make the judgments. The results determine our feelings of value and self-worth.

Because self-esteem is substantially dependent on comparisons, there are any number of ways in which those comparisons can be made. One way is to set an absolute internal standard for what we *should* be like and then gauge how close or how far we are from that standard. Much of the research on these comparison processes has looked at the difference between our *actual self* (i.e., attributes we currently possess) and our *ideal self* (i.e., attributes we think we should possess). Studies have found that the less discrepancy between our ideas of actual self and ideal self, the more positive is our self-esteem and the higher is our sense of well-being. As you might expect, studies have also found that the greater the discrepancy between actual self and ideal self, the more negative are one's self-evaluations and the lower one's sense of well-being (Morretti & Higgins, 1990).

A second way is to compare ourselves with other people. In these comparisons, we ask if other people seem happier, more satisfied, more talented, or more successful than we are. These types of **social comparison processes** are, in fact, one of the most persistent ways that we use to evaluate ourselves. When comparing ourselves with others, however, we can use people who are similar to ourselves (i.e., *lateral social comparisons*), people who we view as better than we are on some dimension (i.e., *upward social comparisons*), or people who we view as less fortunate than we are (i.e., *downward social comparisons*). Our choice of strategy has a relationship to our well-being.

Studies have found that people who report being more happy tend to use downward social comparisons more often than upward comparisons (Lyubomirsky & Ross, 1997). For instance, we know that movie stars are more attractive than most of us, but people who report greater happiness probably do not use movie stars or fashion models as a comparison standard. In fact, the well-being of happy people increases as the number of downward social comparisons increases. People who score higher on self-report measures of happiness are even more selective in the comparisons they make. They are able to select that the types of comparisons with others that will help maintain a feeling of happiness and will also help maintain positive social relationships (Lyubomirsky, 2001). In a sense, they use social comparison processes to their advantage. This finding is a bit complicated. It does say that some aspects of happiness may be related to seeing ourselves as more fortunate than others. If this process is taken too far, however, and people see themselves as "better than" other people, then social comparison processes have turned into arrogance and narcissism. Under those circumstances, comparison processes will eventually lead to problems. In general, higher self-esteem is related to greater consistency between elements of the self, greater clarity and certainty about who one is, and greater stability of the self-concept over time and over different situations (Hoyle, Kernis, Leary, & Baldwin, 1999).

How Self-Esteem Is Maintained

When we engage in self-esteem processes, we must also seek to maintain a sense of self-esteem once it is created. The maintenance of self-esteem involves a number of goals, such as assessment and evaluation, as well as the enhancement of our sense of self. One goal is to look for favorable evaluations of ourselves, or *self-enhancement* processes. Or, we can look for accurate evaluations, or *self-assessment* processes. Finally, we can seek to confirm our current self-evaluations, or *self-verification* processes. So what about people who report greater self-esteem—do they want self-evaluations that are favorable, accurate, or consistent with prior expectations? Studies have shown that people who report greater self-esteem often use more self-enhancement processes (Sedikides, 1993). When evaluating themselves, they often favor information that will enhance their already positive self-esteem. As will be discussed shortly, this information does not have to be correct, just flattering. Interestingly, this tendency toward self-serving bias in self-perception is not consistently found in Asian cultures or when present it is weaker (see Diener, Oishi, & Lucas, 2003). This may reflect a greater tendency for Asian cultures to value humility and harmony in social relationships while placing less emphasis on seeing oneself as "better than" others.

Positive Illusions: Do We Need Rose-Colored Glasses?

In the fourth century BCE, the Greek philosopher Demosthenes said, "Nothing is so easy as to deceive one's self; for what we wish, we readily believe." Some intriguing and provocative contemporary research suggests that happiness, as well as self-esteem, is often not related to an accurate perception of reality (Taylor & Brown, 1988). This conclusion may surprise many people. Do we not need to see the world for what it is in order to be happy? Without that, are we not just living in a "fool's paradise"? On the contrary, interesting evidence suggests that happier people not only choose comparison standards that will be self-enhancing but also hold opinions about themselves that just are not true. They view themselves and their future "through rose-colored glasses." Researchers who agree with this conclusion suggest that having a positive bias about self and one's future is actually better for mental health than valid and accurate self-evaluations. In psychology, this phenomenon is known as having **positive illusions** about self.

Shelly Taylor and Jonathon Brown (1988) began this debate by arguing that overly positive evaluations of self, overly optimistic beliefs about the future, and exaggerated perceptions of control were all associated with better mental health. Taylor and her colleagues have also found that positive illusions can be associated with both better physical health outcomes and better coping with adversity (Taylor, Kemeny, Reed, Bower, & Gruenewald, 2000). One study even found that students who used positive illusions more frequently made higher grades (Wright, 2000). Taylor and Brown's research, however, has sparked considerable debate in psychology.

As you might expect, some people object strongly to the idea that we should all wear rose-colored glasses and deliberately not see the world accurately (e.g., Colvin & Block, 1994). In fact, subsequent studies have found that while positive illusions may be helpful at certain times, they should not be recommended as a universal strategy for increased well-being. First, the impact of positive illusions on mental health depends on how positive illusions are measured (Kwan, John, Robins, Bond & Kenny, 2000; Paulhus, Heine, & Lehman, 2000). For instance, narcissistic people have a tendency to see themselves in a very positive light. However, narcissism is also related to less positive evaluations from others over time (Campbell, Reeder, Sedikides, & Elliot, 2000). Similarly, positive illusions in college students were somewhat adaptive when dealing with immediate threats to self-esteem, but they ultimately resulted in poorer long-term outcomes, such as lower grades and higher drop-out rates (Beer & Robins, 2000).

Whether people should use positive illusions may also depend on the specific judgment being made. For instance, the use of positive illusions seems more likely when the motivation to self-deceive is high or when people are asked to evaluate themselves on highly evaluative traits (Asendorf & Ostendorf, 1998; Robinson & Ryff, 1999). In addition, the use of positive illusions in interpersonal relationships may depend on whom the person is interacting with. Interactions with strangers are more likely to stimulate positive illusions than are interactions with friends (Tice, Butler, Muraven, & Stillwell, 1995). This suggests one reason why we feel more comfortable with friends: we can be more honest and open with them. Therefore, having positive self-esteem is not simply a matter of telling yourself that you are worthwhile regardless of the feedback you receive from other people. People need to pay attention to feedback they receive from others. Actually, as was mentioned, people who report being happier are the ones more likely to accept negative feedback (Aspinwall & Brunhart, 2000). They are able to cope with negative feedback better and motivate themselves to solve the problems.

The Need for Accurate Knowledge of Self and Others

Does all this disprove Taylor and Brown's conclusions that optimal mental health is more related to positive illusions than to an accurate perception of reality? Well, the word *disprove* may be a bit strong. What it does show is that the use of positive illusions and other self-deception strategies is related to well-being in complex ways.

Baumeister (1989) suggested that there may be an "optimal margin for illusions." That is, we can afford to lose some objectivity if it means gaining a bit more optimism about a future that we cannot predict anyway. If the choice is between seeing the glass as "half full" or "half empty" and we have no knowledge on which to base a judgment, then the optimistic viewpoint will often be more helpful. On the other hand, our capacity to see ourselves accurately may have something to do with our initial level of mental health. That is, higher mental health can also be associated with an accurate perception of reality; positive illusions are not completely necessary for good mental health (Compton, 1992; Shedler, Mayman, & Manis, 1993). For instance, Knee and Zuckerman (1996) found that people who were high on autonomy and who felt little influenced by pressures to conform were less likely to use either self-enhancement processes or defensive coping strategies. Finally, Daniel Goleman (1989) urges us all to consider the broader societal implications of positive illusions and self-deception strategies. He persuasively points out that the use of denial, excuse-making, and succumbing to illusions of invulnerability can result in a collective avoidance of problems such as environmental pollution, cultural genocide, and other very real dangers that threaten humanity.

The Pursuit of Goals

As discussed in Chapter 2, one of the other ways that the predictors of subjective well-being may influence happiness and life satisfaction is by helping us to achieve our goals. Theoretical perspectives in this area are based on the idea that it is the successful process of moving toward and accomplishing personally meaningful goals that causes higher levels of subjective well-being. In fact, models of subjective well-being and positive mood that are based on goal setting and achievement have been very successful at predicting increases in positive emotions (Brunstein, 1993; Brunstein, Schultheiss, & Graesman, 1998).

W. Wilson (1967), one of the pioneer investigators of subjective well-being, saw happiness and life satisfaction in terms of the achievement of our goals. He found that a *smaller gap between aspirations and achievements* in life resulted in greater happiness. These smaller discrepancies point to a person whose actual personality and achievements are closer to their beliefs about what they should be like or what they should have accomplished. Although it is quite obvious that people become happier when they achieve important goals, the relationships between goals and happiness cover more territory than just getting what we wish for. As we have seen, not all goals are equally effective in raising levels of happiness and satisfaction. In addition, cultures differ in the types of achievement goals they value.

Evaluation Theory

Diener and Lucas (2000) proposed what they called *evaluation theory* as a way to integrate a number of perspectives on the causes of subjective well-being. They proposed that well-being is determined by how we evaluate the constant flow of incoming information. Well-being depends upon highly active cognitive processes that determine how information is managed. These operations all "share a common purpose: to orient the person and motivate him or her to adaptive future action" (p. 65). Within this theory, certain types of information such as biological needs are more salient. Diener and Lucas suggested, however, that under most circumstances, the most important processes of evaluation concern our progress toward important goals. How we evaluate our progress depends on temperament, the comparison standard we use to measure "progress," our mood, the situations we are in, and our culture. Central to the process, however, is an evaluation of how well our important goals are being met now and how likely they are to be met in the future.

WHAT IS NOT RELATED TO HAPPINESS

Before moving on, it will be helpful to mention some of the factors that research has found to be either not associated with subjective well-being or only mildly associated with it. At this point, let us get rid of some of the myths about what causes happiness.

Money, Income, and Wealth

The first factor that has not been discussed as a predictor of subjective well-being is money, wealth, and income. Are people who have more money happier than other people? One of the most persistent messages of many societies is that money will bring happiness and satisfaction. If you ask people what they believe they need to be happy, one of the most common answers is "more money" (see Myers, 2000). This is not surprising, because in a consumer-based society, having more money is often seen as a way to increase happiness. Increased wealth allows a person to buy a better car, a bigger house, take more vacations, or pamper oneself in any number of ways. Personal wealth is also seen as a means to protect oneself and one's family from unexpected disasters and anxieties of various sorts. Therefore, money is seen as a way to status, pleasure, and security.

Income and Subjective Well-Being

Diener and Biswas-Diener (2002) note that cross-cultural studies indicate that there is a relationship between income and subjective well-being among various countries. Studies have found that the gross national products (GNPs) of countries are positively correlated with average life satisfaction at about .50 (Diener, Diener, & Diener, 1995). This suggests that living in a wealthier country and having more money tend to increase happiness. When the details of the studies are examined, however, this conclusion becomes a little complicated. First, these results do not apply to every country. For example, people in both the Republic of Ireland and Northern Ireland report levels of subjective well-being that are slightly above those reported in the United States. However, when calculated on 1991 U.S. dollars, an index of the per capita GNP in Ireland was less than half the United States index (see Myers, 2000). As a nation, the Irish were less well off financially, but they were just as happy as Americans. Second, within countries, once a person or family's income rises above the poverty level, then further increases in income do not substantially affect levels of happiness. That is, there is a strong relationship between income and satisfaction at lower income levels but an insignificant relationship at higher income levels (Diener, Diener, & Diener, 1995). Third, people who are very wealthy report being only slightly happier than others (Diener, Horwitz, & Emmons, 1995). Fourth, other studies done in the United States indicate that levels of happiness did not rise dramatically from 1946 to the late 1970s. This stability in average levels of happiness is in spite of the fact that personal income rose substantially during that time period (see Figure 3.2). Some reports even show a *negative* relationship between rising disposable income and "I'm very happy" responses over this time period (see Lane, 2000). In other words, happiness ratings may have actually gone down over the past years in spite of increased income. Fifth, one study found that increasing salary levels over a ten-year period were not related to increases in self-reported happiness (Diener, Sandvick, Seidlitz, & Diener, 1993). Sixth, studies done of lottery winners indicate that the initial happiness that comes after the big win does not last very long. Most people return to their prewinning levels of happiness relatively quickly (Brickman, Coates, & Janoff-Bulman, 1978). Some lottery winners actually experience a decrease in their well-being because of the major disruptions in their lives caused by the sudden wealth (see Argyle, 1999). Finally, studies have found that materialists, or people who place a high value on money, are less satisfied with their lives than other people (Kasser & Ryan, 1993; Sirgy, 1998). The more people value money, the less able they are to derive satisfaction from having it.

Does This Mean that Money Cannot Buy Happiness?

What could account for these findings? Could that the old saying, "Money can't buy happiness," actually be true? Most people have seen far too many obnoxious television commercials where ecstatic lottery winners cry and hug each other when they are surprised with the good news. These people win the money, and they are very, very happy. Why are they so happy, and why does it not last?

Adaptation Processes One obvious reason for the increased happiness is that the winners now believe, even expect, that the future will be much easier and more pleasurable. They believe that increased income will allow them to better meet various needs. In addition, people also expect that the future will now

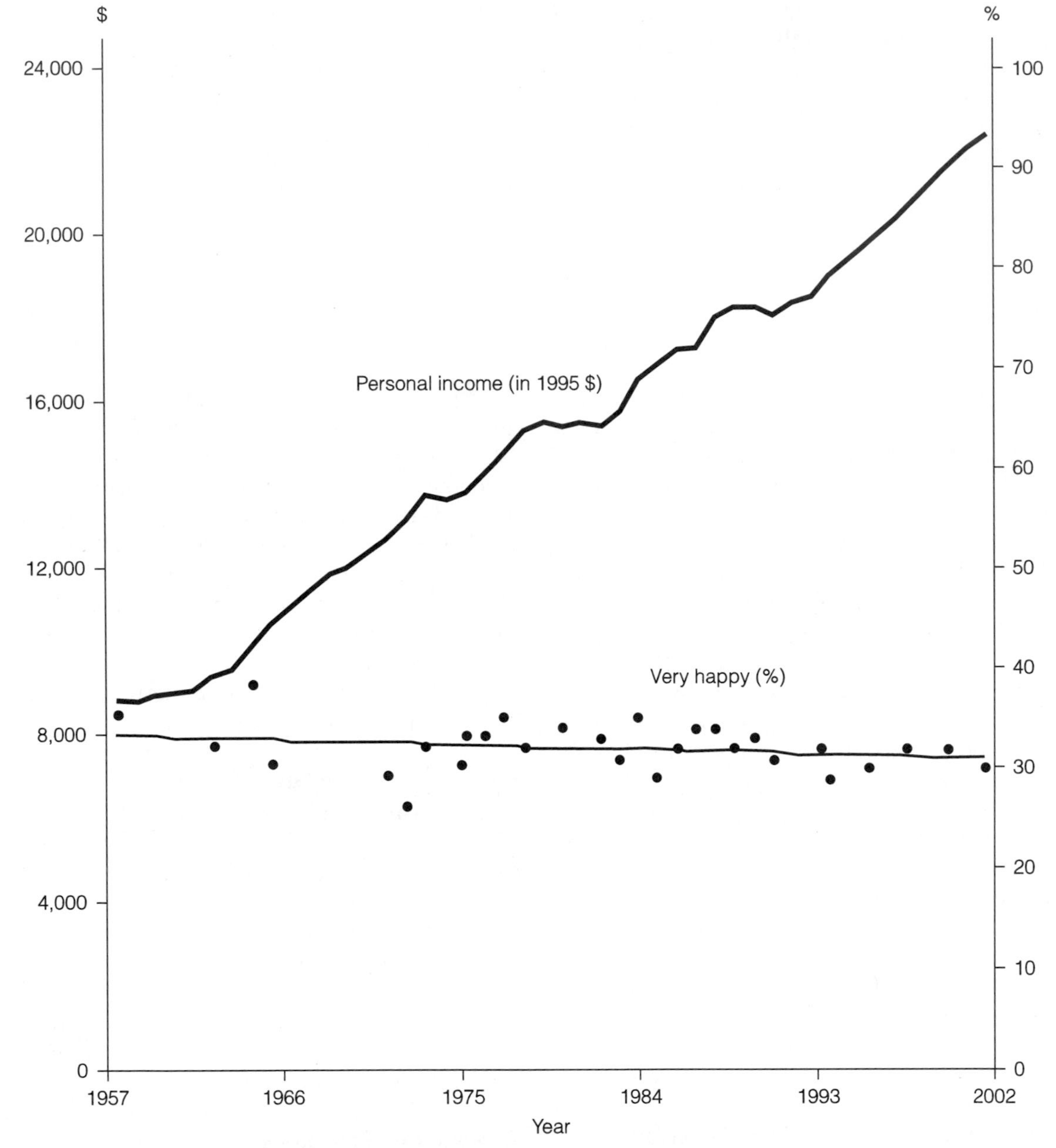

FIGURE 3.2

Income and Percent Very Happy by Years

Source: Income data from U.S. Commerce Department, Bureau of the Census (1975), and *Economic Indicators;* happiness data from General Social Surveys, National Opinion Research Center, University of Chicago; data compiled by David G. Myers. From David Myers, "Funds, friends and faith of happy people," *American Psychologist, 55*(1), fig. 5, p. 61. Copyright 2000 by the American Psychological Association. Reprinted with permission.

bring significant drops in anxiety, worry, and fear. In other words, expectations are extremely high that most of the difficult problems of life will be eliminated and, almost automatically, they will be happier.

The stories told by lottery winners illustrate the fallacy of this expectation. One man, who won five million dollars in the lottery, said that for a short time he was incredibly happy. He said, "I celebrated by throwing a month-long party." Two years after his big win, however, he was less happy than before he won. He summed up the problem rather well by saying, "After all, how many different hats can you buy?" (in Stossel, 1997). In psychology, a similar phenomena is seen in perception and is known as **adaptation level theory** (Helson, 1947). When exposed to a certain level of a stimulus, we become habituated and adapt to that level relatively quickly. In order for us to notice a change from that level, we need to increase the stimuli. The amount of change necessary for us to notice a difference is called the *just noticeable difference.* For instance, if we hold up a two-pound book, we will adapt to the relevant physiological stimuli. When we do, those sensations become normal. Then, if someone places a five-pound dictionary in our hands, we notice a change. The stimuli are now different, and the contrast between the "book-only" and the "book plus dictionary" states is striking because it is new. If, however, we continue to hold the book and the dictionary for some time, then we adapt to that level of stimulation, and it becomes the new standard against which we measure changes in stimuli. In fact, studies have found that we adapt to most changes in life within about three months (see Diener & Lucas, 2000).

When we first get a raise or win the lottery our reaction has much to do with the fact that a baseline level of stimuli has just changed. We notice the change. It grabs our attention. At that moment, the difference between our earlier state and the present one is more pronounced than it will ever be again. Almost immediately, however, adaptation begins to set in, and the new level of income begins the inevitable transformation into our new baseline. When it is the new baseline, then we don't notice it as much. It is then "normal" for us. Lottery winners consistently report this phenomenon. The situation regarding income is even more striking because increases in income do not invariably lead to higher reported happiness—even initially (Diener & Biswas-Diener, 2002).

Will Money Eliminate Worry? A second expectation is also important to the inability of wealth to predict happiness. Most people assume that if they can only decrease the sources of anxiety, fear, and worry in their lives, then they will automatically be happier. In reality, there is occasionally some truth to this assumption. A trip to a Caribbean island can relive the tension of a high-stress job—temporarily. Unfortunately, just like the occasional win at the slot machines in Las Vegas, the increase in happiness that accompanies a decrease in stress can blind someone to the larger relationships involved. As Chapter 1 discussed, however, the factors that predict anxiety, worry, and depression are often different than the factors that predict happiness, satisfaction, and joy. So, for instance, it is quite true that an increase in income can eliminate some worries about mortgage, paying for children's college, and anxieties about having enough money for retirement. It would be foolish to take that truth and say that money can reliably eliminate *all* worries and fears.

Social Comparisons Another psychological process also explains the failure of wealth to bring lasting happiness. This is the idea of **social comparison processes.** As mentioned earlier, psychological research has found that when people are asked to evaluate their self-esteem—or in this case, their income levels—they tend to compare their lives to other people's lives (either real lives or imagined lives). Satisfaction with income often depends upon whom one chooses for the comparison (Argyle, 1999). Some people are less satisfied with their income because of the comparison standards they use. For instance, Sirgy (1998) proposed that materialists use comparison standards that are idealized, global, and remote. The use of global and remote standards results in comparisons that find the person always making "less than" others. Just imagine what would happen if a person used Bill Gates, who is the richest man in the world, as a comparison standard when deciding whether they were satisfied with their income! They would be chronically dissatisfied.

While comparison theory is a useful tool in studying the relationships between money and well-being, more recent studies have found that these processes are fairly complex. For instance, comparison theory does not apply if we compare our current income with our past income. Even though we may be making more money now, that does not satisfy us. The next idea relates to why this might be true.

Rising Expectations One of the more consistent findings about money and happiness is that rising income usually stimulates increasing materialistic aspirations (Sirgy, 1998). Rising income usually translates in rising expectations about what the person "should" have or "needs" to have in order to be happy. It can create an ever-expanding **hedonic treadmill** where each financial goal that is met only leads to rising desires and expanding expectations for what one "really needs" to be happy (Brickman & Campbell, 1971). So, the more money we have, the more money we think we need to be happier. For example, Schor (1998, as cited in Diener & Biswas-Diener, 2002) reported a survey done in 1995 of people who earned more than $100,000 per year (adjusted for inflation, this is approximately $125,00 in 2004 dollars). Incredibly, in that survey 27 percent of the people said they could not afford everything they "really need," while 19 percent said they spent *all* their income on "basic necessities"! In general, people who hold "financial success" as a central and core value tend to report lower global adjustment ratings and more behavior disorders (Kasser & Ryan, 1993).

In a fascinating reversal of the usual assumptions, Diener and Biswas-Diener (2002) suggest money may not cause us happiness—it may be the other way around. They suggest that previously high levels of well-being can be used to predict later increases in income. While they would not go so far as to say that being happy *causes* wealth and prosperity, the personality factors associated with high subjective well-being would certainly be assets in the world of work. That is, it is safe to assume that being a generally cheerful, optimistic, and confident person could be factors in career success. Finally, although most people say they would like more money in order to increase their well-being, does it follow that most people believe that more money is absolutely necessary for their happiness? Laura King and Christine Napa (1998) found that most "folk conceptions" of happiness, or the ideas of ordinary people, do not include wealth as a significant element of happiness. Although most people would like to have more income, they also know that more money is not the ultimate key to happiness.

Gender: Are Men or Women Happier?

Once again, the answer to this question is a little bit complicated. Studies have found all possible answers to this question: no significant differences between the men and women in self-reported happiness or life satisfaction, more happiness for women, and more happiness for men (see Nolen-Hoeksema & Rusting, 1999). In an analysis designed to resolve the inconsistency of findings, Wood, Rhodes, and Whelan (1989) concluded that women generally report slightly higher levels of happiness than men.

The complications with this answer begin almost immediately. On one hand, women report experiencing and expressing *all emotions* both more frequently and more intensely than men. For instance, women report a greater capacity for joy (Fujita, Diener, & Sandvik, 1991). At the same time, it is also well established that women experience and express more negative internally focused emotions, such as depression and anxiety (Nolen-Hoeksema & Rusting, 1999). On the other hand, men are vastly overrepresented in cases involving externally expressed emotions, such as antisocial personality disorder, angry and impulsive behaviors, and alcoholism. In the end, the impact of gender accounts for only about 1 percent of the variability in subjective well-being among people (Nolen-Hoeksema & Rusting, 1999). The good news is that neither gender is inevitably doomed to be less happy than the other.

Age: Is One Age Group Happier than Another?

What about the social message that young people are happier than older people—is it true? Once again, the research does not support the cultural myth. In fact, some studies have found the opposite. Some studies have found that older persons tend to be *more* satisfied with their lives and happier than younger people (see Argyle, 1999). As with gender, there are a number of qualifications to the general conclusions.

First, it does appear that young people experience more intense emotions than older people, but that intensity does not automatically transform itself into higher levels of subjective well-being. Second, there appear to be differences between age groups in terms of how they calculate their subjective well-being. On one hand, older persons often have a smaller discrepancy between their life goals or aspirations and their actual achievements in life. This tends to increase a sense of happiness and life satisfaction. On the other hand, the increased health problems of advancing age do have a negative impact on subjective well-being. When compared to young people, older persons are also more satisfied with their past accomplishments and their present life but less satisfied with their futures (see Argyle, 1999). Satisfaction with social relationships were also more important for older persons (Herzog, Rogers, & Woodworth, 1982).

There may also be differences between the subjective well-being of men and women as they move through the life span. In studies that look at both gender and age at the same time, older women tend to be less happy than older men (Argyle, 1999). In terms of change over time, men's happiness ratings showed a relatively steady increase as they aged, while women's happiness ratings increased up to age 25, then showed a slight dip in happiness from age 25 to 35, which was followed by steadily increasing happiness ratings (Mroczek & Kolarz, 1998). What makes people happy varies by age. With advances in medicine and more emphasis on fitness, it is possible that physically active retirees may eventually turn out to be one of the happiest and most satisfied of all age groups.

Race and Ethnicity

When looking at the relationships between subjective well-being and race or ethnicity, researchers can investigate either differences between racial groups within a specific culture or differences between ethnically diverse cultures. Beginning with differences between racial groups within a specific culture, studies in the United States have found that African Americans tend to have lower self-reported happiness than Caucasian Americans (Argyle, 1999). However, although African American adults often report lower levels of self-esteem, black children may report higher self-esteem than white children (Argyle, 1999). Another qualifier is age, in that in at least one study, black adults aged 55 or older reported being happier than older white adults (Campbell, Converse, & Rogers, 1976). Asian Americans tend to report high self-esteem as well as levels of general well-being comparable to Caucasian Americans (Chang, 2001). However, some studies have also found that life satisfaction is lower and rates of depression higher in Asian Americans than in Caucasian Americans (Oishi & Diener, 2001). Native Americans also report fairly high levels of self-esteem. Unfortunately, the self-esteem of Native Americans drops when they come into contact with white urban culture and face unemployment, discrimination, and cultural clashes (Fuchs & Havinghurst, 1973). In fact, racial or ethnic discrimination within a specific society can negatively influence subjective well-being for all minority groups (see Lewis, 2002). In general, however, when factors such as income, education level, and occupational level within a society are taken into account, then the effect of ethnicity on subjective well-being is quite small (Argyle, 1999).

When questions turn to differences in subjective well-being among cultures, the answers become complex very quickly. These complexities will be explored in Chapter 11. Briefly, however, subjective well-being in all cultures appears to be related to how well people believe they are achieving the things they value (Diener, Oishi, & Lucas, 2003). Because people in different cultures can differ in what they value, paths to well-being also differ among cultures. For instance, Latino cultures tend to place a high value on interpersonal reciprocity and building strong emotional family ties (Lewis, 2002) while Asian cultures tend to value social harmony over individual achievement (Diener & Suh, 2002). Therefore, how people go about pursuing well-being can be somewhat different in different cultures.

Education and Climate

While education is a means to a better job for most people, will it affect happiness? A number of studies have found a small effect from education level on happiness or positive affect (see Argyle, 1999). People with higher education levels have a small tendency to report being happier. Studies in the United States, however, have also found that education is only an important factor in happiness when all income levels are included in the analysis (Diener, Suh, Lucas, & Smith, 1999). Once a person's income is past a certain minimum level, further education does not influence his or her self-reported happiness in any significant way. More education generally translates into more opportunity in the job market, better prospects for income and job satisfaction, and more satisfying use of leisure time. This effect, however, seems to be diminishing in recent years (Argyle, 1999). In today's world, education may have less of an impact on happiness than it once did.

A note for anyone who has dreamed of escaping to a tropical island: studies have shown that climate does not seriously affect levels of happiness and satisfaction (see Argyle, 1987). While changes in the weather can cause variations in daily mood, they do not significantly determine long-term well-being. So, a trip to a warm tropical island may be a good temporary source of relaxation and well-being, but it probably will not produce lasting happiness.

Comments on Subjective Well-Being

A closer look at the traits associated with subjective well-being shows that they appear to tap into both personal characteristics and social interactions. High self-esteem, perceived control, optimism, sense of meaning, and few inner conflicts all suggest a person who has achieved a certain emotional balance in his or her life and believes that this balance is relatively permanent. Because happier people also tend to have more positive social relationships and may be more extroverted as well, this also suggests a person who has achieved a comfortable equilibrium with other people in life. People who report higher levels of happiness appear to have found a way to balance demands to meet their own needs with the needs of other people in their world. Note that this balance is mutually reinforcing. As people perceive themselves in a more positive light, they present themselves to others with a certain level of confidence and optimism, which in turn fosters a more positive reaction from other people and therefore reinforces their initial self-esteem. Finally, this cycle of subjective well-being tends to produce a sense that life has meaning and purpose, because it can lead to a belief that life is predictable and makes sense.

This cycle of well-being can apparently be entered into at any point of the cycle. Zautra and Reich (1981) addressed the question of whether a positive personality causes more supportive social relationships or whether more supportive relationships cause enhanced self-esteem. The answer, interestingly, was that *both* work to increase psychological well-being. Causality is at least bidirectional and appears to operate simultaneously. Therefore, we are engaged in the social world both as creators of our own social reality and as products of the social reality we are embedded in. The variables that are important to happiness and life satisfaction are related to the quality of relationships with significant others and to a variety of attitudes concerning self-evaluation, locus of control, and optimism. Luckily, most of these positive psychological factors are available for anyone to cultivate.

Summary

This chapter introduced the research area of subjective well being. Currently, these studies look at three major variables: happiness, life satisfaction, and low neuroticism. The measurement of subjective well-being is often done with self-report instruments. One of the first questions was whether subjective well-being is a result of summing a number of pleasurable moments together or the result of a general positive orientation to life events. While both of these processes can contribute to subjective well-being, a general positive orientation seems to be the most powerful predictor. Researchers have found a set of six variables that are the core predictors of subjective well-being: positive self-esteem, a sense of perceived control, optimism, a sense of meaning and purpose in life, an extroverted personality, and positive interpersonal relationships. In addition, low neuroticism means that higher subjective well-being is associated with lower scores on measures of anxiety, worry, and depression. These predictors of well-being form what might be called the cycle of well being in that they are mutually reinforcing. Two of the major ways in which these variables influence subjective well-being are by enhancing positive interpretations of life events and by fostering the pursuit of life goals. Next, the topic of selfhood was discussed. The maintenance and enhancement of self-esteem is achieved through a myriad of comparisons, including comparisons with other people, our past experiences, and our hoped-for futures. A fair amount of research supports the idea that our self-concept need not be entirely accurate in order for us to feel good about ourselves. Factors that tend not to be significant predictors of subjective well-being (although they do have an impact) include money, age, gender, education, race, and climate. When these factors do have an impact, it is through the related influence of income, education, and social class.

Note

1. *Neuroticism* is a fairly general term that refers to chronic problems with anxiety, worry, mild depression, and low self-esteem. It is an older term in psychology that is still used for research purposes but is no longer used as a diagnostic label. David Watson and Lee Anna Clark (1984) proposed a more general trait, *negative affectivity,* that describes a combination of trait anxiety, neuroticism, general maladjustment, and

other tendencies to experience distress and discomfort across many situations.

Learning Tools

Key Terms and Ideas

ADAPTATION LEVEL THEORY
BOTTOM-UP THEORY
HAPPINESS
HEDONIC TREADMILL
LEARNED OPTIMISM
POSITIVE ILLUSIONS
REALISTIC OPTIMISM
SATISFACTION WITH LIFE
SOCIAL COMPARISON PROCESSES
TOP-DOWN THEORY

Books

Myers, D. (1992). *The pursuit of happiness.* New York: Avon. A very readable book on subjective well-being by a major figure in positive psychology (popular).

The following two books offer somewhat contrasting views about positive illusions (popular).

Goleman, D. (1996). *Vital lies and simple truths.* New York: Touchstone. Goleman cautions us against unexamined self-deception.

Taylor, S. (1989). *Positive illusions: Creative self-deception and the healthy mind.* New York: Basic Books. Taylor says we should use illusions to our advantage.

Research Articles

Diener, E. (2000). Subjective well-being: The science of happiness and a proposal for a national index. *American Psychologist, 55*(1), 34–43.

Diener, E., Suh, E. M., Lucas, R. E., & Smith, H. L. (1999). Subjective well-being: Three decades of progress. *Psychological Bulletin, 125*(2), 276–302.

Myers, D. (2000). The funds, friends, and faith of happy people. *American Psychologist, 55*(1), 56–67.

Journal of Happiness Studies. Editor-in-Chief: Ruut Veenhoven. A new journal that publishes scientific studies on subjective well-being. The first issue of the journal was published in 2000. Kluwer Academic Publishers. Available at http://www.wkap.nl/journals/johs.

On the Web

http://s.psych.uiuc.edu/~ediener. Ed Diener's home page with links to some of his recent papers on subjective well-being. Includes a copy of the Satisfaction with Life Scale.

http://www.eur.nl/fsw/research/happiness. The World Data Base of Happiness directed by Ruut Veenhoven. Lists thousands of research articles on happiness, life satisfaction, and quality of life.

Personal Explorations

Imagine that medicine has developed a new "happiness pill." If you take this pill everyday it will make you feel positive emotions more frequently. There are also no negative side effects, and it is inexpensive to buy. Would you take it? Why or why not?

Imagine that you have found the famous "Aladdin's Lamp" and the genie has granted you three wishes. What would you wish for (sorry, you can't wish for more wishes)? (a) What do your answers tell you about your idea of happiness or the good life? (b) Are your answers based on any specific assumptions about human nature or the relationships between people and the societies they live in? What are those assumptions?

CHAPTER 4

Leisure, Optimal Experience, and Peak Performance

> On one of those days everything is just right . . . my concentration is so perfect that it almost seems as though I'm able to transport myself beyond the turmoil on the court to some place of total peace and calm. I've got perfect control of the match, my rhythm and movements are excellent, and everything's in total balance. . . . It's a perfect combination of aggressive action taking place in an atmosphere of total tranquillity . . . just totally peaceful.
>
> *Billie Jean King, retired professional tennis player*

Leisure

Any discussion of well-being must eventually take a look at *leisure:* how we spend our spare time, what we do to relax, the activities we engage in to have fun, and how we exercise our passions and interests. A list of activities that could fall under the category of leisure would be endless. People are remarkably creative in finding ways to amuse themselves. The emotions associated with leisure activities also span the entire range of human experiences. Some people prefer active adventure sports that contain an element of danger or risk, such as mountain biking or kayaking. Others are happier with more traditional sports, such as basketball or soccer, that are partially driven by a sense of competition with others. Still others are drawn to quieter activities that foster contemplation and relaxation, such as sailing, walking in the woods, or needlework. Although it may seem obvious to associate leisure with well-being, is there any evidence for a relationship between the two variables? In fact, a number of studies have looked at how leisure is related to life satisfaction and well-being.

Leisure and Life Satisfaction

In a Time-Warner/CNN poll, about 70 percent of people said that they would like to slow down and live a more relaxed life. They especially wished they could spend more time with their families (see United Way of America, 1992). One of the earliest empirical studies of subjective well-being was done by Campbell, Converse, and Rogers (1976). They found that satisfaction with leisure, which was defined as "life outside work," was one of the variables that showed up as a strong predictor of global well-being. Ruut Veenhoven and his colleagues reviewed a substantial number of studies on well-being and found that that happiness and satisfaction with leisure were significantly correlated at typically around .40 and even at about .20 when controls for other variables were added (see Argyle, 1999). One study found that satisfaction with leisure was the most important predictor of satisfaction with community life (Allen & Beattie, 1984).

The impact of leisure on satisfaction may begin in adolescence. A longitudinal study by Mary Glancy, F. Willits, and P. Farrell (1986) in which they followed 1,521 high school students for 24 years found that more participation in leisure activities in high school predicted higher life satisfaction as an adult. Studies have also shown that, at the other end of the life cycle, successful aging is correlated with regular participation in activities. In fact, participation in leisure activities may be the most important contributor to life satisfaction in older women (Kelly & Ross, 1989). Recent research has found that higher activity level could be an effective deterrent to the damaging effects of Alzheimer's disease. Finally, at least one form of leisure has been reliably associated with changes in mood. Studies on exercise have found that increases in aerobic exercise can decrease the symptoms of depression and anxiety, as well as increase levels of happiness (Alfermann & Stoll, 2000). In summary, over the years, researchers have consistently found a positive relationship between our satisfaction with leisure and our satisfaction with our lives (Leitner & Lietner, 1996).

While it is clear that leisure helps people feel better about their lives, it is also true that simply having leisure time does not automatically increase well-being. For instance, higher scores on life satisfaction are associated with participation in a greater variety of leisure activities. In addition, the relationship between leisure and well-being is stronger if people participate in more active types of leisure (Bammel & Burrus-Bammel, 1996). Also, only those older persons involved in activities that are personally meaningful seem to feel happier (Ogilvie, 1987). Therefore, the key is that we must be involved in activities that we personally enjoy or that are meaningful to us in some way. We should be actively involved in an activity that we connect with on an emotional level. Somewhat poetically, Pieper expressed this perspective by saying, "Leisure, it must be understood, is a mental and spiritual attitude—it is not simply the result of external factors, it is not the inevitable result of spare time, a holiday, a weekend or a vacation . . . [it is] a condition of the soul" (Pieper, 1963, p. 40, quoted in Neulinger, 1974).

What Turns an Activity into "Leisure"?

Although leisure is clearly important to the life satisfaction of many people, it is still prudent to ask, "Why do people engage in leisure at all?" Although the easy answer is probably "to have fun," the real answer is more complex than the simple pursuit of pleasure. Some types of leisure provide only necessary relief from stress, while others provide revitalization and renewal. In a study of British citizens, the highest ranked reasons for engaging in leisure were that leisure (1) fulfilled needs for autonomy, (2) allowed the enjoyment of family life, (3) provided for relaxation, and (4) offered an escape from routine (see Argyle, 1987). The suggestion that leisure is associated with autonomy reminds us that for many people leisure activities are those that allow intrinsically motivated behaviors. Related to this is the ability to simply make a choice about how to spend time. Boredom, after all, is not necessarily a state of having nothing to do but rather a state of not being able to choose what to do. The association of leisure with autonomy suggests that leisure may also be related not only to quietude and relaxation but also to challenges. Indeed, people like to challenge themselves to develop and acquire skills, talents, abilities, and to gain knowledge as a way to grow and expand their potential.

The social component of leisure is also extremely important. One of the most powerful reasons for leisure activities is the chance to be with other people. While many activities are done because they involve solitude (e.g., a walk in the woods), there are many, many others that are fun precisely because we do them with other people. One study found that satisfaction with the social component of leisure was the best predictor of overall leisure satisfaction (Crandall, Nolan, & Morgan, 1980). For example, playing music can be very rewarding activity, but playing music with or for other people can make it even more enjoyable. Taking another example, many people enjoy watching Fred Astaire dance his solo numbers in the Hollywood musicals of the 1930s and 1940s. But when he danced with Ginger Rogers, there is magic on the screen that allows the audiences to feel what it is like to be in love.

The relationship between activities that are personally meaningful and leisure satisfaction can also be found in the creation of an identity that can be associated with leisure activities. The sense of identity component of leisure can be seen in what Argyle (1987) called "leisure worlds." One often hears phrases like the "world of ballroom dancing" or the "world of tennis" that refer to the somewhat esoteric bits of knowledge that one must acquire to understand the intricacies of a particular activity. These include the nuances of vocabulary, the types of specialized knowledge, and the esoteric meanings that all combine to make a certain activity special to those who understand its intricacies. A familiar example is the unique "world of *Star Trek*" with its specialized conventions and costumes taken from the television shows and movies. Some people in this "world" ("Trekkies") even choose to learn the fictitious Klingon language.

In summary, leisure activities are important to a sense of well-being and life satisfaction. Activities that provide this sense of well-being should be meaningful to the person, provide for a sense of autonomy, be a break from routine, and involve frequent positive relationships with other people. Another component of leisure has yet to be addressed. So far, this discussion has not addressed what an activity that is "fun" *feels like* to the person. That is, when an activity is intrinsically enjoyable to a person, there may be a common set of psychological experiences that helps to define or identify an activity as "fun." The next perspective on well-being begins by exploring what those common experiences might be.

Flow and Optimal Experience: Being "In the Zone"

Mihaly Csikszentmihalyi began his studies of psychological well-being by asking people to describe in their own words what it felt like when they were doing something really enjoyable and the activity was going particularly well for them (Csikszentmihalyi, 1975). He was interested in studying the experience of enjoyment, fun, play, or the sense of being intrinsically motivated. In his initial study, Csikszentmihalyi interviewed over two hundred people who were deeply involved in activities that required considerable amounts of time and for which they received little or no money or recognition. What he got from a number of his interviewees were wonderfully rich and compelling descriptions of moments of wonder and magic when everything was working just right and all effort just flowed.

During the interviews, chess masters and basketball players told him what it felt like to be totally engaged in a game, dancers spoke about those moments when they were dancing at their best, rock climbers went into vivid detail about the moment-to-moment experience of climbing as one's skill was pitted against the possibility of failure. Csikszentmihalyi and his students also interviewed composers of modern music in order to get a sense of what the creative process was like when it was going exceptionally well. Csikszentmihalyi took these descriptions and performed a *phenomenological* analysis of the experiences. That is, he analyzed the verbal or written descriptions of experience for common themes that appeared in most of the descriptions. These common themes described a fairly recognizable state of consciousness. His initial name for the experience was the *autotelic experience,* but he later settled on the more user-friendly and familiar term *flow*.

Definition of Flow

After the interviews and a content analysis of the responses, Csikszentmihalyi (1975) created a definition of **flow:**

> Flow denotes the holistic sensation present when we act with total involvement. . . . It is the state in which action follows upon action according to an internal logic which seems to need no conscious intervention on our part. We experience it as a unified flowing from one moment to the next, in which we feel in control of our actions, and in which there is little distinction between self and environment; between stimulus and response; or between past, present, and future (p. 43).

Readers who are sports fans may have already recognized the experience that Csikszentmihalyi is describing. In sports, these experiences are commonly referred to as being "in the zone" (Kimiecik & Stein, 1992; Cooper, 1998). Athletes have talked about such experiences for years, although many were reluctant to speak publicly about it for fear of being labeled "crazy" or accused of being on drugs during a game. Today, however, the phrase "in the zone" is commonly used to describe what Csikszentmihalyi termed *being in flow.* Csikszentmihalyi's theory of flow has been very popular, in psychology as well as in the popular press, probably because the experience of being in flow is fairly common, and many people instantly recognize just what he is talking about.

Csikszentmihalyi (1997) reported on surveys that asked people, "Do you ever get involved in something so deeply that nothing else seems to matter, and you lose track of time?" (p. 33). In American and European samples, about 20 percent of people reported having these flowlike experiences often, sometimes several times a day. Only about 15 percent of people reported that they never had that experience. Of course, the percentage of people who have had very intense flow experiences is much smaller. Those who have had the flow experience, either intensely or mildly, reported that they immediately appreciate the association between flow and psychological well-being. Flow feels good and is one element of enjoyment.

Contexts and Situations for Flow

The range of contexts in which people report flow is quite fascinating. Of course, almost any activity that involves active participation in sports could create the context for flow, or being "in the zone." Csikszentmihalyi's original study also included people who were actively involved in creative artistic pursuits of various kinds. In addition to the contexts listed thus far, people report flow when participating in activities such as religious rituals (Han, 1988), using computers (Ghani & Deshpande, 1994), teaching in the classroom (Coleman, 1994), driving a car (Csikszentmihalyi, 1997), being with one's family (Rathunde, 1988), solitary retreats (Logan, 1985), and even while cramming for exams (Brinthaupt & Shin, 2001). One of the most frequently mentioned contexts for flow is when reading for pleasure (McQuillan & Conde, 1996). Csikszentmihalyi has also found that people who enjoy their jobs often report being in a state of flow while at work (Csikszentmihalyi, & LeFevre, 1989). In fact, he speculates that flow experiences may be the key to job satisfaction. In team sports, such as soccer, it is possible for the entire team to experience flow during a game (Cosma, 1999). Csikszentmihalyi has also referred to the experience of **microflow.** These are moments when we are leisurely involved in a relatively simple, almost automatic, activity, such as doodling. In general, Csikszentmihalyi (1990) believes that flow is the experience that allows people to enjoy life, feel happier, and function better in a number of different contexts.

Characteristics of Flow

What exactly is the flow experience like? Csikszentmihalyi said that the state of flow can be described with eight parameters:

1. The Merging of Action and Awareness.

People who experience flow are involved in an activity to the point that they feel "inside" the activity. The person does not have to think about what they are doing before they do it. There is no sense of being an observer who is watching and evaluating the activity. In fact, this type of divided consciousness or "outside" perspective destroys the flow experience. For instance, an expert rock climber told Csikszentmihalyi what it was like when he was on a climb: "You are so involved in what you are doing, you aren't thinking of yourself as separate from the immediate activity. . . . [Y]ou don't see yourself as separate from what you are doing" (p. 46). (All quotations describing the flow experience are taken from Csikszentmihalyi, 1975.)

2. Complete Concentration on the Task at Hand.

The merging of action and awareness is made possible by complete concentration and a centering of attention on the activity of the moment. This concentration appears effortless, however, and is not associated with mental strain or aggressive efforts to control or repress thinking. As a composer described it, "I am really quite oblivious to my surroundings after I really get going [i.e., composing]. I think the phone could ring . . . or the house could burn down . . . when I start working I really do shut out the world" (p. 48).

3. Lack Of Worry about Losing Control that, Paradoxically, Results in a Sense of Control.

The loss of worry apparently allows people to maintain concentration and focus on the task. This focus allows the person to feel as if they are in complete control of their actions. Often they feel more in control than they have ever been. According to a dancer, "If I have enough space, I am in control. I feel I can radiate an energy into the atmosphere. . . . It's not always necessary that another human being be there to catch that energy. I can dance for the walls, I can dance for the floors. . . . I become one with the atmosphere" (p. 51).

4. A Loss of Self-Consciousness.

Once again, this criteria appears to reinforce the merging of awareness and action, as well as the focused concentration. During flow, that part of consciousness that evaluates and plans before acting—the ego—is quieted. We do not have to think before we act, we are not trapped in an internal conflict between various options. A composer described what it felt like when he was writing at his best; "You yourself are in an ecstatic state to such a point that you feel as though you almost don't exist. . . . My hand seems devoid of myself, and I have nothing to do with what is happening. I just sit there watching it in a state of awe and wonderment. And it just flows out by itself" (p. 50). Csikszentmihalyi & Csikszentmihalyi (1988) stated that "In flow the self is fully functioning, but not aware of itself doing it. . . . At the most challenging levels, people actually report experiencing a *transcendence* of self . . . " (p. 33).

5. Time No Longer Seems to Pass in Ordinary Ways.

Time may seem to pass more quickly than usual, or it may appear to be vastly slowed down. This element of flow can be very dramatic and is one of the more distinctive reasons for describing flow as an alternate state of consciousness. People have described this feeling while playing sports. Often, they report that suddenly it seems as if they have all the time in the world to shoot a basket, throw a pass, or position the racket for their next shot. For many, time seems to slow down as they feel a sense of relaxation, a lack of worry, and extreme confidence that their next move will be "perfect." A chess master said, "Time passes a hundred times faster. In a sense, it resembles the dream state. A whole story can unfold in seconds, it seems" (p. 50).

6. Autotelic Nature of the Experience.

This term means that the experience is done for its own sake rather than a means to another goal. A rock climber said, "The mystique of rock climbing is climbing; you get to the top of the rock glad it's over but really wish it would go forever. The justification of climbing is climbing . . . you don't conquer anything except things in yourself. . . . The purpose of the flow is to keep on flowing, not looking for a peak or utopia but staying in the flow. . . . There is no possible reason for climbing except the climbing itself; it is a self-communication." (p. 54).

Csikszentmihalyi (1990) said that there may even be an autotelic personality style. This personality style is associated with a person who consistently does things for their own sake, with involvement and enthusiasm rather than in response to external threats or rewards. Such individuals are characterized by autonomy and independence. According to Csikszentmihalyi (1997), the major characteristic that defines autotelic individuals is that "their psychic energy seems inexhaustible" (p. 123). In addition, he suggests that autotelic persons are less self-centered and generally less concerned with themselves, tending to be "free of personal goals and ambitions" (p. 125).

7. Flow Accompanies a Challenging Activity that Requires Skill.

This criteria of flow describes one of the parameters that Csikszentmihalyi believes is associated with building the feeling of flow. He believes that when the personal challenge of an activity pushes one's skill level, the requisite concentration is produced that can induce the flow experience. If the demands are high and skills are low, then the person will feel anxiety. If the demands are low and skills are high, the person will feel bored (see Figure 4.1). It is only when the demands of the situation present a challenge to the person's skills that flow is possible.

8. The Activity Has Clear Goals and Immediate Feedback.

Once again, this describes the parameters of flow. A chess expert described the experience in the following way: "When the game is exciting, I don't seem to hear nothing—the world seems to be cut off from me and all there's to think about is the game. . . . [A]t times, I see only the positions. . . . If I'm busting a much weaker player, I may think about the events of the day. During a good game, [however] I think over various alternatives to the game—nothing else. . . . Problems are suspended for the duration of the tournament except those that pertain to it" (p. 47). The activity must have clear goals and immediate feedback—as chess does—so that a person does not have to wonder about how well he or she is performing the activity during flow.

Csikszentmihalyi believes that these eight qualities capture the essence of the flow experience. Not all eight are necessarily present in every flowlike experience, but in very intense flow experiences most of them should be pres-

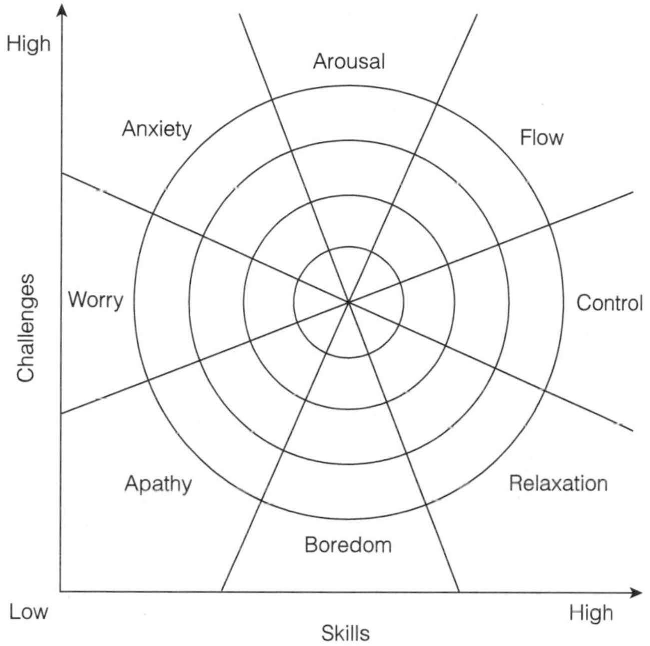

FIGURE 4.1

Current Model of Flow

Source: From M. Csikszentmihalyi, *Finding flow* (New York: Basic Books, 1997), fig. 1, p. 31. Copyright 1997 Basic Books. Reprinted by permission of Basic Books, a division of Perseus Books Group.

ent. Note that the first six characteristics describe what flow *feels like* as one experiences it. They were abstracted from the phenomenological descriptions given to Csikszentmihalyi. The last two characteristics, however, describe the *conditions under which* flow experiences tend to occur. These two are not necessarily descriptions of internal experiencing. Instead, they relate to the fit between the person's level of learned competencies or skills and the demands of the current situation or challenges (see Figure 4.1).

Other Qualities of Flow

The uniqueness of this theory comes from the fact that it proposes that happiness and well-being can be associated with a remarkable experience that involves altered perceptions of self, time, and abilities. It should be obvious by now that when Csikszentmihalyi describes intense experiences of flow he is describing a state of consciousness that is qualitatively different from normal consciousness. As such, Csikszentmihalyi's theory of flow is one of the few theoretical perspectives on psychological well-being that says that higher well-being can be the result of experiencing an alternate state of consciousness—at least in its more intense forms. Because children seem to be able to enter flow states spontaneously and frequently, the ability to experience flow may also be innate. It may be that we do not need to learn *how* to flow, but we can be taught how to *repress* flow. Csikszentmihalyi and his wife, Isabella, also claimed that the flow experience is a universal human experience found in all cultures of the world (Csikszentmihalyi & Csikszentmihalyi, 1988).

There is also evidence that the experience of flow has a physiological counterpart. Daniel Landers and colleagues measured the brain wave activity of athletes (such as archers, marksmen, and golfers) just seconds before they performed (see, Landers, Han, Salazar, & Petruzzello, 1994). The researchers found that being "in the zone" coincides with less activity in the left hemisphere, which is associated with analytical and intellectual thought, and greater activity in the right hemisphere, which is associated with verbal and spatial ability (at least this is true for right-handed people). Jean Hamilton also found that the experience of intrinsic enjoyment is associated with specific patterns of evoked potential in brain waves (Hamilton, Haier, & Buchsbaum, 1983). She also found that the ability to selectively attend to stimuli is a useful way to arrive at different states of awareness or states of consciousness (Hamilton-Holcomb, 1976–1977).

Some researchers have suggested that there may be stages of involvement in the flow experience (Galway, 1974). One suggestion is that there are four stages a person might go through as they move from microflow to very intense flow experiences. The first stage is *paying attention.* The task here is to focus attention on physiological processes. The second stage is *interested attention.* In this stage, the person does not have to concentrate hard on focusing attention and eliminating distractions. He or she is able to stay with the activity and enjoy it. This state of mild flow is the result of persistently maintaining focus on the activity and continually bringing attention back to the present. The third stage is *absorbed attention.* At this point, the person is so absorbed in activity that it is almost impossible for attention to wander or be distracted by what is going on around you. This stage is often accompanied by altered perceptions of time and space. In the fourth stage, *merging,* the person is no longer aware of a separation between self and activity. A transcendent experience, such as being "in the zone," defines this stage (see Edlin & Golanty, pp. 114–115).

Flow and Subjective Well-Being

Any discussion of the relationship between flow and well-being must acknowledge the potential for circular reasoning that comes with this territory. That is, because Csikszentmihalyi originally asked people to describe moments when activities were going extremely well, the theory of flow began by asking people about moments of well-being. So, one answer to the question of whether flow is associated with well-being must be "yes," because feelings of well-being were the starting point of the initial interviews. The real question, therefore, is whether having more frequent flow experiences really increases later feelings of happiness or life satisfaction.

One answer to this question comes from the research on leisure. Because flow is a significant component of many pleasurable leisure activities, flowlike experiences seem to be related to leisure and satisfaction. As noted already in this chapter, research has supported the positive relationship between leisure activities and subjective well-being. It is also obvious that flow may be a significant aspect of intrinsically motivated activities in that people return again and again to activities that allow them to experience flow, even though they receive no recognition or money to do so. But, this still does not get at the question of whether flow facilitates greater well-being after the fact. Is there other evidence?

After almost thirty years of research, a number of studies have found relationships between flow and aspects of well-being (see Nakamura & Csikszentmihalyi, 2002, for a review). For example, Lefevre (1988) found that the more time people spent in flow, the greater was their quality of experience during the day. Higher quality of experience included greater concentration, creativity, and more positive affect. People were not more satisfied, however; they just reported higher quality experiencing. Wells (1988) studied the relationship between self-esteem and flow in working mothers and found that flow was significantly correlated with self-esteem based on perceived competence as a parent. That is, if their interactions with their children were easy, comfortable, and tension free—if they flowed—then women felt they were better mothers. However, their overall sense of self-esteem was not associated with flow experiences. Mothers could feel good about themselves with or without flow. Another study found that adolescents felt more happy, cheerful, excited, involved, and had a higher self-concept when they perceived their family environment at home as more autotelic (Rathunde, 1988). An autotelic family context was one that found the optimum balance between choice, clarity, centering, commitment, and challenge. Taking another approach, Clarke and Haworth (1994) looked at differences between flow (i.e., when skills matched challenges) and optimal experiencing (i.e., when skills slightly exceeded challenges). They found that British college students perceived moments of optimal experiencing to be more enjoyable than moments of flow. Further, students who spent a greater percentage of their time in optimal experiencing had higher well-being scores than students who spent more time in flow. In their study, well-being was related to flow but more strongly to optimal experiencing. American adolescents also reported more happiness when engaged in low-challenge, high skills situations (Csikszentmihalyi & Rathunde, 1993). Finally, Csikszentmihalyi (1997) reported that happiness and flow often go together, but not always. For instance, people report positive experiences of flow at work, but at the same time they may feel less happy at work than in other contexts. Working from the other direction, people report that eating is a very positive experience but report average levels of flow when eating (Csikszentmihalyi, 1990).

Why Does Flow Increase Psychological Well-Being?

In his analysis of why flow increases well-being, Csikszentmihalyi (1990) begins with what he sees as a "simple truth." He believes that the quality of our lives is determined by how we are able to control our consciousness. The ability to exert a measure of control of consciousness leads to order and greater well-being. A lack of this ability leads to disorder, or what he calls "psychic entropy," and various states of dissatisfaction. Control is not some kind of mental muscle, however, that rigidly squashes all unwelcome thoughts and emotions. Rather, control is a learned skill that involves balanced regulation of thoughts, emotions, behavior, and attention. One of the primary reasons that flow leads to well-being is that it helps create order in consciousness. This order allows for the smooth functioning of consciousness. Csikszentmihalyi (1990) said, "When the information that keeps coming into awareness is congruent with goals, psychic energy flows effortlessly" (p. 39). The ability to control consciousness and increase the probability of optimal experiencing also increases the sense of mastery, a sense of participation in life, and the ability to determine the content of life on a moment-by-moment basis. In addition, the ability to control the contents of consciousness can give us the ability to be independent of the social environment, so that external circumstance need not determine our emotional or intellectual states.

Therefore, Csikszentmihalyi looked at what happens both during the flow experience and after experiencing flow. He said that during flow, increased well-being is due to the more efficient organization of consciousness. During flow, currently available information in consciousness is congruent with goals and under this condition psychic energy will flow effortlessly. That is, part of the flow experience is a lack of internal conflict between competing goals. After the flow experience, a further ordering of consciousness occurs. Csikszentmihalyi (1990) suggested that because of the flow experience the organization of the self is more complex. In addition, the sense of self is more integrated after the flow experience as the various elements that make up the increasing complexity work together more harmoniously. Csikszentmihalyi believes that the ability to stay absorbed and interested in our daily experience is one of the key ingredients of a happy and fulfilling life. He said that the "first step" to enjoying life more is to learn how to engineer daily activities in order to foster rewarding experiences

(Csikszentmihalyi, 1997). For him, the engineering of daily experiences has much to do with finding the right balance between skills and challenges.

How to Produce More Flow in Life

If flow were a totally random experience, completely immune from attempts to teach people how to achieve it, then it would be an interesting experience but only a footnote in the psychological literature. As it happens, Csikszentmihalyi believes that the probability of having a flow experience can be increased through certain strategies. Note, however, that he does not believe that flow is entirely controllable. Not every game of tennis, for instance, produces a flow experience. There is always an unknown element in the production of flow. We can, however, increase the likelihood of flow happening under certain circumstances.

So how does one do this? Throughout his writings, Csikszentmihalyi has suggested that if a person wishes to increase the frequency of flow, he or she should find a way to judiciously balance the challenge of an activity with their skill level in a context that provides immediate feedback (Csikszentmihalyi, 1990, 1997). Any activity can be used for this purpose; all that is required is to find a way to challenge oneself, make the task more interesting, and pay attention to what one is doing.

Csikszentmihalyi says that intense flow experiences are induced when the demands of the situation push the person to the limits of his or her skill level. He says, in other words, that we enter a state of deep flow only when two conditions are met. The first is when the demands are so high that we must force ourselves to pay the strictest attention to the task from moment to moment. The second is when the demands of the task force us to move beyond a state where self-consciousness divides our attention between the task and an ongoing self-evaluation of how we are performing it. For instance, when we are just beginning to learn a new skill—playing the piano, for instance—we find it difficult for at least two reasons. First, we do not yet have enough practice to make our bodies perform the unique operations that the task requires. That is why practicing scales on the piano is necessary—to build up dexterity and finesse in the fingers. Second, beginning to learn a new skill is difficult because we have that annoying quality of self-consciousness that sits back and, in a very irritating way, evaluates everything we do. Our awareness is so heightened that we cannot just relax and let the music happen. When we become more proficient, however, we can stop thinking about how to play and simply play the piano. Later, when the piece is challenging, we must pay attention and we cannot divide our attention between playing and some other cognitive task. At this point, flow can happen.

Are Challenges and Skills Necessary for Flow?

Studies have suggested that there may be more to the flow experience than just skills and challenge. McQuillan and Conde (1996) found that the probability of flow during reading was increased if the person had an interest in the subject of the text. In their study, fiction passages were more likely to enhance flow than were nonfiction passages. Webster, Trevino, and Ryan (1993) studied flow and playfulness when using computers. They found that flow was fostered by intrinsic interest in and curiosity about the task. These studies suggest that it is more difficult to experience flow when involved in a task that has no interest for us. Indeed, Csikszentmihalyi (1997) reported that people do not report experiencing flow when doing housework. In fact, many people make boring tasks more interesting by providing some stimulus to help focus their attention. A prime example is listening to music while doing housework. In other words, you can set up your environment so that it is conducive to flow. This could mean removing distractions, noises, and interruptions or creating the external cues that may have conditioned associations with the experience of flow. For example, musicians often have a favorite instrument that increases the likelihood of flow when they play it. Couples often use this strategy as a way to increase the flow that comes with those special romantic evenings. They have dinner by candlelight and listen to "their song." Women wear a special dress, men bring flowers, and if it works, the rest of the world fades away as two people get lost in the flow of a romantic evening.

Comments on the Theory of Flow

Csikszentmihalyi has said that flow is produced by balancing learned skills and the challenges of the situation that requires those skills. The key is to be involved in "just-manageable challenges" (Nakamura & Csikszentmihalyi, 2002, p. 90). Any inquiry must begin by acknowledging that certain types of flow activities—particularly being "in the zone" during sports activities—seem to occur more often when a person is fully exercising learned skills and competencies in a context that provides high challenges and immediate feedback. However, the balance of learned skills and challenges may be problematic for an understanding of flow, leisure, play, and relaxation. A few examples will illustrate the problems.

One of the more frequently observed aspects of the flow experience is that it is not always present in a specific activity, or if it is present, then it may not be present throughout the duration of the activity. Just playing a thrilling game of tennis does not guarantee a flow experience. The challenge of the game may force moment-to-moment attention and bring a person to the very edge of their skill level, and yet the "magic"' doesn't happen and flow is not experienced. We can look at this aspect from the opposite point of view. Even trained musicians may experience flow from pieces that are relatively easy to play but are nonetheless deeply moving. A few years ago, Bill Moyers hosted an entire documentary about the song "Amazing Grace" (Morris, 1990). He found that this nineteenth century song had a very special place in the hearts of many people all over the world. The emotions that this song produces in people seem to transcend barriers of race, religion, social, class, and educational attainment. And yet, the song itself is really quite simple, and even very inexperienced musicians can experience flow when playing the song—or many other simple songs as well.

One of the more relevant contributors to the flow experience is whether the person has an interest in, curiosity about, or facilitation with the activity. Other frequently reported contexts for flow are watching movies, participation in religious rituals, and listening to music (Csikszentmihalyi, 1990). As with reading, getting lost in the movie also requires an emotional connection with the film (also note that the "skills" required to watch a movie are minimal). Similarly, a religious ritual is meaningful only if a person has a personal connection with the underlying belief system or an openness to spirituality. Therefore, the induction of flow experiences appears to be more than a simple matching of one's skills at a certain activity with the challenges presented by that activity.

Last, while deep flow is often associated with the feeling of "being in the zone," does that mean that people actually perform better while in flow? On the contrary, just being in flow and feeling as if you are performing better does not always translate into objectively better performance. Jackson and Csikszentmihalyi (1999) note that athletes often experience flow during those moments when they feel as if they are performing at their best, but is it true that being in flow causes athletes to perform at their best? What does it mean to perform at the "top of your game"?

PEAK PERFORMANCE

> During one particular swim meet which was close, I was delegated to swim "third leg" or slow spot on a freestyle relay team. . . . I vividly remember telling myself that *this time* I was going to make my

> coach proud of me . . . that *this was it!!* Well, I hit the water, and I remember nothing else about the race, except my coach's ecstatic face when I lifted my head. Somehow I had come in ahead of everyone and put our team out front . . . I was so excited and pleased with myself. To this day I can never remember doing that well in another swim meet. It definitely was *not* my usual level of functioning (quoted in Privette, 1981, p. 60).

Peak performance is the term that Gayle Privette (1981, 1983) used to describe those moments when we perform at a level that is beyond our normal level of functioning. Peak performance is conceptualized as behavior that is "more efficient, more creative, more productive, or in some ways better than [the person's] ordinary behavior . . . and may occur in any facet of human activity: intellectual, emotional, or physical" (Privette & Landsman, 1983, p. 195). Almost everyone can recall at least one incident in which they somehow, miraculously, performed far better than they normally do. Some people may recall a superior performance on an exam, others may remember an incident of unusual courage or perseverance, or an episode like the one quoted above of an athletic performance that went beyond what the person believed they were capable of. As a dramatic example of peak performance, Privette (1983) cites the experience of someone who saved farm animals that were trapped by a fire:

> The barn caught fire from a brush fire! The children were safe, but animals in an adjacent shed were not.. . . I had no tools, and the oak boards were thick—nailed with 20-penny nails! I pulled at a board and it came off with ease as if a wrecking bar was being used. The animals were free. After the fire died away it took five minutes to straighten the nails and remove them from the oak plank.. . . . On inspection we verified that the oak board was well attached to the locust posts, and removing it by hand was virtually impossible. But it happened to me (p. 196).

For most people, these experiences are very memorable. Also, most people have no idea how the peak performance happened or how to make it happen again. Note that Privette defines peak performance as "behavior that transcends or goes beyond predictable functioning to use a person's potential more fully than could be reasonably expected " (1981, p. 58). That is, peak performance is superior *behavior* at a task, not just a subjective experience while engaged in the task, as with flow. Privette says that peak performance is not a specific type of activity, but rather it is an especially high level of functioning. That is, peak performance is not specific to any particular context, activity, or situation. It can occur in any activity—it is the "full use of any human power" (Privette, 1983, p. 1362). Some years earlier, Privette (1965) referred to the same phenomena as transcendent functioning. Finally, she saw the ability to exhibit peak performance as a universal potential in human beings. For her, almost anyone could show peak performance under the right conditions (Privette & Landsman, 1983).

Privette's investigations into peak performance have found that it can be described by four parameters:

1. Clear *focus* on self, object, and relationship
2. Intense *involvement* in the experience.
3. A strong *intention* to complete a task.
4. A spontaneous expression of *power.*

Note also that peak performance is defined as a level rather than a type of behavior. While Privette's investigations indicate that many people have experienced moments of peak performance in varied situations, it is still difficult to understand the precise triggers for the experience. Peak performance can also be experienced in two very different ways. The quote about the fire speaks to a spontaneous moment of peak performance that happened in a crisis situation. Incidents like these require no previous training and are not deliberately induced. Examples of this first type would include incidents of unusual courage during a crisis. The other type of peak performance has a more deliberate quality to it.

People will train for years to master a specific skill and may make a conscious effort to induce a moment of peak performance. The quote by the swimmer that opened this section is an example of this second type of peak performance. Often, this type is associated with sports performance, athletic competition, or creativity.

Peak Performance in Sports

Sport psychologists have eagerly adopted Privette's idea of peak performance and applied it to sports and athletics (Williams, 1993). In spite of the difficulty in determining just what it takes to make an athlete "hot," a tremendous amount of work has been done on how to increase the probability of peak performance in athletics. Because the flow experience has often been compared to being "in the zone" during an athletic event, one might reasonably ask if there is a relationship between flow and peak performance. Jean Williams and Vikki Krane (1993) addressed the relationship between peak performance and flow in this way: "One may be in flow and not necessarily have a peak performance; however, when an athlete experiences peak performance, he/she appears to be in a flow state" (p. 140).

Privette (1981) believed that the key to peak performance is in keeping a clear focus on self, object, and the relationship between the two. She believed that peak performance is associated with a strong sense of self in relationship with some object. The object can be almost anything, but it must be something the person is deeply committed to or intensely fascinated by. This helps to produce an intense involvement. She said, "The task that elicits peak performance represents an intrinsic value to the person and culminates in a direct, active engagement with the valued subject" (Privette, 1981, p. 64). In short, peak performance is most often found in activities or situations that a person is deeply involved with, committed to, absorbed in, or emotionally connected with.

In a study that involved interviews with hundreds of elite athletes, Charles Garfield and Hal Bennett (1984) found eight conditions that accompanied those moments when performance was at its best (taken from Williams, 1993):

1. Mentally relaxed, a sense of calm, a sense of high concentration, and often a sense that time has slowed down.
2. Physical relaxation with loose and fluid movements.
3. Self-confidence and optimism even in the face of challenges.
4. Focus on the present and a sense that one's body performs automatically.
5. High energy level along with positive emotions, such as joy, as well as a sense of being "hot" or "charged."
6. Extraordinary awareness of one's own body. Often this is accompanied by an uncanny ability to know what the other athletes are going to do and the ability to respond instantly to them.
7. A sense of total control without undue effort to create or maintain that control.
8. "In the cocoon." This refers to a sense that one is in an envelope that allows one to be protected from distractions. Additionally, it allows easy access to one's powers and skills.

The similarity of these descriptions to flow is very obvious. Almost all of the characteristics of flow are represented in this list. Differences between peak performance and flow begin to emerge when sport psychologists study not just what it feels like to be "hot" or "in the zone," but what it takes to perform better. Research with top athletes has found that in addition to flow experiences, those who actually perform better have a psychological advantage. Williams and Krane (1993) state that most coaches acknowledge that once a certain skill level is achieved, then 40 to 90 percent of athletic success is due to psychological factors.

Training for Peak Performance

Sport psychologists have developed a wide range of training programs to help athletes develop to their full potential. Much to their credit, they have also worked on interventions to help athletes with issues such as burnout, drug abuse, rehabilitation after injury, and forced retirement from sports (see Anshel, 1993). Concerning peak performance, sport psychologists have been working to establish the effectiveness of their interventions from an empirical basis. M. Greenspan and D. Feltz (1989) reviewed a number of studies that investigated the effectiveness of various psychological interventions to increase levels of performance. The studies looked at athletes from diverse sports, including figure skating, baseball, karate, and gymnastics. Their review found support for the effectiveness of education-based psychological interventions. Greenspan and Feltz concluded that psychological interventions can be helpful in improving the performance of adult athletes in competitive situations.

If interventions can be helpful, then how does one go about it? Beginning with flow, or being "in the zone," sports psychologist Susan Jackson and Csikszentmihalyi (1999) gave a number of practical hints for the induction of "the zone" in athletic performance. Their suggestions were to

1. Move beyond one's comfort zone and challenge oneself.
2. Believe in one's skills and stop nagging self-doubt.
3. Focus on the process or the moment-by-moment activity.
4. Be self-aware, not self-conscious.
5. "Set the stage" or do all the necessary preliminary preparations before the competition.
6. Practice a simple meditation exercise to help focus on the present and help control unnecessary and distracting thinking.

These suggestions apply to the induction of flow during an athletic performance. However, as mentioned, flow does not guarantee peak performance. Sport psychologists have added some additional psychological strategies to the suggestions on how to induce peak performance. N. McCaffrey and T. Orlick (1989) listed what they called the essential "elements of excellence" after their study of top professional golfers. The following annotated list of those elements of peak performance includes minor additions from Williams and Krane (1993; see also Jackson, Kimiecik, & Ford, 1998).

1. Total commitment, dedication, and even preoccupation with their chosen sport. (Some studies find that better athletes have more frequent dreams about their sport!)
2. Quality rather than quantity of practice.
3. Clearly defined goals for practice and performance.
4. Imagery practice on a daily basis (for example, they imagine themselves performing at their best).
5. Total focus on each shot.
6. Well-developed coping strategies to deal with anxiety, arousal, and unexpected pressures.
7. Strategies to control distractions.
8. Detailed plans made before games and tournaments.
9. Postgame follow-ups and reviews of their performance.
10. A high determination to win.
11. High self-confidence.
12. Ability to keep the focus on the positive and on their strengths.

In other words, peak performance involves the psychological factors of commitment, dedication, and the intellectual and emotional involvement in—some may even call it an obsession with—all the nuances of the sport.

Additional Avenues to Well-Being

Mindfulness

The next perspective on well-being comes from Ellen Langer (1989) and represents another approach that centers on awareness and the quality of attention that we bring to everyday experiences. Langer found that a certain style of attention was related to increased well-being and better adaptation. She termed this approach mindfulness.

Langer's investigations of mindfulness began with one of the more interesting—and simple—little experiments in the psychological literature. Langer and her colleague Judith Rodin (1976) went to a nursing home and provided a small intervention in order to investigate the sense of control. Some of the residents received a small houseplant to care for and were given minor increases in decisional control over their daily lives. Other residents were not given these opportunities. A year and a half later those who had been given the responsibility for the plants were more cheerful, alert, and active than the other residents. In addition, "less than half as many of the decision-making, plant-minding residents had died as had those in the other group" (Langer, 1989, p. 1). According to Langer and Rodin, the difference between the two groups was the added incentive for the plant group to pay attention to their environment, to notice what was happening around them, and to be more mindful of their own experiences.

Mindfulness is paying attention to one's own on-going experience in a way that allows openness and flexibility. It is being fully present and aware during our daily activities. When people are mindful they are open to new experiences and points of view, are able to create new categories for information processing, and pay attention to process as well as outcome. In other words, Langer says that well-being is not associated with moving through life on automatic pilot but with actively participating in the ongoing experiences of life with openness and creativity. Many people go through life waiting for something important, significant, or meaningful to happen, and all the time they forget to notice their real lives.

Mindfulness, on the other hand, gives us the opportunity to experience our world with fresh eyes and ears. It can help us to create new categories of experience. Mindfulness can also help us to be open to new information and to allow us to see more than one point of view. It can help to break down the rigid categories that we use to make information processing easier at the expense of understanding and complexity. Finally, a mindful approach to life can help us focus on the process of living our lives rather than the goals and hoped for accomplishments. John Lennon once remarked that our life is what happens while we are waiting for our "real life" to begin. The old saying that we have to "stop and smell the roses" is a reminder that we must pay attention to the journey as well as the goals.

In order to get a better feel for what mindfulness is, it is helpful to describe its opposite—mindlessness. When we are in a state of mindlessness, our thoughts wander, we are not paying attention to what is going on around us; in short, we "space out." Yet, often this is helpful. It would be difficult to actively process all of the information that comes to us every moment of the day. When we live in a chronic state of mindlessness, however, we are on automatic pilot and respond habitually to our world without thinking about we are actually doing or saying. Another aspect of mindlessness is that in that state we rely on categories of experience that are too rigid and may actually restrict our ability to respond reasonably or compassionately. In another experiment, Langer and her colleagues sent out memos to some offices at their university. The memos simply said, "Please return memo immediately to room 247" or "This memo is to be returned to room 247." The memos were designed either to look exactly like other ones used at the office or were different from usual memos. When memos were designed to look like usual ones, 90 percent of them were actually returned! Even 60 percent of those that looked different from normal memos were returned. Most people looked at the memo and blindly followed the instructions in spite of the fact that the instructions made no sense (see Langer, 1989). According to Langer, the roots of mindlessness are found in habits, premature cognitive commitments to categories, and in a focus on future goals rather than immediate processes.

As with the flow experience, there are levels of intensity of the mindfulness experience. Some people may experience a mild state of mindfulness simply by paying more attention to their daily activities. Other times—often less frequently—a person may experience a fairly intense form of mindfulness or absorbed attention to experiences of the moment. In a study that looked at mindfulness and subjective well-being, Jeffrey Jacob and Merlin Brinkerhoff (1999) interviewed people who moved out of the city and went back to the country. This group of people had moved to the country in search of a less complicated lifestyle that was closer to nature and that allowed them to live more completely within their ecologically and environmentally based values. One respondent (quoted in Jacob & Brinkerhoff, 1999) described a special moment: "At the moment of a foal's birth or the opening of a newly built gate, time . . . seems to stand still. . . . The world for the moment appears whole and the mind moves toward a stillness. . . . One's being . . . appears to be drawn into the ongoing stream of perceived universal reality, with the potential for finding tranquillity, union and wholeness" (p. 349).

For many of the respondents in this study, these brief moments of intense mindfulness contributed to a sense of subjective well-being. Greater mindfulness throughout the day allowed them to focus on the wonder that could be found in the everyday events of their world.

Savoring

Most people have had the experience of pausing to really experience something that is pleasurable. It could be taking time to really taste ice cream on a hot summer day or absorbing all the sensations while sitting quietly on an isolated beach at sunset. Fred Bryant and Joseph Veroff (Bryant, 1989; Bryant & Veroff, 2004) refer to these moments as **savoring,** an awareness of pleasure along with a quite deliberate attempt to focus attention on the sensation and relish it. In a sense, savoring is the experience of trying to extract every nuance and association that is contained in the complexity of a pleasurable experience.

Bryant and Veroff believe there are four basic types of savoring: *basking,* or receiving praise and congratulations; *marveling,* or getting lost in the wonder of a moment; *luxuriating,* or indulging in a sensation; and *thanksgiving,* or expressing gratitude (see Seligman, 2002a). They also believe that there are five basic ways to enhance savoring and promote the possibility of savoring. The first is *absorption,* or allowing oneself to be immersed in the experience. Because a person must focus on sensations, the second is *sharpening the senses,* or focusing on one sensation while blocking out others. The next way to promote savoring is through *memory building.* Here, the idea is to do something to help remember an experience later on. This is the reason that many people buy souvenirs—to help them remember moments of joy or savoring. Fourth, one can help promote savoring by *sharing with others.* Again, most people automatically seek out other people to share their positive experiences with. The fifth suggestion to promote savoring is *self-congratulation.* This suggestion may seem a bit odd at first. However, the idea is to allow oneself to feel good about having had an experience of savoring, to relish in the experience and even allow oneself a bit of healthy pride. In other words, Bryant and Veroff are saying that we can do more than simply "stop and smell the roses." We can "stop and really savor the experience of the roses."

Comments on Optimal Experiences

A number of ideas discussed in this chapter all are concerned with leisure, play, flow, and the nature of enjoyment. The range of experiences covered by these perspectives is wide: from simple efforts to just pay attention to the details of one's life; to relaxed and focused contemplative experiences, such as lying on the beach or walking in the woods; to the intense excitement and thrills of adventure sports; to the altered state of consciousness termed being "in the zone." Can a central idea be condensed from these different perspectives? What, if anything, can be said about the nature of leisure and enjoyment? In order to answer these questions, it is necessary to note the unique perspective on well-being that has been presented in this chapter. The literature on leisure, flow, peak performance, and mindfulness share a common assumption about happiness and satisfaction. All of these perspectives in one way or another assume that a significant amount of well-being is found through active participation in the ongoing experiences of our lives. They all suggest that a deep appreciation of our moment-by-moment experiences can be satisfying and even fulfilling.

The contrast with some other perspectives on well-being is worth noting. For instance, models based on the goal-achievement gap postulate that people are oriented toward goals, and our well-being depends in large measure on where we currently stand in relation to those goals. Goal-achievement gap models postulate that our current sense of well-being is the result of comparison between our current state and where we would like to be (or where we think we should be). In contrast, the perspectives discussed in this chapter all focus on an *appreciation* of our current experience rather than an *evaluation* of our experience. A person might, therefore, reasonably ask what factors facilitate an appreciation of the moment.

One such factor is a decrease in self-focused attention and internal dialogue. Experiences similar to flow, such as relaxation, hypnosis, and meditation, all seem to be associated with a decrease in the "internal chatter" of our lives. In addition, time is often distorted during flow or peak performance, and the experience of time appears to be related to how we experience the self (Fenchel, 1985). Descriptions of how to induce flow in activities, such as tennis (Galway, 1974) and Zen archery (Herrigel, 1971), often explicitly include instruction on how to lose the sense of self-consciousness and let the body perform without interference. Allison and Duncan (1987) looked at this idea from the opposite perspective. In a study of women and flow, they found that "antiflow" was associated with frustration and boredom. These emotions are characterized by a greater focus on self and an increase in negative "inner chatter." Similarly, neuroticism is associated with increased rumination, which is partially an obsessive preoccupation with thoughts, emotions, or memories.

Further work needs to be done to specify more precisely the differences between various states of optimal experiencing. This chapter has discussed the experiences of leisure, relaxation, flow, peak performance, mindfulness, and savoring. In Csikszentmihalyi's (1975) original

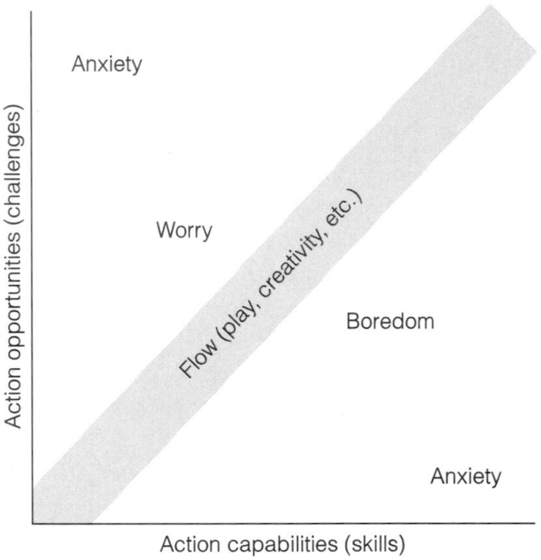

FIGURE **4.2**

Csikszentmihalyi's Original Model of Flow

Source: From M. Csikszentmihalyi, "Play and intrinsic reward," *Journal of Humanistic Psychology, 15*(3), fig. 1, p. 56. Reprinted with permission.

model of flow (see Figure 4.2), a balancing of low skills with low challenges could produce flow. Some of these relatively mindless activities he termed microflow.

Today, Csikszentmihalyi (Nakamura & Csikszentmihalyi, 2002) says that some low-challenge, high-skills activities can be relaxing rather than boring. But low-challenge, low-skills activities are still seen as producing boredom, worry, or apathy (see Figure 4.1). However, many activities that have been studied as precursors to flow, such as reading for pleasure, participating in a religious rituals, or being with close family members, are enjoyable because they demand few skills and present few challenges. Therefore, while research to this point has been helpful, it only begins to define the many differences between intense experiences such as deep flow or peak performance and the quieter experiences characterized by contented relaxation, interested engagement, or delighted easy absorption in an activity.

Finally, at least two alternate pathways lead to greater well-being. One path involves self-enhancement processes. A great deal of the subjective well-being literature speaks to that path. The other path focuses more on temporarily forgetting awareness of self and appreciating the moment. The experiences of flow, mindfulness, and savoring may describe this path.

Summary

This chapter discussed topics that are associated with leisure and optimal experiencing. Satisfaction with life is associated with having adequate leisure time to explore intrinsically satisfying pastimes. The variety of leisure activities speaks to the need to find activities that are personally meaningful and freely chosen. At times, activities can become opportunities for optimal experiences. Many of these states have been described as flow. The intensity of flow experiences can range from mild and pleasurable experiences of being focused and involved to intense experiences where our sense of time, control, and self are all significantly altered. In sports, these intense experiences of flow are called being "in the zone." A related idea is peak performance. These are moments when people perform activities at levels far above what is normally possible for them. The parameters of peak performance and suggestions on how to facilitate it were discussed from the perspective of sports psychology. Finally, the idea of mindfulness and savoring were discussed. This refers to moments when people focus, concentrate, and pay attention to the experiences of the moment. Being more mindful can help to break old habitual patterns and to give people a sense of being more in touch with the ongoing reality of their lives.

Learning Tools

Key Terms and Ideas

FLOW
MICROFLOW
MINDFULNESS
PEAK PERFORMANCE
SAVORING

Books

Csikszentmihalyi, M. (1990). *Flow: The psychology of optimal experience.* New York: Harper & Row. A book intended for the general public by the man who coined the term and the theory. Csikszentmihalyi also has a number of more recent books on flow written for the general public. Look them up at your library or online. The next is one of the more applied books.

Csikszentmihalyi, M. (1997). *Finding flow: The psychology of engagement with everyday life.* New York: Basic Books.

Hayes, K. F., & Brown, C. H., Jr. (2004). *You're on! Consulting for peak performance.* Washington, DC: American Psychological Association. Provides guidance and advice for those seeking excellence (professional/popular).

Jackson, S., & Csikszentmihalyi, M. (1999). *Flow in Sports.* Champaign, IL: Human Kinetics.

Langer, E. J. (1989). *Mindfulness.* Reading, MA: Perseus. A book on the psychological theory of mindfulness by the person who developed it (popular).

Research Articles

Csikszentmihalyi, M. (1975). Play and intrinsic rewards. *Journal of Humanistic Psychology, 15*(3), 41–63. The article that introduced the theory of flow.

Privette, G. (1983). Peak experience, peak performance, and flow: A comparative analysis of positive human experiences. *Journal of Personality and Social Psychology, 45*(6), 1361–1368. A comparison of optimal experiencing states by the researcher who coined the term "peak performance."

Audio Tape

Young, S. (1996). *Meditation in the zone.* Boulder, CO: Sounds True. Instructional tapes that give simple exercises to help people bring more flow into their exercise workouts. Available from Sounds True Catalog. www.soundstrue.com.

On the Web

http://psywww.com/sports/index.htm. Information on sports psychology topics such as training, flow, and peak performance.

Personal Explorations

Have you experienced flow? If so, in what contexts or situations? Do you return to flow activities as often as you would like? The next time you do engage in that activity, practice flow by trying to balance your skills and the challenges of the situation. Describe what happened.

In what contexts or situations do you experience mindfulness? How often do you seek out those contexts or situations? Try to bring more mindfulness into your life by focusing on the details of your moment-to-moment activities. Each time you find yourself "spacing out," return to the experience of the moment. Practice this for a week, and describe what happened.

CHAPTER

5

Love and Well-Being

> At no time in history has so large a proportion of humanity rated love so highly, thought about it so much, or displayed such an insatiable appetite for it.
>
> *Morton Hunt (1959)*

It should be obvious to even a casual observer of human behavior that the search for love and supportive relationships is a significant factor in the lives of many people. References to finding one's "soul mate" or to "living happily ever after" are everywhere in our culture. Why has there been so much attention placed on this single emotion? Is it truly that important to well-being and happiness? In fact, as mentioned, the presence of positive relationships is one of the most significant predictors of happiness and life satisfaction. As we will see in this chapter, romantic love is a predominant factor in psychological and physical well-being. This chapter explores what we know about this somewhat elusive, vigorously sought-after emotion.

The Psychology of Love

Evolution and Love

From an evolutionary perspective, love has properties that help us adapt (Shackelford & Buss, 1997). As social animals, we need to be involved with groups of other people in order to carve out a life for ourselves, our families, and our social group. Within that context, it helps to be able to form tight, close, supportive bonds with a smaller subset of individuals. Speaking from a strictly biological point of view, these bonds compel us to protect those close to us, particularly our children. We must take care of children and others in our group, in spite of the fact that the effort may cause us difficulty and strain. This overtly biological perspective, however, does not describe the emotional experience that leads to romance novels, love songs, sonnets to one's beloved, and that famous commitment vow, "Till death do us part." The experience of romantic love that demands the utmost fascination from most people cannot be totally understood by knowing only about genes, hormones, and neurotransmitters.

Marriage and Well-Being

Recall from the discussion in Chapter 3 on subjective well-being that numerous studies have shown that the quality of our social relationships is one of the central factors of whether we

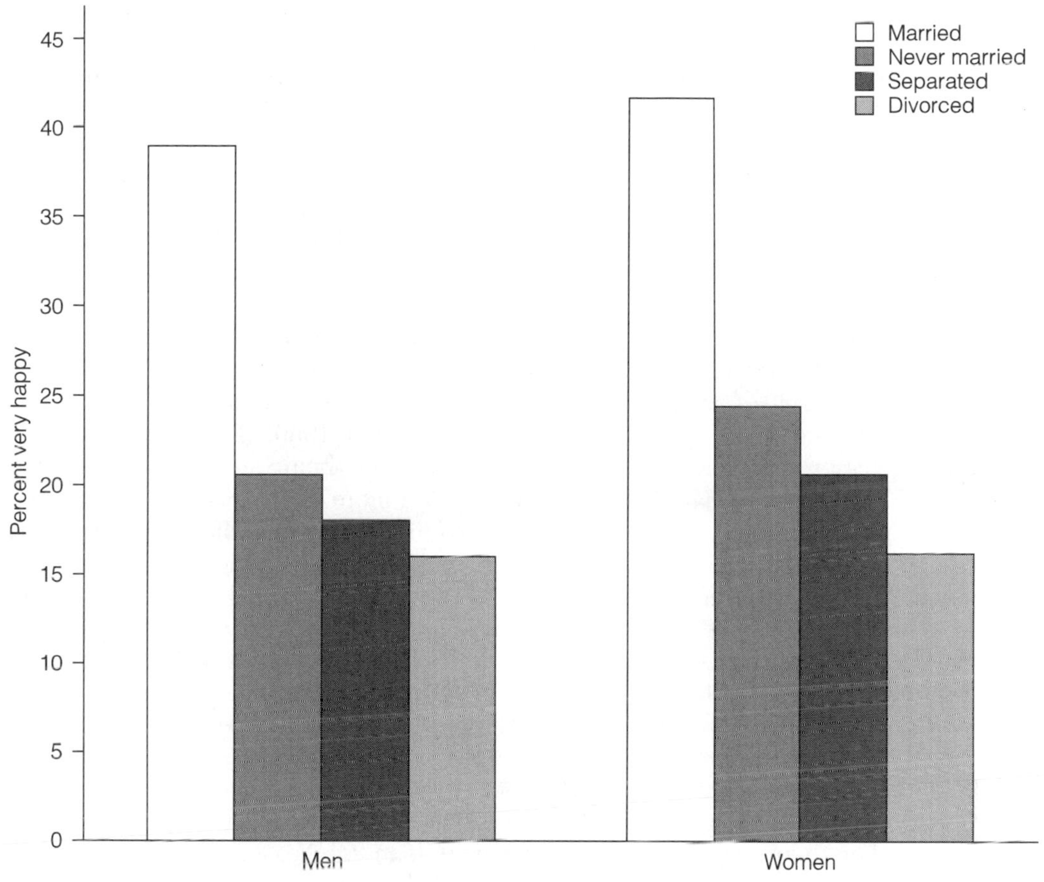

FIGURE 5.1

Happiness by Marital Status for Men and Women

Source: Data from 41,974 respondents from the National Opinion Research Center's General Social Survey, 1972–2002; data compiled by David G. Myers. Adapted with permission from David Myers, "Funds, friends and faith of happy people," *American Psychologist, 55*(1), fig. 6, p. 63. Copyright 2000 by the American Psychological Association.

feel content, satisfied, and happy with our lives. But what about more intimate relationships—do they offer even more to our sense of contentment, joy, and life satisfaction? One of the most frequently found associations in the subjective well-being literature is between being married[1] and higher self-reported happiness and life satisfaction (Argyle, 1987; Diener et al. 1999; Myers, 2000). Studies have shown that married people are both consistently happier and healthier than single people, at least when comparisons are made between groups of individuals (see Figure 5.1). This is true across all ages, income levels, education levels, and racial and ethnic groups. In fact, a number of studies have found that being married is the *only* really significant bottom-up predictor of life satisfaction. For both men and women, being married is associated with feeling happier and more satisfied with life.

Marital quality is also a significant predictor of subjective well-being. Marriages that have more positive interactions, emotional expressiveness, and greater role sharing seem to be associated with greater life satisfaction (see Sternberg & Hojjat, 1997). One of the important variables in these relationships is self-disclosure. Supportive relationships that provide opportunities for emotional intimacy, trust, and openness provide salutary effects in a number of areas of life. On the negative side, problems with interpersonal relationships, particularly intimate relationships, are among the most frequently reported triggers for depression (Paykel, 1979).

Interestingly, the effect of marriage on well-being is stronger for men. In general, single men are less happy than single women, but married men are as happy or happier than married women (Lee, Seccombe, & Shehan, 1991). So while both men and women's average level of happiness increases after they get married, the increase is greater for men. This difference is also seen in ratings that men and women give on how much they love their partner. In a survey conducted by "NBC Today—Weekend Edition" and *Prevention* magazine, 53 percent of the men and women rated their love for their partner a "Perfect 10" or simply perfect. However, when the results were examined more closely, 59 percent of the men rated their love as a "Perfect 10," while only 47 percent of women rated their love that high (Gorman, 1998). Men were somewhat more enthusiastic about their marriages than were women.

Marriage also appears to have positive benefits for physiological health. After reviewing the studies on how marriage is related to health outcomes, Burman and Margolin (1992) concluded that there is good evidence that the psychological and social elements of marriage are related to both physical health and to mortality rates. Positive marital relationships may actually be associated with increased longevity. Couples who interacted in positive ways showed lower blood pressure and lower physiological reactivity to negative interactions (see Gottman & Notarius, 2000). The physiological effects of being married are also greater for men than for women. When compared with unmarried men, married men have fewer infectious diseases and live longer. Married women also benefit physiologically from marriage, but the quality of the marriage is a more significant factor for women. Men seem to benefit simply from being married, whereas women need a good marriage in order to show increased health benefits.

Some studies have also found that the increase in men's well-being is due to increases in happiness after marriage, while women's increases are due to increases in life satisfaction (see Diener et al. 1999). This means that men's increase in well-being after getting married may be due more to the resulting increases in positive emotions, while women's increases may be more attributable to higher cognitive judgments relating to life being good or better than it was before getting married.

A distressing finding is that the strength of the positive relationship between marriage and well-being has declined steadily in the United States since the 1970s . This is because married women seem to be less happy than they once were, while single men seem to be getting more happy (Glenn & Weaver, 1988). Rogers and Amato (1997, 2000) found decreased satisfaction and increased levels of conflict in younger couples when compared to older couples who had fallen in love during an earlier generation. They believed that this effect was due to increased tensions surrounding work-family conflicts that come from new gender roles. The implications of this decline are unclear. Of course, this does not mean that the solution is to return to the old gender roles. If new gender roles are creating new conflicts, then solutions need to be found for these conflicts that will allow both relationship satisfaction and gender equity.

The Varieties of Love

Because love is so important to emotional well-being, it is surprising that comparatively little research has been devoted exclusively to love.

As we will see, however, considerable research has been done on what makes people satisfied with their relationships and what factors seem to predict the stability of relationships. A few theoretical perspectives on the types and varieties of love will be helpful in understanding this all-too-puzzling emotion.

Michael Barnes and Robert Sternberg (1997) group the perspectives on love into *explicit* and *implicit* theories of love. Perspectives that attempt to analyze love into its core elements or dimensions are grouped as explicit theories. Not surprisingly, a few of these perspectives view love as a single dimension. Among the first to view love in this way was Freud. He saw love as a single phenomenon (Freud, 1921/1952). Essentially, love is one emotion that can take a variety of forms. According to Freud's theory, any attempt to decompose love into constituent parts will destroy the essential experience. While some research supports the single-dimension theory of love (see Barnes & Sternberg, 1997), most perspectives on love view it as a multidimensional experience.

A Two-Factor Theory of Love

The first of the multidimensional perspectives to be discussed is the two-factor theory of love (see Hatfield, 1988; Barnes & Sternberg, 1997). A number of researchers propose two factors: **passionate love** and **companionate love.** They see these two elements as the fundamental and primary elements of love, and from them can be derived all the varieties of love that people experience—both the good and the bad. Passionate love is the intense longing for the beloved. It can take the form of the terrible despair of rejection or the joy of emotional union and sexual fulfillment. Companionate love is often a quieter form of love that is associated with affection, companionship, friendship, and long-term commitment to relationships. Interestingly, Elaine Hatfield (1988) believes that both ecstasy and misery can intensify the feeling of passionate love while only pleasurable experiences can deepen companionate love.

Multifactor Theories of Love

The Love Styles The next multidimensional theory of love is the notion of *love styles* from Susan and Clyde Hendrick. They expanded on work done by John Alan Lee to create six styles of love (Hendrick & Hendrick, 1992). The first love style is *eros.* This type of love has been discussed for thousands of years. It is passionate love or the experience of love that draws one to someone with an almost irresistible pull and a desire to be the exclusive focus of that person's attention. Under the influence of eros, one becomes obsessed with thoughts of one's lover. A person may even physically ache when they cannot be with his or her lover. Eros is the stuff of countless novels, love poems, music, art, and is what most people mean when they say they want to be in love. The second type is *ludus.* This style has been described as "game playing" love. It is a style in which relationships are seen as a way to play with experiencing feelings of affection and attraction. People who enjoy being flirtatious are having fun with the ludus style of love. Those who are fascinated with this style of love often like to have more than one lover at the same time, or they like to toy with their lovers by deliberately making them jealous, playing "hard to get" to increase passion, using their sexuality as a tease, or any other number of strategies that seem to make love into a game. The third style of love is *storge,* a rather boring sounding word that is used to describe a type of love that is primarily affectionate and close but not always exciting. Storge is also related to long-term commitment and qualities that allow relationships to endure.

The fourth love style is *pragma.* This style of love describes a very practical and pragmatic approach to love. A person who prefers this style of love is seeking a person who fulfills certain conditions or who has certain rational and objective qualities that are necessary for a suitable partner. While everyone looks for certain qualities in their lovers, the person who prefers the pragma style sees rational and objective qualities as the primary reason for choosing their relationship partners. For instance, a person focused on the pragma love style might look for a partner who has financial stability and would reject someone who did not have sound financial prospects, even though they felt passionate love for that person.

Mania is the fifth of the six love styles. This style is somewhat similar to eros in that both involve passionate emotionalism and an almost obsessive focus on one's lover. In mania, however, the experience of love always seems to be painful. As one song put it, "Love is sharp, it cuts like a knife . . . love is cold, it chills your soul in the middle of the night" ("Love is Sharp," by Chris Michie, Kulberg/Michie Music). Many readers probably know people whose relationships seem to always be in turmoil and marked by many alternating periods of wonderful highs and awful lows. In fact, some people prefer these types of relationships and may believe that the emotionality indicates "true" love. The last love style, *agape,* is a selfless love. It is a style of love that asks nothing from the lover and is oriented toward giving, not getting. Again, while this quality is present in most relationships, the lover who exhibits this style is not so much engaged in a relationship as in a one-sided expression of compassion for the other person.

All of these styles of love would only be an interesting exercise in scholarly research pursuits if they did not have some practical significance. At first, the Hendricks thought that each of the love styles could be the source of a satisfying relationship. Later studies showed that this is not the case. They did a study using fifty-seven dating couples in which they looked at associations between the love styles, relationship satisfaction, and relationship stability (Hendrick, Hendrick, & Adler, 1988). They found that a person's preferred love style was related to both attraction and satisfaction. First, they found that couples showed similarity of their love styles. For example, people who scored high on the eros style tended to be paired with someone who also scored high on the eros style. So, similarity of love styles was related to whether people were attracted enough to each other to even begin forming a relationship. Second, they also found that higher satisfaction with the relationship was related to higher scores on the eros style for both men and women. For everyone, passion seemed related to satisfaction. On the other hand, the ludus style was a negative predictor for men, and the mania style was a negative predictor of satisfaction for women. The Hendricks also found some evidence that the love style expressed by the woman in a relationship may be more important to her partner's satisfaction than his style is to her satisfaction. They found that when women were more passionate (eros) and altruistic (agape) then their male partners were more satisfied with the relationship. Men's scores on these same love styles, however, seemed to be unrelated the women's satisfaction. Finally, relationship stability over a two-month period was related to more eros and less ludus for both men and women.

Sternberg's Love Triangle The most frequently mentioned of the multidimensional perspectives is Sternberg's (1986) triangular theory of love. Sternberg said that all experiences of love are built on three emotional components: passion, intimacy, and commitment. Passion, an intense emotional response to another person, is the eros love style. Intimacy is warmth, closeness, and sharing of self in a relationship. Commitment is the decision to maintain the relationship. From these, three types of singular love can be described: *infatuation* (passion only), *liking* (only intimacy), *and empty love* (commitment only). By combining two types, one gets three other types of love: *romantic love* (intimacy plus passion), *companionate love* (intimacy plus commitment), and *fatuous love* (passion plus commitment). Finally, **consummate love** is passion plus commitment plus intimacy. Certainly, most people wish for consummate love in their lives. Figure 5.2 illustrates Sternberg's types of love schematically in the love triangle.

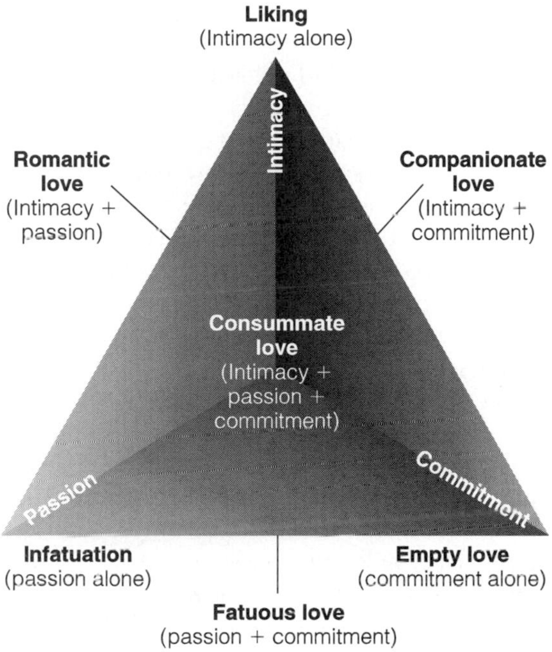

FIGURE **5.2**

Sternberg's Love Triangle

Source: From R. J. Sternberg, "A triangular theory of love," *Psychological Review, 93:* 119–135. Copyright 1986 by the American Psychological Association. Reprinted by permission.

Sternberg said that the three components of love often progress differently across the lifespan. At the beginning of a relationship passion is very high. Over time, however, passion may decrease. Sternberg believes that intimacy, on the other hand, may increase steadily throughout the relationship. Commitment may start out very low but increases over time until it reaches its highest point and then remains steady. That is, in Sternberg's model, most relationships begin as infatuation and end up as companionate love (Sternberg, 1986). However, recent research suggests that this model may be biased by a subtle ageism. Studies of elderly persons have found that sexual activity and interest in sexuality remain strong into the seventies and even the eighties (see Belsky, 1997). So, consummate love may be more frequent in long-lived relationships than Sternberg believed. Finally, Sternberg did not say how one goes about achieving consummate love, but his ideas emphasize how many different types of emotion get lumped together under the heading of "love." It is no wonder the simple exclamation, "I love you," can be interpreted so very differently.

Love as a Prototype or an Ideal

Implicit theories of love view it as a very personal experience in which people define their own ideas of love. These models try to address the question of how we know when the feelings we have for another are actually love. From this perspective, the answer is that we compare our current feelings with a standard or ideal and see how closely the two match. So people's ideas of love are organized around a prototype or ideal that is composed of numerous factors that seem to co-occur when a person recognizes that they feel love.

Studies have found that the core aspects of our prototypes of love seem to be intimacy, passion, and commitment (Fehr, 1988). While this appears to be saying the same thing as Sternberg's model, note that there is a difference. In this model, what each person means when they say, "I'm in love," can be similar and still somewhat different. For example, two best friends may both view love as a combination of intimacy, passion, and commitment, but the way that intimacy, passion, and commitment need to be expressed in order to match each person's "ideal love" may be slightly different. In other words, what ignites a sense of passion in one person may be quite different than what sparks passion in another. In implicit theories of love, the dimensions of love are important but are secondary to the match between one's real lover and one's "ideal" lover.

The Love Hierarchy

All of the intriguing ways that people express and experience love may be a bit confusing and overwhelming. Barnes and Sternberg (1997) noticed the variety of perspectives on love, and to bring some order to the different types, researched hierarchical classifications of the types of love. They asked people to report what was important to them in their romantic relationships (both the good and the bad aspects). They also gave people questionnaires that measured relationships satisfaction. Barnes and Sternberg took the results and used statistical techniques to find eight clusters of responses that were highly related to each other and not as related to the other responses.

After this procedure, they found three levels of hierarchically arranged meanings that people applied to love. At the lowest level in their hierarchy they listed the eight clusters that described the qualities people valued in their relationships: trust, sincerity, mutual understanding, compatibility, fulfillment, sexuality, intimacy, and mutual needs. The next higher level consisted of *"compatibility"* (the first five traits on the list) and *"passion"* (the last three traits). They described compatibility as the "warm" factor that allows for commitment over time and feelings of companionship, friendship, and respect (i.e., companionate love). Passion the "hot" factor that defined feelings of desire, romance, and sexual need (i.e., passionate love). The highest level was the single factor called *love.* Their analysis suggested that what we call "love" could be described at a number of levels by a number of emotions and behavioral components.

FINDING ROMANCE, INTIMACY, AND LOVE

In order for love to develop in the first place, people have to be attracted to each other. Research has found that some of the most important variables that influence attraction are proximity, physical attractiveness, attitude similarity, and the mutual exchange of positive evaluations or reciprocity. *Proximity* simply means that the two people spend some time near each other. It takes time for two people to get to know each other and to learn whether they feel comfortable and attracted to one another. Some people might read this last statement and say that they know someone whose relationship began with a single glance across a room and a "spark" that told the person, "This is love at first sight." In spite of the romantic elements of these chance encounters, they are far from the norm and do not necessarily guarantee either deep satisfaction or stability. *Physical attractiveness* is another factor in attraction, but it is not as important as many people think (see "personality traits" below). Nonetheless, attractiveness is a factor in whether people are initially interested in another person. After all, one does not even know if another person is kind or intelligent unless one is motivated to meet him or her. An interesting sidelight to this is a study by Diener, Wolsic, and Fujita (1995) that found no significant relationship between attractiveness of the person and their self-reported happiness. That is, attractiveness may be a factor in initial attraction, but it seems to have little to do with overall happiness and satisfaction. Notions of attractiveness also differ among cultures. For instance, Americans tend to rate smiling faces as "more attractive," while Japanese tend to rate smiling faces only as "more social" (see Matsumoto, 1994).

Another factor in attraction is a *similarity of attitudes and values.* In the research literature, this quality has been termed **homogamy,** or the pairing of like with like. In one of the first psychological studies of married couples, Lewis Terman (Terman, Buttenweiser, Ferguson, Johnson, & Wilson, 1938) found that, at least in terms of romantic relationships, opposites do not attract. Happy couples tended to be very similar to each other in terms of a variety of attitudes. These were as specific as whether or not to have a pet canary and what each thought of insurance salesmen! Over the years, a high similarity of attitudes and values between happily married couples is one of the most frequent findings in the research. One study found that the similarity of interests and values that are shared initially by married couples often lasts throughout the years of their marriage (Caspi, Herbener, & Ozer, 1992). Mahzad Hojjat (1997) also hypothesized that similarity in philosophy of life was an overriding factor that determined much of relationship satisfaction. So, studies tend to disprove the old adage that "opposites attract." However, it is also true that people can be happily paired with someone who has complementary personality traits, such as an introvert with an extrovert. When it comes to our basic values and attitudes, however, the rule of the game seems to be similarity.

Finally, we tend to be attracted to people who show that they like us. The obvious advantage of this *reciprocity*, or mutual exchange of positive emotions, is that it allows us to feel good about ourselves. It may also help us to self-disclose more to the other person and they to us. This can create an interpersonal cycle of risking self-disclosure, being validated by the other person, building trust, and then risking more self disclosure. This pattern is one of the more familiar ones seen in building close relationships of any kind.

Relationship Satisfaction: What Makes Relationships Good?

One of the first issues to clarify when discussing satisfaction in intimate relationships is that "satisfaction" is not a state that couples achieve at one time and then no longer worry about. Satisfaction in any intimate relationship is a dynamic process that changes over time in response to situations, stresses, and the personal growth of each person. Given that satisfaction is a fluid process that can at times be hard to capture, it is nice to know that there are some consistencies that are shared by people who report their relationships as more satisfying and meaningful. Researchers look at three major categories when they investigate satisfaction for couples: (1) intrapersonal qualities, or factors that describe something about one or both of the partners; (2) interpersonal qualities, or factors that describe something about the relationship between the two people; and (3) environmental influences, or external factors that impact the relationship in either a positive or a negative way.

Personality Traits, Attributions, and Illusions

Personality Traits

Turning first to qualities that describe one or both of the partners, studies have found a number of variables that seem to influence the quality and satisfaction of intimate relationships. One factor that occurs rather quickly to most people concerns personality traits. In fact, in surveys of men and women that ask what qualities they look for in a partner, one of the highest ranked qualities for both men and women can be summarized as having a "healthy personality." For instance, surveys have found that the most desirable personality traits in a romantic partner listed by both men and women include: confidence, integrity, warmth, kindness, intelligence, dependability, emotional stability, a good sense of humor, loyalty, and being affectionate (Lauer, Lauer, & Kerr, 1990; Sternberg & Hojjat, 1997). Physical attractiveness is not a major predictor of relationship satisfaction. It is true that "beauty is only skin deep."

At the opposite end, one of the most frequently found predictors of poor relationship quality is the trait of neuroticism (Sternberg & Hojjat, 1997). This is not to say that people must be completely free of worries, nervous habits, or little quirks of personality in order to have happy relationships. Everyone has little anxieties and insecurities. Problems enter relationships, however, when one or both people in the relationship are persistently anxious, worried, fearful, and suffer from very low self-esteem. Part of the damage comes from the fact that chronic neuroticism often leads to chronic focus on the self, leaving little time for attention to one's partner. Without that sense of mutual support and validation most relationships will suffer. Neuroticism is also related to the capacity to be loved, as well as to the capacity to love. The distinction is between loving others and allowing others to love you. Neuroticism can inhibit a person's capacity to be loved. If a person is constantly engaged in self-reproach, then they cannot allow positive feedback and affection from others to influence them in any way. One of the interesting qualities of love is that most people enjoy telling those they love how they feel about them and seeing how the support and validation enlivens and uplifts the other person. Without the capacity to be loved, this does not happen and relationships can suffer.

When looking at personality from another perspective, a number of researchers have searched for the fundamental dimensions of personality. One of the best-known models is the five-factor model, which says that five basic personality traits are the foundation of human behavior: conscientiousness, agreeableness, neuroticism, openness to experience, and extroversion (McCrae & John, 1992). One study that looked at the five-factor model of personality found that four of the five traits are related to higher satisfaction and happiness in couples (Kelly & Conley, 1987). This study found that happier couples were more agreeable, more conscientious, more open, and more emotionally stable (i.e., low on neuroticism). The fifth factor, extroversion, was not reliably related to satisfaction with the relationship but, as discussed in Chapter 3, it is a significant predictor of self-reported happiness. In addition, similarity of personality styles is a significant predictor of marital happiness (Caspi & Herbener, 1990). What people want in their long-term relationships are personality traits that will keep them interested in the other person and will allow trust, stability, and nurturance to develop.

One of the difficulties with predicting relationship satisfaction or stability from personality traits is that traits are descriptions of broad summaries of behaviors over time. Personality traits tend to describe consistencies and regularities in behavior over time and across different situations. While these descriptions are helpful, they do not illuminate the psychological processes that may underlie relationship satisfaction. At the individual level, a great deal of what makes a relationship good is determined by smaller behaviors that define the unique relationship between two people. For instance, there are many men and women in the world who are warm, tolerant, affectionate, considerate, funny, and capable of forming secure attachments to others. Now imagine yourself in a room with a hundred of these people. Could you fall in love with every one of them simply because they had those personality traits? Of course not. Love at the individual level must involve more than general personality traits—although they are very important. Therefore, in order to further understand satisfaction and stability in relationships, researchers have looked at cognitive variables that describe how we think about our partners and how we create our impressions.

Attributions

Attributions are judgments we make about the causes of behavior. In the context of intimate relationships, these refer to how we decide about the causes of our partner's behavior. A number of investigators have found strong relationships between the attributions people make about their partners and their relationship satisfaction (see Hojjat, 1997). One might ask, if we need to guess about why our partner behaves in a certain way, why not just ask them? This is, of course, a reasonable solution—as well as one that can help improve relationship satisfaction and stability. However, often we do not have time to continually ask why someone did something. In addition, prior attributions may have made us decide beforehand that the person does not understand him- or herself because the person is motivated by "unconscious" needs that he or she does not understand or, even worse, that the person is not telling the truth. Before proceeding, however, note that studies have found a wide variety of cultural variations in how people use attributions (Matsumoto, 1994). Therefore, the following discussion applies mainly to the use of attributions by people from Western cultural backgrounds. Unfortunately, there are few cross-cultural studies on the use of attributions in romantic relationships.

One of the most studied attribution processes in psychology is the *fundamental attribution error* (Gilbert & Malone, 1995). This error in judgment involves the tendency to attribute the causes of other people's behavior to enduring personality dispositions or traits, while at the same time seeing the causes of our own behavior as due to temporary aspects of the situation. If, for instance, we ask our partner to send in the car payment and the partner forgets, then we generally engage in an attribution process to determine why the partner forgot. If we decide that a partner is "under too much stress" (i.e., a temporary and situational attribution), we may respond with increased support. On the other hand, if we decide that our partner forgot because he or she is "too self-centered" (i.e., an enduring disposition or personality trait), then our response may be to blame the partner for his or her negative personality trait. The first attribution may enhance the quality of the relationship while the second will hurt it. In fact, this pattern is exactly what research has found.

Couples who are more satisfied with their relationships tend to make dispositional and stable attributions for their partner's positive behavior along with situational and unstable attributions for their negative behavior (see Bradbury & Fincham, 1990; Hojjat, 1997). Relationships are further enhanced by using different attributions for positive and negative behaviors. So, if one's lover stops to help a stranger on the street, that is evidence that he or she is always a "compassionate person" (a stable disposition). But, if a lover is curt with a waiter, it is because of "too much stress at work" (a temporary and unstable reaction). In this example, note how both politeness and rudeness are explained in a way that helps to enhance the relationship. As might be guessed, this pattern is reversed for couples that are distressed and less satisfied. Some research studies suggest that the basic problem with inaccurate attributions for our partner's behavior is that the attributions result in less effective problem-solving strategies (Bradbury & Fincham, 1990). That is, when we are wrong about why our partners behave the way they do, we have a much harder time trying to work out differences. Each person assumes motives that are not actually present in his or her partner, so everyone starts out misunderstanding the other.

Note also that the fundamental attribution error is not always an error. Sometimes we are really quite correct! The difficulty comes into play because people simply assume that they are correct. In addition, people are often not aware of their own attribution processes because these are so automatic. We often do not recognize how or when we use them to create our impressions of our partners.

Another personality factor related to attributions is the use of optimistic or pessimistic explanatory styles. We saw in Chapter 3 that optimism is an important predictor of subjective well-being. In a similar fashion, couples who are more optimistic usually have a better chance of making marriage work (Karney & Bradbury, 1995). In light of what has been discussed so far in this chapter, this makes perfect sense. If the wife consistently explains her spouse's behavior in optimistic terms, she will be more likely to support and validate her husband and less likely to bring overly negative attacks into their disagreements. Studies of optimism in marriage have found that the more positive the explanations are for the partner's behavior, the more satisfied and stable are the relationships (Bradbury & Fincham, 1990).

Positive Romantic Illusions: Is Love Really Blind?

The importance of how we view our partners cannot be overestimated in relationship satisfaction. Some readers may have already surmised that these cognitive processes have one curious feature. In many instances, the ways we describe our partners to ourselves need not be accurate. These are called **positive romantic illusions.** The old adage "love is blind" is sometimes true. Of course, most people know a young couple who are so enamored of each other that they are completely oblivious to faults that are obvious to everyone else. Who has not observed a friend who is madly in love and thought, "What does she see in him?" Most people, however, believe that these illusions fade with time and that they are not important in long-term relationships.

Sandra Murray and John Holmes (1997; Murray, Holmes, Dolderman, & Griffin, 2000) investigated relationships and found that positive illusions may be more characteristic in successful relationships. As stated in Chapter 3, a slight positive bias toward oneself can at times enhance one's own sense of happiness. Similarly, couples that idealized their partner's attributes, had exaggerated beliefs about their control over the relationship, and were overly optimistic about the future of the relationships were happier. Interestingly, those relationships were also more stable and did actually last longer! For many couples, the strength of their illusions about their partners increased as the relationship progressed. In fact, the more idealizations used by one person, the more satisfied was the partner. Murray and Holmes (1997) said, "Such findings suggest that the willingness to make a leap of faith—to possess hopes for a relationship that reality does not seem to warrant—is critical for satisfying dating and marital relationships" (p. 598). In other words, they suggest that we would all be better off if we learned how to use positive illusions in our relationships. They suggest that we need to see through those famous rose-colored glasses in order to make relationships work. Why would they make such a suggestion?

In romantic relationships, this tendency for partners to view the other person in slightly more positive terms than others might can result in a form of mutual reinforcement. Each person tends to reinforce and support the qualities in their partner that the partners most like about themselves. The style of interaction for happily married couples is such that it validates and supports each person's self-concept (Clark & Bennett, 1992). Happy couples seemed to implicitly "negotiate" areas of self-evaluation so that neither partner's esteem was threatened. Happy couples avoided topics, situations, comments, and behaviors that would tread on each other's self-esteem. It is not too surprising that people with positive self-esteem were more committed to spouses who also saw them in a positive light (Swann, Hixon, & DeLeRonde, 1992).

Couples also seem willing to deliberately distort information about their partner in order to enhance or maintain the relationship. Simpson, Ickes, and Blackstone (1995) found a phenomenon they termed *motivated inaccuracy.* When couples tried to infer information about their partners, their accuracy was lower only when the information could be threatening to the relationship (e.g., "Does your partner ever think about leaving you?"). In essence, each member of the couple deliberately (and unconsciously) guessed wrong about their partner's thoughts, attitudes, or motives *only* when knowing the truth would be problematic to the relationship. Unfortunately, for many people the first indication that they have been using positive illusions comes when the relationship breaks up. It is at that very difficult time that many people "see" those qualities in their former partner that they had not seen before. As one song put it, "You won't really know her 'till you've seen her walking away" ("You Won't Really Know Her," by William D. Collins, Power Diamond Music).

In many ways, this is analogous to the self-esteem literature. On one hand, holding positive illusions can be helpful to both self-esteem and to relationship satisfaction. On the other hand, the very nature of love is such that a person sees qualities and potentials in a partner that he or she does not see in himself or herself. One must wonder if these positive perceptions represent "illusions" or other qualities such as optimism, compassion, understanding, and confidence that others who know the person less intimately simply cannot see. In fact, Murray and Holmes (1997) suggest that the use of positive illusions in relationships may actually be related to greater self-esteem. People with higher self-esteem tend to have more successful relationships; they also tend to be more positive, more optimistic, and may be more likely to project their own positive self-ideals onto their partners. It is an interesting irony: because they are probably more likely to have successful relationships, their optimism is justified! Murray and Holmes (1997) used the term *resilient illusions* for illusions that occur in the context of healthy self-esteem and realistic optimism. They also cautioned, however, that if distortions of one's partner are based on avoidance of important information, denial, or attempts to escape conflicts, then illusions are harmful. The trick is to see your partner in her or his best possible light—even an illusory light—and yet still remain open to danger signs and clues that might indicate problems in the relationship.

Interpersonal Factors

Both psychologists and the general public have often given interpersonal factors in relationships the most attention. By far, the most studied aspect of interpersonal relationships is the style of communication expressed. In numerous studies of married couples, communication is the primary determinant of marital satisfaction (Gottman, 1994). In the NBC Today-Weekend Edition/*Prevention* poll, couples listed the following elements they would like to improve about their relationships: be able to spend more time together (31 percent), better communication (30 percent), less worries about money (21 percent), more romance (6 percent), and more sex (3 percent). In other words, the majority of couples wanted more time and better talks, not more sex (Gorman, 1998).

Studies have found that compared to dissatisfied couples, those who report being more satisfied are more supportive, laugh together more, withhold comments that might be taken negatively, and agree more about a variety of topics. Dissatisfied couples exhibit communication characterized by more disagreement, less humor and laughter, more negative emotion expressed, fewer helpful or supportive comments, and more criticism (Gottman, 1998). John and Julie Gottman found that a simple index can help distinguish satisfied from unsatisfied couples (see Gottman & Silver, 1999). In these studies, couples that are more satisfied will turn toward each other more often and seek little gestures that indicate attention, support, humor, or affection. These and other small gestures indicate what the Gottmans call **bids for attention**—small gestures that help each person stay connected to the other. They are usually not grand expressions of love but rather small interactions in which one person invites the other to respond with support or affection. For example, imagine a couple on their way to dinner and the wife says, "I just don't know if I should spend the money on that new dress for the office party next week." Her husband turns to her, looks her in the eyes, and says, "It's up to you, but I think you would look nice in that dress." The wife's bid for attention has succeeded. In an unsuccessful bid for attention the husband might respond with a noncommittal, "uh-huh" or launch into an angry attack about how she is reckless with her money.

Indeed, these little moments can add up, both positively and negatively. Gottman and Levenson (2000) found that couples who were low on fondness, low on a sense of togetherness as a couple, high on feeling a sense of chaos, and high on feeling disappointed in the relationships were also more likely to experience communication that lead to more negativity and less positive strategies for problem solving.

Environmental or Social Factors

One of the stressors that most families face is the arrival of children. Studies have found that satisfaction with the marriage decreases after the arrival of children. Figure 5.3 shows that, as might be expected, marital satisfaction is high during the initial years of marriage.

Average satisfaction levels begin to drop as children arrive in the household. This drop continues until it bottoms out when the children are in early adolescence. As the children leave home, however, the "empty nest syndrome" turns out to be a myth. When couples are once again alone and free of parental responsibilities, their satisfaction with the marriage goes back up to about the same levels it was when they first got married. Note that even though the couple's satisfaction with the marriage goes down, satisfactions with the parental role and other elements of family life rise during this period. This pattern might be described as the "parental paradox."

Studies have shown that the decline in marital satisfaction after the arrival of the first child is due mostly to declines in the wife's satisfaction (Shapiro, Gottman, & Carrere, 2000). This may the result of the increased anxiety of being a new mother and the increased demands placed on the wife for child care. Shapiro et al. also found that if the couple felt their life was more chaotic after the baby arrived they were less satisfied with the marriage. So, the decrease in marital satisfaction after the first child seems to be the result of the wife feeling that her life went out of control after the baby was born.

The good news in the study was that about one-third of couples did not experience a decline in satisfaction after the first child. New mothers were more satisfied if their husbands continued to express fondness and if the couple continued to pay attention to the relationship in spite of the demands of the new baby. These couples seemed to find ways to build fondness and affection into the relationship, to keep in touch with each other's lives, and to approach problems as something they could resolve together. In other words, they stayed in tune with each other's lives in spite of the added stress and saw parenthood as a team effort.

Relationship Stability: What Makes Relationships Last?

While satisfaction with one's relationship is an important variable, the stability of relationships is also at the very heart (pun intended!) of what makes relationships so central to well-being. Right at the start of this discussion, however, it must be made clear that high satisfaction with a relationship does not necessarily translate into long-term stability. It is possible, after all, to be very satisfied with each separate relationship in a series of relatively short-term relationships. Indeed, some people seem to prefer passion and intimacy without long-term commitment. It is also possible to be in a long-term relationship that is marked by frequent arguments—this is a relationship termed the *volatile couple*. In spite of these caveats, for the majority of people the real joys and benefits of intimate relationships come from those that remain satisfying through the ups and downs of a lifetime.

Most researchers also begin with the assumption that people remain committed to relationships because they are satisfied with them and end relationships when satisfaction wanes. As Ellen Bersheid and Jason Lopes (1997) note,

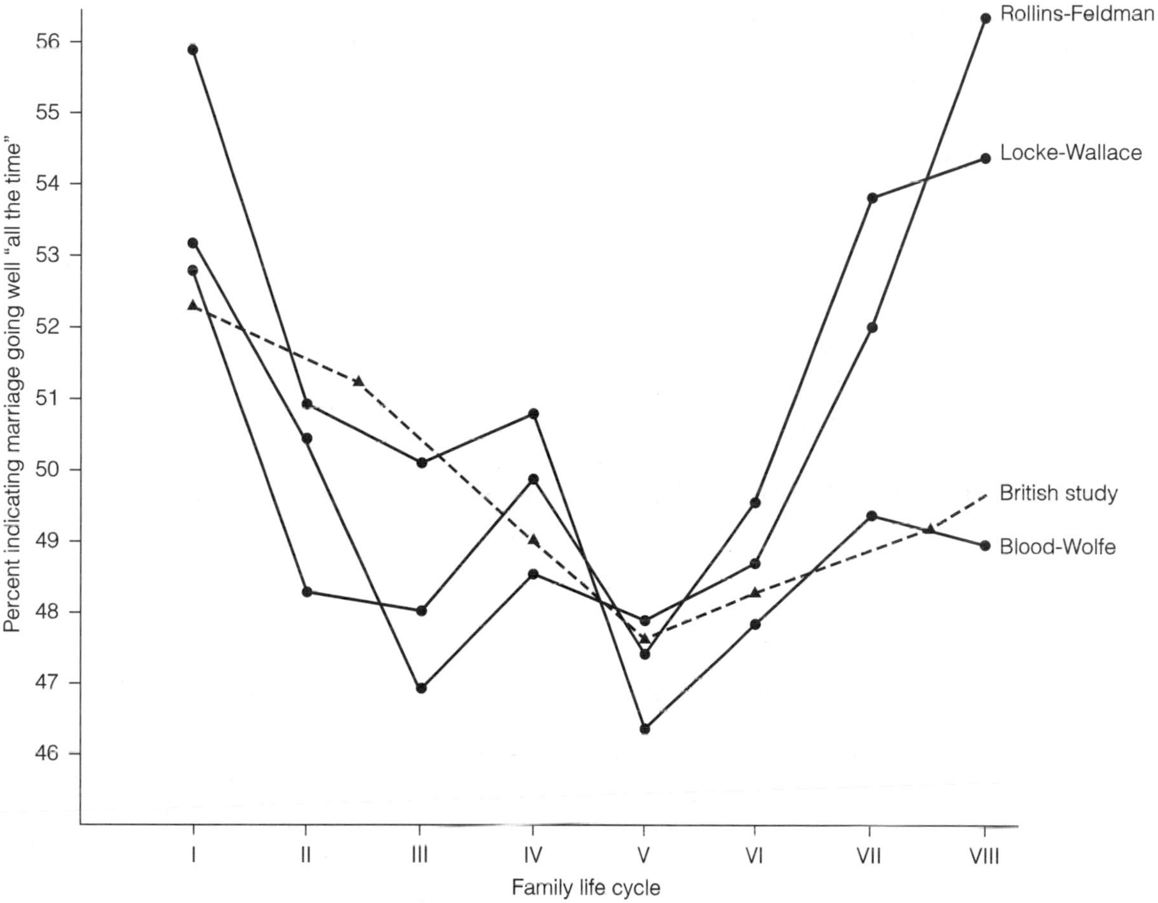

FIGURE 5.3

Marital Satisfaction over the Life Cycle. Stage I, Beginning families; Stage II, Child-bearing families; Stage III, Families with preschool children; Stage IV, Families with school-aged children; Stage V, Families with teenagers; Stage VI, Families as launching centers; Stage VII, Families in the middle years; Stage VIII, Aging families.

Source: Table 18.4, "Marital Satisfaction by Stage of Family Life Cycle," in *Well-Being: Foundations of Hedonic Psychology*, D. Kahneman, E. Diener, and N. Schwarz (eds.) © 1999 Russell Sage Foundation, 112 East 64th Street, New York, NY 10021. Reprinted with permission.
Note: The lines on the graph indicate four different studies that have looked at marital satisfaction and the life cycle.

however, "It is surprisingly difficult to find hard empirical evidence to support this seemingly obvious assumption, at least with respect to marital relationships" (p. 130). For instance, it is also possible to dissolve a satisfactory relationship in order to form another one that seems to offer a potential for even greater satisfaction. Given this, what do we know about relationship stability?

What Do Happy Couples Say about Their Relationships?

One way to judge what may help maintain relationships is to ask couples who have been together for years what they think is important. Robert and Jeanette Lauer studied over three hundred married couples who had been together for at least fifteen years (see Lauer,

Lauer, & Kerr, 1990). Interestingly, both husbands and wives listed the same seven qualities as being important to a successful marriage:

1. My spouse is my best friend.
2. I like my spouse as a person.
3. I believe that marriage is a long-term commitment.
4. We agree on aims and goals.
5. My spouse has grown more interesting over the years.
6. I want the relationship to succeed.
7. Marriage is a sacred institution.

People with these long-term success stories also said that they had to recognize that marriages would inevitably have hard times. Therefore, partners need to accept that marriage will be rough at times, and they need to tolerate differences between them, as well as relish the similarities they share.

Theories of Relationship Stability

Balance Theory

The balance theory of relationship stability assumes that every couple will express both positive and negative behaviors. Therefore, it is not the presence of negative emotions or behaviors but how they are regulated that is important to stability. One idea about stability in relationships says that it is the result of finding a balance between positive and negative behaviors in marriage. Couples who have stable, long-lasting relationships where patterns of emotionality are balanced and predictable are termed *regulated couples.* Regulated couples who seem to be stable and free from undue conflict are called *validating couples.* However, note that having a stable but argumentative relationship can also describe a regulated couple. An example is a couple that has been together forever and yet is quarrelsome and curt to each other at the drop of a hat. Although they quarrel often, this pattern is predictable and stable.

According to balance theory, those couples that tend to be unstable and short-term are called *nonregulated* couples. In these relationships, positive and negative behaviors are not predictable. These types of relationships are characterized by more negative emotionality, more severe problems, less positive affect, lower satisfaction, and greater likelihood that the relationship will end. Wives in these types of marriages also showed greater sympathetic nervous system arousal (e.g., faster heart rates) and poorer health (see Gottman & Notarius, 2000). Two types of nonregulated marriages are the hostile and the hostile/detached marriages (see "Conflict" section later in this chapter).

Social Exchange Theories

Probably the most relied-upon theoretical perspectives in the research on relationship stability are social exchange theories. In these theories, relationships are assumed to be an exchange of rewards and costs. This perspective assumes that satisfaction is the result of a cost-benefit analysis that evaluates the ratio of positive interactions to negative interactions. If there are more positive than negative, the result is satisfaction. From this perspective, determining the probability of any relationship staying together is a relatively simple calculation. If rewards outnumber costs, then it is more likely that the relationship will continue. If the costs outnumber the rewards, the relationship will probably end if the situation continues for too long. While this general statement holds much validity, how people make the initial judgments about what is "positive" and "negative" can be a bit more interesting.

Kelly and Thibaut's (1978) social interdependency theory postulates that people make separate decisions about (1) whether they are satisfied in the relationship and about (2) whether they should maintain the relationship. The decision about satisfaction is one's *comparison level,* or how "attractive" the relationship is. To arrive at this judgment, people evaluate other relationships they have had or have observed. It is a judgment about the type of relationship a person believes he or she deserves.

The stability judgments involve a *comparison level for alternatives,* or an evaluation of the best alternatives to the current relationship. People may also look at what the alternatives are to the current relationship and decide if a change will be preferable and worth the costs of leaving. In truth, often people engage in both types of analyses. So, stability could result from any one of the following outcomes of the comparisons: high satisfaction with few alternatives, low satisfaction with few alternatives, or high satisfaction with many alternatives—but the person chooses not to pursue alternate relationships. Interestingly, some studies have shown that people who are highly committed to a relationship will often devalue alternative partners as a way to keep satisfaction high (Johnson & Rusbult, 1989).

The mention of commitment brings up Rusbult's (1991) perspective, which looks at the role of commitment in maintaining relationships. Here, commitment is defined as a combination of three elements: relationship satisfaction, the alternatives to the relationship, and the investments one has made in the relationship. That is, commitment also increases if we have invested a considerable amount of time and emotional effort into the relationship. Commitment can also entail the degree to which people believe they ought to maintain the relationship—the moral dimension. The term "barrier forces" is used to describe factors that present difficulties or costs to the dissolution of relationships. These could include financial concerns, worries over the emotional health of the children, or family pressures. In terms of social exchange theories, the influence of barrier forces is a cost that has decreased over the last forty years.

What Does Research Say about Stability?

John and Julie Gottman concluded from their research studies that friendship is absolutely essential to a satisfying and stable relationship (Gottman & Gottman, 1999). By friendship, they are referring to specific ways that happy couples interact with each other. They found that happy couples frequently communicate affection, fondness, admiration, and interest in the other person. Happy couples have a genuine interest in their partner's lives. Happy couples turn toward each other more often during their conversations and invite the other to respond to them in positive ways (bids for attention). The Gottmans feel so strongly about this predictor that couples who attend the Gottmans' marital enrichment seminars are asked to spend at least 5 minutes every day simply expressing sincere appreciation to their partners for specific behaviors (Gottman & Gottman, 1999). The Gottmans also ask couples to take time every morning to find out one specific thing that their partners will be doing during the day. In other words, they remind them that it is important to express real interest in each other and not take the other person for granted.

The nature of the courtship and age are also related to marital stability. One of the more practical factors is that successful relationships tended to have longer courtships (Skolnick, 1981). Successful couples take the time to get to know one another before they make a commitment. Related to this is the fact that people who marry when they are older tend to have longer marriages (Skolnick, 1981). People who marry at a very young age begin married life at a disadvantage. Studies have also found that a few specific correlates of satisfaction do change over the course of long-term relationships. The factor that predicts satisfaction may be different for newer and older or long-lasting couples (Levenson, Carstensen, & Gottman, 1994). In newer couples, the effect of passion may still be strong, and resilient illusions may be operating to conceal differences. Older and long-lasting couples have often found a way to acknowledge, accept, and work with their partner's shortcomings and foibles. Gottman says, "They give each other the message that they love and accept each other, 'warts and all'" (Gottman & Silver, 1999, p.154).

Arlene Skolnick (1981) reports on a longitudinal study of marriage that followed couples for up to twenty-seven years. In her data set, the best predictors of marital stability were a few demographic variables, attitudes, and personality traits. Specifically, couples who married when they were older and had higher incomes, higher education, and higher religious participation tended to have more stable marriages. She also found that similarity of attitudes and values was important for stability. Finally, the personality traits of self-confidence and nurturance were significantly correlated with stability. In general, she found that the most salient quality in marriages that were high on satisfaction was a "strong affective commitment to the spouse, that is, an affectionate and enjoyable personal relationship between husband and wife" (1981, pp. 288–289).

Skolnick noted that each marriage is really two marriages: the husband's and the wife's. All marriages in her study tended to show slightly different predictors of satisfaction for each partner. Skolnick also observed that among both her satisfied and unsatisfied couples there was tremendous variation in the behaviors that comprised each marriage. She concluded that the important elements of satisfied marriages are the relational processes rather than the specific behaviors. In other words, from her perspective a successful marriage is built on a variety of behaviors that lead to specific processes, such as affection and support. What is less important is how people behave, just as long as those behaviors enhance affection, support, and the other necessary processes.

Because positive psychology is defined as being in part the search for strengths and virtues, one might wonder if these are also important in relationship satisfaction and stability. Blaine Fowers (2000, 2001) emphasizes the importance of virtues in his theory of marital happiness. He believes that the important relationship processes involve the development and strengthening of core virtues and strengths. Specifically, he advises couples to build the virtues of loyalty, courage, generosity, and justice. Fowers argues that relationships need a strong commitment to these virtues in order for difficulties to be managed and overcome. His point can be illustrated by imagining a couple that is trying to increase satisfaction by deliberately using more "bids for attention" every day. This is an important strategy that is backed up by quality research on relationships. However, if this couple does not exercise the virtues of loyalty, generosity, and justice, it is unlikely that any satisfaction they may have gained will be maintained over time. With a relationship foundation built on these virtues, however, the increased bids for attention may be able to rekindle necessary feelings of closeness and intimacy.

Relationships as a Vehicle for Personal Growth

Much of the discussion so far has focused on how to create stable relationships that can withstand the ups and down of life and maintain a sense of mutual respect, friendship, and love in whatever form it may take. According to some researchers, this dynamic quality of relationships can actually be used as a vehicle for personal growth. That is, a couple can use their relationship as an impetus for self-exploration, as a way to challenge their own assumptions, as a way to take emotional risks, and as a means to deepening their understanding of their partner and of themselves. There is virtually no empirical research on this aspect of long-term relationships. However, couples often mention personal growth as a unique benefit to long-term committed relationships. How might this work?

All relationships will eventually experience some difficulties. The source of those issues might be external, such as job stresses or the birth of children. The source might also be internal, such as the fading of certain positive illusions—the familiar "the honeymoon is over" phenomenon. Whatever the cause of the inevitable difficulties, each partner may be forced to look at how their own expectations, personal desires, needs, or unconscious issues are impacting the relationship. When partners successfully cope with these psychological challenges, they are also propelling themselves and their relationship toward greater psychological maturity and development (Welwood, 1997; Tashiro, Frazier, Humbert, & Smith, 2001). This element of romantic relationships is a promising area for research on relationship satisfaction and stability.

What Hurts Relationships?

Conflict

One way to understand healthy relationships is to know something about the factors that tend to erode and destroy relationship satisfaction. Stated quite boldly, conflict is the number-one cause of marital dissolution, and communication problems are the number-one reason given for getting divorced (Gottman, 1994). However, studies have found that the number of conflicts people have and the things they argue over are less important to stability and satisfaction than how they handle conflicts. Conflict can lead to at least two different ways of being a nonregulated couple. The first is the hostile couple. The name of this one says it all—anger, recriminations, accusations, and hostility define the relationship. Gottman also identified a pattern of communication often found in these couples that is particularly destructive to relationships: *negative reciprocity* that is often signaled by the *harsh setup.* This style describes a sequence where an initial negative comment only serves to stimulate a negative response from the partner and an increasing cycle of disagreeable comments (Gottman & Gottman, 1999).

Another sequence defines the hostile couple. In this sequence, one person is demanding, critical, or strongly expresses a number of complaints while the other partner responds by withdrawing. The Gottmans referred to this pattern as the **demand-withdraw pattern** (Gottman & Gottman, 1999). This four-step pattern is particularly destructive to satisfaction in relationships. It begins with (1) criticism and complaining from one partner, which results in (2) a sense of contempt from the other, that (3) leads to defensiveness, and (4) ends with withdrawal. When the withdrawal becomes so extreme that one person may leave the room or withdraws attention in a passive-aggressive and hostile attempt to punish the other person, then step 4 becomes what the Gottmans call **stonewalling.** The Gottmans see this four-step pattern with stonewalling as being so destructive that they called it "the Four Horseman of the Apocalypse," in reference to the Biblical horsemen whose appearance will signal the end of the world. Interestingly, the stonewalling pattern is more common in men than in women.

The Gottmans found that at times the negativity and ferocity of personal attack from one partner can overwhelm the other partner. The other person becomes shell-shocked and retreats into a mode of responding that seeks protection more than anything else. The Gottmans call this response pattern **flooding.** The Gottmans' study found that flooding results in a number of physical reactions, such as increased heart rate and blood pressure, as well as a stimulation of the "fight or flight" stress response. These responses result in an inability to engage in positive problem solving. Objectively, they result in body language that indicates fear, anxiety, and the simplest of basic responses—to fight or to flee. The idea of **repair attempts** is also related to flooding. These are efforts to calm down a tense situation or to de-escalate tension so that flooding does not occur. When repair attempts fail or are not attempted, the couple is in trouble. Finally, distressed couples often chose to remember the negative moments in their shared history. They used to remember the positive moments together; now, they cannot help but recall the difficulties, the hurts, and the disappointments. Their shared history gets rewritten negatively.

In a longitudinal study that followed couples for fourteen years, Gottman and Levinson (2000) found that answers to questionnaires, plus direct observation of the couple in discussions, helped predict later divorce at a very high accuracy level. They found that examining the level of marital satisfaction, the presence of negative affect during conflicts, the lack of positive affect in day-to-day interactions, the number of thoughts about divorce, the number of bad memories, and the demand-withdraw communication pattern helped predict future divorce at over 90 percent accuracy. Note that such high accuracy of prediction is nearly unheard of in psychology. Note, too, that for some couples, these interaction patterns were present very early in their relationships, for some as early as just a few months after they were married.

Finally, some researchers have estimated that negative and destructive acts are more important to satisfaction and stability than are positive acts of kindness and respect. They have estimated that one very destructive act toward one's partner can erase five to twenty positive acts of kindness (Greg Schmidt, Ph.D., personal communication, October 10, 2000). In other words, one cruel and thoughtless act or comment can wipe out an entire month of affection and tenderness.

Social and Cultural Factors

The influence of society and culture on long-term commitments can be significant. Within a society, changes in social expectations over time can create unforeseen stress. For example, when issues such as social mores and economic need are no longer significant barriers to divorce or single parenthood, then relationships can suffer. Social exchange theory posits that we evaluate relationships by looking at costs and benefits. If the social costs of leaving (i.e., single parenting, social stigma) are reduced, then people must look for other reasons for maintaining the relationship. Under these circumstances, one of those other reasons must be the strength of the emotional relationship between the people. People's reasons for maintaining a relationship can then become focused exclusively on the emotional interaction between themselves and their partners. What can happen is that people then spend a much greater amount of time being preoccupied with the quality of their relationship. As Bersheid and Lopes (1997) put it, "Few barriers to relationship dissolution often signal that both partners must spend much time and energy 'taking the pulse' of the relationship and attending to even the slightest symptom of malaise, for fear that it ultimately will prove fatal to the relationship" (p. 135). This very contemporary perspective suggests that if we are not careful, we can pay a price for our new financial, economic, and social freedoms. The price is that we base all decisions about relationship commitments on the shifting and changeable emotional quality of the relationship. In the worst of circumstances, this can lead to a somewhat obsessive preoccupation with the emotional tone of the relationship.

Within highly pluralistic societies, differences between the ethnic or cultural backgrounds of two people can also create stress for the relationship. In the United States, for example, a romantic relationship between two people from different ethnic backgrounds can create unique stresses and tensions (see Menard, 2003). Differences among cultures can also force us to acknowledge that the rules for finding satisfying and stable relationships may depend on cultural contexts. For instance, the idea of marriage in other cultural contexts can include polygamy (a man having more than one wife), polyandry (a woman having more than one husband; see Price & Crapo, 2002), or arranged marriages in which the bride and groom have played no part in choosing their partners. While the cultural contexts are different, evidence suggests that these marriages can be both stable and satisfying. The reasons that these marriages work vary, depending on how different cultures value love. For instance, one study found that Americans and Europeans tend to place a much higher value on experiencing feelings of love than do Japanese (see Simmons, von Kolke, and Shimizu, 1986, in Matsumoto, 1994). Simmons et al. suggested that romantic love is more highly valued in more Westernized cultures that have fewer extended-family ties and are influenced less by strong traditional kinship networks. One of the benefits that positive psychology can bring to investigations of love and relationships—hopefully in many different cultural contexts—is an emphasis on how virtues and strengths can help create healthy interdependent relationships.

How to Nurture Relationships

The Gottmans are currently the most preeminent researchers working on marriage enrichment. They have done more to understand what makes marriage satisfying and stable than any other people working in the field. In *The Seven Principles for Making Marriage* Work (Gottman & Silver, 1999) John Gottman summarizes the techniques and suggestions they offer in their marriage enrichment seminars:

1. *Enhance your love maps.* Love maps are the stored information about your relationship and about your partner. They can include the likes, preferences, habits, and quirks of your partner, as well as the memories of important events and significant moments of your relationship. This principle suggests that people should pay attention to and take an interest in their partner.
2. *Nurture Your Fondness and Admiration.* While the principle is fairly obvious, it also means that couples should use positive attributions and optimism to focus on the positive qualities of their partner. It is particularly helpful to remember the positive events of the relationship and to view a shared past in positive terms.
3. *Turn toward Each Other Instead of Away.* This principle refers to "bids for attention." In essence, couples need to take time throughout the day to "stop, look, and listen" to the other person.
4. *Let Your Partner Influence You.* This principle says that couples need to share power. Put another way, it says that being stubborn and always insisting on getting one's own way is damaging to relationships.
5. *Solve Your Solvable Problems.* This principle applies to how couples go about solving problems. From their research, the Gottmans suggest the following five steps for conflict resolution:
   a. Soften your setup.
   b. Learn to make and receive repair attempts.
   c. Soothe yourself and each other.
   d. Compromise.
   e. Be tolerant of each other's faults.

   Their research suggests that these steps can help couples reach better solutions to solvable conflicts. If a conflict cannot be solved (and some issues simply cannot be), these steps at least help maintain a healthy relationship.
6. *Overcome Gridlock.* The goal of this principle is "not to solve the problem, but rather to move from gridlock to dialogue" (p. 217). The movement toward dialogue is partially accomplished by acknowledging and nurturing what the Gottmans call each person's "dreams." These are the hopes, goals, aspirations, and wishes that each person has for his or her life. Often these involve deep commitments or beliefs about

what makes life important or special. For example, "deep" dreams can be a need for a sense of unity with one's past or a desire for a unity with nature. Dreams define our identity on a deeper level. Often, conflicts are based on differences between dreams, and the differences must be acknowledged and respected before a compromise can be found.

7. *Create Shared Meaning.* This principle says that couples should create a "culture" in which their shared life together is appreciated. Creating a number of customs, rituals, myths, or symbols that help to define their unique relationship can do this. For example, couples may listen to "their song," fall into little habits, like always allowing the husband to make Sunday brunch, or even more obviously, hang their wedding photographs in the bedroom. When they do this, they are creating their own culture that builds a sense of shared meaning into their relationship.

The Gottmans also urge couples to work on building their relationship every day. They say that an extra five hours per week is enough to change relationship in a more positive direction. Referring to the research on marriage and physical health they say, "Working on your marriage every day will do more for your health and longevity than working out at the health club" (Gottman & Silver, 1999, p. 261). While no one should neglect their physical health, the well-documented benefits of intimate relationships do illustrate their importance to well-being and happiness.

Comments on Love and Well-Being

There is little doubt that love is one of the most significant factors in well-being. This is especially true for people in Western cultures. Evidence shows that the need for some type of companionship and the capacity for caring are both biologically given. It is also true that the social environment is extraordinarily important to how we perceive love. Morton Hunt (1959) noted, "The physical isolation and rootlessness of modern life, however, is only half the reason love has assumed such great significance. The other half lies in the fact that our society, more so than most others, conditions us from earliest childhood to measure and rate ourselves by the amount of love we receive" (p. 373). Interestingly, it also seems that in order to create loving relationships, we must risk being hurt and self-disclose to another. The more we remain isolated in our apparently secure self, the less love we can experience. Self-imposed isolated individualism leads to loneliness, not love. It is also apparent that love need not be directed at another human being to be important to well-being. Many people direct their affection toward pets and find deep satisfaction from the relationship (Keil, 1998). Finally, the examples of those engaged in monastic practices suggest that the object of love need not be corporeal. A love for God or something of ultimate concern can be as fulfilling as a love for a sentient being.

Summary

This chapter covered the topic of love. The search for love is one of the most significant ways that people pursue well-being. The need for love and intimacy seems to be biologically given and innate. Most theoretical perspectives on love see it as a multifaceted experience that combines at least two elements: passion and compatibility. Relationship satisfaction is associated with similarity of attitudes and values, honesty, trust, the types of attributions that people make to explain their partner's behavior, and the use of healthy communication. It may also be associated with forming positive illusions about one's partner. Relationship stability is associated with factors such as friendship, commitment, how a couple deals with conflict, and the effects of external stressors. The major cause of relationship instability and dissolution is conflict. Conflict styles that involve coercion, contempt, or the demand-withdraw pattern appear to be particularly predictive of failing relationships. Suggestions for enhancing relationships tend to be focused on creating more opportunities for deeper involvement in the activities and emotional lives of our partners.

NOTE

1. Throughout this chapter, the term "marriage" will denote an emotionally intimate and committed relationship between two people. The discussion deals primarily with heterosexual relationships because that has been the focus of most marriage research. Unfortunately, we do not know how many of these findings apply to same-sex couples. Researchers do know, however, that same-sex relationships tend to be shorter—on average, they last about six years. The difference may be the result of social factors (e.g., fewer legal factors involved in breakups, usually no children) that tend to keep heterosexual couples together. Nevertheless, John Gottman, Ph.D., believes that same-sex couples have an advantage in that they tend to discuss issues more positively and with greater affection and humor than heterosexual couples (see Lemonick, 2004).

LEARNING TOOLS

Key Terms and Ideas

BIDS FOR ATTENTION
COMPANIONATE LOVE
CONSUMMATE LOVE
DEMAND-WITHDRAW PATTERN
HOMOGAMY
PASSIONATE LOVE
POSITIVE ROMANTIC ILLUSIONS
REPAIR ATTEMPTS
STONEWALLING

Books

Fowers, B. (2000). Beyond the myth of marital happiness: How embracing the virtues of loyalty, generosity, justice, and courage can strengthen your relationship. San Francisco: Jossey-Bass. Fowers argues that virtues, not behavioral techniques, are what make a solid relationship (popular).

The Gottmans have a number of books on making marriages work. Here are two written for the general public.

Gottman, J., & Declaire, J. (2001). The relationship cure: A five-step guide for building better connections with family, friends, and lovers. New York: Crown.

Gottman, J., & Silver, N. (1999). The seven principles for making marriage work. New York: Crown.

Cultural issues within pluralistic societies can create unique problems for relationships. The following books address two examples of this potential challenge.

Menard, V. (2003). Latinas in love: A modern guide to love and relationships. New York: Marlowe & Company.

Whitfield, K., Markham, H., Stanley, S., & Blumberg, S. (2001). Fighting for your African American marriage. San Francisco: Jossey-Bass.

On the Web

http://www.gottman.com. John Gottman's Web site with information on what makes relationships work.

Personal Explorations

Use a five-point scale and rate yourself on the six love styles listed in this chapter. What kind of lover are you? What kind of love style are you attracted to?

What qualities do you look for in a romantic partner? What are the most important three qualities? What qualities are you attracted to in your friends? Are these the same or different?

Is love blind? What are the advantages and disadvantages of positive illusions in relationships? How vulnerable are you to positive romantic illusions? How can you tell if you are seeing someone through those "rose-colored glasses"?

CHAPTER 6

WELLNESS, HEALTH PSYCHOLOGY, AND POSITIVE COPING

> Health is a state of complete physical, mental, and social well-being, and not merely the absence of disease and infirmity.
>
> *World Health Organization (1948)*

The idea that physical health and vitality are important to the good life is one of the oldest assumptions of psychological well-being. Peoples of many early societies often believed that physical health could influence psychological or emotional factors. The Greeks believed that certain mental illnesses such as depression were caused by the imbalance of physical elements in the body, which they called the four humors.[1] Quite logically, the Greeks prescribed physiological interventions such as a change in diet or exercise to help cure the disorders (Kemp, 1989). Unfortunately, interest in physical well-being as a necessary component of the good life was another component of Greek thought that was lost during the development of Western civilization. During the Middle Ages, the dominant philosophical position tended to denigrate the "flesh" in the quest for the "spirit." Christian perspectives also tended to view the body as a source of temptation and sin.

Although traditional religious doctrine was often uncomfortable with the physical self, at the same time it is also true that throughout history many people saw physical vitality as a source of well-being. To take an example from the early part of the nineteenth century, the Romantic movement in literature and the arts emphasized the emotional and physical as important to well-being. The American writer and philosopher Henry David Thoreau suggested that in order to find emotional well-being one had to "first become a good animal." In other words, a healthy, realistic, and vital physical self was necessary for mental health.

Western science had also come to view mind and body as relatively isolated elements of persons. Therefore, another consequence of history was that twentieth century science inherited the centuries-old belief that there exists a split between mind and body. In fact, the professional specialties of today reflect that division: physicians study the body and psychologists study the mind. Note that many traditional cultures do not share these ideas about mind, body, or disease. Native Americans, for instance, see disease as a disruption in the balance of life (see Lewis, 2002). In the West, although Freud had helped to popularize the idea that psychological factors could impact physical states, there was a lack of good reliable scientific evidence to support the idea of mind-body interaction. For many scientists, the mind and the body would forever remain separate aspects of the person. Not until the 1970s did science begin to find good evidence that pointed beyond the traditional boundaries between our psychological lives and our physical being. Even before scientific evidence became available, however, people expanded the definition of well-being to include both mental and physical health.

WELLNESS

Until recently, it was traditional to define physical health as the lack of illness or disease. That is, physical health was defined as the absence of some other state. This situation is analogous to defining psychological well-being as the absence of mental illness. In scientific terms, this is a fairly poor way of defining any phenomenon. Defining a phenomenon by what it is *not* fails to set specific criteria for the object under scrutiny. The problem with this approach is that it allows *any* other phenomena to be included in the definition. Imagine what it would be like to define love as the absence of hate. This type of definition would place emotions such as indifference, boredom, joy, curiosity, lust, and love all in the same category. Obviously, using such a strategy would not produce an acceptable definition of love. However, this is exactly the strategy that has most often been used to define physical health—as the absence of disease.

Recently, researchers have begun to focus on more expanded specifications of physical health and well-being. The World Health Organization (WHO), however, was years ahead of most scientists on this point. In 1948, their official position on health was, "Health is a state of complete physical, mental, and social well-being, and not merely the absence of disease and infirmity." WHO has recognized for almost sixty years that while being disease free is a worthy goal, there is also a state of enhanced vitality that would help define a more encompassing sense of well-being.

Initially, researchers who focused on the state of physical vitality studied physical health as a pathway to increased energy and longevity. This perspective assumed that vigorous exercise, along with good diet and nutrition, would produce greater physical health and would also have positive consequences in terms of emotional health as well. However, the emphasis was clearly on physical well-being. Researchers realized, however, that true vitality might be possible only if people are healthy in a number of areas of their lives. The situation began to change in 1961 when Halbert L. Dunn coined the term "high-level wellness" to describe a state of enhanced physical and emotional well-being. Thereafter, the term **wellness** was used to refer to states of optimal physical, mental, and emotional health. For Dunn, wellness was a state in which a person had

1. A zest for life
2. A way of living that maximized potential
3. A sense of meaning and purpose
4. A sense of social responsibility
5. Skills for adapting to the challenges of a changing environment.

The wellness perspective has also had a distinctly practical and applied emphasis. As a consequence, a whole new research agenda, educational focus, and occupational category have been created to fulfill the interest in this area. Today, the wellness perspective encompasses the benefits of exercise, nutrition, stress management, emotional self-regulation, social support, and personal growth (Edlin & Golanty, 1992). Today, even the United States Department of Health and Human Services sees health promotion as one of its central objectives (U.S. Department of Health & Human Services, 2000).

HEALTH PSYCHOLOGY

As mentioned earlier, psychology in the twentieth century had been somewhat involved in health-related issues through research in the area of psychosomatic medicine. However, in the early years of the century most of this interest was focused on specific diseases such as ulcers or hypertension. It was obvious to many people that psychology could play a much larger role in many more aspects of health and the delivery of health services. In the 1970s, the American Psychological Association created a new specialty area that focused on the contributions that psychology could make to an understanding of illness and disease. This new division of psychology, called health psychology, would focus on all the behavioral factors that might affect a person's health (Brannon & Feist, 2000). Health psychology would include interest areas such as using psychological knowledge to help prevent risk factors for disease, increasing compliance with health directives, and creating public policy investigations into how the health care system can work better (Brannon & Feist, 2000). Interestingly, an early focus of health psychology was one that would also be compatible with positive psychology: how to use the knowledge of psychology to enhance health status beyond the curing of disease and toward greater wellness.

Note that the issues discussed so far have focused on how psychological processes might impact physical health. The more difficult question for scientists has always been if mental processes could actually cause changes to the chemical processes of the body. Of course, at the turn of the century, Freud had demonstrated that mental processes could mimic physiological disorders, and hypnosis has a long history of demonstrating dramatic examples of pain suppression. In addition, the placebo phenomena and spontaneous remission of disease were both well known to medicine. As interesting as these phenomena were, however, they could not qualify as acceptable scientific evidence for direct mind-body causal transactions. In fact, no one had provided scientifically acceptable evidence for the direct effects of psychological processes on the chemical processes of the body. If evidence could be found, it could convince scientists to view people as integrated systems rather than collections of isolated components. This evidence could break down the old scientific barrier between the "mind" and the "body." Is there any evidence to support the idea that the mind and the body interact in complex and significant ways to ensure or hinder better health status? In fact, scientific studies have supported causal linkages between cognition, emotion, and physiological processes. Scientists in a new area of research have begun to publish research findings that are turning scientific thinking on its head.

Psychoneuroimmunology

Research in the new area of **psychoneuroimmunology** (PNI is the accepted acronym) has looked at the relationships between psychological processes (especially emotion), the functioning of the nervous system, and the body's immune system. David Felton, John Williams, and others at Indiana University provided some of the first evidence of a direct neuronal connection between the immune system and the brain (see Locke & Colligan, 1986). They examined slides of tissue that included cells associated with the immune system and found that many of the nervous system's synapses were located near those immune system cells. Felton (cited in Grubin, 1993) described the dilemma that he and his colleagues faced at that moment: "Everybody says that nerves are associated just with blood vessels—why are they here? Certainly the thought crossed our minds, 'I wonder if nerves might be controlling some immune responses?' But it was almost dogma that the immune system was autonomous and doesn't have any outside controls. We were afraid to publish . . . afraid we'd look like [fools]."

As it turned out, rather than looking like fools, Felton and his colleagues broke new scientific ground by providing scientific evidence that the brain may be "hard wired" into the immune system. Another pioneer in PNI research was Robert Ader. In the mid-1970s, Ader and immunologist Nicholas Cohen performed an experiment where they conditioned the immune system of rats to respond to saccharin as if it were an immunosuppressant drug (Ader & Cohen, 1975; see also Ader & Cohen, 1993). Their experiment provided evidence that the immune system could "learn" and suggested a direct influence between the brain and immune responses. Ader and Cohen's results were met with considerable skepticism and resistance.

As late as 1985, an editorial in the *New England Journal of Medicine* stated that belief in a connection between disease and mental state was "largely folklore." However, once it became scientifically respectable to do scientific studies on the links between psychological functioning and the immune system, a number of studies have supported the hypothesis that psychological factors can influence the immune system.

One of the first studies to provide strong evidence for a *direct causal* connection between health status and psychological factors was published in 1991. The study suggested a direct connection between psychological stress and vulnerability to the common cold (Cohen, Tyrrell, & Smith, 1991, 1993). Later, Cohen, Doyle, Skoner, Rabin, and Gwaltney (1997) used a more rigorous test of the stress-cold connection hypothesis and found that the greater the extent of a person's social ties, the less likely they were to develop a cold. In fact, those with lower social support were four times more likely to become ill than those with higher social support.

Currently, a substantial amount of research has found scientifically measurable relationships between cognition, emotions, and the immune response. For instance, studies have found measurable decreases in immune system functioning for a number of stressors including caring for Alzheimer's patients, stressful living, and widowhood (see Brannon & Feist, 2000).

Psychological Factors Important to Health

The research on PNI and the immune system has shown that psychological factors can have a measurable impact on the working of our immune system. Arguably, one of the most fascinating research areas in PNI concerns the possibility of consciously influencing the immune system through psychological interventions. Studies have demonstrated that people have much greater control over some aspects of their physiological processes than was ever believed possible. Specifically, studies have found that some people, under certain circumstances, can be taught how to either increase or decrease the number of cells in their own bodies associated with immune functioning (e.g., T-cells or S-IgA antibodies) (e.g. Benson, 1983). Only thirty years ago, no respectable scientific journal would have published the results of these studies. It would have been assumed that the researchers were philosophically naive, intellectually incompetent, and possibly frauds. From a logical standpoint, however, if human beings are actually holistic organisms rather than a collection of parts, then all the elements of the organism must be able to communicate with each other and must have some influence on each other.

The next question is: can those changes in immune system functioning translate into better health for people? For instance, while it may be that psychological factors can enhance the functioning of the immune system, it may also be true that the enhancements do not go far enough to improve a person's actual health status. That is, one might ask if psychological interventions have shown any real-world improvements in health. Therefore, we now turn to the ways in which psychological factors appear to improve health status and the functioning of the immune system.

Social Support

Social support can include emotional support such as caring and empathy, getting positive feedback about our behavior, receiving helpful information, the willingness of others to give us their time or other tangible forms of assistance. Often, the perception that we are loved or supported is important to our health status. It is beneficial to see ourselves as embedded in a mutually supportive social network. The positive effects of social support on health have been documented in numerous studies (Cohen & Syme, 1985). The presence of social support has been associated with positive health outcomes such as greater resistance to disease, lower rates of coronary heart disease, faster recovery from heart disease and heart surgery, and lower mortality. Social support can also help increase compliance with medical treatments, may help reduce the levels of medication, and may speed up recovery (see Salovy et al., 2000). Support from family and friends has also been associated with less arterial blockages in patients with Type A personalities (Burg, Blumenthal, Barefoot, Williams, & Haney, 1986). A classic epidemiological study in Alameda County, California, found that a lack of social support was as strongly related to mortality as was smoking (Berkman & Syme, 1979). For ethnic minorities, a perceived closeness to one's ethnic or racial group as well as a positive racial identity may serve to reduce health risks (Williams, Spencer, Jackson, & Ashmore, 1999). Conversely, perceived racial or ethnic discrimination can have a negative impact on health (see Lewis, 2002).

For women, social support has been correlated with lower complications during pregnancy and delivery (Nuckolls, Cassel, & Kaplan, 1972). For instance, one study found that women in labor who have a supportive person present showed a decreased mean delivery time of more than 50 percent compared to women who did not have a supportive person present (Sosa, Kennell, Robertson, Klaus, & Urrutia, 1980). This effect, however, was greater for women who were under high stress. The benefits of social support and relaxation training may even extend to problems of infertility. Alice Domar (see Kolt, Slawsby, & Domar, 1999) gives workshops for infertile women and has found that a program based on support groups and relaxation training can show significant increases in pregnancy rates and decreases in depression.

One of the better-known studies in health psychology involves social support and cancer. David Spiegel and his colleagues ran support groups for women who were diagnosed with breast cancer (Spiegel, Kraemer, Bloom, & Gottheil, 1989). They found that women in the support groups lived an average of 18 months longer than women who received only conventional treatment. Some of the women also received training in self-hypnosis, and they experienced lower levels of pain than women who did not have similar training.

As discussed in Chapter 5, positive physiological effects for married people have also been found. These effects are particularly evident for men. When compared with unmarried men, married men have fewer infectious diseases and even live longer. For example, effects have been found for positive marital relationships and love on heart disease. A study in Israel of 10,000 married men who were over 40 years old found that those men who believed their wives showed them love had a smaller chance of developing symptoms of angina pectoris (chest pain caused by poor blood supply to the heart). Incredibly, the belief in his wife's love and support was a *better* predictor of future angina for a man than physical factors such as cholesterol levels, age, and blood pressure (Medalie & Goldbourt, 1976). The perception of being loved by one's wife has also been associated with decreased risk for ulcers (Medalie, Strange, Zyzanski, & Goldbourt, 1992). Married women also benefit physiologically from marriage, but the quality of the marriage is a more significant factor for women. Men seem to benefit simply from being married, whereas women need a good marriage in order to show increased health benefits. Women also seem to benefit more from general social support than do men (see Brannon & Feist, 2000). Finally, the perception that one is loved or that one was loved as a child has been associated with a number of health benefits, including less risk for heart disease, ulcers, hypertension, and alcoholism (Russek & Schwartz, 1997).

Social support may have an effect on health in at least two ways. Higher levels of social support may either impact health directly, or it may provide a "buffer" during stressful times that helps to decrease the negative effects of the stress. In either case, social support may help to increase positive emotions such as hope, confidence, or a feeling of security. In a reciprocal fashion, an increase in positive mood from better social support may also increase the probability that a person receives more social support (Salovey et al., 2000). Others have suggested that one of the critical factors in positive relationships with others and social support is empathy. People who empathize with others are liked better by other people and feel closer to others as well (Feshbach, 1984). High levels of empathy are also associated with lower levels of anger and aggression , and hostility has been related to heart disease.

Social Support and the Immune System In the 1980s, Janice Kiecolt-Glaser and her husband Ronald Glaser began collecting immunological and psychological data on medical students as they progressed through the academic year. They found that the stress of medical school and final exams was related to a decrease in certain cells associated with immune functioning (Kiecolt-Glaser, Garner, Speicher, Penn, Holliday, & Glaser, 1984). Interestingly, they also found that the effect was greater for medical students who reported more feelings of loneliness. Similarly, Kielcolt-Glaser and Glaser also studied couples that had either happy or unhappy relationships. They found that those who were happy were more likely to have healthier immune systems than those in unhappy relationships (Kiecolt-Glaser, Fisher, Ogrocki, Stout, Speicher, & Glaser, 1987; Kiecolt-Glaser, Newton, Capioppo, MacCallum, Glaser, & Malarkey, 1997). Other researchers have also found that psychological factors, such as loneliness, can have negative effects on immune functioning, health, and psychological well-being (see Green & Shellenberger, 1991; Brannon & Feist, 2000).

Social Support from Pets? The health benefits of relationships even extend to pets. A number of studies have found that pets can enhance health in many ways, including lowering blood pressure, reducing rates of angina, and increasing longevity (Keil, 1988; Siegal, 1990). While the benefits of a having a loving and supportive dog are fairly clear, people are able to gain health benefits by caring for a variety of pets. Even watching a stress-free environment such as a fish tank can help some people lower their blood pressure. It seems that social support from whatever source can be a positive resource for health and well-being.

Compassion and Health

An interesting study by David McClelland looked at the association between empathy and health. He suggests that simply watching someone be kind and sympathetic to others may even influence changes in our immune system responses. McClelland (1985; McClelland & Kirshnit, 1982) showed people two films and measured immune system functioning prior to viewing the films and just after viewing them. He showed *Triumph of the Will*, a World War II

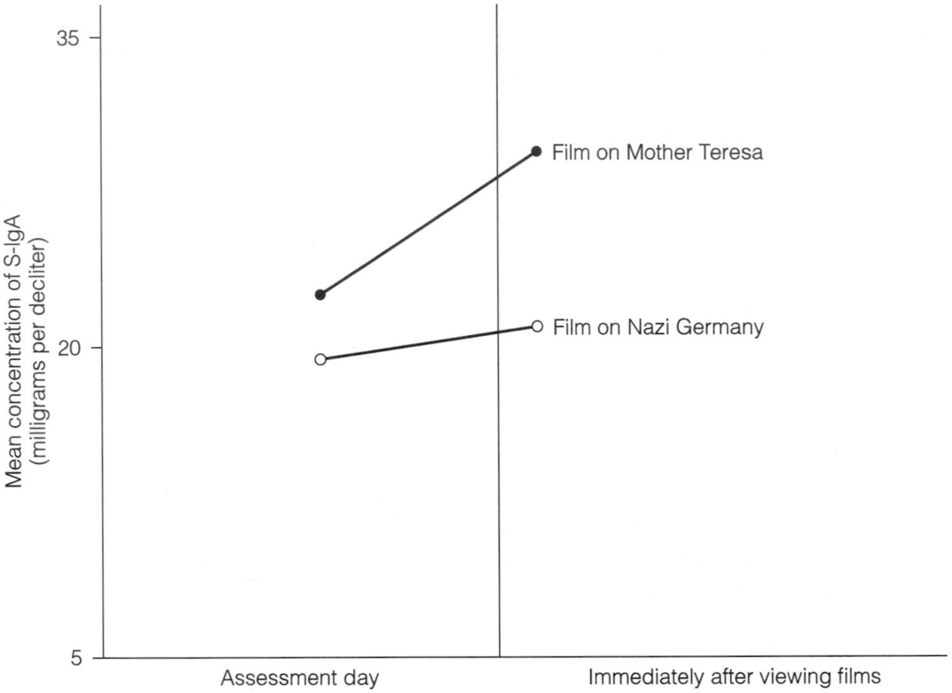

FIGURE 6.1

Effects of Watching *Triumph of the Will* and *Mother Teresa* on Immunoglobulin A

Source: From David McClelland, *Human motivation* (Scott Foresman, 1985), fig. 6.1, p. 368. Copyright 1985 Scott Foresman. Reprinted by permission of Scott Foresman, a division of Pearson Education.

propaganda film produced by the Nazis showing their early victories and their anti-Semitic attitudes. He also showed *Mother Teresa,* a film about the life of Nobel Peace Prize winner Mother Teresa as she worked among the sick and dying in India. Immediately after seeing the film on Mother Teresa, the immune system functioning of all subjects was increased (see Figure 6.1). Some people were also asked to recall times in their lives when they had felt loved. After watching the Mother Teresa film, the immune responses of those people remained high for up to an hour.

McClelland also measured the affiliation and power motives of his volunteers. Someone with a high affiliation motive is more oriented to engage in social interactions and to have more positive social relationships. Someone with a high power motive tends to be focused on competition, achievement, and individualism. What McClelland found was that the Nazi film had little effect on the immune responses of those high in affiliation but lowered the response of those high in the power motive. In other words, watching Mother Teresa had a positive effect on everyone's immune system response while watching the Nazi propaganda film had a negative effect on the immune system response of only those high in the power motive. McClelland's results showed how personality style could interact with environmental events to impact immune system responses.

Humor and Health

Another area of research suggests that physicians should prescribe jokes! Even Hippocrates, the father of Greek medicine, prescribed laughter to his patients as early as the fourth century BCE (Viney & King, 1998). More recently, George Vaillant (1977, see Chapter 8) found that the defense mechanism of humor, or being able to laugh at either oneself or at the situation, was associated with greater adjustment and well-being.

Research on humor and health gained considerable recognition after writer Norman Cousins helped cure himself of a degenerative and possibly fatal illness, ankylosing spondylitis. Cousins refused to accept the fatal diagnosis given by his physicians and added an unusual component to his treatment. In addition to high doses of vitamins, Cousins watched old "Candid Camera" television shows and Marx Brothers movies (Cousins, 1981). Cousin's unorthodox treatment apparently contributed to the cure of his disease. Later experimental studies have found that laughter can increase S-IgA antibodies that help fight off infections (Dillon, Minchoff, & Baker, 1985–86), can increase natural disease fighting killer cells, and can lower blood pressure (Lefcourt, 2002). Thorson, Powell, Sarmany-Schuller, and Hampes (1997) found that people who scored high on a sense of humor scale also tended to score high on measures of optimism, extroversion, and capacity for intimacy and scored low on neuroticism. High scorers also showed less negative self-esteem and tended to use better coping strategies to deal with stress. In general, studies have found that having a sense of humor can help people recover from illness, can help us cope with life stress and anxieties about death and mortality, helps enhance immune system functioning, and helps reduce the psychological experience of pain (Lefcourt, 2002).

The use of humor in the healing process has sparked considerable interest in both medicine and psychology. Today, professional journals, as well as the American Association for Therapeutic Humor, are devoted to the research on this topic. As interesting as these studies have been, Willibald Ruch (2001) cautions that scientists still do not know if the positive benefits come from the physical act of laughing or from simply having a sense of humor.

Music and Health

In a similar fashion, some researchers and physicians are now proposing that music can aid the healing process. James Pennebaker (see below) studied the process of coping with trauma and found that nonverbal expression of emotions through art or music can be helpful (Pennebaker, 1997). Relaxing sounds have also been shown to lower stress hormones and blood pressure as well as increase immune system functioning and raise endorphin levels which increase positive moods (Halpern & Savary, 1985; Charnetski, Brennan, & Harrison, 1998). Cancer specialist Mitchell Gaynor has had success using music as an adjunctive therapy with his cancer patients (Gaynor, 2002). He uses a variety of music in this process, including the sounds of Tibetan singing bowls, Gregorian chants, the singing of Jewish prayers, and even drumming.

A fascinating series of studies has even suggested that the normal human heartbeat may sound musical. Cardiologists C.-K. Peng, Ary Goldberger, Gene Stanley, and colleagues recorded human heartbeats and discovered that it was possible to graph the intervals between beats and convert them into a series of musical notes (Peng et. al., 1993; Peng, Havlin, Stanley, & Goldberger, 1995). They found that healthy heartbeats sounded musically pleasing, while unhealthy hearts sounded a bit off key or out of rhythm (check out the Web site: http://polymer.bu.edu/music; http://reylab.bidmc.Harvard.edu/heartsongs). The Boston Museum of Science took this research and created an exhibition that allows museum-goers to record their own heartbeats and turn them into music.

Emotional Expression and Health

James Pennebaker's research is also relevant to health. He completed a number of interesting studies on the use of writing as a way to deal with trauma and difficulties. Of course, for years many people have kept diaries or journals of their experiences, and they may have known something about stress that psychologists have only recently discovered. What Pennebaker was really looking at was the effect of emotional suppression on health and well-being. The basic research question was whether psychologists were right to assume that "keeping it all inside" is bad for one's mental and physical health. Pennebaker's research has looked at the effects of a number of stressors; he has studied Holocaust survivors, people who lived through the San Francisco earthquake of 1989, and Gulf War veterans, among others.

Pennebaker concluded from his studies that confiding in others or sharing one's experiences can be therapeutic, and, as mentioned above, even the nonverbal expression of emotions through art or music can be helpful (Pennebaker, 1993, 1997). His most surprising finding was that even the simple act of writing down one's thoughts about a traumatic event could be helpful. In one study, Pennebaker, Kiecolt-Glaser, and Glaser (1988) asked one group of college students to simply write about a personal traumatic experience. Another group was to write about superficial topics. The group who wrote about their traumatic experiences showed a significant decline in visits to the university health center, showed better immune system responses, lower blood pressure, as well as less distress. The largest improvement in these areas was found for those students who wrote about traumatic events that they had not shared before with others. Further benefits were found for those who were more self-reflective, open to their emotions, and thoughtful (Smyth & Pennebaker, 1999). One of his more interesting findings was that sharing negative emotions was more helpful to the resolution process than trying to focus only on positive emotions. However, Laura King (King & Miner, 2000; King, 2001) found that people who also wrote about how they have grown and benefited from a trauma gained the same health benefits as those who wrote only about trauma.

Does this mean that we sometimes have to feel worse in order to feel better? Apparently, people who keep diaries and daily journals do know something the rest of us should learn: efforts to use control to suppress negative emotions related to traumatic events are counterproductive. There is one caution for those who wish to use writing as a tool for emotional healing. Pennebaker did find that people often report feeling worse immediately after writing about difficult experiences and memories. The positive effects from the exercise only come a few days later (see Pennebaker's suggestion in Chapter 9).

Does Having a Good Cry Help?

James Pennebaker's research suggests that at times it is helpful to feel bad briefly in order to feel good. Could it then be true that having a good cry is an effective stress reducer? The research on crying does not support the view that crying is always a good stress reliever (DeFruyt, 1997; Vingerhoets, Cornelius, Van Heck, & Becht, 2000). Not everyone seems to benefit from crying. Part of the reason is that there are a number of crying styles and a number of reasons for crying.

For instance, crying can be used as a coping mechanism to help deal with negative emotions, it can be used in order to manipulate others, or it can even be a response to very happy events such as weddings. Studies have found that only people who are extroverted and emotionally stable often find relief and experience an increase in positive feelings after crying (DeFruyt, 1997). In contrast, people who score high on neuroticism tend to cry more often and tend to use weeping as a coping style but may not experience significant relief from crying. Apparently, "having a good cry" is not universally helpful.

Finally, crying may also be a generalized response to powerful emotions—regardless if they are negative or positive. Being more open to aesthetic experiences and being deeply moved by works of art is related to the frequency of crying (DeFruyt, 1997). Similarly, Anderson (1996) looked at a phenomenon termed "transformative weeping." This type of crying occurs in response to profound spiritual experiences. In this instance, it is weeping for joy.

POSITIVE COPING

Up to this point in the chapter, we have seen how a variety of emotions and behaviors can impact health and wellness. These have included better social support, the use of humor, increased compassion, and for some people at least, taking time out for a good cry. One of the ways in which all these enhance wellness is that they all help foster positive coping with the events of life. One obvious reality is that at times life is challenging. In fact, researchers who study positive coping define psychosocial adjustment in terms of a positive outcome to psychological conflict or struggle. Note that the emphasis is not simply on adaptation but on successful adaptation. Research perspectives on positive coping tend to focus on those individuals who cope with the challenges of life more successfully than other people who deal with the same types of events with less success.

A Definition of Positive Coping

One definition of coping says that it is "a response aimed at diminishing the physical, emotional, and psychological burden that is linked to stressful life events and daily hassles" (Snyder & Dinoff, 1999, p. 5). Effective coping should reduce the burden of challenges of both short-term immediate stress and should also contribute to longer-term stress relief. The long-term effects are found primarily when positive coping helps to build resources that will inhibit or buffer future stressful challenges. Those resources can be physiological, such as better health status, psychological, such as greater subjective well-being, or social, such as helping to foster more intimate social support networks. More effective coping programs will generally take a multidimensional approach and impact many core areas that can be used for resource building (see Snyder, 1999).

The goal of many newer perspectives on stress management is to describe adaptations to challenges that do not simply return a person to homeostasis but instead help propel a person toward a better quality of life. This is not just coping, but *positive coping*. In line with a positive psychology orientation, Virginia O'Leary and Jeannette Ickovics (1995) termed such a process as psychological **thriving.** Elissa Epel, Bruce McEwen, and Ickovics (1998) expanded this concept so that thriving includes both enhanced psychological and physical functioning after successful adaptations. They found that women who had come away from a major life trauma with a greater appreciation for life and a deeper religious faith showed a faster physiological adaptation to a laboratory induced stressor. That is, we are engaged in thriving when we adapt to stress and challenge, and as a result of that process, we create even better adaptations and acquire even more refined coping skills in the future. Just as in the broaden-and-build model of positive emotions, some ways of dealing with stress may actually help to build more effective coping resources for the future.

The Importance of Daily Hassles

The definition of coping given above included responses to both major life events and to daily hassles, those minor irritations that stop life from going smoothly. An important question is, which is more detrimental to our well-being, the big and significant life events that must be confronted from time to time or the smaller daily hassles that must be coped with on a daily or weekly basis? Surprisingly, studies have shown that it is the smaller daily hassles that can be more problematic for us (Lazarus & Folkman, 1984). Why might this be so? One of the reasons is that many of the significant life events, such as marriage, a death in the family, or the birth of one's first child, actually occur quite infrequently. Many of these events are also associated with socially prescribed rituals, such as weddings and funerals, to help people deal with the changes involved. Eunkook Suh, Ed Diener, and F. Fujita (1996) found that the impact of recent life events on long-term well-being was quite short-lived. In their study, the stressful impact of various life events lasted only about three months. This seems to be the result of the fact that daily hassles are more likely to impact a person's current mood, and persistent negative mood is more likely to effect well-being. In other words, this research suggests that the cumulative effects of many smaller stressors in a relatively short period of time may be more important than the impact of relatively infrequent major life events. Note this conclusion also suggests that stress management and positive coping need to be built into a person's daily routine.

Dimensions of Positive Coping

Considerable work has also been done on how to deal with the effects of stressful challenges. In general, approaches to positive coping strategies take two forms. The first tends to focus on external environment, physical health, or health behaviors. For instance, this approach might suggest using voice mail to decrease the annoyance of a constantly ringing telephone or an increased exercise regime to enhance physical resistance. The second approach tends to focus on psychological factors. Usually these cognitive factors are the expectations, attitudes, or beliefs that people use to interpret life events and give them meaning. These interpretive habits are often habitually stimulated by potential stressors and then, if the resultant interpretation is negative, actually produce or exacerbate the stress. That is, the interpretive meaning systems are seen as intervening between the actual objective event and the psychological effects on the person. In practice, any good stress management program will combine these two approaches.

Bruce Compas (1987) suggested that the large variety of coping responses can be understood better by dividing them into three different dimensions or categories: (1) coping styles, (2) coping resources, and (3) coping strategies. Coping styles are the basic and fundamental approaches we use to deal with challenges. Coping resources are more specific skills and resources we can draw upon when under stress. Coping strategies are the more complex behavioral strategies we use over time to cope with challenges.

Coping Styles

Richard Lazarus and Susan Folkman (1984) believe that a large number of specific coping styles can be grouped into three subtypes: (1) those in which a person attempts to change negative emotions, (2) those in which a person attempts to change the situation that caused the stress, and (3) those that just seek to avoid the problem. These are called emotion-focused coping, problem-focused coping, and avoidance, respectively.

According to Lazarus and Folkman (1984), **emotion-focused coping** is "directed at regulating emotional responses to problems" (p. 150). The goal is to release the tension, forget the anxiety, eliminate the worry, or just release the anger. Emotion-focused coping can be further divided into two subtypes: cognitive and behavioral. *Cognitive emotion-focused coping* is often involved with what Lazarus and Folkman term "defensive re-appraisals." These are ways of thinking that attempt to draw attention away from the more painful elements of a situation by reinterpreting the situation, using positive thinking to block out negative emotions, or by the use of selective attention. *Behavioral* *emotion-focused coping* involves doing something to regulate one's emotions, such as exercise, meditation, or simply venting anger.

At first glance, these coping behaviors appear to be the very heart of stress management. However, what these behaviors may fail to do is focus on ways to change the precipitating factors that caused the stress in the first place. For instance, if a person has fairly regular arguments with a supervisor at work and tends to follow them with a night of drinking, then he or she is using emotion-focused coping. A night in the bar may help a person forget negative emotions, but it does nothing to solve the heart of the problem with the supervisor. Less obviously, if a person uses a different strategy and follows the arguments at work by having long discussions with their spouse, he or she may also be using emotion-focused coping. In this instance, while the discussions with one's spouse may help the marital relationship and ease anger, they nonetheless focus just on one's emotional responses.

The other coping style, **problem-focused coping,** involves the use of realistic strategies that could make a tangible difference in the situation that causes the stress. Problem-focused coping styles can be divided into those directed at changing the situation and those directed at changing the self. A person could change the situation mentioned above by talking the problem out with his or her supervisor or even leaving the job and finding one that provided more respect. Problem-focused coping directed at the self often involves cognitive reappraisals. In this approach, a person changes how he or she thinks about the situation but does so in a realistic and honest manner. We can change our attitudes, beliefs, or expectations about an event and decrease our stressful reaction to it.

Of course, in many instances, people combine the two types of coping. For instance, if a person consistently takes work problems home to their spouse, but the discussions help that person decide on a course of action that could change the situation, then he or she has combined emotion-focused and problem-focused coping to help solve the problem. Last, another way of dealing with stressors is to simply use avoidance. Here, a person attempts to run away from stress, refuses to confront difficulties presented by life events, or attempts to deny their impact and importance. Under most circumstances this strategy is not very adaptive.

The three major styles of coping are not equally effective as coping strategies in all situations. In general, the use of problem-focused coping tends to increase self-esteem, a sense of control, and leads to effective coping. Problem-focused coping strategies are more likely to be associated with higher well-being (see Snyder, 1999). Emotion-focused coping can be beneficial. For instance, emotion-focused coping helps if people use emotions to approach and engage stressors (Stanton, Parsa, & Austenfeld, 2002). In most instances, avoidance is clearly detrimental to well-being. However, denial or avoidance can be helpful under certain restricted circumstances. For instance, denial can help protect a person against overwhelming anxiety during the early stages of coping with a serious illness even though denial is usually a poor long-term solution to the anxiety associated with illness.

There are interesting differences in how culture and gender may influence the types of coping used. Chang (2001) found that in Asian American groups the use of emotion-focused coping was just as important to well-being as was problem-focused coping in Caucasian American groups. Seiffge-Krenke and Shulman (1990) found cultural differences in coping between German and Israeli adolescents. German youth tended to use active coping behaviors such as seeking advice and social support. Israeli adolescents tended to use a more internal behaviors such as thinking through a solution on their own (see Price & Crapo, 2002). They also found that both German and Israeli girls tended to seek social support more than boys. German girls were the most likely to use withdrawal as a coping behavior.

Coping Resources

Recall that in Compas's classification, coping resources are those we can draw upon as we rise to meet various challenges. These resources may be either external or internal. Earlier in this chapter, we saw how the presence of one external resource—available social support—can have a positive effect on health and well-being. Lazarus and Folkman (1984) also mention another external resource that can help people meet various challenges: money or sufficient income to help with unexpected challenges (remember, however, that income has very little effect on subjective well-being). Although these external resources can be quite important, the following discussion will focus on internal psychological resources that help people meet challenges and adjust well.

Positive Emotionality In a recent study, the presence of positive emotions relative to negative emotions appeared to impact health status and longevity. Danner, Snowdon, and Friesen (2001) analyzed the two-to-three page autobiographies written by 180 Catholic nuns as part of their applications to the order. The autobiographies were written as early as 1930 and were analyzed for the number of positive emotions expressed. Of the nuns who expressed the lowest number of positive emotions in their early autobiographies, only 34 percent were still alive at age 85. Of those who expressed more positive emotions in their autobiographies, fully 90 percent were still alive at their 85th birthday. By age 94, there were 54 percent still alive from the happiest group and only 11 percent still alive from the least happy group.

Cognitive Interpretation of Events A number of researchers have proposed that between life events and our reactions to those events can be found our cognitive interpretations of the events. These approaches focus on how we interpret the events of our lives and how we can learn to modify beliefs that are contributing to stress and poor health behaviors. These approaches evaluate how we think about challenges and, in particular, how we interpret the meaning of events for our own lives. Overly negative or unrealistic interpretations can lead to unnecessary increases in stress, worry, or unwise reactions. For instance, imagine a "straight-A" student who gets a "B" on his first chemistry test and reacts by telling himself, "Oh, this is awful! Now I'll never get into law school! My life is ruined!" More than likely, he is driving up his own negative emotions with his irrational thoughts about a single test grade. If this student tells himself that it is only one grade and he has time to pull up his final grade in the course, then his emotional reaction should be less extreme and more reasonable. As in this example, Higgins (1987) presents an interesting idea about the source of stress. He suggests that the perceived challenge of an event is related to how much personal redefinition it will involve. He says that if an event challenges our basic definition of self, then it will be more stressful than if the necessary adjustment leaves our self-concept or identity intact.

Lazarus and Folkman also suggests that what is crucial to this cognitive mediation approach is the meaning that we bring to the situation. Also implied in his formulation is that stress is viewed not as a quality of either the person or the situation but rather as a quality that emerges from the relationship between the person and the situation. Current mood, health, past experience, and a number of other factors also influence these judgments. Because of factors like these, what is viewed as stressful is a highly individual judgment that is sensitive to the situational context. Almost all stress management programs incorporate the idea that we can change our emotional reactions to events by changing how we think about or interpret those events. Studies have also shown that a few styles of thinking may be extremely important to positive coping. Some of the more important will be discussed next.

Optimism Martin Seligman (1975) proposed a very influential perspective on depression with his theory of learned helplessness. He said that when faced with seemingly inescapable stressors, people learn to respond with helplessness and expect defeat. Later he also proposed the opposite response, called **learned optimism** (Seligman, 1990). In this theory, if we focus on the positive and the possible, we can learn to respond to stressors with an attitude of optimism and hope. As a general statement, we can say that optimists tend to have better health outcomes than pessimists (Peterson, Seligman, & Vaillant 1988)

M. Scheier and C. Carver (1987, 1992) produced compelling evidence that optimism is related to both physical and psychological well-being. Their research on dispositional optimism was mentioned earlier in reference to subjective well-being. Scheier and Carver have also looked at potential consequences for health for being optimistic. They found that optimism, or the generalized expectancy that good things will happen in the future, is related to better health outcomes including less distress in women with breast cancer and faster recovery from surgery (Scheier & Carver, 1992). They have also looked at what factors might account for these relationships. One of their findings is that optimists have a tendency to use problem-focused coping strategies to deal with challenges and stress. This was especially the case under circumstances that were actually controllable. At the same time, optimism was positively correlated with seeking social support, which also helps health status. A related finding is that women who were more hopeful were more informed about risk factors for breast cancer, more willing to visit health professionals, and more likely to perform self-examinations for early signs of cancer (Irving, Snyder, & Crowson, 1998).

Optimism may also be related to longevity. A study that followed over 2,000 Mexican Americans for two years found that those who were more optimistic tended to live longer (see Seligman, 2002a, p. 40; also Ostir, Markides, Black, & Goodwin, 2000). Similar results were found in a study from the Mayo Clinic. That study looked at optimism scores obtained at admission and related them to survival rates forty years later. When comparing expected life spans, optimists had a 19 percent greater longevity when compared to the pessimists.

Perceived Control As is the case with subjective well-being, there may be a relationship between a perceived sense of control and health. Most discussions of control begin with Julian Rotter's (1966) work on internal and external locus of control. One would expect that this factor would be related to health behaviors at the very least. Bonnie Strickland's (1978) review of the research on locus of control and health behaviors concluded that people who are more internal tend to engage in more adaptive coping styles and engage in more health-related behaviors. However, the review also noted that this conclusion is quite tentative and is qualified in some ways. One of the most important caveats to the general conclusion is that internals have an advantage over externals in terms of positive coping and adaptations only under circumstances where some control is actually possible. Last, a perceived lack of control can be associated with negative affectivity (or neuroticism), but that trait has been related only to complaints about one's health and not to actual health status (Watson & Pennebaker, 1989).

The phenomenon of *placebo response* is related to optimism and control. In medicine, the placebo response is activated when a patient believes that a medicine or treatment will work. In research studies, people who receive the placebo are given a treatment that looks like it should work even though there is no scientific or logical reason that it should work. The idea is to separate out the psychological effects of hope or optimism from the physiological effects of a real drug or accepted treatment. For many years, the placebo response was a nuisance in medicine. Many researchers thought that it complicated the search for the "real" medical treatments. All that time the acknowledgment that people actually got better—apparently by simply believing they would get better—was neglected. Herbert Benson (Benson & Stark, 1996) reinterpreted the placebo response. He argued that to view the placebo response as just false belief misses the point because that belief can lead to measurable changes in physiology. He renamed the placebo response as "remembered wellness," indicating that it just might be an untapped power for healing that all people posses. Albert Bandura (1977) indicated that a person's belief in the effectiveness of a placebo may release endorphins or other natural pain killers of the body.

Self-Efficacy Bandura's (1977) theory of self-efficacy is very well known. He postulated that people are able to make changes in their behavior if, and only if, they have specific beliefs and expectations about personal effectiveness. **Self-efficacy** is the belief that we have the ability to perform, or the capacity to learn, the behaviors necessary for us to reach desired goals. Bandura said that it is our beliefs about our ability to change that determine how we will work for change. People who are high in self-efficacy tend to believe that they have more control over their own health and are able to manage pain better (see Brannon & Feist, 2000). They also show better adherence to programs that attempt to increase their health, such as smoking cessation programs.

Bandura (1986) also said that our self-efficacy beliefs come from four major sources: our actual performance, vicarious experiences, verbal persuasion, and physiological (usually emotional) arousal. For instance, if we cannot play tennis very well, but we wish to learn, then we need to slowly increase our sense of efficacy. First, to increase our actual performance we can begin with relatively simple exercises in tennis (e.g., just hitting the ball over the net). We learn those simple skills until we feel somewhat competent at them (that is, we increase our sense of efficacy), and then move on to a slightly more difficult exercise. Second, we can watch professionals and other good players as they play tennis. By watching how they move and their strategy we can increase our understanding of the game and increase our sense of efficacy. Third, we can take tennis lessons and get encouragement from a good coach. More important, we can pay attention to the cognitions that may hinder our performance (for example, thinking, "I'll never learn this game!") and then take steps to modify those cognitions (for instance, thinking, "I can learn this game if I continue to work at it"). Last, we can monitor our emotional reactions (e.g., anxiety) and take steps to reduce it. Bandura recognized that our beliefs and expectations play a primary role in how we cope with life and how we feel about ourselves.

Personality Styles

It is obvious from the above discussion that a number of individual personality factors have been studied as they related to health, positive coping, and well-being. A few researchers have taken this information and proposed that a more general personality style may combine some of these coping resources. Two of the proposals for a "stress-resistant" personality style will be discussed next.

Hardiness Suzanne Kobasa[2] (1979) examined coping resources by looking at physical illness as an indictor of poor coping. Kobasa found that three factors differentiated a group with high stress and low illness from a group with high stress and high illness. She used the term **hardiness** to describe those in the high stress and low illness group who coped better. More specifically, she believed that she found evidence for a hardy personality style that helped people cope with stress. Kobasa found that a person with a hardy personality appears to cope better with stress such that hardiness is associated with better mental and physical health status (Kobasa, Maddi, and Courington, 1981; Kobasa, Maddi, & Kahn, 1982; Gentry & Ouellette-Kobasa, 1984; Kobasa, Maddi, Puccetti, & Zola, 1994). Kobasa also found that low hardiness was most detrimental to health status under conditions of high stress.

Hardiness is defined as a combination of three cognitive factors involved with how people interpret life events. Those who were hardier tended to have:

1. A sense of *control* over their lives. They may not have known how they would cope with the crisis, but they felt confident that they would be able to cope. This factor included a sense of (a) decisional control, or autonomy in decision making; (b) cognitive control, or "the ability to interpret, appraise, and incorporate various sorts of stressful events into an ongoing life plan and, thereby, deactivate their jarring effects" (Kobasa, 1979, p. 3); and (c) more coping skills or a greater variety of available strategies to deal with stressors.
2. A sense that the stress they were facing presented them with a *challenge* rather than a crisis. They tended to see that each problem could be used for some potential good. They saw change as a catalyst for growth and many even have sought out change and variety. In addition, this quality referred to greater cognitive flexibility.
3. A sense of *commitment* to the various areas of their lives. This third characteristic involved (a) a belief system that minimized the perceived threat of a stressor, (b) a sense of purpose that prevented surrender in the face of stressors, and (c) an involvement with others in positive social relationships. Kobasa believed that of primary importance was a commitment to self and one's unique values and goals that allowed the maintenance of internal balance and a strong sense of self.

What is it that people who are hardy do that is different? People who are high in hardiness may engage in transformational coping. They are not willing victims of threatening change, but rather they become active determinants of the direction that change will take (Gentry & Ouellette-Kobasa, 1984). In addition, the same cognitive processes that help produce a positive self-concept and subjective well-being may also help create a sense of hardiness. Compton, Seeman, and Norris (1991) found that high hardiness was related to positive self-concept, the low use of attributions to luck, and strong self-enhancement processes.

When looking at the three qualities of the hardy personality, it is obvious that a hardy person is one who can use certain cognitive skills to reinterpret the events of his or her life in more adaptive ways. In many ways, Kobasa is also saying that the events of our life may not matter as much as our interpretation of those events. However, Kobasa has suggested that the concept of hardiness may be more applicable to people who are seeking a sense of meaning and purpose and who are motivated by existential themes such as freedom, responsibility, and independence (Ouellette, 1993).

Sense of Coherence Aaron Antonovsky (1979; 1987) also developed a theory of the stress-resistant personality as he explored issues around how people coped well with stress. He placed his research into a broader context, however, than most other scholars who investigate positive coping. He was interested in redefining some of the theoretical assumptions most often used by researchers in the field of stress and stress management.

Antonovsky believed most researchers assumed that homeostasis, or a state of balanced equilibrium, was the desired and baseline state of the human organism. If one assumed homeostasis was "normal," then stressors were pathogens that disturbed the equilibrium and were "abnormal." Therefore, stress was not normal and stressors were inherently bad. In contrast, Antonovsky began with the assumption that human beings are inherently active, curious, exploratory, and variety-seeking. If this is true, then people do not really want equilibrium. Instead, people seek active involvement in life changes that foster a sense of growth, development, and positive change. Antonovsky (1987) stated, "The pathogenic orientation invariably sees stressors as pathogenic, as risk factors, which at best can be reduced, inoculated against, or buffered.... But the assumption that stressors are inherently bad is tenuous" (p. 7). Taking this line of reasoning one step further, Antonovsky stated that stress management interventions that merely return a person to a state of homeostasis will be different from interventions that enhance active and exploratory coping. Therefore, researchers interested in stress should focus on how to enhance an active, exploratory, and variety-seeking orientation to life rather than focusing on how to return people to a homeostatic repose that is impossible to maintain. This approach is similar to that taken by positive psychology.

Taking these basic ideas as his starting point, Antonovsky developed his model of positive coping, which he called **sense of coherence.** He saw sense of coherence as a unique set of personality traits that combine to create an orientation to life that allows people to interpret life stressors in a positive and adaptive way. That is, life seems coherent and understandable in spite of the ups and downs. Antonovsky began his empirical research into the sense of coherence concept by examining the lives of people who met two criteria. First, they had undergone a severe trauma that involved inescapable consequences for their lives, such as the death of a loved one, concentration camp internment, severe disability, and economic deprivation. Second, the person had to be functioning remarkably well. In other words, Antonovsky began by investigating the lives of people who showed evidence of highly adaptive coping skills and competence in spite of experiencing extreme stress and trauma in their past. For example, here is an excerpt from one interview with a 90-year-old man who had a strong sense of coherence: "How we overcame all difficulties in our lives? You need patience. You have to believe in the Promise, a word I learned in Bulgaria. . . . It doesn't have to be God. It can be another force, but you have to have faith. Otherwise you can't suffer so much and go on" (Antonovsky, 1987, p. 68). Contrast that interview with the following excerpt from a 50-year-old woman with a weak sense of coherence: "I'm a sick woman, I always suffered from something, and even before the tragedy three years ago when my husband died. . . . I believe in fate. True, I don't know who runs it, because I don't believe in God anymore. . . . My life has been full of losses even from before. . . . Things are rough, I don't have any faith left in anyone. . . . All of life is full of problems, only in dying there are no problems. . . . I don't even think of going out with a man or of getting married again" (1987, p. 72). The difference is quite obvious between the hope and determination of the first interview and the despair and hopelessness of the second.

Antonovsky postulated that the sense of coherence consisted of three major factors.

1. The first, and most important, factor he called *meaningfulness.* Antonovsky defined this as the extent to which life makes sense on an emotional level—not just theoretically. It is a motivational component that gives a person the willingness to take up the challenges of life. It gives a person the sense that he or she is "a participant in the process shaping one's destiny as well as one's daily experience" (Antonovsky, 1979, p. 128). Meaningfulness gives a person the sense "that at least some of the problems

and demands posed by living are worth investing energy in, are worthy of commitment and engagement, are challenges that are "welcome" rather than "burdens." Interestingly, he said that this factor does not imply that when life makes sense, then we will always be happy. Instead, a life that is meaningful allows people to accept the disappointment and suffering that are inevitable in life.

2. The second most important factor in sense of coherence is *comprehensibility,* the extent to which life events appear ordered, consistent, structured and clear. Comprehensibility means that life does not appear to be chaotic and random. Someone who scores high on the comprehensibility dimension "expects that the stimuli he or she will encounter in the future will be predictable or, at the very least, when they do come as surprises, that they will be ordered and explainable" (1987, p. 17). Note that this factor does not imply that life events are desirable. It also does not imply that we are always pleased with the accidents and circumstances of our life. It does imply that when events happen, there seems to be a reason for them or that we find a way to derive meaning from them.
3. The third factor is *manageability,* the belief that our personal resources and coping skills are adequate to meet the demands of the task that confronts us. It is "the extent to which one perceives that resources are at one's disposal which are adequate to meet the demands posed by the stimuli that bombard one" (1987, p. 17). A person who scores high on manageability will not feel victimized by life events or unfairly treated by life. In essence, this factor is a sense of control factor derived from confidence in coping skills.

In general, research on the sense of coherence concept has shown that it can be useful as a measure of psychological well-being (Frenz, Carey, & Jorgensen, 1993). Note that having a strong sense of coherence implies that life events are meaningful and understandable. It usually means a person experiences positive emotions more frequently.

Coping Strategies

The last category in Compas's system was the behavioral strategies that people use over time to help adjust in positive ways to challenges and to build future resources for positive coping. We saw some of those strategies earlier in the chapter during the discussion of health psychology and the enhancement of health status. Included in that discussion were strategies such as maintaining positive social contacts and keeping a sense of humor and optimism. Healthy physiological strategies can include following a healthy lifestyle (Edlin & Golantry, 1992) that includes frequent exercise (Rostad & Long, 1996), regular meditation (Benson, 1975), and even having a good massage (Rich, 2002). Strategies from Eastern psychology such as yoga and tai chi chuan have also been effective methods for using the physical body to impact psychological well-being. What is important here is the regular and consistent use of various techniques for maintaining positive relationships with one's emotional and social well-being.

Comments on Wellness and Health Psychology

Note that coping styles, resources, and strategies all interact in rather complex ways. Our appraisals of events can be impacted by our sense of optimism, which can be enhanced by being in good physical condition, which in turn can be impacted by a sense of control or self-efficacy that allows us enough discipline to maintain a consistent exercise regime. Positive emotions seem to be central to at least some of the processes that lead to the development of positive health and even longevity. Research is just beginning to investigate how these factors interact to help enhance health status. Nonetheless, the results so far imply that emotions are important to our health. Further, the results also imply that the old distinction between the "mind" and the "body" is slowly being replaced with a more interactive model of a very dynamic system that includes both psychological and physical factors in our health.

SUMMARY

The chapter opened with a discussion of wellness or the idea that total well-being is an interaction of physical, emotional, physical, and spiritual well-being. The field of health psychology and psychoneuroimmunology were introduced. Study in these areas has begun to change how scientists believe the mind and body interact. Scientists now believe that psychological factors can have a direct influence on certain physical processes, such as our immune system responses. Some of the important psychological factors that impact health were then reviewed, such as social support, an optimistic orientation to the future, and a confidence in one's ultimate ability to bounce back from temporary difficulty. Positive coping strategies were then discussed. Helpful positive coping often involves the way in which we interpret the events of our lives—the meaning we give to those events. Some effective positive coping styles take on the qualities of a personality trait. The coping styles of hardiness and a sense of coherence clearly focus on our reactions to the events of our lives rather than the events themselves as the most important elements of stress management. One caution is that coping is very personal. The coping strategy that works for each person is often determined by a unique combination of personality and situational variables.

NOTES

1. Note that this idea is almost exactly the same as the contemporary idea that psychological problems are caused by a "chemical imbalance." Today the chemicals are neurotransmitters rather than the four humors, but the concept is the same.

2. Kobasa has also published under her married name, Ouellette, and as Ouellette-Kobasa.

LEARNING TOOLS

Key Terms and Ideas

EMOTION-FOCUSED COPING
HARDINESS
LEARNED OPTIMISM
PROBLEM-FOCUSED COPING
PSYCHONEUROIMMUNOLOGY
SELF-EFFICACY
SENSE OF COHERENCE
THRIVING
WELLNESS

Books

Lefcourt, H. M. (2001). *Humor: The psychology of living buoyantly.* New York: Plenum/Kluwer (professional/popular).

Lewis, M. K. (2002). *Multicultural health psychology: Special topics acknowledging diversity.* New York: Allyn and Bacon (an undergraduate textbook).

Research Articles

Salovey, P., Rothman, A., Detweiler, J., & Steward, W. (2000). Emotional states and health. *American Psychologist, 55*(1), 110–121.

Taylor, S., Kemeny, M., Reed, G., Bower, J., & Gruenewald, T. (2000). Psychological resources, positive illusions, and health. *American Psychologist, 55*(1), 99–109.

On the Web

http://wellness.uwsp.edu/Health_Service/services/stress.htm. A wellness Web site from the University of Wisconsin–Stevens Point. It provides stress and wellness evaluations and stress balancing strategies.

http://reylab.bidmc.harvard.edu/heartsongs and http://polymer.bu.edu/music. Two sites that introduce the Heartsongs project by the cardiologist's son who turned heartbeats into music.

http://healthpsych.com/links.html. A Health Psychology Library that provides general information, listing of books, research, and other resources.

Video

Healing and the Mind, hosted by Bill Moyers (1993). This four-part video series explores issues such as mind-body interaction, emotions and health, and how psychological interventions can influence health and well-being. A number of the important figures in health psychology and psychoneuroimmunology (PNI) were interviewed for the series.

Personal Explorations

Because much of stress seems to be produced by our thinking, take one stressful incident and (1) notice how your thinking feeds the stress, and (2) find an alternative way to think about the incident. Practice changing your stressful thoughts whenever you notice them for a week. What happened? How did it change the way you feel?

List everything you do from time to time to relieve stress: from the small treats (e.g., taking a bubble bath) to the large commitments (e.g., exercising daily). How often have you done these in the past month? During the next week try to increase the time you spend in stress-balancing activities by at least 2 hours. How did it change your level of well-being?

PART

iii

POSITIVE TRAITS

CHAPTER 7

EXCELLENCE, AESTHETICS, CREATIVITY, AND GENIUS

> Genius is 1 percent inspiration and 99 percent perspiration.
>
> *Thomas A. Edison*

THE PURSUIT OF EXCELLENCE

We can define excellence as the acquisition of extraordinary skill in a specific area of expertise (Ericsson & Charness, 1994; Ericsson, 1996). People who exhibit excellence are able to perform some behavior, talent, or skill much more fluently and expertly than are other people. The skill or talent can be anything—from basket weaving to theoretical physics. The ability to perform it extraordinarily well is the primary focus of this chapter. In addition, the ability to deeply appreciate beauty or excellence in the works of others will be discussed.

The Foundations of Excellence

The first question for consideration is whether expertise or excellence is the result of innate ability. In other words, is it genetically determined, and, therefore, are experts born but not made? The ancient Greeks, for example, described those who had special talents as "blessed by a gift from the gods." It is quite understandable that this view might be prominent. After all, the achievements of certain creative artists, for example, do seem to be beyond what "normal" people can accomplish. Mozart's youthful accomplishments—he composed his first symphony at age 9 and first opera at age 12—seem so far out of reach for other children's abilities that the innate genius hypothesis may appear the only reasonable explanation. In fact, one of the foremost researchers in this area, Howard Gardner (1993), partially endorses the view that extraordinary talent is related to innate biological factors.

In spite of the intuitive appeal of the innate abilities theory, a considerable amount of research suggests that learning is more important to the acquisition of extraordinary skills than is biology (Ericsson & Charness, 1994). For the most part, this research has focused on demonstrating that amateurs who are given opportunities for intensive practice can, in fact, mimic the superior abilities of experts. In addition, studies have also shown that even child prodigies learn their skills in the same way as others. The difference is not so much in innate knowledge but in the fact that prodigies start to learn their craft earlier than others and they work harder at perfecting their skills.

Although evidence such as this is compelling, some researchers are still persuaded that biological factors are at the core of high-level excellence. Some of these researchers cite savants as an obvious example of how innate biological factors must be involved in excellence (see Winner, 2000). Savants are mentally impaired but show amazing abilities in a limited area. Some can multiply very large numbers almost instantly. Others can name the day of the week for any date in any year in history, or they can memorize musical pieces after only one hearing. In spite of these impressive abilities, studies have shown that motivated college students in a laboratory setting can learn most of the remarkable abilities of savants. Therefore, even savants appear to learn their extraordinary skills. Savants may focus all of their available cognitive capacities on one unusual area of talent and develop it to extraordinary levels (see Winner, 2000, for an alternate view).

Finally, the learning perspective on excellence is supported by the fact that for many abilities, the accomplishments of absolute top performers are constantly bested by the next generation. The most obvious example is in sports. For example, the winning time for the first Olympic Marathon almost 100 years ago was "comparable to the current qualifying time for the Boston Marathon [which is] attained by thousands of amateur runners every year" (Ericsson & Charness, 1994, p. 737). Similarly, in classical music, pieces that are part of a standard performance repertoire today were considered unplayable when they were written in the nineteenth century.

Does this mean that hereditary factors have no influence on expert performance? Probably not. A number of researchers believe that if any portion of excellence is inherited, it is likely to be physical characteristics that match with the requirements for certain sports or personality dispositions that match with specific interest areas. In other words, what may be partially inherited are physical or emotional characteristics that make it more likely for interest to develop in a specific area. K. A. Ericsson and N. Charness (1994) put it boldly when they said, "Our analysis has shown that the central mechanism mediating the superior performance of experts is acquired; therefore acquisition of relevant knowledge and skills may be the major limiting factor in attaining expert performance" (p. 737).

Much of the research today supports the view that excellence can be learned. However, before anyone runs out and tries to buy a book on how to compose like Mozart or paint like Picasso, a few very important caveats should be heeded. First, expert performance is almost always specific to a certain domain. While there have been a few "Renaissance" men like Leonardo Da Vinci, who excelled as a painter, a sculpture, an architect, and an inventor, in almost all other cases a person's expertise is restricted to a single domain. As Ericsson and Charness (1994) note, elite athletes are able to react faster and make better decisions in their realm of expertise, but they are not any better than others on standard reaction time and decision-making tasks that are unrelated to their sport. Second, excellence takes considerable effort. This aspect will be discussed next.

The Development of Excellence

If the superior performance of those who exhibit excellence is learned, then the obvious question, is how do they do it? The studies that began much of the research in this area provide the first hints. In 1946, Adrian de Groot (de Groot, 1965), an expert chess player, published his studies of chess masters. In his initial studies, he demonstrated that chess masters could remember the positions of chess pieces on a board with incredible accuracy after only a brief exposure to the chessboard. He assumed that the expertise of the chess masters was a result of their superior memory abilities. Later studies, however, showed that the chess masters were no better than others at remembering positions of pieces on a chessboard if those pieces were placed *randomly* on the board. What appeared to be a simple advantage of memory was apparent only if the pieces on the board were placed so that they were *meaningful* and represented arrangements that might be found in a real chess game. Therefore, the chess masters were not better at basic memory skills but were better at recognizing familiar chess patterns—patterns learned over years of experience with chess (see Ericsson & Charness, 1994).

The first elements of real excellence appear to involve cognitive skills. And the first of these is a *large knowledge base* in the specific domain. Expertise in tennis, for example, takes a thorough knowledge of the game, including familiarity with different strategies; different styles of potential opponents; the different types of equipment, such as rackets and shoes; and even knowledge of the game's history. Expert performers often have an almost endless curiosity about their specific domain and can become quite enthusiastic about the minutiae of their area.

In addition to memory skills for *relevant* aspects of their interest area and a large knowledge base, studies have found that expert performers also possess other cognitive abilities. They often learn shortcut strategies for reaching decisions that allow them to leap to conclusions faster than others. Related to this is the finding that expertise also involves tapping into well-organized cognitive schemas related to the specific discipline (Bedard & Chi, 1992). That is, the knowledge base of an expert is not just a random collection of facts. Rather, it is an organized cluster of information that involves numerous links between concepts that allow quicker and easier access to memory and problem-solving strategies. These skills allow experts to find solutions quicker because they do not get sidetracked into as many blind alleys as other people do. The ability to utilize these cognitive shortcuts has lead many people to associate expertise with intuition. The literature on excellence, in general, views intuition as simply the rapid access to information facilitated by shortcuts and schemas. Studies indicate that many of these cognitive skills can be taught. For instance, a study of over four hundred school children in Venezuela found that creative problem-solving skills could be learned (Hernstein, Nickerson, Sanchez, & Swets, 1986). Even more interesting is the fact that the children were all from economically and educationally deprived families. Yet, they still learned these skills.

A second element in expert performance is the motivational factor of *commitment.* People who excel are committed to their particular domain. They are determined to succeed and can persevere in spite of difficulties. This commitment to learn all they can about their area usually leads to the formation of mentor relationships. The type of detailed and specific knowledge that one needs in order to develop superior skills is often found only in another person who has also committed him- or herself to the same area. In certain areas, such as classical music, the necessity for a mentor is even somewhat formalized. In classical music circles, there exists a fairly well known list of potential teachers at various levels of expertise who are expected to guide the next phase of the person's training. It is, in fact, common for the best young students to compete for the chance to study with famous teachers.

Finally, the single most important factor in the acquisition of expert performance is *practice.* This is important in at least three ways. First, those who truly excel at a specific discipline often begin to practice earlier in life. Studies have found that people who reached higher levels of expertise tended to begin regular practice schedules from 2 to 5 years earlier than less accomplished—although still very highly talented—performers. Second, those who were most accomplished practiced more hours than others did. Ericsson, Krampe, and Tesch-Romer (1993) found that by age 20, top-level violinists had practiced on average about 10,000 or more hours over the years. This figure was about 2,500 more than those violinists who were at the next lowest level of accomplishment. Ericsson et al. pointed out that this figure represented a few years' worth of extra practice, or the difference between the experience of a freshman and a senior at a school for the performing arts. Again, remember that the next lowest level of expertise is still filled with musicians who are extremely accomplished.

Consistency of practice is also important to the development of expertise. Across domains, those who are the most accomplished practice approximately four hours per day, seven days a week. The great classical pianist Arthur Rubinstein was purported to have said that if he missed practice for one day, then he knew it; if he missed practice for two days, then his colleagues knew it; if he missed practice for three days, then the public knew it. This dedication to constant practice is one of the most important factors in determining who will reach the highest levels of excellence.

Third, in addition to the time put into practice, studies have also found that a certain style of practice, called **deliberate practice,** is important. It is defined as practice that is focused, planned, concentrated, and effortful (Ericsson & Charness, 1994). Anyone who has taken music lessons and ended up half-heartedly running through musical scales while their mind wandered to other more pleasant topics can understand how that experience was the opposite of deliberate practice. In deliberate practice, the focus is on the task at hand with attention to what the person is doing correctly, or incorrectly, at each moment. Interestingly, while this type of practice is highly motivated, this type of dedication is not always intrinsically motivating. In contrast to the intrinsic motivation found in leisure activities and flow (see Chapter 4), the effort required to attain advanced levels of expertise or excellence often involves periods of simple discipline. However, even though excellence requires extensive practice, also note that too much practice might be harmful. Particularly in sports, overtraining is a recognized danger. People who achieve high levels of excellence usually keep practice to a set amount of time—about four hours a day—that allows them to perfect their skills and also make sure that they get needed rest and sleep. Excellence, therefore, requires a sensible balance of hard work and rest.

So, for people who are knowledgeable, motivated, and dedicated to fairly intense practice schedules, how long does it take for them to become elite performers? Interestingly, the answer is fairly consistent across various disciplines. The **ten-year rule** states that it takes at least ten years of dedicated, consistent practice before a person can obtain excellent performance levels (Gardner, 1993).

Table 7.1 illustrates how the ten-year rule seems to fit the careers of a few well-known people who achieved excellence in their respective fields. While a minimum of ten years is usually necessary for excellent performance, the age at which people generally attain recognition and make their big breakthroughs does vary across disciplines. For instance, the peak age for creative achievement in mathematics, physics, and lyric poetry occurs in the late twenties and early thirties, while the peak age in philosophy and for writing fiction is the late forties and early fifties (Simonton, 1988). Remember, though, that these ages are group statistics or averages and vary by individual.

One of the most unusual examples of how excellence is not tied to age is the American architect Frank Lloyd Wright. By the time Wright

TABLE 7.1 **THE TEN-YEAR RULE AT WORK**

	Origin	10 Years	20 Years	30 Years and Beyond
Freud	Charcot's hysteria research	"Project"* *The Interpretation of Dreams***	*Three Contributions to the Theory of Sex*	Social works
Einstein	Light-beam thought experiment	Special theory of relativity*	General theory of relativity**	Philosophical works
Picasso	Barcelona circle	*Les demoiselles d'Avignon** Cubism	Neoclassical style	*Guernica***
Stravinsky	Rimsky-Korsakov influenced works	*Le sacre du printemps**	*Les Noces***	Later styles
Eliot	"Prufrock" Juvenilia	*The Waste Land**	*Four Quartets***	Playwright/critic
Graham	St. Denis troupe	First recital	*Frontier**	*Appalachian Spring*** Neoclassical style
Gandhi	Anti-Indian laws in Natal	South Africa Satyagraha	Ahmedabad*	Salt march**

Source: From Howard Gardner, *Creating Minds* (New York: Basic Books, 1993), table 10.1, p. 371. Copyright 1993 Basic Books. Reprinted by permission of Basic Books, a division of Perseus Books Group.
*Radical breakthrough
**Comprehensive work

was in his fifties, he was world famous and had already firmly established himself as one of the most creative architects of the twentieth century. At this point in his life, however, he was revered more as an historic figure than as a relevant force in architecture (Norwich, 1979). In spite of this assumed irrelevance by his colleagues, Wright surprised everyone by renewing his creativity and his career at the age of 69 with the completion of one of his masterpieces—the private home known as Fallingwater. From that point on, Wright designed some of his most memorable buildings. In fact, after the age of 80, Wright was busier than he had ever been in his professional life. This period of creativity culminated in another of his masterpieces, the Guggenheim Museum in New York City, which was completed only a few months after Wright's death at the age of 92.

Resonance

Another perspective on excellence comes from the work of Doug Newberg and colleagues (Newberg, Kimiecik, Durand-Bush, & Doell, 2002). They created the concept of the **resonance performance model,** which they use to describe the cyclical process that guides the development of excellence in many different areas of expertise. They found that "performance excellence was the byproduct of living . . . life in such a way that [people are] fully engaged in what they do" (p. 251). However, in an interesting twist to other perspectives on excellence, their model assumes that excellence is grounded in a desire to experience specific emotions. The emotions are those associated with how people feel when fully engaged in their preferred activity. Therefore, in the resonance model, people who achieve excellence "consciously identify unique feelings they want to experience in their daily pursuits and place themselves in situations and environments that elicit these feelings" (p.257).

The resonance performance model (RPM) Newberg et al. created is a four-stage model that begins with what they call (1) "the dream," or the feelings a person seeks when engaged in an activity. Note this is not a goal for the future, but a sense of what the person wishes to feel like in the present. Next, the person must be involved in intense (2) "preparation." This stage involves intense practice, but it is *engaged practice* rather than drudgery. Inevitably, a person encounters (3) "obstacles." In the RPM, however, when obstacles are encountered, one does not simply try harder. That is, a person does not necessarily believe that "when the going gets tough, the tough get going." Instead, she or he (4) "revisits their dream," or reconnects with the feelings that give spark their dream. This reconnection with original feelings allows a person to embrace the obstacles, to avoid the trap of trying harder and enjoying it less, and to move forward with the development of skills. This model, although quite new, has shown promise as a method to help people achieve excellence in a number of areas.

Aesthetics and the Good Life

Why is a discussion of aesthetics important to a book on positive psychology? Perhaps the relevance is easiest to understand if you try a little thought experiment. Imagine that you lived in a world where all the buildings were simple gray, concrete-block structures; all the clothes were the same, gray in color with no ornamentation; and nowhere in the society was any attempt made to beautify the environment or the people in it. Would you enjoy living in such a world? Most people would find that it lacked an important quality—beauty—that enhances our experience of being human. Actually, some people do live in this "world"—it is the prison environment. In fact, in the world of prison, the lack of aesthetics is part of the punishment. So, at first a discussion of aesthetics may seem a bit out of place in a book on well-being, but a moment's reflection shows that it is quite consistent with the other topics presented. One may still be wondering why a discussion of aesthetics appears in a chapter on excellence and creativity. First, there is an obvious relationship between aesthetics and creativity. Second, one way to think about the aesthetic sense is that it is the appreciation of excellence.

Why Is the Aesthetic Sense Important to Well-Being?

Even a casual study of history shows that people have applied their artistic sense since before recorded history. We know that societies have always had some forms of artistic expression. The compelling and beautiful cave paintings at Lascaux and Vallon-Pont-d'Arc, France, are 12,000 to 20,000 years old and are but one example of artistic expressions that most likely included music, dance, and story as well. Even nomadic peoples, who own relatively little property, use beadwork on leather or cloth, paintings on pottery, as well as feathers, bones, or beautiful stones to enhance the aesthetic value of their everyday property. This adornment may not be done for extrinsic reasons, such as increasing the value of the object to others, but rather simply to make everyday objects more beautiful to the owner. Looking at the object increases a sense of well-being—even if only momentarily. This particular impulse toward the aesthetic is one that does not disappear as cultures advance in complexity or technological sophistication. In fact, as societies become more advanced, people's desire to bring aesthetics into their lives only increases. Witness today's world, where a large percentage of disposable income is spent on jewelry, the latest fashions, new furniture, new cars, or new "dream" homes, all intended to bring their owners a greater sense of beauty. Although some objects are acquired simply for the social status they bring, many more are obtained for the aesthetic pleasure they give.

In short, the desire to stimulate the aesthetic sense has been around since the beginnings of humanity. But what purpose does it serve? From the psychological point of view, it can serve many purposes. Chapter 4 discussed the pursuit of leisure in its importance to well-being. One type of place that people often like to visit for leisure or vacations are natural areas, such as national parks or beaches. When asked what is important about these areas, people often reply, "the scenery." In other words, they go to appreciate the beauty of the natural world. In fact, research studies have found that landscapes that are both mysterious and yet somewhat easy to understand reliably arouse people's interest (see Franklin & Kaplan, 1994).

Artwork, photographs, drawings, and other objects that people place in their homes also serve to remind us of places we have been or things and people that we love. Often, these objects serve as stimuli for positive emotions either by helping us recall pleasant memories and experiences or by taking us away, even for a moment, from the day-to-day concerns that can consume our emotional lives if we are not careful. A sense of aesthetics can also help us learn about the world around us. Interesting objects, curious patterns, and unexpected color combinations can stimulate our sense of curiosity. Such objects in our world help keep us interested in life and provide variety and new stimulation. Even children only a few weeks old show preferences for objects that are interesting and stand out from the rest of their environment. Art can also be used to express emotions, intuitions, and meanings that people feel but find it hard to express in words. Even poetry is the art of using words to express a meaning that is beyond the words themselves. Finally, a desire for aesthetic experiences seems to be growing in our society. Attendance at museums, the theater, music events, and dance has grown significantly in the past decades.

Art as a Doorway to Personal Growth

Another use of aesthetics—although a less common one—is to see art as a pathway toward greater personal growth. According to this approach, art should challenge people to view the world, others, and themselves in new ways and stimulate people to think and feel differently. This view that art should point the way toward a new vision of the future was the rallying cry of the *avant-garde* movement that began in the nineteenth century. Artists of the avant-garde deliberately set out to shake up the bourgeoisie, whom they saw as rigid, afraid of emotions, and stifled by a social system that demanded conformity rather than creativity (Hughes, 1980). While this is the extreme position, art can be used to shake up our complacent sense of who we are.

An example of this use of aesthetics comes across in a story in which the author described his young niece and her first experience of Beethoven's Ninth Symphony. The young woman was simply overwhelmed by the music. She had never heard music like it before. She was speechless as she left the concert hall. Her first words to her uncle were a stammering question, "What do I do now? Now that I know such music exists." Her reaction indicated a person whose view of the world had just been shattered. She had no idea that she could experience so many new and intense emotions as a result of music. Dramatically, the old boundaries of her experiential world had been proved limited, or even wrong. She knew she must adjust to the shock and discover how to react to the newer, expanded vision of life's possibilities. Her confusion called for creative adaptation in terms of developing new beliefs about the boundaries of her life.

The famous American philosopher and psychologist John Dewey (1934) proposed a similar function for art in his book *Art as Experience*. He believed that an appreciation of art builds on "[experience] which intensifies the sense of immediate living" (quoted in Sarason, 1990, p. 86). According to Dewey, a sense of the aesthetic is necessary for well-being because it creates a heightened vitality that is restorative. In other words, the aesthetic sense helps us to transcend the mundane and overly familiar by intensifying our relationship with our immediate experience. A sense of the aesthetic heightens our awareness, energizes our appreciation of the human experience, and allows a more complete "interpenetrating of self and the world of objects and events" (Sarason, 1990, p. 86). In Dewey's perspective, art and a sense of the aesthetic must not be separated from our everyday lives. The aesthetic sense should not be confined simply to those experiences that are deemed works of art.

Seymour Sarason (1990) agrees and proposes that the need for artistic expression or appreciation is universal. He also says that artistic expression is often suppressed in childhood as children get the message that "art" is something to be judged, that only "creative" people can do it correctly, and that one pursues art for external recognition or gain rather than for internal satisfaction. Sarason believes that in adults this suppressed need for artistic expression creates a "festering source of dissatisfaction in quotidian living" (p. 5). In other words, the fallout to the suppression of the aesthetic need is a sense that life is boring and uninteresting. Ken and Mary Gergen (2001) reported on successful programs designed to help older persons rekindle "the expressive, playful, and innovative impulses so characteristic of child development, but so often obscured or suppressed during 'maturity'" (p. 2). The good news is that the creative magic is not lost forever.

A powerful example of how art may have an impact on us occurs when art pushes our personal boundaries of what is "acceptable" art. One of the most famous examples of unwelcome changes in aesthetics comes from the first performance of Stravinsky's *Le Sacre du printemps* ("The Rite of Spring") in Paris in 1913. The audience at that premier was so outraged that they revolted! Stravinsky had composed a piece of music that was so counter to the audience's acceptable sense of the aesthetic that the normally conservative Parisian society simply exploded in a unanimous outburst of anger and outrage. The following passage describes the most famous premiere in the history of Western music (adapted from Brockway & Weinstock, 1958):

> The first performance of *Le Sacre du printemps,* at the Theatre Des Champs-Elysées, on May 29, 1913, was a scandal unmatched in the annals of music. . . . The *Great Sacred Dance* [movement] . . . is the high-water mark beyond which the brutal modern [musical] technique has not gone, possibly cannot go. Its constantly changing rhythms thudded out in screaming, searing discords engender a physical agitation in the listener that is closely akin to sexual excitation, acting chiefly on atavistic, deeply veneered strata of being. . . . Jean Cocteau, the star reporter of *Smart Paris,* so describes it: "The audience behaved as it ought to; it revolted straight away. People laughed, booed, hissed, imitated animal noises . . . and a handful of musicians, carried away by their excessive zeal, insulted and even roughly handled the public in the loges. The uproar degenerated into a free fight.
>
> Standing up in her loge, her tiara awry, the old Comptesse de Pourtales flourished her fan and shouted, scarlet in the face, 'It's the first time in sixty years that anyone's dared to make a fool of me.' The good lady was sincere; she thought there was some mystification."
>
> The cause of this disturbance was the most beautiful, the most profoundly conceived, and most exhilarating piece of music thus far composed in the twentieth century (pp. 599–601).

Although this example is somewhat comical, it serves to remind us that artistic expression can have a profound impact on our sense of identity and emotional security. Again, this can be either as a stimulus that reminds us of our joy and our strengths or as a one that pushes us to look at the unexamined boundaries we have created for our lives.

Art as an Aid to Healing and a Boost to Intelligence

Compare the example given in the preceding discussion to some new research on music. Recently, the New York Academy of Sciences published a collection of research papers on music, entitled *Biological Foundations of Music* (Zatorre & Peretz, 2001). These papers, as well as others, indicate that music can help patients heal faster after surgery, can help cancer patients with the healing process, can help Alzheimer's patients remember events from their past, can help people cope better with severe pain, can boost our immune systems, and can even help children raise test scores. Some evidence finds that music can actually lead to increases in brain size. Gottfried Schlaug and his colleagues (Schlaug et al. 1995; Schlaug, 2001) compared brain scans of thirty nonmusicians and thirty musicians and found that the corpus collosums of musicians were measurably larger. (The corpus collosum is the thick bundle of neurons that connects the right and left hemispheres of the brain.) For musicians who began playing a musical instrument at an early age, the difference was even greater. Recent findings indicate that while listening to music can be beneficial, many of the real benefits come from playing music. Studies have found that 3- and 4-year-old children who learned how to play the piano scored 34 percent higher on tests of abstract reasoning skills than children who were taught computer skills. Other studies found that children with attention deficit hyperactivity disorder learn to concentrate better and control their aggression better after playing games based on musical rhythms (see Zatorre & Peretz, 2001). It turns out that music really can heal.

Finding Beauty Outside the Arts

An appreciation of beauty need not be confined to traditionally recognized forms of art. A person can appreciate beauty in many other forms. The "beauty" of a special theory or a unique equation or the immensity of the universe moves even scientists. Some scientists have even said that a scientific theory should be judged partially on its "elegance." Susan Fitzpatrick (2001) recalls how she entered science because she was moved by "the elegant, spare functionality of the Kreb's Cycle." She advises her fellow scientists to tell their students about "the moment you recognized beauty in the work of another scientist and fell in love" (p. 4).

Fitzpatrick (2001) also tells a story about beauty, but this time it is in the context of sports competition. She writes about an event at the world's most demanding bicycle race, the Tour de France.

> One image I see over and over is the moment in the race when [Lance] Armstrong decided the time had come for him to put his definitive mark on the grueling 21-day event, ending all speculation about the eventual outcome. A French rider, Laurent Roux, out in front, all alone, was leading the day's stage for more than 60 miles when, during a mountain climb, Armstrong blew by him. Literally. There is no other way to describe it. In the post race interview Roux was quoted as saying, "When he passed me, I had the impression that it was a motorcycle at my side. It was beautiful to see." It was beautiful to see? Can you imagine that you have been riding as hard as you can, drawing on every fiber of your mind's and body's strength, will, and determination to power yourself up a long climb? Can you imagine that you are a Frenchman within sight of claiming victory of one of the most demanding stages of your country's most famous athletic event when some kid from Texas passes you like you are standing still? It was beautiful to see. That's how Laurent Roux described it. That's one of the images I cannot get out of my mind. These athletes ride for glory, and for fame, and because cycling is how they support a very comfortable lifestyle—but they could not achieve the

> sheer monumentalism of what they do unless there was something more. They ride for the sheer beauty of the sport (p. 4).*

Anyone who has been involved with high-level athletic competition will tell you that one of the appeals of athletics is that at certain times during a competition, the grace, precision, or even the audacity of the athletes is "beautiful."

Origins of the Aesthetic Sense

Where does the sense of aesthetics come from? Some researchers have proposed that being interested in and intrigued by landscapes may have had evolutionary significance (see Franklin & Kaplan, 1994). In this view, as humans evolved, such curiosity would be advantageous because it encouraged early humans to explore their environment. That helped them seek out new information and extend cognitive maps of their environment. The more they knew about their world, the better able they would be to adapt to it. Another evolutionary theory of aesthetics comes from a totally different source. Swiss psychologist Carl G. Jung suggested that our emotional responses to certain forms and images might be the result of innate response patterns from what he called a "collective unconscious" (discussed in a later chapter).

Although there may be some element of evolution in the aesthetic sense, it is also quite true that many judgments of what is beautiful are learned from our respective cultures and the periods of history in which we live. A need for artistic expression may be innate, but the psychological significance is the singular feature of aesthetics, and this is most often learned. For example, many people in Western societies find the traditional singing style of India to be odd and not particularly pleasing. This is primarily because the Indian system of music uses quarter tones while Western music uses a half-tone scale. In Indian music, for instance, there is a note that exists between "B" and "C," whereas in Western music there is no note between those two. Therefore, to most Westerners, Indian music sounds strange, off-key, and makes the listener slightly uncomfortable. Similarly, *Noh*, the highly stylized form of Japanese drama, is completely incomprehensible for most Westerners even though the aesthetic of Japanese gardens is very accessible. Nevertheless, a new appreciation of any art can be gained by anyone who takes the time. That is, we can also learn to appreciate new aesthetic experiences that we initially find quite unappealing.

Can Tragedy and Sadness Be Beautiful?

This discussion of aesthetics and positive psychology brings up an interesting question about the role of tragedy in art. Why is it that people are drawn to plays, books, poetry, movies, and other art forms that portray tragic stories? For instance, Shakespeare's tragic play, *Romeo and Juliet,* is one of his most popular in spite of the fact that both lovers die unnecessarily at the end of the play. A recent example of the power of tragedy is the movie *Titanic.* In the latest film version, Leonardo DiCaprio and Kate Winslet portray two people who fall madly in love only to be separated by the death of DiCaprio's character as the ship sinks into the Atlantic. In spite of this tragic ending, the film grossed hundreds of millions of dollars, and some fans returned to see the movie over twenty times. After each viewing, these fans left the movie theater with tears in their eyes, having wept as the lovers were separated forever by fate. So, we return to the original question. Why would people voluntarily engage themselves with an artistic creation that they know will make them feel negative emotions? The research on this question is sparse, but some cautious speculations can be made.

* From Susan M. Fitzpatrick, "Commentary," *The Scientist* (October 1, 2001), p. 4. Reprinted by permission of The Scientist.

People know that tragic events are part of life; they know that in order to deal with this aspect of being human they must confront the sadness in some way. Through the medium of art, people can experience tragedy and gain at least three benefits. First, the sense of empathy for the characters in the creation reminds us of our shared humanity and may even serve to increase qualities such as compassion and charity. Second, this new sense of compassion can also build a resolve not to allow such tragedies to occur if we can do something about it. Tragedy can serve to build a dedication to help stop future tragedy in the real world. Third, experiencing life's sad and tragic moments in a work of art can allow us to feel certain emotions without having to live through the actual experience itself. After all, people *do not* want to *really* lose their lovers in tragic deaths—they just want to experience a sympathetic and empathic reaction to fictional others who have gone through such a tragedy. Paradoxically then, the power of tragedy is that we can feel real negative emotions that under the right circumstances can lead us to experience emotions of compassion, hope, relief, empathy, or courageous resolve. As a blues musician put it once, "There's nothing like the blues to make you feel good."

Creativity

One of the more interesting ways that people pursue well-being is through creativity. Using creativity as a vehicle through which one derives pleasure, satisfaction, and a sense of well-being is quite common. Every day, people around the world are engaged in hobbies, crafts, and amateur performances in the arts. In a more general sense, creativity is responsible for practically all of the major advances that humans have made over the centuries. We literally would not have emerged from the caves or the savannas without it! What is unusual in terms of history is the use of creativity as the *major* road that a person can travel on his or her journey toward enhanced well-being. Indeed, for some people, creativity and the actualization of creative potential is the primary goal in life and can even supersede most other goals. However, the fact that our culture allows some people to be professional artists and expects this type of dedication to the arts from them is a social role that is really quite new. It is only within the last three hundred years that the social role of "artist" has been created in contemporary society.

What Is Creativity?

Just what do we mean by the elusive term *creativity?* The quest for a simple definition has baffled psychologists. Creativity is one of those qualities that is enormously difficult to pin down. One criterion is that it seems to be a process that produces novel responses that contribute to the solution of problems (Simonton, 2000). Another perspective says that, in general, other people must deem those contributions novel. According to this criterion, if an artist is the only one who sees her latest painting as inventive, inspiring, and original, then it is not really creative. In all honesty, however, given the fact that a number of creative breakthroughs were not recognized as such when they were produced, this restriction needs to be qualified. John Nicholls (1972) also adds that the solution must be original and "make a meaningful contribution to culture." From his point of view, if we find a novel and unique solution to the problem of how to dust our apartment, it may be considered clever but it may not be true creativity. Part of the problem is that there is a very wide range of behaviors that fall under the label of creativity. When people speak of someone being creative, they can mean anything from an unexpected and unusual use of mulch in a vegetable garden, to a clever new ad campaign for diapers or a breakthrough in fiction that transforms the way the world looks at literature. Therefore, two basic types of creativity need to be specified.

Basic Types of Creativity

Psychologists distinguish two types of creativity. The first, termed primary or **process creativity,** refers to a personal and somewhat more psychological type of creativity. It is associated with increased openness to experiences, a willingness to accept and even relish change, the ability to improvise and adapt quickly to situations, and a greater than average ability to think in unexpected directions. Secondary or **product creativity** is what most people think of when they use the term *creativity.* It is the process of finding highly original and inventive solutions to problems. Most of the psychological research on creativity has focused on product creativity. In fact, most of the tests that psychology commonly uses to measure creativity involve generating solutions or artistic products of some type. Another distinction is made between *small-C* and *big-C creativity* (Simonton, 2002). Small-C creativity enhances life with superior problem-solving skills. Big-C creativity is the kind associated with genius—the type that makes lasting contributions to a field of study or a culture. Small-C and big-C creativity may represent degrees of creativity that fall along the same continuum (Simonton, 2002).

Frank Barron (1988) has called into question the sharp distinction between product and process creativity. He suggests that the relationship between persons and products or problems is more akin to an "open system" where the two are "mutually interdependent" on each other. It is the relationship between persons and products or problems that ignites creativity. Twila Tardif and Robert Sternberg (1988) also note that one quality of creative people is "what seems almost to be an aesthetic ability that allows such individuals to recognize 'good' problems in their field and apply themselves to these problems while ignoring others" (p. 435). Creative people seem to sense where the "fit" will be between their talents and the problems that are just waiting for a creative solution.

The Measurement of Creativity

As mentioned, creativity is a fairly slippery concept to grasp. As a result, it has also been a difficult subject for researchers to measure. Measurement scales usually rely on interval measurement where one indicator is higher or lower than another indicator—if we score "8" on a happiness test and our friend scores "6," then we are "happier" than they are. But how does one measure creativity on a 10-point scale? In fact, most psychologists do not try to be that precise. Rather, they measure relative degrees of creativity. For instance, Todd Lubart and Robert Sternberg (1995) asked forty-eight adults to tap into their creativity and gave them tasks such as making a drawing that depicted "hope" or designing a television ad for the Internal Revenue Service. The participants' work was rated by several people for such qualities as novelty, overall creativity, and perceived effort. The raters were not very interested in whether one person's drawing of hope was a "6" or an "8" on a 10-point scale. Instead, they were interested in a more global assessment of whether the drawing was "creative" or not. In this study, as in a number of others, the first finding was that there was considerable agreement among the raters in terms of which solutions were creative and which were not. The study found that, in general, many people can recognize creativity when they see it.

The next interesting finding that emerged from the Lubart and Sternberg study was that creativity in one domain, such as art, was only moderately associated with creativity in a different domain, such as writing. In many ways, this is not surprising, given what we know about excellence. As mentioned, excellence and expertise seem to be confined to a single domain for most people. The same is to be true for creativity. For instance, Andy Warhol transformed twentieth century art with the invention of pop art. He was also very involved in creating films. Although Warhol's films are interesting experiments, they did not transform the world of filmmaking the way his paintings changed the world of art. Similar examples of how excellence in one area does not translate into excellence in another can be cited for numerous artists. The one caveat to this general rule is that certain crossovers are possible within related artistic disciplines. For instance, it is fairly common for artists to be creative at both painting and sculpture because the mediums are closely related. Note that researchers do not say that the very nature of creativity is different for different domains or different problems. There are a few commonalties in creativity that seem to transcend the medium, the problem, and the situation (Tardif & Sternberg, 1988).

Another difficulty with the psychological study of creativity is that each discipline of psychology tends to study it from its own perspective. In this way, social and personality psychologists study the personality traits associated with creativity, cognitive psychologists look at cognitive processes, and some others focus on motivational theories. Situations like this are analogous to the parable of five blind men each trying to describe an elephant only by the sensation of touch. The first man, holding the trunk, says that elephants are long and round and like a snake. The second man, holding a leg, says that elephants are round but thick and have toes like a horse. The third man, holding the ears, says that elephants are wide and flat and have wings like a huge bird, and so on. Each man explains the "reality" of an elephant only from his particular perspective. In a similar manner, J. P. Guilford (1950) explained creativity as a cognitive function that is composed of multiple factors. Therefore, some researchers have tried to group the various approaches to creativity knowing that each approach represents only one piece of the entire pie. The **confluence approach** to creativity assumes that multiple factors need to be in place in order for real creativity to occur. The confluence model proposed by Lubart and Sternberg (1995) states that six resources need to work together in creativity: intellectual abilities, knowledge, personality traits, a motivational style, thinking styles, and an environment that is supportive of the creative process and creative output. Tardif and Sternberg (1988) summarize all the research and group creativity studies into four general areas: the creative person, the creative process, creative products, and creative environments.

The Creative Person

First, most of the characteristics of creative people overlap with the characteristics of people who achieve excellence. However, this relationship seems to be a one-way street, because not all people who achieve excellence are highly creative. Creative people are intensely interested in their field and willing to work hard and work for a long time (recall the ten-year rule). Creativity generally takes time. People work to find solutions and must often wait for insights and practical solutions to problems.

For many people, the first hypothesis about the origins of creativity involves intelligence (see the confluence approach discussed earlier). The hypothesis is that if highly creative people are better at problem solving, then they should be more intelligent. This hypothesis seems logical, but the data do not support it completely. Studies have found that the correlations between tests of creativity and scores on standard IQ tests are usually between .10 and .30, or in the modest range (Barron & Harrington, 1981). Research studies have generally concluded that having an average to moderately high IQ is often associated with creativity and may even be beneficial to it, but it is not necessary in order to be creative. Again, these conclusions should sound familiar given the earlier discussion of excellence.

The next factor that is part of the confluence approach is a firm and thorough *knowledge of one's area of expertise or one's artistic medium.* Creative people seem to be experts in their field as well as creative within it. This makes quite a bit of sense if one ponders the definition of creativity. That is, if a truly creative product is novel, original, and "breaks new ground," then one must know what the "old" ground was like in order to do something new that differs from it. While this factor for creativity may be significant in most cases, examples do exist where it does not seem to apply.

In the art world these days, there is considerable interest in what is called folk art—art that has been created by people who have no formal training in, or often even knowledge of, the elements of art such as design, color, and composition. For instance, in Nashville, an African American man named William Edmonson created stone sculptures without having any formal training in art, principles of design, or theories of composition. Yet, he created objects that seem to capture the essence of his subjects in powerful and moving ways. He carved his works in relative obscurity, often as tombstone ornaments for friends, until a Nashville artist who had friends in New York saw his work. In 1937, Edmonson was the first African American to have a one-person show at New York's Museum of Modern Art. In 2000–2001, a major retrospective of his works traveled around the United States to rave reviews from the critics. Occasionally, a firm knowledge base is not a requirement—although this exception may be more common in the visual arts than in other disciplines.

One area of research that has found a somewhat dizzying array of associations with creativity is the search for the personality characteristics of creative people (Tardif & Sternberg, 1988). In some ways, highly creative people are different than other people, and those differences enhance their ability to find the novel, the unique, and the unexpected. Yet, Tardif and Sternberg (1988) note that no single personality trait has overwhelmingly emerged from studies as the key to creativity.

Creative people do tend to share a number of traits that could be classified as *openness to experience* (Tardif & Sternberg, 1988; Sternberg, 2000). Greater openness implies a person who is more willing to consider the unusual, the unexpected, the out of the ordinary, and the unconventional. Therefore, creative people tend to *be highly flexible in their thinking* and quite *tolerant for ambiguity* or even outright disorder. In fact, they may even have a preference for complexity. They often delight in looking for the simplicity that lies beneath apparent complex, difficult, and even chaotic problems. As a result, they may also have a *higher tolerance for frustration* because these more complex problems can lead to more dead ends and more exasperating failures than problems with a more simple structure to them.

Studies have also found that highly creative people tend to be very *independent.* This can manifest itself in being able to resist social pressures to behave and think in conventional ways. Of course, many young aspiring artists seem to only mimic this unconventionality and in so doing may paradoxically be quite conforming to the conventional stereotype of "artist." Truly creative people do more than just resist social pressures so they can be different. They may resist convention because it is stifling to the creativity they need for their work. They also may prefer to work alone so they can take their own path toward their own solutions. Because of this, many creative people see themselves as loners. Highly creative people also seem *willing to restructure problems* or play with ideas, concepts, and solutions. More than many other people, they are willing to restructure a problem, an idea, a form, or a pattern. Many researchers also agree that creativity involves tension and conflict. Creativity involves a struggle to resolve seemingly incompatible questions. Creativity also is associated with being *intrinsically motivated.* Creative persons love the activity that they use to stimulate their creative impulses. Often, they seem to have a passion for their area. Working on a creative endeavor may actually seem to give them more energy rather than deplete energy. Gardner (1993) found that creative people are often productive in some way every day.

Other personality characteristics that have been associated with creativity include receptivity, sensitivity to problems, fluency in thinking, and a willingness to take risks (Arieti, 1976; Sternberg, 1999). Therisa Amabile (1983) summarized many of these qualities into three major characteristics of creative persons. First, they are experts in the chosen field or artistic medium. Second, they possess and utilize the cognitive skills and personality characteristics that have been mentioned earlier. Third, they are intrinsically motivated.

The Creative Process

One of the most common characteristics associated with creativity concerns thinking styles. The first idea about how thinking style is related to creativity came from Freud (1901/1960). He believed that creativity was associated with *primary process thinking,* or the type of thinking engaged in by the id process in the unconscious. Primary process thinking is illogical, emotional, and symbolic. Freud's idea lead to the notion that creativity is related to one's ability to tap into unconscious processes. Jung also believed that creativity comes from unconscious processes but at a deeper level of the unconscious that is central to creativity, invention, and spontaneity. Later psychodynamically oriented theorists proposed that creativity was not based on unconscious processing but on preconscious thinking (Kris, 1952; Kubie, 1958). One of the more influential of these perspectives is that of Ernst Kris (1952), who said that creativity resulted from a specific cognitive process that he called **regression in service of the ego.** This is the ability to temporarily submerge the rational and control functions of the ego and tap into cognitive processes that were more allegorical, symbolic, and holistic.

The Four Stages of the Creative Process

The idea that creativity is somehow connected with unconscious or preconscious processes is also related to the famous four-stage theory of creativity proposed by Joseph Wallas (1926). In this theory, the first stage is *preparation,* or the time when information is gathered, initial attempts to solve a problem are attempted, a variety of ideas are tossed around, and, in general, the stage is set for a creative solution. If a solution is not found, then the second or *incubation* stage begins. In this stage, attempts to find a creative solution are handled at an "unconscious" level of processing. This stage can last hours or years. Numerous stories about how creative breakthroughs were reached will include this stage of latency and an apparent—though not actual—abandonment of the problem. Recent research suggests that while a period of incubation is often associated with a new solution, it is normal cognitive processes that are operating beneath the surface and not the primary process thinking of the id (Trotter, 1986).

The third stage, *illumination,* is initiated when a creative solution emerges often rapidly and unexpectedly as an insight, for example, when a person emerging from a dream has the answer to a difficult question. The insight may be stimulated by everyday occurrences. The following excerpt from an interview with Paul McCartney, who with the late John Lennon was part of the most successful song-writing team in history, will serve to illustrate the mysterious quality of illumination that creativity has for many artists,

> *Interviewer:* You've said that [the song] "Yesterday" emerged fully formed from a dream. What is your personal understanding of inspiration?
>
> *McCartney:* I don't understand it at all. I think life is quite mysterious and quite miraculous. . . . Every time I come to write a song, there's this magic . . . and I just sit down at the piano and . . .

> suddenly there's a song there . . . it's a faith thing . . . with creativity, I just have faith. . . . It's a great spiritual belief that there's something really magical there. And that was what helped me write "Yesterday." Something to do with me, something to do with my love of music, and my faith in the process. But I don't quite know what it is and I don't want to know ("Getting better all the time," pp. 85–87).

The American photographer Ansel Adams referred to these first three stages of the creative process when he described creativity as, "Chance favoring the prepared mind."

Many researchers on creativity also recognize that what is commonly known as insight can be an important part of the creative process. What may be surprising to many people is that while most researchers who study creativity recognize that insight plays a role in creativity, they also assign it a somewhat small role in the overall creative process. As mentioned, many researchers who study creativity and excellence also believe that insight is not a special unconscious process but rather the use of rather ordinary cognitive skills at a preconscious level. Similarly, renowned choreographer Twyla Tharp (2003) believes that creativity is found primarily through discipline and hard work rather than insight.

The last stage in this theory of the creative process is *verification*. In this stage, the creative breakthrough must be worked into its final form. Often, this involves working on how to turn the illumination and insight into a real-world solution that can be applied practically.

Thinking Styles and Creativity

The most common thinking styles mentioned in the research literature on creativity are convergent and divergent thinking (Guilford, 1950). **Convergent thinking** is the process we use when various problem-solving strategies converge on a single, correct answer to a problem. Tests of convergent thinking often are scored by counting the number of correct answers. In contrast to this, **divergent thinking** is the ability to think in many different ways, using a number of strategies that, at least initially, may or may not show any direct relevance to the solution. It is the ability to produce many different solutions to the same problem. Tests of divergent thinking are usually scored by counting the number of different but plausible solutions that have been generated. For instance, a divergent thinking test might ask someone to generate as many uses as possible for a burned-out light bulb.

At first glance, divergent thinking seems to be more related to creativity than convergent thinking. Unfortunately, neither style is highly correlated with creativity (Barron & Harrington, 1981). Actually, both may be necessary—divergent to generate ideas and convergent to take those ideas and hone in on a solution (Rathunde, 2000). Research has shown that attempts such as this one to find a single style of thinking that is associated with creativity have been overly simplistic (Sternberg, 1999).

Finally, the research on right- and left-brain thinking styles must be mentioned. In the 1980s, there was a popular theory that logical and rational thinking was produced in the left hemisphere of the brain while creative, holistic, and generally artistic styles were products associated with the right hemisphere. A number of popular books and workshops were offered to the public to teach people how to "use right-brained thinking." Researchers at first completely dismissed this idea, but there actually is some support for the distinction between cognitive processes utilized by the left and right hemispheres. This research, in fact, has found that there *is* a small advantage of the left hemisphere for logical thought and the right hemisphere for symbolic thinking (at least in right-handed people). The overall conclusion, however, is that both hemispheres are involved in both styles of thinking. The difference is the relative emphasis shown in each hemisphere (Trope, Rozin, Nelson, & Gur, 1992).

Creative Environments

Creativity is also associated with supportive environments, which can range from family environments to social or even historical environments. The families of creative people seem to share a few common characteristics. Often the childhoods of creative people were not the happiest or the most stable. Many highly creative people seem to have come from turbulent childhoods in which they received comparatively little emotional comfort. Interestingly, these families strongly encouraged their children to achieve and also provided many opportunities and resources for learning and new experiences. Speaking of families, one of the factors that does *not* seem to be important to creativity is heredity. Twin studies that looked at identical twins who were raised apart have found that correlations between the twins' creativity scores are lower than the correlations between the twins' IQ scores (Nicholls, 1972).

Sometimes a unique group of people together can create a special synergy that allows for greater creativity. Again, the Beatles are an instructive example. They are universally seen as four of the most creative innovators in the history of popular music. However, after the breakup of the group, the individual members never quite created the magic that they had had as a group. Their producer, George Martin said, "It is absolutely true that the sum of the four of them was much, much greater than the sum of the individual parts" (Hertsgaard, 1995, p. 135). John Lennon commented on the group of which he was a part: "Beatlemania is when we all get together. The Beatles go into the studio and IT [i.e., creativity] happens" (Herstgaard, 1995, p. 135). Work environments that encourage exploration and diversity of thinking can also foster creativity. Certain places seem to foster creative magic more than others do. Places that come to mind immediately are Paris in the 1920s and 1930s and New York City in the 1950s and 1960s. Creative people who may see themselves as loners will also tend to congregate in areas where they can mingle with other artists and get their creative "juices" flowing.

TABLE 7.2 COMPARISONS BETWEEN EXCELLENCE AND CREATIVITY

Excellence	Creativity
Large Knowledge Base	Large Knowledge Base
Commitment	Commitment
Practice: Consistent	Practice: Consistent
Deliberate	Deliberate
Ten-year Rule	Ten-year Rule
	Openness to experience
	Flexible in thinking
	Tolerance for ambiguity
	Tolerance for frustration
	Independent
	Intrinsically motivated
	Willing to restructure problems

Source: K. Ericsson & N. Charness (1994), Simonton (2000), & R. Sternberg (1988)

Some historical periods of time have seen surges of creativity, such as the Renaissance—especially in Italy, particularly in Florence—and the end of the nineteenth century in America. The last decades of the nineteenth century and the first decades of the twentieth century in the United States saw an astounding number of inventions. Someone who lived during the fifty years between 1875 and 1925 saw inventions such as the automobile, the airplane, the telephone, and the phonograph. The number of patents filed at the United States patent office hit an all-time high during this period. This all suggests that creativity in some ways is not a totally individual product. In fact, Csikszentmihalyi (1988) proposed that in order for creativity to be nurtured and really flower, a special synergy of person, environment, culture, and the historical time needs to take place. Table 7.2

compares factors related to both excellence and creativity.

Genius

Before leaving the topic of creativity, a few words should be mentioned on the concept of *genius*. It is an often-stated myth that the word "genius" was invented during the Renaissance to describe Leonardo Da Vinci. Although Da Vinci certainly deserves to be called a genius, the term actually comes to us from the ancient Greek, who used the word to describe a creative spirit. During the Renaissance (probably, in part, because of people like Da Vinci), it began to take on the meaning of some special talent or ability that goes beyond the normal range. Since that time, it has taken on its current meaning of *someone who shows extraordinary levels of creativity and inventiveness.*

Gardner's (1993) study of genius investigated such luminaries as Freud, Picasso, and Einstein. He found that these well-known geniuses were quite similar to and also somewhat different from others who were also very creative. First, those who we have labeled "genius" showed the same qualities associated with people who achieve excellence in their fields. They are extremely dedicated and committed to their area of expertise, they are extremely motivated, they are willing to work long and hard, and they are absorbed in a search for more knowledge about their craft. Second, they were different in that while they were often loners, they were so intensely involved in their work that they appeared self-absorbed. Third, in contrast to those who were creative (but not geniuses), the geniuses tended to exhibit extremely high levels of self-confidence that bordered on arrogance. Freud's stubborn confidence in the correctness of his theories, for instance, was the primary reason for the difficult splits with both Adler and Jung. Fourth, Gardner found that many geniuses would probably not be very good friends. Often they made friends only when they needed support, but they could abandon those friendships easily, quickly, and sometimes heartlessly if they felt they needed to. For instance, Picasso's relationships with other people—especially women—were once described as "ruthless." Similarly, Frank Lloyd Wright was famous for his egotism and could occasionally seem cruel in his personal relationships. In spite of this, creative geniuses all tended to find one person—often prior to a big breakthrough—who served as a mentor. Even this very important person in their lives, however, could also be abandoned quickly. Finally, Gardner believed that many creative geniuses had made what he called a "Faustian bargain" in order to be creative. This is a reference to the medieval legend of Faust, a character who sold his soul to the devil in order to gain knowledge and power. Gardner believes that creative geniuses "strike a deal" with themselves that they will sacrifice something important in order to become creative and famous. Often what is sacrificed is the quality of their personal relationships. Genius has its costs as well as its rewards.

One of those costs for some very creative people has been mental illness. The association between creativity and mental problems is part of the popular conception of the creative artist. Even Aristotle said, "There was never a genius without a tincture of madness." In general, however, this is a myth. Albert Rothenberg (1990) argues quite logically that the types of cognitive skills that seem to be associated with creativity have absolutely no inherent relationship to mental illness. There is one interesting caveat to this, however. Recent research has found that there may be a slight relationship between some very notable creative people and certain forms of mental illness. Fredrick Goodwin and Kay Redfield Jamison (1990) found that a number of Pulitzer Prize winners for poetry suffered from either depression or bipolar disorder (the newer term for manic-depression). Specifically, they found that about 20 percent of well-known twentieth century American poets exhibited signs of bipolar disorder compared to 1 percent in the general population. N. Andreasen (1987) found similar results when looking at famous fiction writers. Before anyone begins to romanticize bipolar disorder and creativity, remember that bipolar disorder is extraordinarily difficult for the person and for his or her family, and it is a disorder that often ends in suicide.

Ruth Richards, Dennis Kinney, Inge Lunde, and Benet (1988) did an interesting study that looked more directly at the genetic contributions to creativity. In this study, they looked at rates of bipolar disorder and cyclothymia, which is a milder form of bipolar disorder. They reasoned that because bipolar disorder has a very strong genetic component, close relatives of creative artists who have bipolar disorder should show higher rates of both bipolar disorder and also higher rates of creativity. They found, as expected, that first-degree relatives of artists with bipolar disorder or cyclothymia were more creative than a comparison group. When they looked further, however, the higher creativity scores were found for either relatives with cyclothymia or relatives who did not have a mood disorder. They did not find higher creativity scores for relatives with bipolar disorder. In other words, creativity was more easily expressed in those who did *not* have all the symptoms associated with bipolar disorder. Therefore, their study suggested that if there is some shared genetic contribution to both creativity and bipolar disorder, then serious mental illness such as bipolar disorder may actually *inhibit* the expression of creativity. Last, while not all creative people suffer from a mood disorder, it may well be that creativity is related to an openness to negative emotions. Rathunde (2000) proposed that creativity is a dialectic process that builds on the unique contributions of both positive and negative emotions to fuel the development of unique solutions to problems.

Finally, childhood experiences may have an impact on creativity and genius. There does seem to be a relationship between genius and early loss in childhood. Dean Simonton (1999) notes that a higher than expected percentage of very creative or accomplished people experienced a loss of a parental figure early in life. He reports that 55 percent of highly creative writers lost a parent before the age of 15. When looking at eminent mathematicians, 25 percent of them lost a parent before age 10 and almost a third before age 14. This supports the idea that early adversity can be a stimulus to creativity and achievement.

Summary

This chapter covered a number of topics related to excellence. First, the research on excellence was reviewed. Much of this research says that excellence is learned rather than the result of innate genetic factors. Key factors in excellence include dedicated and frequent practice, a strong intrinsic interest in one's area of expertise, and the persistence to develop one's expertise for many years. The relevance of aesthetics for well-being was discussed next. The appreciation of beauty serves a number of functions that can enhance a sense of wonder and appreciation of the world. Research on creativity was explored. The development of creativity shares most of the characteristics of excellence but adds certain cognitive styles. These include, but are not restricted to, openness to experience, cognitive flexibility, a tolerance for ambiguity, and a willingness to consider unconventional solutions. Characteristics of the creative person, creative process, and creative environments were discussed. Finally, there was a discussion of genius. Genius builds on the qualities of both excellence and creativity but seems to add an intense drive to succeed that may involve a willingness to sacrifice even the most basic needs in order to achieve goals.

Learning Tools

Key Terms and Ideas

CONFLUENCE APPROACH
CONVERGENT THINKING
DELIBERATE PRACTICE
DIVERGENT THINKING
PROCESS CREATIVITY
PRODUCT CREATIVITY
REGRESSION IN SERVICE OF THE EGO
TEN-YEAR RULE

Books

Adams, J. (2001). *Conceptual blockbusting: A guide to better ideas.* Reading, MA: Perseus. Helpful hints on how to think more creatively (self-help).

Edwards, B. (1999). *The new drawing on the right side of your brain.* Los Angeles: J. P. Tarcher. A best selling book on how to draw (self-help).

Goldberg, N., & Guest, J. (1986). *Writing down the bones: Freeing the writer within.* Boulder, CO: Shambhala. Helpful book on how to use writing as your creative passion (self-help).

Tharp, T. (2003). *The creative habit.* New York: Simon & Schuster. Renowned choreographer Twyla Tharp gives her ideas on learning how to be creative (self-help).

Research Articles

Ericsson, K. A., & Charness, N. (1994). Expert performance. *American Psychologist, 49*(8), 725–747.

Simonton, D. K. (2000). Creativity: Cognitive, personal, developmental, and social aspects. *American Psychologist, 55*(1), 151–158.

Winner, E. (2000). The origins and ends of giftedness. *American Psychologist, 55*(1), 159–169.

Film

Everyday Creativity. A film by National Geographic photojournalist Dewitt Jones that invites people to use ordinary skills to be more creative. Distributed by Star Thrower, St. Paul, MN.

On the Web

http://psychology.ucdavis.edu/Simonton/homepage.html. Dean Simonton's homepage with links to his articles on creativity, genius, and other topics.

http://ericec.org/fact/myths.html. Web site on the myths and realities of gifted children.

Personal Explorations

Describe the most creative thing you have ever done. Why did you consider it creative? Was there anything unique about you or the situation that allowed you to be more creative (from www.positivepsychology.org/teachingresources.htm.

For this exercise, get a blank piece of paper and some crayons or colored pencils. Your instructions are to "draw something creative." (If you are an artist, this exercise will not work for you—sorry!) Now take a second piece of paper, and draw something with your nondominant hand. Did it feel different? For many people drawing with their nondominant hand allows them the freedom to draw "badly," and this allows them to experiment and take themselves less seriously.

This exercise must be done in a small group. Start with a few pieces of blank paper. Each person begins by drawing something—anything—on the paper and then passes it to the next person. That person can add anything to the paper he or she wishes, and it is passed to the next person. Continue this process until at least four to six people have added to the evolving drawing. Then, all the pieces of paper are collected, and the group discusses which ones are the most "creative." Interestingly, consensus can usually be reached. What criteria did you use? Did the shared responsibility for the final drawing allow you to feel more freedom to express yourself?

CHAPTER 8

Positive Mental Health: Thriving and Flourishing

> The hell to be endured hereafter, of which theology tells, is no worse than the hell we make for ourselves in this world by habitually fashioning our characters in the wrong way.
>
> *William James (1890)*

Positive Development across the Life Span

Psychologists have long been concerned with how people grow and develop over the course of a lifetime. Early perspectives, however, were based on an image of human beings as simply reacting to events—people merely responding to stimuli. Further, these responses were seen as the result of past conditioning that allowed little room for independent action. Newer perspectives on development assume that we are more active participants in shaping our own development. These newer theories assume that in addition to reacting to events, people can also anticipate upcoming changes and prepare for them before life challenges turn into crises. According to these perspectives, people not only monitor their progress toward goals but also look at how realistic those goals may be in light of current realities. Therefore, adult development is a continuous process of anticipating the future, appraising and reappraising goals, adjusting to current realities, and regulating expectations so as to maintain a sense of well-being in the face of changing circumstances.

Resilience: Healthy Adjustment to Difficult Childhood

One of the assumptions of early theories of child development was that a poor family environment inevitably leads to less healthy adult personality development. Recently, some studies have found that poor early environments do not necessarily result in psychological problems for the children as adults. In fact, what is surprising is that some children who grow up in very difficult homes turn out to be quite well adjusted as adults (Anthony, 1987). These studies are relatively consistent in finding a group of children who thrive in spite of difficult backgrounds that include chronic poverty, parental neglect, parental psychopathology, abuse, and living in the midst of war. However, these findings should not be taken as evidence that early family environments are unimportant—they are extremely important. Rather, these findings point to the fact that some children learn how to adjust to the difficult environments and are less affected than other children. Emily Werner (1995) notes that researchers have come to describe children who do exceptionally well in spite of their environments as *resilient* in that they seem to know how to bounce back from life's difficulties. Ann Masten and R.-G. Reed (2002) define **resilience** as a "pattern of positive adaptation in the face of significant adversity or risk" (p. 75).

N. Garmezy, A. Masten, and A. Tellegen (1984) describe one such child, an 11-year-old boy, who came from a poor home with an alcoholic father, a troubled mother, two brothers who were involved in crime, and two other special-needs siblings. In this home, both parents were depressed and approached life with a sense of hopelessness and helplessness. In spite of this background, the school principal described this boy as someone who got along well with others and was liked by everyone. The boy was a good athlete who had won several trophies and was well-mannered, bright, and "a good kid."

Werner (1995; Werner & Smith, 1992) followed the progress of children in Hawaii for over 30 years and also found exceptional children who emerged from difficult childhoods. In her study, she found that approximately one third of the children from difficult backgrounds emerged as competent and caring adults. Werner (1995) described a core group of characteristics that she believed were typical of resilient children across various studies. First, they were able to find a nurturing surrogate parent. The ability to emotionally detach from a disturbed parent was only the first step. In addition to distancing themselves from unhealthy relationships, the children had to be able to find someone else who could fill the role of caring and supportive parent. This ability to find a surrogate parent may have been in part the result of a temperament that was "active, affectionate, cuddly, good-natured, [making them] easy to deal with" (Werner, 1995, p. 82). Often, the children also managed to form a close relationship with at least one teacher who served as a role model. Second, the children had good social and communication skills and at least one close friend. They also seemed to have a desire to help others and provide some nurturance to other people. Third, the children had creative outlets, activities, or hobbies that they could focus on when life became even more difficult. Competence with this activity gave them a sense of pride and mastery. Fourth, these children seemed to believe that life would somehow work out well. In other words, they were fairly optimistic, seemed to have an internal locus of control, and a positive self-concept. They also developed a style of coping that combined autonomy with the ability to ask for help when necessary. Last, their families held religious beliefs that provided meaning in difficult times.

Werner (1995) also mentioned that family factors that promote resiliency were different for boys and girls. For resilient boys, the important factors were a household with good structure and rules, a male role model, and encouragement of emotional expressiveness. Resilient girls needed homes that emphasized risk taking and independence and also provided reliable support from an older female. She noted that a particularly positive influence on girls was a mother who was steadily employed. Werner also notes that these "protective buffers" could be found in resilient children regardless of differences in ethnicity, social class, and geographic location.

One of the more intriguing conclusions of these studies is that resilient children seem to be actively involved in creating or finding environments and people who will be supportive and reinforce their competencies. That is, when their own homes do not provide those qualities, resilient children do not react passively to the loss and neglect. Rather, resilient children seek out what they need and avoid as much as possible relationships that are unhealthy. Similarly, E. J. Anthony (1987) followed three hundred children of schizophrenic parents for twelve years and found that about 10 percent of the children were very well adjusted in spite of some very bizarre home environments. In contrast to attachment theory, Anthony also believed that these children thrived because they could detach themselves emotionally from their schizophrenic parents.

Generativity: Nurturing and Guiding Others

A growing body of research has looked at a quality similar to altruism called *generativity,* a term used by Erik Erickson (1950) to describe the successful resolution of stage 7 of his theory of psychosocial development. Eric Erikson, Joan Erikson, and Helen Kivnick (1986) defined generativity as "the responsibility for each generation of adults to bear, nurture, and guide those people who will succeed them as adults, as well as to develop and maintain those societal institutions and natural resources without which successive generations will not be able to survive" (pp. 73–74).

Dan McAdams and his colleagues spearheaded much of the newer research in this area (McAdams & de St. Aubin, 1998). In general, studies have shown that higher levels of generativity are associated with greater well-being (e.g., Ackerman, Zuroff, & Moskowitz, 2000). As Erikson predicted, generativity is also associated with other factors that are related to increasing maturity or greater personal growth. For instance, studies have found an association between generativity and the use of more principled moral reasoning, a balance between individualistic and communal concerns, and an increasing importance of less egocentric behaviors in midlife (Mansfield & McAdams, 1996; Nauta, Brooks, Johnson, Kahana, & Kahana, 1996; Pratt, Norris, Arnold & Filyer, 1999). In other words, generativity is related to many traits that are central to the concept of the good life in positive psychology. Greater generativity is also associated with having more education and being at least middle-aged (see McAdams & de St. Aubin, 1998). However, women tend to be more generative than men, possibly because women tend to show more empathic concern.

Dan McAdams, A. Diamond, E. de St. Aubin, and E. Mansfield (1997) suggested how generativity might be related to well-being. They found that the identities of highly generative people, as revealed through their life stories, were often partially constructed with a **commitment script.** A common theme in this type of life narrative was that initial difficulties in life were faced, which then lead to a greater sensitivity to other's suffering, and finally, to a positive outcome that benefited society. So, part of the self-identities of highly generative people were based on personal life stories that emphasized overcoming difficulties and, as a result, growing into greater understanding, empathy, and compassion for others. Another very interesting finding was that highly generative people had not experienced either more positive events or fewer stresses compared with less generative people. The difference was in how those life events were interpreted. For generative people, both positive and negative life events were seen as events that fostered empathy, compassion, and a deeper understanding of others. Once again, the important factor was not the number or types of events encountered in life, but how the person perceived them or made the events meaningful.

Flourishing and Thriving as We Age

Paul Baltes (1993) proposed a model of adaptation to aging that, like resilience, is based on how people adapt to difficult circumstances. Baltes called his model **selective optimization with compensation.** According to his model, optimal adjustment to aging is accomplished by accepting that certain capacities decline with age and by finding ways to compensate for those necessary losses. By doing this, a person can retain optimum enjoyment from activities that give a sense of satisfaction. Baltes (1993) used the following example to illustrate his idea. Classical pianist Arthur Rubinstein continued to perform into his eighties. As he aged, Rubinstein realistically could not expect to play at the same technical level that he could when younger. Therefore, he selected fewer pieces to perform, practiced more often, and deliberately slowed down his playing just prior to the faster passages in order to compensate and give the impression that he was playing faster. These strategies allowed him to continue performing music—an activity that gave him deep satisfaction.

Laura Carstensen (1992, 1995) also proposed a theory that is relevant to how people may actively regulate aspects of their emotional lives throughout the life span. Carstensen begins by noting that older people are often found to regularly bypass opportunities for social contact, and yet they report levels of subjective well-being that are as high or higher than younger people. If, as we saw in Chapter 3, positive social relationships are correlated with well-being, then how can this be true? Carstensen's answer involves her theory of **socioemotional selectivity,** which says that basic psychological goals such as the development of a positive self-concept or the regulation of emotion remain throughout the life span. But the salience of those goals changes depending on a person's place on the life cycle. Specifically, she believes that the drives to seek out information and to develop a positive self-concept are most important during adolescence and become less important with age. The drive for emotional regulation, however, is somewhat less important during adolescence and then rises in importance with age until in old age it is dominant. Further, Carstensen (1995) says that as people enter old age, they have fewer and fewer peers who can provide novel and interesting information. Therefore, people are "less motivated to engage in emotionally meaningless (but perhaps otherwise functional) social contacts and will make social choices based on the potential for emotional rewards" (p. 153). In other words, for older persons, reductions in social contacts can be adaptive. This process, however, is more akin to social selection than to social withdrawal. This means that intimate relationships may become more important but less numerous with age.

In a study designed to test some of these ideas, Carstensen and her colleagues (Carstensen, Mayr, Nesselrode, & Pasupathi, 2000) found that while age was unrelated to the frequency of positive experiences, extended periods of positive emotionality were more likely to be found in older persons. In other words, how often people felt positive emotions was not related to age, but how long those positive emotions endured was related to age—they stayed around longer for older persons. They also found that older persons felt more complex and more poignant emotional experiences than younger people. They suggested that older people have learned how to recognize more nuances of emotional experience and how to regulate their emotions in more adaptive ways. Carstensen's theory is yet another approach to well-being that suggests that the types of goals people seek in life are intimately related to issues that may be salient at their own places in the life cycle.

Wisdom: What Was It That King Solomon Had?

Throughout Western history, "wisdom" has been one of the most frequently used terms to describe optimal maturity. The Bible tells us that King Solomon was "wise," and the Greek philosophers speculated for centuries about wisdom and how it should be the *ultimate* goal of life. In the past, research psychologists tended to avoid the term because of its highly abstract nature. Nevertheless, a few researchers have attempted to describe what people mean by the term wisdom (e.g., Sternberg, 1990).

In general, wisdom implies a positive outcome to long developmental processes. Erik Erikson (1950) saw wisdom as the result of a successful resolution of the last stage of psychosocial development, one that involves an acceptance of life as it had been lived and accepting the reality of approaching death. He also saw it as "involved disinvolvement" or a commitment to the process of life with a calm detachment from any requirement that life turn out a specific way. Therefore, wisdom is not simply a storehouse of information or opinions. Rather, wisdom implies knowledge that is social, interpersonal, and psychological. Wisdom also implies knowledge that may be difficult for the average person to grasp. Hence, the wise person is the one to go to when wrestling with the most difficult questions in life. One does not seek out the counsel of the wise just to ask them the best place in town to buy Chinese food! Kramer (2000) has said that wisdom is "exceptional breadth and depth of knowledge about the conditions of life and human affairs" (p. 85). Vivian Clayton (1982) stated, "Wisdom is . . . the ability that enables the individual to grasp human nature, which operates on the principles of contradiction, paradox, and change. Human nature is being used here to refer to understanding of self and understanding of others" (p. 316). Paul Baltes and Ursula Staudinger (2000) take the definition even further and imply a relationship with ethics. They state that wisdom is "knowledge with extraordinary scope, depth, measure, and balance . . . a synergy of mind and character; that is an orchestration of knowledge and virtue" (p. 123). They also see the concept of wisdom as complex, highly differentiated, and associated with diverse cultural meanings. They even suggest that the concept may be so complicated that it "may be beyond what psychological methods and concepts can achieve" (p. 123). In other words, the idea of wisdom may be too complex for the necessary restrictions of the scientific method. Nonetheless, being enterprising psychologists, they have taken this particular bull by the horns and undertaken a series of empirical studies into the construct of wisdom.

Despite difficulties with definition, psychologists are fairly sure about what wisdom is *not*. The first point is that wisdom is not the inevitable outcome of advanced age (Clayton, 1982). Having said that, however, it is also true that profound wisdom is seen more often, although not exclusively, in persons who are at least middle-aged. Baltes and Staudinger (2000) even suggest that the optimal age to attain wisdom may be about 60 years old. It is also true that wisdom is not simply intelligence as measured by IQ tests. Clayton (1982) points out that IQ tests measure domains of knowledge that are essentially nonsocial and impersonal (e.g., facts, vocabulary, ability to manipulate objects in space. and so on). Most psychologists assume that wisdom cannot be totally understood by only looking at these nonsocial domains of intelligence.

Theories of Wisdom

Baltes and Staudinger (2000) see three related research traditions that utilize explicit theories of wisdom. The first tradition involves perspectives that look at personality traits and how they may be related to wisdom. Erikson's (1950) theory of psychosocial development is an example of the first tradition. The second tradition views wisdom in terms of postformal cognitive thought and dialectical methods of thinking. For example, both Juan Pascual-Leone (1990) and Gisela Labouvie-Vief (1990) see the ability to deal with contradiction and paradox as central to any definition of wisdom. Both also state that wisdom, however defined, must be a type of thinking that is more complex than simply being able to use abstract ideas and concepts. Labouvie-Vief (1990) believes that wisdom must involve the integration of two forms of knowledge: *logos* and *mythos*. Logos is knowledge gained through the use of analytical, propositional, and other formal structures of logic. Mythos is knowledge gained through speech, narrative, plot, or dialogue. It is exemplified in oral traditions, social relationships, and many forms of art. Mythos is a type of knowledge that is embedded in the context of social relationships and social experiences. It includes intuition and openness to unconscious processes.

Pascual-Leone (1990) sounds similar themes in his perspective on wisdom but adds a theoretical statement on what he calls the "ultraself" or "transcendent self" as a hallmark of wisdom. The ultraself operates as a higher, more encompassing, center of information processing that is able to integrate cognitive and emotional processes, particularly, love and care. In a similar way, Deirdre Kramer (2000) refers to wisdom as a form of self-transcendence that is a "detached, but encompassing, concern with life itself" (p. 86).

Kramer (2000) has also reviewed a good deal of the research on wisdom. She sees the two major elements of wisdom as greater openness to experience and a "capacity to reflect on and grapple with difficult existential life issues" (p. 99). One of the other qualities that she found in studies on wisdom was an ability of wise people to find meaning in both positive and negative life experiences. Kramer believes that persons who are wise are able to transform negative experiences into life-affirming experiences. Through this process, they may even exhibit a sense of serenity that others lack. Wise people may also possess a self-effacing sense of humor that recognizes life's ironies (Webster, 2003). A study by Ravenna Helson and Paul Wink (1987) suggested there are two forms of wisdom. The first is *practical wisdom,* which consists of exceptional abilities such as good interpersonal skills, clarity of thinking, greater tolerance, and generativity. The second form they called *transcendental wisdom,* which has a spiritual or philosophical quality. It deals with the limits of knowledge, the rich complexity of the human experience, and a sense of transcending the personal and individual aspects of human experience. Kramer also views wisdom as a potential resource for communities. She urges communities to recognize that wise people do exist and to utilize them to a greater extent.

The third research tradition of explicit theories sees wisdom as a specific example of excellence (see comments on excellence in Chapter 7). In this instance, wisdom is defined as excellence in the performance of one's life. In their research studies on wisdom, Baltes and Staudinger (2000) found it useful to conceptualize wisdom as a multifaceted phenomenon that can be understood only by looking at many different predictors. This is similar to the confluence approach that is used with creativity. In addition, any search for the causes of wisdom must acknowledge that many paths can lead to wisdom. In another interesting parallel with creativity, Baltes and Staudinger also assume that wisdom is a joint product of the person and the culture. Wisdom, therefore, is partially carried in the knowledge and expertise of the culture at a specific point in time. Wise people recognize and utilize the knowledge that is around them in the culture.

The Predictors of Wisdom

The research studies of Baltes and Staudinger (2000) have found that wisdom can be predicted by looking at four general categories of factors: intelligence, personality dispositions, cognitive styles, and life experiences (see Figure 8.1).

Their first finding was that all the factors except age contributed significantly to wisdom, although the strength of the individual contributions varied. In addition, the significant predictors interacted with each other to help produce wisdom. Baltes and Staudinger concluded that wisdom is partially the ability to coordinate multiple personality attributes and life experiences. In terms of the specific factors, they found that high scores on measures of intelligence were significant predictors of wisdom

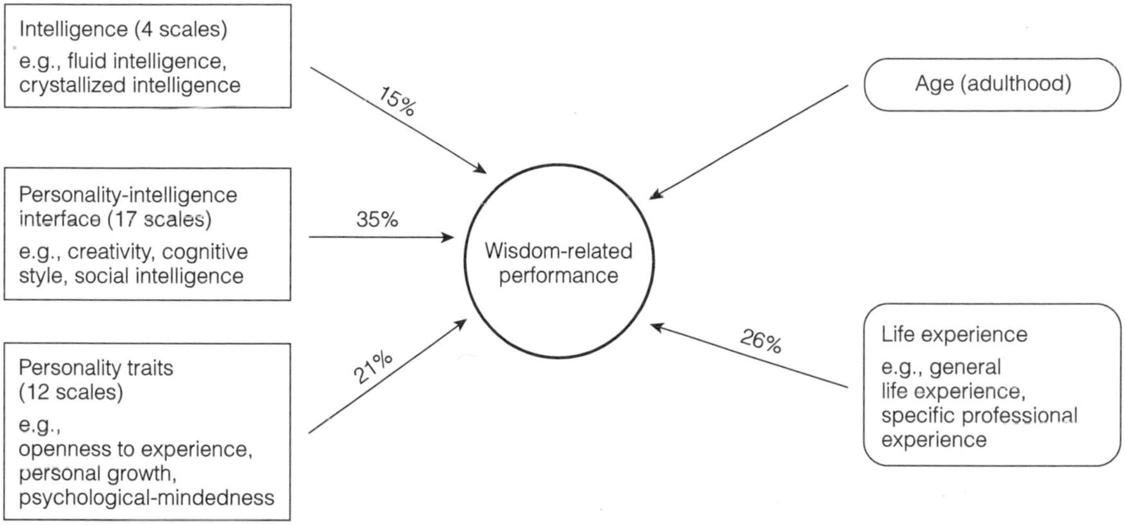

FIGURE **8.1**

The Pattern of Predictive Correlates of Wisdom-Related Performance in Adults

Source: From P. Baltes and U. Staudinger, "Wisdom: A metaheuristic . . . excellence," *American Psychologist, 55*(1), fig. 3, p. 130. Copyright 2000 by the American Psychological Association. Reprinted with permission.
Note: Percentages indicate shared influence. Age is not significant.

(15 percent of wisdom-related performance). These factors, however, were the least important. Personality dispositions such as openness to experience and psychological-mindedness were better predictors of wisdom. The type of life experiences people had was an important predictor of wisdom-related performance. In this regard, Baltes and Staudinger looked at clinical psychologists as part of their study, assuming that people who deal with life's difficulties, complexities, and meanings in the course of psychotherapy may learn something about wisdom along the way. In fact, they did tend to score better on the tests of wisdom. Last, measures of cognitive styles and creativity showed the strongest relationships to wisdom. Among the better predictors in this factor were creativity and the "judicial" and "progressive" thinking styles. These describe the ability to evaluate and compare issues and the ability to move beyond the rules while showing a tolerance for ambiguity, respectively. To Baltes and Staudinger, all of this implied that wisdom is "metaheuristic"—that it implies a highly organized strategy for searching out relevant information from multiple sources and combining that information into solutions that optimize both knowledge and virtue. Note the reference to virtue; it implies an ethical component to wisdom.

While wisdom is a universal goal, is there any evidence that it actually increases well-being? A study by Ardelt (1997) found that wisdom is significantly correlated with life satisfaction for both men and women. In Ardelt's study, wisdom actually was a better predictor of life satisfaction than objective life circumstances such as physical health. Although psychological research into the concept of wisdom is in a fairly early stage of development, positive psychology will probably spark a new interest in this area. New research continues to be done, and new tests of wisdom are being developed (see Webster, 2003). The willingness of certain researchers to venture into this very abstract territory speaks to a great interest in defining one of the ideals of positive personality development.

Positive Mental Health

Of psychology's many achievements during the twentieth and early twenty-first centuries, one of the most successful is the study of mental illness and how to treat it. Advances in theory and research on mental illness have been accompanied by a variety of ideas on what constitutes positive mental health. Attempts to describe psychological adjustment began in the earliest days of psychology. William James, often cited as the "father of American psychology," was quite interested in mental health issues and especially in exceptional states of well-being (see Rathunde, 2001). James stated that the psychologically healthy person has a personality that is harmonious and well balanced (1902/1958). However, for many people, ideas on mental health begin with Freud.

Freud's vision of humanity was a pessimistic one. He saw people as inevitably trapped in a stalemate between the incessant needs for aggression and sex and the socially oriented ego that must keep these needs in check. Happiness and satisfaction in life are essentially compromises that leave a bitter taste because we know they are less than perfect solutions. He said of the pursuit of happiness, "The goal toward which the pleasure principle impels us—of becoming happy—is not attainable; yet we may not, nay cannot, give up the effort to come nearer to realization of it by some means or other" (Freud, 1930/1961, p. 94). The concept of genital character served as the model of maturity for Freud. When Freud was asked what a mentally healthy person should be able to do, he quite succinctly stated, *"lieben und arbiten"*—they should be able "to love and to work." Freud also suggested that maturity was marked by a brotherly concern for other people and a desire to do something good for society (Maddi, 1972). While Freud's simple goals for humanity do require substantial effort, they do not speak eloquently to the ultimate possibilities for psychological growth and optimal mental health.

Most of the theorists who followed Freud created more optimistic models for positive mental health. In fact, there are quite a number of perspectives on positive mental health (see Jahoda, 1958; Coan, 1977; Schultz, 1977; Fadiman & Frager, 1994). Only a few of those perspectives will be reviewed here. For clarity, the perspectives are grouped into those that (1) assume innate needs drive the search for positive mental health and those that (2) assume positive mental health is a product of developing specific personality traits or the development of character. Of course, these two approaches should not be seen as strict divisions; rather, each represents a relative emphasis.

Positive Mental Health as Innate Potentials

Early Psychodynamic Formulations

Alfred Adler was an early colleague of Freud's. In contrast to Freud, Adler focused on an instinctive striving for creative self-realization. Adler believed that self-realization was driven by an innate striving for prosocial interactions and even altruistic concern for others. The term that is most closely associated with Adler's theory of optimal mental health is *Gemeinschaftsgefuhl,* a German word created by Adler that has no exact equivalent in English. It was first translated as "social sense" and then later as **"social interest"** and "social feeling" (Adler, 1964; Ansbacher, 1992). *Gemeinschaftsgefuhl* is a feeling of an intimate relationship with humanity, empathy with the human condition, and a sense of altruism. Adler believed social interest could propel a person toward a type of self-realization that would inevitably include more empathy and compassion for others. In fact, Adler believed that a therapist could tell if psychotherapy was working or not by observing how much the client was being motivated by social interest. The more social interest present in the client, the better therapy was working.

Carl G. Jung was also part of the early inner circle of Freud's colleagues. Jung, like Adler, believed that people possess an innate potential for optimal mental health that needs to be actualized. For Jung, optimal mental health was characterized by a balance between elements of the personality, an openness to messages from a deeper level of the unconscious, and a growing sense of spirituality (Jung, 1964, 1965).

Carl Rogers and the Fully Functioning Person

Carl Rogers developed his theory of mental health from his experiences as a psychotherapist. One of the major thrusts of his approach to psychotherapy was to address ways that people can be allowed to develop their own unique approach to life in the context of a supportive psychotherapeutic relationship.

Rogers began by assuming that we have an innate need to develop our potentials. Rogers termed this need the **self-actualizing tendency** (Rogers, 1959). He assumed that given the right circumstance, people can find ways to fulfill their potentials that will also be both socially responsible and personally fulfilling. The problem, according to Rogers, is that many people lose touch with their innate impulses toward self-actualization. The process of losing touch with our own self-actualizing tendency begins when we deny our own experiences of self and the world in order to gain conditional acceptance from other people. Therefore, the process of self-actualization is fueled by honest self-awareness. Rogers believed that when people exist in environments defined by unconditional love, empathic understanding, and genuineness, then they can grow psychologically toward their fullest potentials (see Firestone, Firestone, & Catlett, 2003).

The Fully Functioning Person

For Rogers, the definition of psychological adjustment rested on the idea that mental health exists when all the relevant experiences of the person can be integrated into a coherent and flexible self-concept. As people grow toward their fullest potentials, a few recognizable traits indicate their progress. Rogers chose the term **"fully functioning person"** for someone who achieves this ideal (Rogers, 1961). Three major criteria and two auxiliary ones characterize the fully functioning person: (1) openness to experiences, (2) existential living, and (3) trust in one's own organismic experiences (i.e., sensations, physiological experiences, or our "gut" feelings). These three result in (4) a sense of freedom and (5) enhanced creativity.

By "openness to experience," Rogers suggests a personality that is aware of both internal and external stimuli, one in which the uses of defense mechanisms are kept at a minimum. Actually, Rogers hypothesized that it is possible to live without *any* defense mechanisms. One consequence of this openness is that both pleasant and unpleasant experiences are allowed equal access to consciousness. A person must have a sufficiently grounded sense of self so that he or she will not be overwhelmed by emotions. Therefore, although Rogers does not specifically mention it as a criterion, the fully functioning person would also exhibit substantial fortitude and courage.

The second criteria, existential living, implies that the fully functioning person favors experiences that come from life as it is lived in the moment. This criterion is similar to the old saying that one must "stop and smell the roses." It implies a strong process orientation to life. It implies that life should be lived as a fluid and dynamic sense of awareness of current experiences, deciding what to do with the experiences, taking action, and moving on to deal with the next experience (note the similarity to the theory of flow in Chapter 4).

People who are open to the moment are also open to the cues that come from their physiological reality—they trust their own organismic experiences. The fully functioning person is aware of, trusts, and values his or her instincts, intuition, and hunches. Because the fully functioning person is nondefensive, open to the experience of the moment, and willing to experience life as a process, it is obvious that he or she would also experience a sense of freedom. Finally, because the fully functioning person is continually adapting to new experiences, a certain degree of creativity in that adaptation seems necessary. Creativity in Rogers's sense means an approach to life that is open to unique and unusual ways of problem solving. It also implies a willingness to be challenged by new experiences. Therefore, Rogers said that if people relate to their immediate and on-going experiences in a certain way, then their innate need for self-actualization will emerge and motivate behavior.

Living as a Fully Functioning Person

What is a fully functioning person like? Rogers (1961) provided some clues when he stated,

> It seems to mean that the individual moves toward *being*, knowingly and acceptingly, the process which he inwardly and actually *is*. . . . He is not trying to be more than he is, with the attendant feelings of insecurity or bombastic defensiveness. He is not trying to be less than he is, with the attendant feelings of guilt or self-deprecation. He is increasingly listening to the deepest recesses of his physiological and emotional being, and finds himself increasingly willing to be, with greater accuracy and depth, that self which he most truly is (pp. 175–176).

The movement is toward self-direction, openness to experience, acceptance of others, and trust in self. The movement is not toward any particular state. Rather, it is a way of approaching and even welcoming life experiences. Again, in Rogers's (1961) words,

> It seems to me that the good life is not any fixed state. It is not, in my estimation, a state of virtue, or contentment, or nirvana, or happiness. It is not a condition in which the individual is adjusted, or fulfilled, or actualized. To use psychological terms, it is not a state of drive-reduction, or tension-reduction, or homeostasis (pp. 185–186).

Rogers seems to be describing a person who can balance rationality and intuition but who shows a slight preference for the intuitive mode of understanding the world. His idea of optimal mental health borrows heavily from the image of the creative artist (see "the creative person" in Chapter 7).

Abraham Maslow and Self-Actualization

The next theory to be discussed is Abraham Maslow's theory of **self-actualization.** In general, self-actualization refers to the process of living up to one's potentials. Although Maslow's theory of the self-actualizing person is one of the most well-known theories of personality development, it is also widely misunderstood even in psychology. For instance, his theory has nothing to do with self-indulgence or preoccupation with self. Originally, Maslow (1954) stated that self-actualization "may be loosely described as the full use and exploitation of talents, capacities, potentialities" (p. 200).

Early Studies of Self-Actualizing People

According to Maslow, self-actualization does not describe a state but rather an on-going process of development. He began with a question about how some people seem to adjust extraordinarily well. In order to approach this question, he began to search for exemplars of optimal mental health—people who showed evidence of fulfilling their potentials. Who were these people who exemplified the process of self-actualization? They were not, in any sense, the average person off the street. To get a feel for the elite nature of his candidates, one only has to look at how some historical figures fared in this classification system. Maslow's "fairly sure they are self-actualizers" candidates included Abraham Lincoln (only in his last years) and Thomas Jefferson; the "highly probable group" included Eleanor Roosevelt and Albert Einstein; Beethoven and Freud were in his "partial" group; while George Washington Carver and Albert Schweitzer he placed in his "potential" group. In addition to studying public figures for evidence of self-actualization, well-known people from history, and acquaintances, Maslow also screened three thousand college students. In this group, he only found one person who fit his criteria—and that person was only in the "probable" category. He concluded that self-actualization "was not possible in our society for young, developing people" (Maslow, 1954, p. 200). He believed that a person needed some life experience before he or she could be considered self-actualizing. Later, Maslow would estimate that less than 1 percent of the adult population could be called self-actualizing people.

Maslow developed his definition of self-actualization through an iterative process. That is, first he chose subjects, then he evaluated those people, and next he adjusted the original definition based on the first evaluation. Then he followed by choosing the next group to be evaluated based on the revised definition, and so on. Using this process, Maslow's (1954) more expanded explanation of self-actualization was, "Such people seem to be fulfilling themselves and to be doing the best that they are capable of doing, reminding us of Nietzsche's exhortation, 'Become what thou art!' They are people who have developed or are developing to the full stature of which they are capable. These potentialities may be either idiosyncratic or species-wide, so that the self in self-actualization *must not have too individualistic a flavor*" [italics added] (p. 201). Part of this last quotation is italicized to emphasize that, right from the beginning, Maslow did not equate self-actualization with self-absorption or excessive individualism. Later, many interpreters of Maslow would forget this point.

Maslow's Hierarchy of Innate Needs

Once Maslow had identified examples of the self-actualizing person, he began to develop a theory of personality development that might explain how those people came to be the way they were. He proposed a theory that was based on an idea relatively common in psychology at the time—the examination of basic needs.

Maslow (1954) initially delineated five basic human needs that must be met in order for people to feel fulfilled in life. Graphically, Maslow presented these needs in the shape of a pyramid (Figure 8.2). The pyramidal shape suggested that the lower needs were more pervasive and that the higher needs were more tenuous and more easily overwhelmed by the influence of lower needs.

Maslow assumed these five basic needs to be innate:

1. *Physiological.* People need to have their basic needs met for food, shelter, comfort, and freedom from disease.
2. *Safety and security.* People need to believe that they are relatively safe from physical harm and societal chaos and that they have some degree of control over their own destinies.
3. *Love and belongingness.* People need to feel connections to the social world and need to feel that they are loved and cherished for who they are as individuals.
4. *Self-esteem.* People need to feel a sense of competence and achievement and that they are respected and valued by other people in their life.

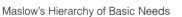

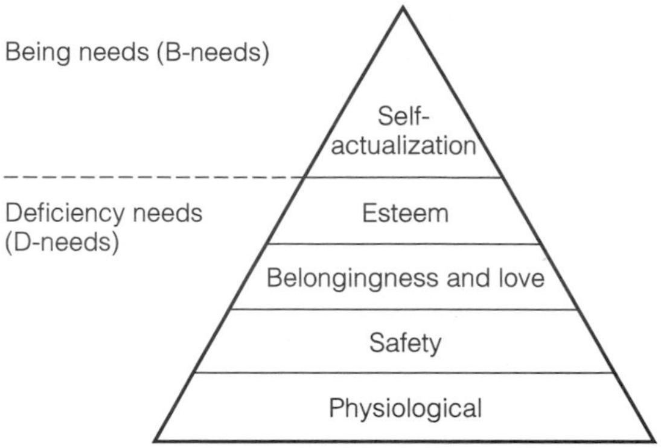

FIGURE **8.2**

Maslow's Hierarchy of Basic Needs

5. *Self-actualization.* People have a need to develop their unique potentials.

Maslow (1954) also postulated that certain preconditions were necessary for satisfaction of the basic needs: specific *freedoms* (i.e., freedom of speech, expression, inquiry) and necessary *ethical principles* (i.e., justice, fairness, honesty, orderliness). He also believed that the needs *to know* and *to understand* formed a second, smaller-needs hierarchy that was interrelated and synergistic with the basic-needs hierarchy. Finally, Maslow stated that some people have a basic need for *aesthetic expression.* For these people (e.g., creative artists), the failure to satisfy their need for creativity and beauty resulted in ennui, boredom, and meaninglessness.[1]

Maslow believed that the first four needs have to be met in a relatively sequential fashion. However, it is not necessary to meet each need fully before moving on to concerns of the next higher need. For the sake of illustration, Maslow (1954) stated that a person might have satisfied 85 percent of his or her physiological needs, 70 percent of safety needs, 50 percent of belongingness needs, 40 percent of self-esteem needs, and 10 percent of self-actualization needs.

Motivation According to Maslow

The first four stages were also based on what Maslow termed **deficiency needs** or **D-needs.** If the D-needs are not met, then we are motivated by a sense that we lack qualities that are necessary for basic psychological adjustment. In this case, we lack a positive sense of self, a sense that we are loved, or a sense of security that allows some optimism for the future. If these needs are not met satisfactorily, then the basic foundation of personality and adjustment has not been built. Once one feels relatively secure, connected to others, loved, and holds a healthy respect for who one is as a person, then the need for self-actualization becomes more important. However, this need creates a new tension, which comes from the difference between who we are and who we imagine that we can be. Because we acknowledge that our potentials are unrealized, this distance between the real and the potential produces a desire to fulfill our potential.

Maslow's term for the self-actualizing need and the peripheral needs associated with it was **being needs** or **B-needs.** Some of the B-needs are truth, justice, beauty, wholeness, richness, playfulness, meaningfulness, and goodness (Maslow, 1968, 1971). One unique characteristic of self-actualizing people is that they are motivated by the B-needs more than the D-needs. Maslow (1954) said, "Our subjects no longer strive in the ordinary sense, they develop." (p. 211). Note that the self-actualization and the B-needs arise in a person who has already found relatively healthy adaptation and adjustment. Therefore, part of the tension created by the need for self-actualization comes from a conflict between the security of current happiness and the risk of change. Maslow saw this type of choice as a common conflict in life that illustrates a general principle: the tension between **security versus growth.** For Maslow, the self-actualizing person is characterized by a willingness to risk the security of the known and comfortable for the potential growth that can come from embracing a new challenge. Therefore, he believed that self-actualizing people are motivated by the B-needs. They are, in a sense, pulled toward a possible future for themselves that is in many ways defined by the need to develop their unique potentials as well as the needs for truth, justice, beauty, and the other B-needs. Self-actualizing people also acknowledge, accept, and may actually embrace, the tensions created by these unfulfilled B-needs. Their response to these tensions is, more often than not, to risk the current security of the familiar and to risk possible failure in an attempt to actualize their potentials.

Maslow also knew that many people reject personal growth changes because they fear that other people in their lives will not accept those changes. Maslow (1971) called this fear the **Jonah complex.** Nelson Mandela spoke of this fear in his presidential inaugural address in South Africa:

> Our deepest fear is not that we are inadequate. Our deepest fear is that we are powerful beyond measure. It is our light, not our darkness that frightens us. We ask ourselves, "Who am I to be brilliant, gorgeous, talented and fabulous?" Actually, who are you not to be? You are a child of God. Your playing small doesn't serve the world. There's nothing enlightening about shrinking so that other people won't feel insecure around you. . . . And as we let our light shine, we unconsciously give other people permission to do the same.

As mentioned before, Maslow assumed that only a small percentage of the population could manage to be self-actualizing on a consistent basis. For those who did manage it, what would they be like?

The Personality Traits of Self-Actualizing People

In his study of self-actualizing people, Maslow abstracted fifteen personality traits that he believed were characteristic of their behavior. Not every self-actualizing person he studied showed evidence of all fifteen traits. Therefore, the list was a useful tool, not a rigid checklist, for an understanding of how self-actualizing people interacted with the world and themselves. Maslow also recognized that his subjects were not perfect. They were not completely free of guilt, anxiety, sadness, or conflict. He felt compelled to remind people that his subjects "are not angels." For the most part, however, they were free of neurotic anxieties and conflicts. With this in mind, Maslow (1954) presented a list of fifteen personality traits for self-actualizing people. For the sake of clarity, the fifteen traits are grouped into four categories.

The first is *openness to experience.*

1. *More efficient perception of reality and more comfortable relations with it.* Maslow believed that self-actualizing people have a keen sense for deception, dishonesty, and superficiality in other people. Because they have settled many questions about self-esteem, they are more able to perceive the world without the distorting bias of their own wishes, hopes, and anxieties. They can view the world without positive illusions or defensive distortion.
2. *Acceptance (self, others, nature).* It follows logically that self-actualizing people should also be better able to detect deception, weakness, and shortcomings within themselves. This attitude toward their shortcomings distinguished Maslow's self-actualizing people. He said, "Our healthy individuals find it possible to accept themselves and their own nature without chagrin or complaint or, for that matter, even without thinking about the matter very much. They can accept their own human nature in the stoic style, with all its shortcomings, with all its discrepancies from the ideal image without feeling real concern" (1954, pp. 206–7). He also said that self-actualizing persons had a lack of defensiveness. When they do feel guilty or dysphoric, it is from recognition of the

discrepancy between what is and what could be or ought to be. They can see the possibilities inherent in humanity and are acutely aware of how far short we fall.

3. *Continued freshness of appreciation.* This characteristic describes an openness to life, joy, and a gratitude for moment-to-moment experiences. According to Maslow (1954), "Self-actualizing people have the wonderful capacity to appreciate again and again, freshly and naively, the basic goods of life with awe, pleasure, wonder, and even ecstasy, however stale these experiences may have become to others" (pp. 214–215).
4. *Spontaneity.* Maslow also found his subjects to be more spontaneous than other people. They showed behavior that was marked by simplicity, naturalness, and a lack of artificiality. This does not mean their behavior was necessarily unconventional, and it certainly was not overly impulsive. By simplicity, Maslow meant that his subjects were neither boastful nor supercilious but easy-going and natural.
5. *Creativeness.* Maslow referred to creativity as process more than as product. The creativity he saw was originality, inventiveness, adaptability, and spontaneity in the solution of problems—both the large and the small.
6. *The mystical experience; the oceanic feeling.* Maslow (1976) would later describe these fairly brief moments of heightened awareness and intense positive emotionality as "peak experiences." (They will be discussed in more detail in Chapter 10.)

The second category is *autonomy.*

7. *Autonomy; independence of culture and environment.* Maslow's subjects also seemed to be relatively self-contained. Their self-esteem was not based on how other people thought of them or on culturally defined criteria for success. They could remain fairly stable, even serene and happy, in the midst of frustrations and stressors. They found intrinsic satisfactions rather than relying on extrinsic responses from others.
8. *The quality of detachment; the need for privacy.* Maslow believed that his subjects showed a distinct tendency to enjoy solitude and privacy. They were not unsociable, but they did not need people around them at all times. In this context, Maslow also mentioned a greater ability to concentrate and a quality of detachment that allowed them to "remain above the battle, to remain unruffled, undisturbed by that which produces turmoil in others" (1954, p. 212).
9. *Resistance to enculturation.* Maslow (1954) begins his description of this criterion with the very provocative sentence, "Self-actualizing people are not well adjusted" (p. 224). By this, he meant that his subjects seemed to be able to maintain a certain detachment from the culture in which they lived. They lived in their society, usually without overt rebelliousness or unconventionality, but their inner attitudes and beliefs were not shaped and dominated by the messages from that society. They were able to look at their culture more objectively and see the contradictions, inconsistencies, and errors that existed.

The third category is *positive relationships with others.*

10. *Gemeinschaftsgefuhl ("social interest").* Maslow borrowed the name of this criterion from Adler's criteria for optimal mental health. Maslow's subjects seemed to have a deep feeling of empathy, compassion, and humanitarian affection for people, despite a piercing awareness of others' imperfections. Self-actualizing people have a genuine desire to help the human race that is based on a sense

of shared identity. They feel a need to be of service to others in some way. Self-actualizing persons can be simultaneously autonomous and deeply connected to others.

11. *Interpersonal relations.* Maslow believed that his subjects experienced deeper, more intense, and more profound interpersonal relationships than the average person. They seemed to be able to drop defensiveness and find greater love. In this context, Maslow also stated that self-actualizers tend "to be kind or at least patient to almost everyone. They have an especially tender love for children and are easily touched by them." (1954, p. 218). Maslow also stated that their friendships were extremely close but not numerous.
12. *Philosophical, unhostile sense of humor.* Maslow's subjects did not find humor at other people's expense. They laugh not at but rather with other people. They found the foibles of the human condition—their own included—to be the greater source of humor. More often the source of their humor was irony rather than malicious attack or sarcasm.
13. *Problem centering.* Maslow found that his subjects tended to be oriented to some problem, vocation, or mission in life. The goal of this mission was, in general, not oriented toward personal gain and was unselfish rather than egocentric. Maslow said, "Generally the devotion and dedication is so marked that one can fairly use the old words vocation, calling, or mission to describe their passionate, selfless, and profound feeling for their "work" (Maslow, 1971, p. 291). In other words, his self-actualizers tended to devote a good deal of energy to tasks they believed would be of service to others. How they defined service to others often came from a "framework of values that [was] broad and not petty, universal and not local, and in terms of a century rather than the moment" (1954, p. 212).

The fourth category is *strong ethical standards.*

14. *The democratic character structure.* Part of this criterion describes a lack of pretense, hypocrisy, and status manipulation in his subjects. Maslow found them more than willing to listen to and learn from anyone who might have something important to say. Issues of rank, class, status, or educational attainment meant very little to them (although a number of them had considerable achievements in these areas).
15. *Discrimination between means and ends.* This is a somewhat confusing title, and, in fact, it is the least clearly defined of the original fifteen criteria. What Maslow was trying to capture with this unwieldy term was a strong sense of ethics and morality. He stated that his subjects were quite clear about the differences between right and wrong and lived their lives according to those values. The reference to "means versus ends" suggests that self-actualizing people would not use unethical means to obtain an ethical end.

Although Maslow did not use terms from contemporary positive psychology, it is fairly obvious that his fifteen traits of self-actualization are a list of strengths and virtues. Therefore, Maslow's theory postulates that the process of self-actualization involves two primary characteristics. First, self-actualizing people exhibit a specific set of strengths and virtues. Second, they tend to show an uncommon style of motivation: they are motivated more often by needs for personal growth than by needs for psychological security, safety, and self-esteem.

Research Studies on Self-Actualization

One of the criticisms of Maslow's theory is that there is no research support for it. This is a more complicated issue than it might seem.

First, it is true that most studies fail to support Maslow's proposed ascendancy of needs through the needs hierarchy (Wahba & Bridwell, 1976), although some recent studies have found partial support for the needs hierarchy (e.g., Hagerty, 1999). Studies of self-actualization as a descriptor of optimal mental health, however, offer a striking contrast to research on whether people meet innate needs in a hierarchical fashion as Maslow proposed. The research literature on the traits of self-actualization contains over a thousand studies, and many of them support Maslow's self-actualization criteria as useful indicators of positive mental health (see Welch, Tate, & Medeiros, 1987; Knapp, 1990; Jones & Crandall, 1991). For instance, Mahmoud Wahba and Lawrence Bridwell (1976) did not find support for Maslow's needs hierarchy, but they found support for his distinction between deficiency needs (D-needs) and being needs (B-needs). Apparently, some people *are* motivated by the self-actualization needs more than others (also see Helson & Wink, 1987). In general, studies have found that people who score higher on measures of self-actualization also score higher on other indices of mental health. Finally, for those interested in applied self-actualization, Maslow's last book, *The Farther Reaches of Human Nature* (1971), described how people can help themselves move toward being more self-actualizing.

Positive Mental Health as Character Development

The necessity for some degree of valid self-knowledge has been recognized at least since the time of the ancient Greeks. The most famous mandate on self-knowledge was inscribed in marble at the Oracle at Delphi: "Know Thyself."

Authenticity: Finding One's "True Self"

Over the centuries, this requirement for honest self-examination has changed from one that asks us to be aware of our talents to one that places more emphasis on valid knowledge of our interior lives and psychological realities. The other side of this coin involves honest presentation of oneself to other people. The assumption is that, under most circumstances, it is better to present an honest portrait of oneself to other people in order to facilitate trust and help develop good will.

Positive psychology uses the term **authenticity** to describe this combination of behaviors. Authenticity involves both the ability to recognize and take responsibility for one's own psychological experiences and the ability to act in ways that are consistent with those experiences. Susan Harter (2002) described authenticity as follows: "At one level, authenticity involves *owning* one's own personal experiences, be they thoughts, emotions, needs, wants, preferences, or beliefs, processes captured by the injunction to 'know thyself.' The exhortation 'To thine own self be true' further implies that one *acts* in accord with the true self, expressing oneself in ways that are consistent with inner thoughts and feelings" (p. 382). This quotation uses terms and ideas from psychology that may also help describe authenticity. Terms such as the "true self" or the "real self" are often used to describe core elements of authenticity.

If we are to speak of a true self or a real self, then obviously there must be some conceptualization of a false or an unreal self. Indeed, we have seen similar ideas presented already in terms of positive illusions about self (see Chapter 3). Therefore, one of the guiding assumptions of authenticity is that people can deceive themselves about their real motives, true emotions, or actual beliefs. The call for greater authenticity says that in many instances, this self-deception is harmful to the development of the good life. Of course, at times it may be helpful or more appropriate to have a little self-deception (e.g., "I know that I have the talent to be a best-selling author") or to tell a polite little white lie (e.g., "Of course, you look great in that new dress"). In spite of these caveats, the authenticity literature assumes that honest self-examination and self-presentation are necessary components of creating a satisfying life.

One other guiding assumption runs through the authenticity literature. This one concerns the reasons for inauthentic presentation and the blocks to authentic presentation. In general, the culprit is the social world. On the one hand, it is assumed that the need for false self-presentation is socially implanted by parents, friends, or society (Harter, 2002). On the other hand, even if someone wishes to present in an authentic manner, social restrictions and demands may forcefully inhibit that expression. In short, inauthentic self-presentation can be created by social pressures that either reward the presentation of a false self or punish expression of the true self. Erich Fromm (1941) spoke to the consequences of compulsively denying one's own perception of truth: "What then is the meaning of freedom for modern man? He has become free from the external bonds that would prevent him from doing and thinking as he sees fit. He would be free to act according to his own will, if he knew what he wanted, thought, and felt. But he does not know. He conforms to anonymous authorities and adopts a self which is not his" (p. 254).

Authenticity and Well-Being

Richard Ryan and Edward Deci (2000, 2001) see their self-determination theory as a newer perspective that attempts to explain how the real or true self can be actualized. According to self-determination theory, the true self is actualized through activities that promote and foster the three basic psychological needs for autonomy, relatedness, and competence. Among the many research findings that support their ideas, Ryan and Deci have found that greater well-being is associated with the pursuit of goals that are more meaningful, more integrated with the self, more aligned with the true self, and more autonomous. That is, when greater authenticity is used as the foundation for pursuing our goals, then greater well-being is the result.

In a study that looked at both the true self and authenticity, Kennon Sheldon, Richard Ryan, Laird Rawsthorne, and Barbara Ilardi (1997) found that greater authenticity was related to greater self-esteem, more identity integration, and greater sense of autonomy. Greater authenticity was also related to less depression, less perceived stress, and fewer complaints of physical problems. They also found that the more genuine and self-expressive people felt in a given role, the more free they felt to express their basic personality traits. Harter (2002) has looked at the development of authenticity in childhood and adolescence. She found that the ability and willingness to find one's true "voice," or to express one's real opinions and feelings, are related to higher authenticity. She also found that adolescents who had higher authenticity also had higher self-esteem, more hope, felt more positive emotions, and were more cheerful. Harter also believes that greater authenticity can be created through more positive interpersonal relationships. She encourages us to build close relationships that are based on genuine empathy, a willingness to be truthful, unconditional positive regard, and on both autonomy and connectedness to others.

Existentialism

Any discussion of authenticity requires at least a brief discussion of existentialism, because existentialist thinkers actually created the concept of authenticity. However, existentialism is a very diverse movement in European philosophy that many people find difficult to summarize (see Barrett, 1962). Nevertheless, all existentialist thinkers objected to a society that they saw as superficial because it supported the denial and repression of certain aspects of human experience. They saw society as fostering a restricted awareness in order to maintain the social order. In other words, they saw society as selling the inherent freedom and responsibility of being human in order to purchase a false security. The existentialists believed that the consequences of this bargain were that people no longer confronted the world openly and honestly but instead lived inauthentic lives. For existentialists, a full life was one in which all aspects of our humanity were accepted into awareness and people were allowed or compelled to wrestle with how those aspects would be incorporated into their own sense of identity. One of the goals of existentialism is to point people in the direction of authenticity so their lives can accommodate full honesty, self-awareness, and openness.

The focus on honest awareness also implied that we are aware of the finitude of our lives. This knowledge inevitably creates anxiety or dread (i.e., angst). At this point, most other theoretical approaches to mental health would say that if we feel dread, then the solution is to live in a way that we can be free from the dread. That is, most other approaches postulate that some escape from guilt and anxiety is possible. As is normally the case with existentialist philosophers, they do not provide such an easy solution. According to them, living an authentic life does not allow us to completely escape certain negative emotions. If we retreat or hide from guilt, we have chosen to live an inauthentic life. Therefore, the truly authentic life is one in which we live with full awareness of choice, responsibility, freedom, anxiety, guilt, fate, and the impossibility of escape from the full range of our human experience—both the joyous and the tragic. The existentialists argued that we must take responsibility for our lives and create meaning out of whatever situation we find ourselves in. Our ability to create authentic meaning is dependent upon our willingness to confront and honestly deal with the existential givens or fundamental realities of life. The following quotation from Henry David Thoreau's book *Walden* (1854/1980) may illustrate the existentialist's drive to extract deeper levels of honesty, understanding, and meaning from life experiences.

> I went to the woods because I wished to live deliberately, to front only the essential facts of life, and see if I could not learn what it had to teach, and not, when I came to die, discover that I had not lived.
>
> I wanted to live deep and suck out all the marrow of life, to live so sturdily and Spartan-like as to put to rout all that was not life, to cut a broad swath and shave close, to drive life into a corner, and to reduce it to its lowest terms, and, if it proved to be mean, why then to get the whole and genuine meanness of it, and publish its meanness to the world; or if it were sublime, to know it by experience and be able to give a true account of it in my next excursion . . .
>
> Let us settle ourselves, and work and wedge our feet downward through the mud and slush of opinion, and prejudice and tradition, and delusion, and appearance, that allusion which covers the globe . . . till we come to a hard bottom of rocks in place, which we can call reality (p. 66).

Healthy and Adaptive Defense Mechanisms

Even though Freud held a relatively pessimistic view of our potential for optimal mental health, almost all of the perspectives that followed his have agreed with one of his points: people can sometimes hide their true feelings or their true motives from conscious awareness. Psychology now accepts that at times people can keep unpleasant emotions or thoughts out of awareness (Cramer & Davidson, 1998). That is, under certain circumstances, people will use what are called *defense mechanisms*. George Vaillant has focused on how the use of various defense mechanisms can help or hinder our progress toward positive mental health.

The story of Vaillant's research study began in 1937 when philanthropist William T. Grant and Dr. Arlie V. Bock decided to begin a systematic inquiry into the kinds of people who are healthy and function well (Vaillant, 1977, 2000). That is, they believed that too much medical research was weighted toward the disease end of the spectrum and studies of healthy functioning were needed. The Grant study began by selecting a group of 268 Harvard sophomore men because they appeared to be healthier than their peers—they were the "best and the brightest." The study followed those men for the next 40 years. Vaillant joined the staff of the Grant study in 1967 and began to summarize the research on what differentiated people who continued to adapt well throughout life from those whose earlier promise was not maintained in later years. Later, Vaillant also examined data gathered from two other longitudinal studies. The first was a study that began in the late 1950s and looked at adolescent boys from disadvantaged neighborhoods in Boston. The second looked at women who were part of the Terman study of gifted women that began at Stanford in 1920 (see Vaillant, 2000, for more details).

Vaillant (1977) began by recognizing that an adequate definition of mental health or adaptation is a very slippery concept. He felt that mental health could *not* be defined by an average or by reference to "normal" behavior. He felt that this criteria represented the "average amount of disease and incapacity present in the population" (1977, p. 5). Vaillant also rejected the absence of psychological conflict because all of the men in the Grant study had at times been despondent, anxious, too temperamental, or reacted childishly to stressors. Vaillant followed the advice of Frank Barron (1963) and assumed that good mental health was "a way of reacting to problems and not an absence of them" (p. 64). In addition, Vaillant decided that he would define positive adaptation in terms of a person's actual behavior (rather than how he or she feels) and the number of areas in life in which people functioned well.

Mature Defense Mechanisms

Vaillant found that what differentiated healthy adaptation from unhealthy was the type of defense mechanisms used when people confronted conflicts and difficulties. Surprisingly, Vaillant found that the type of defense mechanisms used as a young man could predict well-being twenty years later (Vaillant, 2000). He classified the defense mechanisms as "psychotic," "immature," "neurotic," and "mature" or "adaptive" styles (Vaillant, 1977). In Vaillant's system the degree of unconsciousness and involuntariness involved in defense mechanisms is on a continuum from extreme to mild. The psychotic defense mechanisms were clearly unhealthy and involved extreme distortions of reality in an attempt to avoid anxiety. These mechanisms included delusional projection or psychotic denial. Vaillant believed immature defense mechanisms were often used by adolescents and by people with severe depression. These mechanisms included projection, hypochondriasis, passive-aggression, and acting out. In contrast, Vaillant saw the neurotic defense mechanisms as the "average" or "normal" styles that people use to cope with anxiety, threat, and conflict. They included repression, intellectualization, reaction formation, displacement or conversion, and neurotic denial or dissociation. Finally, the **mature** or **adaptive defense mechanisms** that Vaillant identified were sublimation, altruism, suppression, anticipation, and humor. These defense mechanisms deal with anxiety by attempting to maximize gratification, but at the same time allow awareness of underlying feelings, impulses, ideas, and consequences of behavior. The mature defenses "synthesize and attenuate rather than deny and distort conflicting sources of human behavior . . . " (Vaillant, 2000, p. 97).

Vaillant found that in the Harvard and Boston samples, those men who used adaptive defense mechanisms more often and the other defenses less often had higher incomes, better psychosocial adjustment, more social supports, more joy in living, better marital satisfaction, and higher self-rated health (but not actual health status). He also found they had jobs that fit their ambitions, were more active in public service, had rich friendship patterns, had happier marriages, and still engaged in competitive sports in midlife. In the Boston sample from the disadvantaged neighborhood, those who used mature defenses were more likely to have escaped poverty as adults.

Interestingly, Vaillant also found that self-perceptions of happiness were not always associated with better adjustment. In fact, those in the "mature" category did not always score higher on self-report measures of happiness. Specifically, only 68 percent of the men in the mature category were in the top third of self-reported happiness. Interestingly, 16 percent of the men in the immature category rated themselves in the top third of happiness (Vaillant, 1977). Note how his findings may relate to the issues of positive illusions discussed in Chapter 3. Vaillant's results suggest that if positive illusions about self are based on immature defenses, then the resulting happiness may be fragile and short-lived.

Strengths and Virtues

Recall from Chapter 1 that positive psychology has been partially defined as a branch of psychology that investigates human "strengths and virtues." Similarly, most of the theories described in this chapter list certain behaviors that could be viewed as strengths and virtues. In Western culture, the legacy of the Hebrews, the Greeks, and Christianity combined in the Middle Ages to produce the four cardinal virtues and the three theological virtues (i.e., justice, prudence, fortitude, temperance, faith, hope, and charity; see Chapter 1). These virtues were seen as the core elements of an admirable life. In the twentieth century, however, many perspectives in scientific psychology adopted an attitude of ethical relativism so the proscriptive nature of advocating certain values or virtues was suspect (Schimmel, 2000). Today, this picture is changing. Research has shown that certain psychological characteristics such as optimism, self-respect, and self-control can have advantageous effects on both psychological and physical well-being. It is not too large of a stretch to see these characteristics as strengths or virtues.

Why Strengths and Virtues Are Important

Robert Emmons and Cheryl Crumpler (1999) define virtues by saying, "Virtues are acquired excellences in character traits, the possession of which contributes to a person's completeness or wholeness. Virtues represent ideal states that facilitate adaptation to life" (p. 57). Therefore, strengths and virtues are more than just useful tools for adaptation to stress or difficult circumstances. They serve those functions, too, of course, but they are important because they help a person to grow psychologically toward optimal character development. Virtues operate in many situations throughout life. McCullough and Snyder (2000) provide a helpful definition that emphasizes the social aspect of virtues: "any psychological processes that enable a person to think and act so as to benefit both him- and herself and society" (p. 1). Seligman (October 2000) proposed that positive psychology as a discipline must embrace the study of virtues and strengths in order to study the goals or desired outcomes of development. He recognized that in order to define a positive psychology, one must know how to recognize a positive outcome. Therefore, he stated that a positive outcome is an outcome that follows from the exercise of the strengths and virtues.

Recognizing Strengths and Virtues

Strengths and virtues can be recognized because they have certain effects:

1. They contribute to fulfillment.
2. They are valued in their own right.

3. They are celebrated when present and mourned if lost.
4. They are taught by parents and social institutions.
5. There are parables and morality tales in the society that teach them.
6. People hold and express them in different degrees.
7. They are malleable or learnable.
8. They prompt joyful responses from others when expressed.

Peterson and Seligman (2004) state that the outcomes of the exercise of strengths and virtues are *fulfillments.* The expression of the strengths and virtues leads to fulfillments that are recognized because they make the individual and the society better. Peterson and Seligman found that in different cultures at different times, these human qualities are *valued in their own right* and not just as a means to another end. For instance, it may be simply better to possess wisdom than not to, even though being a wise person has no obvious and immediate practical consequences. Most strengths and virtues are also *recognized by the societies and culture* in which they occur. The more valued they are by the society, the more likely it will be that the society has developed institutions and rituals to help develop those qualities. Societies or communities also celebrate role models who embody the strengths and virtues. Recently, there has been a resurgence of interest in people, or even generations of people, who might serve as exemplary role models or heroes. For instance, Maurice Ashley is the first African American chess Grand Master. He volunteers his time to teach chess to kids in Harlem and serves as a role model to the children. Luckily, role models do not have to be real to be effective. Luke Skywalker or Yoda of the *Star Wars* movies and, even more recently, Harry Potter of the now-famous Hogwarts training academy for wizards and witches, can also serve as models for character, integrity, and courage. To identify a virtue, one might also ask, what would a parent generally wish for their newborn child? For instance, most people hope that their child develops positive character traits like honesty and integrity. Finally, strengths and virtues do not diminish other people when they are exercised. In fact, they may often *prompt a feeling of elevation or joy* when people witness someone expressing a strength or virtue. When someone expresses genuine humility after a courageous act, most people feel uplifted, expansive, or even compassionate. Peterson and Seligman (2004) said that the display of a strength by one person does not diminish or belittle other people. Indeed, it is frequently the case that others are elevated by their observation of virtuous action. Everyone benefits by the exercise of strengths and virtues.

In general, strengths and virtues support enabling conditions that help strengthen education, opportunity, family, and community. Furthermore, strengths and virtues are more than temporary or infrequent spontaneous reactions to the world. They should be consistent enough to be seen in different situations and present across time. Last, Peterson and Seligman differentiate talents and abilities from strengths and virtues. For them, talents are valued because they result in more tangible outcomes, and virtues are valued in their own right. For instance, musical talent is valued because it leads to better musical abilities, but a deep sense of humanitarian justice—a virtue—is valued in its own right.

Another perspective on virtues is that of Steven Sandage and P. Hill (2001), who define virtue by six dimensions. They believe that virtues "(a) integrate ethics and health, (b) are embodied traits of character, (c) are sources of human strengths and resilience, (d) are embedded within a cultural context and community, (e) contribute to a sense of meaningful life purpose, and (f) are grounded in the cognitive capacity for wisdom" (Emmons & Paloutzian, 2003, p. 387). The last dimension implies that virtues should emerge from a larger perspective on life that takes into consideration how current actions might have an impact on the welfare of self, others, and the community.

Good Character

One final clarification is necessary. That concerns the difference between virtues and character. On one hand, virtues are composed of specific strengths that benefit self and others. On the other hand, character is a higher-order concept that reflects the possession of several virtues. Consulting psychologist H. Skipton Leonard (1997) has written about a number of important issues concerning character. First, he notes that it has always been an important element of human society because people "needed to find ways to quickly predict whether a stranger could be trusted to act honorably. . . . Having a good reputation meant that people could depend on an individual to act consistently and in ways that took into consideration the welfare of others and the greater good of society" (p. 235). In other words, character has always counted. Second, Leonard also gives some guidelines for defining character, or at least recognizing it when we see it. He notes that character always implies behavioral consistency over time. However, it is not the same as temperament or dispositional personality traits. Instead, character must be learned and developed over time through experience, training, or socialization. Good character is also recognized as involving certain capacities of the self, including self-regulation, strong self-identity, and empathy. Character is also recognized in the exercise of good judgments. Leonard describes this as "the ability to think effectively while emotions of fear, greed, pity, disappointment, and so forth are raging, it identifies those individuals who will be able to demonstrate sound judgment and character consistently over time and in a wide variety of situations" (p. 242). According to Cloniger, Svrakic, and Prybeck (1993), good character is also seen in displays of high ethical standards and self-transcendence. They believe that good character must involve the ability to "get out of" oneself, to transcend one's personal concerns, and to empathically identify with another's feelings or situation. Therefore, character implies a summation of one's virtues, a willingness to behave in accordance with those virtues even in difficult social situations, and the ability to be empathic.

Authentic Happiness

One of the most recent perspectives on positive mental health comes from Martin E. P. Seligman (2002a). Consistent with this discussion of strengths and virtues, Seligman focused his theory on what he terms **signature strengths,** positive personality characteristics that are representative of each person and add to his or her uniqueness. Everyone has a number of positive qualities that represent their strengths, but some of those are more important and more central to their identity. When people exercise their signature strengths, they tend to feel invigorated, enthusiastic about displaying them, and have a sense that their "real self" is being expressed. The strengths are also recognized more easily by others (see Seligman, 2002a). Therefore, for Seligman (2002a), **authentic happiness** is found by "identifying and cultivating your most fundamental strengths and using them every day in work, love, play, and parenting." (p. xiii). Further, the consistent exercise of signature strengths results in recognizable core virtues that over time become identifiable positive character traits for individuals.

Taking the idea of signature strengths further, Seligman defines **gratifications** as our emotional responses to activities that allow us to enact our signature strengths and virtues. For example, imagine someone who has a number of positive qualities but is especially recognized by others for her courage, perseverance, self-control, caution, and passion for life. This woman also enjoys rock climbing—a somewhat dangerous sport. Seligman would say that she enjoys rock climbing because the activity allows her to experience the gratifications that result from using her signature strengths and virtues in that activity.

For Seligman, the *good life* is using one's signature strengths to obtain gratifications in the important areas of one's life. The *meaningful life* is using signature strengths in the service of something that is larger and more significant than the individual self. The *full life* is feeling and savoring positive feelings about the past, present, and future to obtain abundant gratifications. These come from exercising strengths and using strengths to foster meaning by placing efforts into the service of something larger and more significant.

Recently, Seligman teamed with *USA Weekend* magazine to find and evaluate "America's happiest person" (McCafferty, 2003). The man they located scored "off the charts" on all standard measures of happiness. Seligman then applied these six principles of authentic happiness to help their "happiest man" gain even more fulfillment in life:

1. *Everyone benefits.* Authentically happy people negotiate life by fostering an "every body wins" strategy, as opposed to focusing on threats of other negative possibilities.
2. *Savoring success.* Authentically happy people not only savor good moments and successes but also tap into past successes to help deal with problems in the present.
3. *Social intelligence.* Authentically happy people know which strengths to use and which to avoid with a particular person or situation.
4. *Opening doors.* Authentically happy people find open doors when others find closed doors. As in the old saying, "when life hands you a lemon, make lemonade."
5. *Strengths in couples.* Authentically happy people enhance their romantic relationships by joining both partner's personal strengths.
6. *Finding meaning.* Authentically happy people leave a legacy.

Although this collaboration was done for the popular press rather than for the scientific journals, it nevertheless illustrates Seligman's theory (which is based on scientific research). Note that in his perspective a hedonic focus on positive emotions is combined with a eudaimonic focus on virtues and personal growth in order to produce authentic happiness.

Summary

This chapter covered a number of topics related to positive mental health. Recent studies of resiliency in children have shown that in spite of difficult early environments, some children grow into healthy adults and may even thrive. Similarly, studies of aging have found that many people adapt to changes with remarkable ingenuity as they age. Research has found that wisdom is related to sensitivity to interpersonal issues, more varied life experiences, perspective taking, and the ability to grapple with paradox. A number of major criteria for positive mental health were reviewed. Perspectives on self-actualization, authenticity, and mature defense mechanisms were reviewed. The unique perspective on human strengths and virtues offered by positive psychology was reviewed. Studies of both development and mental health have found that people sometimes show remarkable adaptability in response to life's difficulties. The ability to use strengths and competencies has been shown to influence quality of life and mental health in positive ways.

Note

1. Later in his life, Maslow added a sixth need at the top of his hierarchy (Maslow, 1968): the need for transcendence or to expand one's sense of meaning in life through development of a more "spiritual" per-

spective. Maslow came to believe that people need to connect with something larger than the individual self. Much of his later work was devoted to the exploration of the need for transcendence.

LEARNING TOOLS

Key Terms and Ideas

AUTHENTIC HAPPINESS
AUTHENTICITY
FULLY FUNCTIONING PERSON
GRATIFICATIONS
MATURE OR ADAPTIVE DEFENSE MECHANISMS
RESILIENCE
SELECTIVE OPTIMIZATION WITH COMPENSATION
SELF-ACTUALIZING TENDENCY
SOCIAL INTEREST
SOCIOEMOTIONAL SELECTIVITY
WISDOM

Books

Anthony, E. J., & Cohler, B. J. (Eds.). (1987). *The invulnerable child.* New York: Guilford. A collection of articles on resilience in children (professional).

Maslow, A. (1968). *Toward a psychology of being.* (2nd ed.). New York: John Wiley. Maslow's best introduction to what he meant by self-actualization (popular/professional).

McAdams, D. F., & de St. Aubin, E. (1998). *Generativity and adult development: How and why we care for the next generation.* Washington, DC: American Psychological Association.

Rogers, C. (1961). *On becoming a person.* Boston, MA: Hougton-Mifflin. Rogers's best introduction for the public on his ideas about therapy and optimal mental health (popular/professional).

Seligman, M. E. P. (2002). *Authentic happiness: Using the new positive psychology to realize your potential for lasting fulfillment.* New York: Free Press. The founder of positive psychology discusses his ideas on happiness and the good life (popular).

Research Articles

Baltes, P., & Staudinger, U. (2000). Wisdom: A metaheuristic (pragmatic) to orchestrate mind and virtue toward excellence. *American Psychologist, 55*(1), 122–136.

Masten, A. (2001). Ordinary magic: Resilience processes in development. *American Psychologist, 56*(3), 227–238.

McCullough, M. E., & Snyder, C. R. (Eds.) (2001). Classical sources of human strength [special issue]. *Journal of Social and Clinical Psychology, 19*(1). This special issue was devoted to an exploration of human strengths and virtues such as gratitude and forgiveness.

Vaillant, G. (2000). Adaptive mental mechanisms: Their role in a positive psychology. *American Psychologist, 55*(1), 89–98.

Personal Explorations

Some theories of well-being say that our perspective on life changes as we age and, therefore, how we think about well-being also changes. For this exercise, interview someone who is at least 25 years older than you (if you are past middle age, then interview someone from a different generation than yourself). How did his or her answers differ from yours?

The theories of Rogers and Maslow take a eudaimonic approach to well-being (see Chapter 1). Do their ideas on well-being differ from ideas from the subjective well-being literature discussed in Chapter 3? If so, how?

Maslow said that self-actualizing people tended to chose growth over security. That is, they took healthy risks to expand their potentials. Describe a time that you took a risk and felt that you grew as a person because of it. Remember, you can grow as a person both when you succeed and when you fail. How did the experience help you grow as a person?

Think of an incident when you "found your voice" or you felt that you acted very authentic. How did it make you feel? What aspects of yourself or the situation helped you be more authentic?

CHAPTER 9

INTERVENTIONS FOR ENHANCED WELL-BEING

> We have discovered that there are human strengths that act as buffers against mental illness. . . . Much of the task of prevention in this century will be to create a science of human strengths whose mission will be to understand and learn how to foster these virtues in young people.
>
> *Martin E. P. Seligman (2002b)*

THE DISEASE MODEL OF MENTAL ILLNESS AND ITS PROBLEMS

The last chapter covered a number of perspectives on positive mental health that have emerged over the years from psychological theory, psychological laboratories, and clinics. With this variety of perspectives, one would expect there to be a standard method used to assess levels of positive functioning in human beings. Surprisingly, no standard method for assessing positive psychological functioning is in use today. A number of theorists have produced measurement scales to measure their own theoretical perspective on mental health; however, for the most part, these assessments exist as research tools and are not found in applied settings. Almost all assessment and diagnostic systems that are in common use today focus not on positive functioning but rather on mental illness or psychopathology.

In Chapter 1, we saw that before World War II psychology had three distinct missions: to cure mental illness, to make people's lives more fulfilling, and to nurture talent. As psychology and other professions that work with mental illness began to focus on curing mental illness, they developed a diagnostic system to help identify the types of mental illness. The standard manual used for this purpose is the *Diagnostic and Statistical Manual for Mental Disorders,* 4th edition, or the *DSM-IV* (American Psychiatric Association, 1994). This manual has helped professionals identify mental illness and has helped researchers discover real cures for a number of disorders. While the *DSM* has been helpful to millions of people, it has also been criticized because it is based on a disease model and because it may create victimology (Maddux, 2002; Seligman, 2002b).

Any diagnostic system of mental illness that is based on the disease model views psychological problems in the same way that medicine views disease. Under a **disease model,** any mental illness is a distinct deviation from normality that can be identified by a unique cluster of symptoms that are caused by a specific pathogen. Most of the ways in which psychology and the other mental health professions have thought about mental illness are based on a disease model. Note that even the terms used so far in this discussion are based on a disease model—mental "illness," mental "health," "pathogen," psycho-"pathology." Is there any evidence that psychological problems are analogous to diseases?

Actually, little evidence exists that problems such as depression or anxiety operate like diseases (Seligman, 2002b). Psychological problems are generally based on normal human emotional experiences that are either unnecessarily over- or undercontrolled. Psychological problems can also be ineffective patterns in living that exist between people in social interactions rather than "inside" people as diseases (Maddux, 2002). In general, the disease model is a poor fit with psychological problems.

One of the most unfortunate consequences of the disease model has been the creation of a victim mentality in the health professions and in clients or patients (Seligman, 2002b). Just as people can be the unfortunate victims of germs, viruses, and other disease causing agents, psychology has come to view people as victims of their unconscious drives, their innate needs, the families they grew up in as children, or the environments in which they exist as adults. In other words, people were seen as passively reacting to stimuli such as dysfunctional families that inevitably caused responses such as excessive anxiety and depression. If health professionals and psychotherapists treat patients as helpless pawns or victims, then two things can happen. One, the professionals begin to react to the patients as if they are helpless and need to be fixed. They take on the total responsibility for treatment. Two, the self-fulfilling prophecy begins to operate, and the patients see themselves as helpless and passively allow themselves to be poked, probed, and pilled. They relinquish any responsibility for their own treatment. As this victimology has continued, each new edition of the *DSM* has included more and more new types of mental "illness."

Toward a Classification of Strengths

One of the tasks for positive psychology is to develop a classification of human strengths (Seligman, 2002b). It is quite apparent that human beings are capable of exhibiting a wide variety of extraordinary behaviors that foster well-being in themselves and in those around them. Beatrice Wright and Shane Lopez (2002) said, "In positive psychology we must challenge a common error of professional psychology today: making diagnostic, treatment, and policy decisions primarily on deficiencies of the person instead of giving serious consideration to . . . strengths of both person and environment" (p. 26). We know that even people who are caught in states of deep depression or are plagued with debilitating anxiety can still exhibit amazing courage, resilience, fortitude, and compassion for other people. Further, good evidence suggests that a critical factor in curing distress is the psychological strengths that people bring to the task.

Take the hypothetical example of a client who presents herself in a therapist's office. Three months ago, Sarah's husband unexpectedly walked out on her, and their fifteen-year marriage ended. Since then, she has been experiencing low-energy levels, a lack of enthusiasm for life, poor self-esteem, and a sense of hopelessness about the future. In addition, she has lost weight because of poor appetite and is plagued with insomnia. According to the *DSM*, she may be clinically depressed. However, Sarah has also shown evidence of adaptability, fortitude, perseverance, and the ability to emotionally connect with other people. Sarah is also intelligent, creative, and determined to fight her problem. Currently, there is no way to adequately classify the strengths that Sarah is bringing to therapy. Further, no systematic body of research exists that would help illuminate for the clinician how Sarah's strengths will help her beat depression. It is important to note that there is no doubt that Sarah's strengths will help. We simply do not know exactly how they will help her as she deals with her depression.

Therefore, one of the tasks for positive psychology is to create a classification system of strengths. Some work has already been done by people who have designed assessment tools for their particular theory of well-being. The next section will explore a few theories and assessment tools that focus on positive behaviors and positive well-being. One of the advantages that positive psychology brings to the research in this area is a renewed sense that we need to identify those human strengths that foster positive growth. Another advantage will be a call to develop reliable and valid assessment instruments that can adequately address previous work in this area and expand that research into more comprehensive classification systems of human strengths.

The Dimensions of Positive Mental Health

By the late 1950s, some researchers were frustrated by a lack of classification systems for positive mental health. Many were also frustrated with trying to use a single personality factor to index a person's degree of mental health. So, those researchers began to propose multiple dimensions of well-being that could be used to form a profile of mental health for any specific person. The following perspectives on positive mental health have all adopted multidimensional models.

Marie Jahoda and Positive Mental Health

The first attempt to summarize the relevant literature on positive mental health was undertaken by Marie Jahoda in the late 1950s. The resulting book was the first systematic cross-theoretical exploration of twentieth-century concepts of positive mental health (Jahoda, 1958).

Jahoda began her analysis with a listing of three unacceptable criteria for positive mental health: (1) the absence of mental illness, (2) conformity to social norms, and (3) permanent states of being. The first criterion is problematic because defining mental health as an absence of some negative emotional state such as depression or anxiety does not describe what it is but rather what it is not. Such lack of specificity makes the definition functionally meaningless. Conformity to social norms is a problematic criterion because norms change with history, they may be different for subgroups within a population, and they may actually be destructive to mental health (e.g., rigid sex-roles may be the norm in some societies, but they may also be unhealthy). Finally, basing a definition of mental health on permanent states of being ignores the fact that no one can feel certain emotions at all times. Our emotions constantly change. Mental health must be defined by how one adapts to inevitable changes.

Jahoda's (1958) review and analysis resulted in six criteria for positive mental health. In addition, each criteria has subcategories associated with it.

1. *Attitudes toward the self.* This criterion addresses ideas such as self-acceptance, self-confidence, or self-reliance. There are four main subcategories: (a) adequate self-awareness, (b) accurate self-concept, (c) self-acceptance, and (d) a positive and "globally benevolent" view of the self.

2. *Growth, development and self-actualization.* Jahoda associated mental health with a striving toward goals in the future including efforts to realize potential. This involved: (a) the ability to accept challenges and tension in the present in the interest of future goals and (b) investment in living or an extension of the self through involvement in different pursuits, a concern for other people, and a desire to help others and be of service.
3. *An integrated personality.* This criterion refers to a balancing of the important aspects of self that allows for efficient functioning. It is composed of three elements: (a) desires, impulses, and needs are balanced with rationality, responsibility, and social concerns; (b) a unifying philosophy of life or a sense of meaning and purpose is present; and (c) the person exhibits anxiety tolerance, frustration tolerance, and the ability to delay gratification.
4. *Autonomy.* This criterion has two aspects: (a) regulation of behavior from within and (b) independent behavior. This element speaks to the ability to act independently of environmental pressures. It involves the strength to resist unnecessary conformity or obedience to authority.
5. *Perception of reality.* An ability to see the world and self accurately. According to Jahoda, it involves two aspects: (a) the ability to see self and others without one's own needs distorting perception of other people or situations and (b) empathy and social sensitivity. She suggests that if people are free from need distortion, then they are better able to see others clearly and honestly and are thus more able to empathize with them.
6. *Environmental mastery.* This criterion refers to successful adaptation to situational demands and expectations. It includes six different subcategories: (a) the ability to love, (b) ability to work and play, (c) good interpersonal relations, (d) ability to meet the demands of situations with a sense of mastery and self-efficacy, (e) ability to balance efforts to change the external world with efforts to change one's own psychological world, and (f) ability to use adequate problem-solving strategies.

In general, Jahoda's perspective on positive mental health presents a picture of a person who is able to balance a number of personality factors. For instance, the person is able to balance independence with dependence, self-concern with concern for others, and honest self-awareness with healthy self-enhancements. Because of this balance, the person can form healthy relationships with others and has the capacity to reach desired goals in life. Although Jahoda's analysis was completed in 1958, many of her comments remain relevant today.

Carol Ryff and Psychological Well-Being

Carol Ryff has also attempted to summarize the positive mental health literature. Ryff (1985, 1995) reviewed the work of the classic theories of positive mental health and added more recent research from developmental, clinical, and personality psychology. Ryff's studies produced six criteria for what she called psychological well-being, along with subcategories (1989a, 1989b, 1995).

Ryff's six-dimensional model of **psychological well-being** includes the following factors:

1. *Self-acceptance:* (a) positive self-evaluation, (b) the ability to acknowledge multiple aspects of self, and (c) the ability to accept both positive and negative qualities into a balanced picture of one's abilities.
2. *Personal growth:* (a) capacity to grow and develop potentials, (b) personal changes over time that reflect growing

self-knowledge and effectiveness, and (c) openness to new experiences.

3. *Positive relations with other people:* (a) close, warm, and intimate relationships with others, (b) a concern about the welfare of others, and (c) empathy and affection for other people.
4. *Autonomy:* (a) independent and self-determined, (b) ability to resist social pressures, and (c) ability to regulate behavior from within.
5. *Purpose in life:* (a) a sense of purpose and meaning to life and (b) a sense of direction and goals in life.
6. *Environmental mastery:* (a) a sense of mastery and competence and (b) the ability to choose situations and environments that are conducive to meeting goals.

Ryff developed the Psychological Well-Being Scale to measure these six dimensions of psychological well-being. Her research with this scale and others has supported the dimensions of psychological well-being as a valid measure of positive mental health in a variety of populations (Ryff, 1995; Ryff & Keyes, 1995). Ryff has also found that different dimensions of psychological well-being may be more important than others at different points throughout life. High psychological well-being in younger people tends to be based less on environmental mastery but more on personal growth, while high well-being for middle-aged persons tends to require more autonomy and environmental mastery (Ryff, 1989b). She has also found that the ways in which people find a sense of psychological well-being may be different at different points in the life span. Younger persons associate well-being with pleasant activities, middle-aged persons associate it with positive relationships with family and friends, while older persons associate well-being with positive work experiences in the past and current opportunities for educational experiences (Ryff, 1995; Ryff & Heidrich, 1997).

Richard Coan and the Modes of Fulfillment

Another way to think about criteria for the positive mental health or the good life is to consider that there may exist multiple ways to search for fulfillment in life. Richard Coan's particular approach to well-being involved what he called the five basic **modes of fulfillment** (Coan, 1974, 1977), which are the basic directions that people take in their search for happiness and well-being. The modes are the person's core focus in his or her search for the good life. They are the goals pursued, but sometimes never fully realized, in the search for well-being and fulfillment. Note that the modes of fulfillment Coan described are not specific emotions. Each individual's search may contain various degrees of struggle and disappointments as well as satisfactions, joys, and moments of happiness.

Coan's five basic modes of fulfillment include:

1. *Efficiency.* This refers to a focus on the exceptional use of one's talents or skills. People who pursue excellence in specific endeavors are focused on this mode of fulfillment.
2. *Creativity.* This mode is the one chosen by artists or people who have an artistic temperament. It is an approach to well-being that relies on openness to experience, freedom of expression, spontaneity, and independence from social convention.
3. *Inner harmony.* As might be expected, this mode refers to a focus on psychological criteria for psychological well-being. Characteristics associated with this mode would be personality integration, balanced emotional responding, absence of debilitating anxiety or depression, and resolution of psychological conflicts.
4. *Relatedness.* This mode has as its focus the development of interpersonal relationships and the presence of love. Anyone whose

definition of happiness revolves around love, family, or emotional intimacy is committed to this mode

5. *Self-transcendence.* This mode takes as its focus the person's relationship to God, spirituality, or whatever they conceptualize as the ultimate being.

Coan says that fulfillment can be found through any of these modes. He implies that if we are diligent, committed, and persistent in our pursuit of the goals associated with that mode, we can find fulfillment. Happiness is certainly associated with fulfillment, but the quality, quantity, and character of happiness can vary as people pursue these goals.

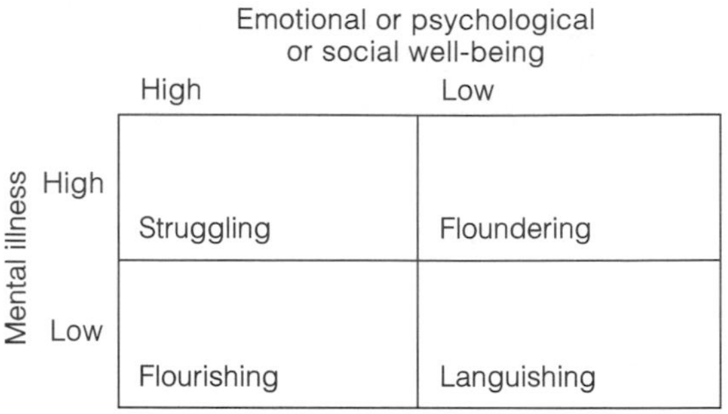

FIGURE **9.1**

Complete Mental Health According to Keyes and Lopez

Source: Keyes & Lopez (2002).

Keyes and Lopez and Complete Mental Health

One of the newer perspectives on the classification of mental health comes from Corey L. M. Keyes and Shane Lopez (2002). First, they are in agreement with one of the basic assumptions of positive psychology: that mental health is not merely the absence of mental illness. Second, they suggest that positive mental health is also not merely the presence of high levels of subjective well-being. Keyes and Lopez took these ideas and created a four-fold typology of well-being. In their system, people who are high on subjective well-being and low on mental illness are *flourishing.* People who are low on well-being and high on mental illness symptoms are *floundering.* When someone shows signs of low well-being, but they are also low on mental illness, they are *languishing.* Finally, *struggling* is found when someone exhibits both high well-being and high mental illness (see Figure 9.1).

Keyes and Lopez take their idea a bit farther and look at how well-being has been defined in the past. They believe that other systems of classifying mental health and well-being are incomplete because they focus on only a portion of what it means to be mentally healthy. Instead, they suggest that **complete mental health** is a combination of three types of well-being along with low mental illness: (1) high emotional well-being, (2) high psychological well-being, and (3) high social well-being. High *emotional well-being* or emotional vitality is present when people are happy and satisfied with their lives—when they have high subjective well-being (see Chapter 3). High *psychological well-being* is found when people are competent, autonomous, self-accepting, when they have a purpose in life, exhibit personal growth, and when they have positive relationships with others (see the earlier discussion of Ryff's criteria for psychological well-being). High *social well-being* is found when people have positive attitudes toward others in their social world, believe that social change is possible, when they make a contribution to society, when they believe the social world is understandable, and when they feel a part of a larger social community. Therefore, the complete model could include twelve basic classifications of well-being (i.e., high and low well-being by high and low mental illness by three types of well-being).

TABLE 9.1 **VALUES IN ACTION CLASSIFICATION OF STRENGTHS AND VIRTUES**

Wisdom and Knowledge	**Justice**
Curiosity and interest in world	Citizenzhip
Love of learning	Fairness
Open-mindedness	Humane leadership
Creativity	**Courage**
Perspective	Bravery
Humanity	Persistence
Kindness	Honesty and integrity
Love	Zest and vitality
Social intelligence	**Transcendence**
Temperance	Appreciation of beauty and excellence
Self-control	Humor and playfulness
Prudence	Gratitude
Modesty	Hope
Forgiveness and mercy	Religiousness

Source: C. Peterson and M. E. P. Seligman, eds., *Character strengths and virtues* (New York: Oxford University Press, 2004). Reprinted with permission.

The Values in Action (VIA) Classification

Recently, Christopher Peterson and Martin E. P. Seligman (Peterson, 2001; Peterson & Seligman, 2004) began to develop a classification system for strengths and virtues (recall the discussion in Chapter 8). They proposed that strengths can be broadly classified into cognitive strengths, emotional strengths, strength of will, relational and civic strengths, and strengths that help create coherence of personality. Working with Katherine Dahlsgaard and others, Peterson and Seligman reviewed the important virtues that have been promulgated in cultures throughout history. They also looked at how these virtues were regarded in different cultures as they compiled their list of strengths and virtues. They included in their **Values in Action (VIA)** classification system strengths and virtues that have universal significance because those strengths have been valued across different cultures throughout different periods of history.

In their classification, Peterson and Seligman list 24 different strengths that help define six different core virtues. Their list, which is shown in Table 9.1, includes cognitive, emotional, and interpersonal strengths as well as strengths that promote healthy community life, protect against excess, and forge connections to a larger universe.

The similarities to Aristotle's virtues and the cardinal and theological virtues listed in Chapter 1 are quite striking suggesting a degree of historical validity to the list—at least in terms of Western civilization. However, Peterson and Seligman note that their list is certainly not a comprehensive list of strengths and virtues because they recognize that other virtues may be useful in specific social contexts (Peterson, 2001). For instance, in certain religious or spiritual contexts, the virtue of "selflessness" may be prized and fostered. One of the tasks for positive psychologists in the future is to continue efforts to classify strengths and virtues. Researchers and therapists can then use those classification systems to develop positive therapy interventions to help people accentuate modes of flourishing in their lives.

Positive Psychology Interventions

So far, this chapter and the previous chapter have addressed the major criteria for positive mental health as well as the classification of positive mental health and well-being. If we know what the goals for positive well-being should be and we know how to evaluate progress, then the next step is to devise intervention strategies that will help people reach those goals.

Positive Psychotherapy

Seligman (2002b) suggests that "treatment is not just fixing what is wrong, it is also building what is right" (p. 4). **Positive therapy** is an approach to treatment that is built on the enhancement of positive traits, the building of strengths, and helping clients find untapped resources for positive change. As was mentioned in Chapter 1, a number of studies have found that processes that help to eliminate negative emotions are not necessarily identical to the factors that help enhance positive emotions. The reduction of negative emotions and behaviors does not automatically result in positive emotions or psychological flourishing (Keyes & Lopez, 2002). Therefore, just fixing what is wrong is only half of the challenge.

A relevant example comes from research on the outcomes of psychotherapy. Seligman points out that research on psychotherapy has repeatedly shown that most people report substantial benefits from psychotherapy. One study found that over 90 percent of clients felt they benefited from therapy (Seligman, 1995). He further points out that the benefits of psychotherapy are not the result of any particular form of therapy. Instead, Seligman believes that therapy is beneficial because it does more than eliminate symptoms of psychological distress. He argues that good therapy enhances already existing strengths in clients. In fact, studies of what makes psychotherapy effective have found that "client factors," which include psychological strengths, can account for up to 40 percent of the improvement seen in therapy (Lambert, 1992).

Just what are the strengths that all good therapy seems to provide? One example comes from Jerome Frank (Frank & Frank, 1991), who for many years has said that all good therapies will "instill hope." Seligman agrees that the development of hope is one of the basic strengths that all good systems of psychotherapy can enhance. Good therapy may also enhance courage, insight, optimism, honesty, perseverance, and the ability to dispute one's own negative thinking. A positive orientation to therapy also recognizes that positive traits and adaptive behaviors may also serve as buffers against future stressors and difficulties. People who know how to dispute their irrationally negative thinking, for instance, are in a better position to deal positively with unexpected setbacks.

In addition to facilitating the building of strengths, positive therapy may also view clients or patients in a different light. Many traditional systems of psychotherapy view clients as passive recipients of the intervention strategies provided by the therapist. Therapists working from this perspective view themselves as "change agents" who intervene by doing something that stimulates a passive (or resistant) client to change in specific directions. The therapist usually determines those directions and the goals of therapy.

In positive psychotherapy, however, therapists see clients as "active seekers of health" (Keyes & Lopez, 2002). This is an important distinction, because even in times of extreme psychological difficulty, most people are actively trying in many ways to solve their own problems. In fact, most people successfully use a wide variety of techniques to help them regulate their moods on a daily basis (Thayer, Newman, & McClain, 1994). Pause for a moment and think about the variety of ways that a person uses to put him- or herself in a good mood or shake off a bad mood. If one wants an emotional boost, one can exercise, listen to music, do something for fun, go shopping, or go out with a friend. People can be very creative problem solvers if therapists just work with their clients to nurture already existing skills, talents, and strengths. Therefore, one of the tasks of good therapists should be to amplify client strengths as well as to help decrease debilitating negative emotions.

Early Perspectives on Positive Therapy

As seen earlier, Adler, Jung, and others in the beginning of the twentieth century all saw their systems of psychotherapy as ways for some people to achieve enhanced well-being and positive mental health. All these early pioneers believed that optimal mental health involved both the elimination of debilitating emotional conditions and the development of more fulfilling, creative, and meaningful lives. Most of these approaches to positive mental health, however, were relatively isolated from mainstream psychology, which focused almost exclusively on the treatment of psychopathology.

As a result of this exclusive focus on serious pathology, in the 1940s some psychologists began to see a need to create a new specialty area. Because clinical psychology seemed to focus on the most serious forms of mental illness, a new specialty area was needed that would focus on making normal lives more fulfilling. In 1951, these psychologists created a new specialty area in psychology called *counseling psychology*. Today, counseling psychology continues to focus more on relatively undisturbed clients who need assistance with life adjustment problems, career plans, relationship difficulties, and other problems in living. Over the years, the distinctions between clinical and counseling psychology have blurred, but counseling psychology still remains focused on helping normal people lead lives that are more fulfilling.

Personal Growth and Human Potential

Therapists associated with humanistic psychology have also developed a number of intervention strategies aimed at helping people to achieve states of enhanced well-being (Schneider, Bugental, & Pierson, 2001; Cain & Seeman, 2002). During the 1960s, a number of people associated with humanistic psychology created a style of intervention termed *personal growth therapy or human potential* (Mann, 1979). These approaches focused on helping people who were functioning fairly well to reach more of their potentials. The basic principle behind the human potential approach is that normal psychosocial adjustment represents a point of departure, rather than a goal (Mann, 1979). It is assumed that people utilize a very small part of their potentials and that all people have the capacity to expand and develop their skills, talents, and potentials.

There is a second approach to personal growth that may or may not be associated with humanistic psychology. This type of personal growth experience tends to be more educational and tries to help people overcome their self-imposed limits. For instance, people may choose workshops designed to tap into their creative potential, or they may take part in exercises designed to help them build self-confidence and increase their motivation for success. Or, they may choose a workshop to just help relax and communicate better with their colleagues. Personal growth experiences like these, as well as many other types, are offered to a variety of clients in a variety of settings—to individuals, church groups, and corporate boardrooms.

Unfortunately, the usefulness and long-lasting effects of many personal growth experiences and techniques from the human potential movement have not been determined. In the past, a number of humanistically oriented personal growth interventions had not been adequately researched (Mann, 1979). Even today, many personal growth intervention techniques of both types still remain untested for their usefulness. However, more recently, many of the well-established styles of humanistic psychotherapy, as well as a few basic assumptions behind humanistic psychology, have developed a good initial research foundation that supports their usefulness (Bohart & Greenberg, 1997; Greenberg & Rice, 1997; Cain & Seeman, 2002).

Recent Contributions to Positive Therapy

A few of the newer theoretical and applied perspectives in clinical and counseling psychology are in agreement with positive psychology's perspective on psychotherapy. In fact, a few years prior to the introduction of positive psychology, some psychotherapists were already beginning to suggest that therapy needs more focus on client strengths, capacities for problem solving, and demonstrated competencies.

One of the more well-known of these approaches is called *solution-focused therapy* (de Shazer, 1985; Berg, 1994; O'Connell & Palmer, 2003); as its name implies, it places the focus on solutions rather than on problems. Therapists help their clients to find strengths they have used in the past, remember how they have solved problems similar to the current one, and set realistic goals for newer healthy behaviors. The idea behind this therapy is that fixing what is "wrong" with clients may actually do little to help them solve their current problem and can end up as an exercise in self-reproach and self-pity for the clients. Therefore, therapy should focus on strengths and let the negative emotions and behaviors fade away as strengths are enhanced and goals reached. Therapists who use these ideas generally assume that people not only are competent, but that they can build upon that competence (Durant & Kowalski, 1993). Many view their clients as the true "experts" in the treatment and their own job as helping clients get "unstuck" and back on track.

Other new techniques of therapy and counseling have taken their theoretical cues more directly from a positive therapy orientation. *Well-being therapy* is an eight-session treatment package based on Ryff's proposed dimensions of psychological well-being. Developed by Giovanni Fava, well-being therapy helps clients to restructure the way they think about aspects of their lives in terms of Ryff's six dimensions of psychological well-being (Fava, Rafanelli, Cazzaro, Conti, & Grandi, 1998; Fava, 1999). Clients are helped to identify episodes of high well-being in their past, find ways in which well-being has been hindered in their lives, and identify the processes of change that can be used to enhance well-being in their lives. Clients are taught self-observation or self-monitoring skills, how to use a structured diary to record episodes of well-being, and how to change their thinking habits away from negative thoughts to more positive interpretations of events.

Similarly, Nossrat Peseschkian has developed a system of therapy he calls *positive psychotherapy* (Peseschkian, 1997; Peseschkian & Tritt, 1998). This system is based on the hypothesis that every person has within him or her a number of capabilities for dealing with problems. These capacities have developed over the years but are underutilized by the person. As positive psychotherapy is practiced with both individuals and families, the therapist uses procedures to assess the person's abilities and possibilities as well as problems. Positive psychotherapists point out that in traditional therapy, a client gets the therapist's attention by reporting negative symptoms, difficulties, and weaknesses. Therefore, the very nature of traditional psychotherapy tends to reinforce client problems because reporting problems is rewarded with the therapist's attention! Instead of reinforcing disturbances, positive psychotherapy attempts to enhance a person's actual capacities. The actual capacities are positive traits such as punctuality, courtesy, reliability, patience, or confidence (Peseschkian, 1997). In addition, positive psychotherapy also emphasizes the social, cultural, and transcultural aspects of therapy, just as positive psychology emphasizes the social contexts of our lives.

Another way that a positive psychology orientation may be used to help people change their lives comes from the work of Christine Robitschek (1998). She created the idea of *personal growth initiative* to describe how some people are able to foster personal growth changes. Personal growth is defined as a person's sense that he or she is growing psychologically, and the direction of that growth indicates progress as an individual. Personal growth initiative is the "active, intentional engagement in the process of personal growth" (Robitschek, 1998, p. 184). People who are high on personal growth tend to be open to experiences, seek improvement in themselves, have a sense of direction, and have goals in life (Whittaker & Robitschek, 2001). Robitschek has found that people who have high levels of personal growth initiative know the directions in which they would like to grow. They seem to be able to capitalize on opportunities for personal growth and seek out avenues for creativity and adaptive solutions (Robitschek & Kashubeck, 1999). For instance, college students who had high personal growth initiative also had stronger vocational and career directions and were more open to exploring different experiences in their environments (Robitschek & Cook, 1999).

Interventions that take a positive psychology orientation have also focused on training people to increase hope. *Hope therapy* is based on the idea that hope drives the emotions that define well-being (Lopez, Floyd, Ulven, & Snyder, 2000). It is derived from hope theory, which assumes that well-being is enhanced when people have well-developed goals and believe that they have the capacities and resources to reach those goals (see Chapter 2). Therefore, hope therapy attempts to help people conceptualize clearer goals, see numerous paths to those goals, and summon the energy and commitment to reach their goals. Researchers have studied the effect of hope training on people with psychological distress (see Keyes & Lopez, 2002). Training in hopeful thinking has helped people decrease anxiety and depression and increase positive coping skills and overall level of well-being.

One of the long-established interventions in counseling psychology is designed to help adults who find themselves at an impasse in their lives or who seem to have lost their sense of meaning and purpose in life. *Values clarification* is a process by which people can explore and clarify their values in order to refocus their lives in more meaningful directions or to simply reconnect with the values they use to ground their lives in more significant and meaningful ways (Simon, Howe, & Kirschenbaum, 1972). For a number of people, the stress and strain of contemporary life and the multiple, and often conflicting, values presented in society have combined to create a sense of confusion. Therefore, when people find themselves pulled and pushed by various choices and floundering with no sense of direction, they may seek to clarify the basic values that can be used to focus their lives. Many values clarification workshops are based on Louis Raths' seven criteria for a useful value. Raths, who built his ideas on the work of John Dewey, was concerned not with the content of values but with the process of valuing (see Simon, Howe, & Kirschenbaum, 1972). He focused on how people go about creating values in their lives and how those values turn into behavioral patterns. According to Raths, seven criteria can describe the process of creating values and turning them into behavioral traits (see Simon, Howe, & Kirschenbaum, 1972, p. 19):

1. Prizing and cherishing one's beliefs
2. Publicly affirming values, when appropriate
3. Evaluating alternative values

4. Choosing after thoughtful consideration of the consequences
5. Choosing freely
6. Acting on one's beliefs
7. Acting with some pattern, consistency, and repetition.

Over the years, a number of techniques have been developed to help people explore and clarify their values. These techniques can be used by people of all ages when they need to clarify their basic values or modify old values that no longer help them adjust to change (Hart, 1978).

Positive Interventions with Children

Seligman, Reivich, Jaycox, and Gillham (1995) created an intervention strategy to help children increase their optimistic thinking and build an optimistic orientation to life. In the Penn Optimism Program, Seligman and colleagues developed a twelve-week program for groups of children who were at risk for depression. Their *learned optimism training* program taught the children techniques of causal reattribution among other skills. That is, the children were taught to recognize the differences between positive and negative thoughts and to change their negative attributions for events through the use of role-play and story telling. Along with this strategy, Seligman and his colleagues also taught the children the skill of "disputing" (Seligman, Schulman, DeRubeis, & Hollon, 1999). This is a common cognitive skill that many people use everyday. In learned optimism training, however, people are taught to use the skill systematically and strategically. People use disputing, for instance, when someone says something about them that they know is false. Under many circumstances, people will immediately begin to dispute the other person's statement. They will marshal arguments to defend what they know is correct. For instance, both children and adults in Seligman's learned optimism training seminars are taught to recognize their own catastrophic thinking and to counter it by being skilled disputers. The children were also taught problem-solving skills and how to apply the principles in real-world settings. Research with the program has found that children who learn the skills are at less risk for later depression. In fact, children who went through the training were half as likely to experience depression later as were children who did not receive the training.

Seligman (2002b) gives some suggestions for how to dispute pessimistic thoughts and increase optimism and hope. His suggestions are based on the ABCDE model. In this model, "A" is the event that stimulates adversity. "B" is the beliefs that automatically occur in response to that event. "C" is the usual consequences of the belief. So far, the model describes the following sequences: an event occurs (A); it is interpreted in some way and given meaning (B); and because of how it is interpreted, certain emotional or behavioral responses reliably occur (C). Those emotional responses are often negative if the beliefs were pessimistic or unrealistic. Optimism or hope can be the emotional response if a person disputes their usual belief (D) with other more hopeful or realistic interpretations. If this is successful, then the person will feel more energized (E). This basic sequence is used often in various forms of cognitive therapy and will be discussed later in the section on happiness training programs.

Using a similar approach, Snyder, McDermott, Cook, and Rapoff (1997) developed a narrative approach to help build hope in children (see also "learned hopefulness" in Zimmerman, 1990). In their intervention strategy, children are taught to include hopeful themes in stories that they write. Shane Lopez has also brought the perspective of positive psychology into the schools. He and his colleagues have developed a series of classroom experiences designed to develop and foster hope in junior high-school students (Lopez, Bouwkamp, Edwards, & Teramoto-Pedrotti, 2000).

Positive Psychology in Educational Settings

As mentioned, schools are one of the more obvious settings to implement training and education based on positive psychology. What is this training like? First, the training workshops on optimism and hope can also be implemented in school systems. However, most studies up to this point have targeted children who are at risk for psychological problems. It is also possible to include lessons in the normal school curriculum that are based on a positive psychology perspective. For example, Michael Wehmeyer (1996) has worked for a decade with students in special education populations. He and his colleagues believed that students who leave school as self-determined persons will adapt to the world in more positive and healthy ways. To this end, they developed instructional methods to enhance *self-determination* and have found that students who learn greater self-determination skills do adjust better after graduation. Similarly, Pajares (2001) found that personal qualities associated with positive psychology, such as optimism and authenticity, were higher in public middle school students who were high in achievement motivation and goal oriented.

The discussion of *emotional intelligence* in Chapter 2 is also relevant to the school setting. Because one of the stated goals of education is to nurture "intelligence," it is logical that some schools might want to encourage emotional intelligence as well. In fact, some schools have begun to teach emotional intelligence skills. The Self Science curriculum developed at the Nueva School in Hillsborough, California, is offered to children in the first through the eighth grades and teaches them skills essential to emotional intelligence (see Salovey, Mayer, & Caruso, 2002). Among a number of skills, the curriculum helps children to recognize and label their emotions, be more aware of multiple feelings, take responsibility for their emotions, and teaches both listening and communication skills (Stone-McCown, Jensen, Freedman, & Rideout, 1998). A number of other programs that fall under the general category of social and emotional learning programs and character education also offer training in skills essential to emotional intelligence.

For a number of years, one of the goals of most school systems has been to promote character development. Formally, many of these programs have been called *character education* or *moral education* programs—although this last term has been the more politically sensitive descriptor. The aim of these programs is to teach students about positive moral values and virtues. At the most basic level, character education tries to teach children how to distinguish "right" from "wrong," but the goals may also include teaching how to recognize ethical dilemmas and resist peers who pressure students to violate personal values, good decision making, and the promotion of citizenship (Murphy, 1998). Almost all these programs teach a set of virtues that are fairly universal and transcend specific religious or cultural contexts. Over the years, school systems have found that positive values can be taught, and some schools really stand out from others because they do such a good job of providing quality character education (Murphy, 1998; Stirling, Archibald, McKay, & Berg, 2000).

Interventions to Increase Resilience

Strategies to promote resilience in children and adolescents are already underway, although the number of programs is still quite small (see discussion of resilience in Chapter 8). Intervention efforts that are aimed at promoting, enhancing, or maintaining resiliency focus on two major goals. The first is to reduce risk factors that may decrease or destroy resilience. The second is to promote and build resilience in children and adolescents. In general, efforts to reduce risk factors have focused on risk factors within the family and community (Masten & Reed, 2002).

Important factors within the family that build resiliency include caregivers who value the child's education, an authoritative parenting style (i.e., consistent and clear rules but respect and caring for the child), and socioeconomic advantages. Early interventions for families at risk can have a positive impact on within-the-family factors. Helpful factors outside the family include the presence of a supportive adult and forming relationships with prosocial peers. Relationships outside the family can be enhanced through organizations such as Big Brothers and Big Sisters or the Girls and Boys Clubs. Advantages within the community include good schools, good public health services, and cohesive and connected neighborhoods (Masten & Reed, 2002). A number of interventions that foster social life also help improve the quality of life for neighborhoods and communities. Other strategies attempt to promote and build resilience within the child. "Within-the-child" qualities include positive self-esteem, good social skills, problem-solving and academic abilities, a positive outlook on life, and a good sense of humor.

The work of Sybil and Steve Wolin (2000) illustrates how intervention strategies enhance and build resilience. The Wolins taught resilience skills to troubled adolescents as a way to increase their chances for better social adjustment. They began by interviewing adolescents who seemed to be resilient and asked them how they managed to thrive while others succumbed to poverty and other risk factors. From the answers they received, they abstracted seven traits of resiliency (see www.projectresilience.com):

1. *Insight.* The resilient adolescents asked tough questions to provide clarity and to pierce through denial and confusion.
2. *Independence.* They were able to distance themselves emotionally and physically from trouble in order to ensure safety and to open up opportunities.
3. *Good relationships.* They were able to create healthy emotional ties to nurturing people.
4. *Initiative.* They took charge of problems to create a sense of self-efficacy.
5. *Creativity.* They could transform their emotional pain into creative works that could benefit others as well.
6. *Humor.* They could keep a sense of humor and the ability to laugh at difficulties.
7. *Good moral standards.* They were able to act from a sense of conscience even when surrounded by others who did not.

The Wolins then began to teach resiliency to at-risk adolescents. Although their results are still quite new, they seem to have been successful in teaching certain psychological qualities to children and adolescents that promote and enhance resiliency. In conclusion, the results of some studies on resiliency illustrate one of the basic themes of positive psychology. That is, if therapists, teachers, or parents want to enhance resiliency, then they must both decrease negative risk factors and enhance, build, and maintain positive emotional experiences, positive traits, and positive institutions.

Positive Interventions Targeted toward Specific Emotions

This section will discuss a few interventions that have been designed to increase relatively specific emotions or build specific strengths and resources. Of course, some intervention strategies have been discussed earlier in the book as well. We have already seen suggestions on how to increase flow and peak performance as well as ideas on how to enhance intimate interpersonal relationships. The use of exercise, relaxation, and the reattribution of stressful events to enhance wellness was also covered. What follows is a list of interventions and strategies that can also help increase well-being, can foster strengths and virtues, and can help build a more enjoyable life.

Increasing Positive Emotions

Barbara Fredrickson (2000), who developed the "broaden-and-build" model of positive emotions (Chapter 2), also suggested a number of ways in which positive emotions may be fostered and cultivated. She recommends that relaxation strategies such as meditation, positive imagery, massage, and muscle relaxation can be useful in this regard. In addition, she proposes increasing a sense of meaning and purpose as an effective way to increase positive emotions. Finally, she also suggests that positive emotions can be created through laughter, using one's sense of humor, engaging in activities that are intrinsically motivating, by enhancing empathy, and with activities that involve both challenges and skills (see "Flow" in Chapter 5).

People have devised a number of ways to enhance positive mood. Most people have a number of different strategies that they use to change a bad mood into a good mood. These can include talking to a friend, listening to music, reading, exercising, taking a warm bath, walking outdoors, and trying to look on the bright side of a situation. In a survey of how average people improve their mood, Thayer, Newman, and McClain (1994) found that one of the most effective ways is to increase one's level of exercise. Other effective strategies are listening to music, talking to others, trying to think positively, and simply distracting oneself with activities. Other researchers have also found that increasing activity level is an effective way to stimulate positive mood (Watson, 2002; Williamson, 2002).

Increasing Happiness

Any discussion of interventions to increase happiness must begin by acknowledging that this general goal has been present throughout history. In one sense, the goal of religion, philosophy, social reform, the arts, and psychology has been to increase happiness and well-being. Throughout this book, various ideas have been presented on how to enhance well-being and one's ability to experience the good life—however it is defined. The interventions in the sections that follow, however, have all been designed specifically to promote and facilitate increases in happiness or positive emotions.

Behavioral Interventions for Happiness

Recently, psychology's earlier reluctance to investigate happiness has been replaced by a growing body of work that uses psychological research knowledge to increase happiness. A number of these strategies use behavioral principles; that is, they tend to begin with the behaviorist assumption that happiness can be defined as the ratio of positive emotion to negative emotion: if a person experiences more positive emotions than negative, then he or she is happy. Therefore, these studies all share the common premise that by increasing the frequency of positive emotions on a daily basis a person will experience an increase in his or her happiness. People are asked to read positive self-statements, watch happy movies, simply increase positive activities, and listen to cheerful music (see Argyle, 1987, pp. 200–217). Following these ideas, Lewinsohn, Sullivan, and Grosscup (1980) developed an approach they called "pleasant events therapy." In their study, people were asked to list activities that they enjoy and then simply to do more of the activities that produced the greatest increase in positive mood.

All of the strategies listed in this section have demonstrated an ability to increase the frequency of a person's self-reported happiness—at least on a temporary basis. Of course, most people use these strategies throughout their lives to increase frequency of happiness (Thayer, Newman, & McClain, 1994). Anytime we do an activity for fun, we are using the basic behavioral formula to increase our own happiness. However, a strict application of the behavioral formula for happiness is somewhat limited. Other factors are also important. The research on intrinsic motivation has shown that the activity chosen must be pleasurable to the specific individual, it must be freely chosen by the individual, and he or she must choose to engage in the activity (that is, it is hard to force someone to have fun).

Cognitive Interventions for Happiness Some psychologists have designed happiness interventions that tap into cognitive processes. As an example, a group of psychologists in New Zealand developed a happiness training course that was based on cognitive-behavioral principles (Lichter, Haye, & Kammann, 1980). In their study, the researchers taught volunteers some basic principles of cognitive retraining that could be applied to beliefs and attitudes about happiness. For instance, a person might believe that "It is absolutely necessary that I be loved by most people in order to be happy." The researchers would then point out the irrationality or the impossibility of that belief and suggest a substitute belief that was more amenable to lasting happiness (e.g., "I would like to be loved by those people who are important to me"). They found that a relatively brief course focused on increasing happiness through cognitive retraining could be effective in raising happiness and life satisfaction scores.

Fordyce's Happiness Training Program Probably the most extensive attempt to develop a happiness training program was developed by Michael Fordyce (1977, 1981, 1983, 1988). For a number of years, Fordyce has concentrated on creating a method for teaching people how to be happier. Combining a review of the literature on subjective well-being with a knowledge of counseling and cognitive-behavioral therapy, he devised a package designed to teach what he called the "Fourteen Fundamentals of Happiness" (1981):

1. Be more active.
2. Spend more time socializing.
3. Be productive at meaningful work.
4. Get organized.
5. Stop worrying.
6. Lower your expectations and aspirations.
7. Think optimistically.
8. Orient yourself to the present.
9. Work on a healthy personality.
10. Develop an outgoing, social personality.
11. Be yourself.
12. Eliminate negative feelings.
13. Develop and nurture close relationships because they are the number-one source of happiness.
14. Value happiness—put it first in your life.

The similarities between this list and the subjective well-being literature should be very obvious. Fordyce's program and the subjective well-being literature both view these factors as central to happiness and satisfaction with life: increased socialization, close personal relationships, optimism, increased meaning (meaningful work in Fordyce's program), and decreased neuroticism. Fordyce's (1977, 1983) research studies have found that scores on standard measures of happiness can be increased following implementation of his program. Of course, other factors are also helpful. For instance, Smith, Compton, and West (1996) found that happiness scores could be increased even further when people practiced a simple meditation technique in addition to implementing Fordyce's program for happiness.

While there are many obvious similarities between Fordyce's fourteen fundamentals and the subjective well-being literature, two of Fordyce's fundamentals deserve special attention. The sixth fundamental states that people should "lower their expectations and aspirations." The research basis for this comes from studies that show greater satisfaction and higher self-esteem in people whose ideal self and real self or their goals and achievements are more similar or closer together. That is, subjective well-being is higher in people when their image of who they would like to be is similar to who they believe they actually are. Fordyce means that people should not be so perfectionistic about themselves and others and should not set their goals unrealistically high. The problem, however, is that it is difficult to distinguish how "realistic" a goal actually is for any particular person. For instance, was it "unrealistic" for a young African American girl born into poverty on a farm in Mississippi in the 1930s to believe that she might one day be Surgeon General of the United States? In many ways, this dream was completely unrealistic. Nonetheless, that dream became reality for Dr. Joslyn Elders. It is better to allow people to set their goals high and then teach them how to use the struggle, challenge, and even failure for personal growth.

The fourteenth fundamental states that people should place the pursuit of happiness "first" in their lives. In contrast, many other theorists believe that happiness is a by-product of other activities and is, in fact, more elusive when relentlessly pursued. Also, there is any number of definitions of happiness. Some even advise us to focus our attentions and efforts on other people first. It may be that Fordyce is trying to say that subjective well-being is an extremely important element of our lives and we should not neglect its importance. In this respect, at least, the studies on positive emotions support his suggestion.

General Comments on Increasing Happiness

Research on use of interventions to increase happiness has shown that it is, in fact, possible to increase scores on measures of happiness and life satisfaction through psychological interventions. One caveat is that the research on the heritability of positive affect suggests that there may be biological limits to how we experience positive emotionality. That is, just as in the development of intelligence, a person's genetic inheritance may produce a range of positive emotionality that is generally and easily available. Within that range, the environment and training can lead to experiencing either the low end of the "happiness continuum" or the higher end. Everyone, however, can use psychological interventions to increase their level of positive emotionality on a daily basis (see "happiness set point" in Chapter 2). The relationships among emotions and a sense of well-being are complex—like life itself—and the psychological models used to explain them have just begun to explore the intricacy involved in creating an apparently simply judgment that "Life is good."

Writing as a Tool to Allow Emotional Expression

James W. Pennebaker has given suggestions on how to use writing to help deal with difficult emotions resulting from trauma or other problems. One of the more interesting aspects of Pennebaker's strategy is that people are not told to deliberately alter their thoughts in any way—positive or negative thoughts are all just grist for the mill, and relief comes after the writing exercise. He has found that "keeping it all inside" may be harmful after all.

Pennebaker's studies give people a method for acknowledging and dealing with difficult emotions in a healthy way. He developed the following instructions (adapted from Smyth & Pennebaker, 1999, and Pennebaker, quoted in Sattler & Shabatay, 1997, pp. 262–266) for using writing as a way to deal with stress, difficult emotions, and painful memories.

1. Write about any issue that you are currently living with. If you find yourself thinking about or stressing about an issue or events, then sometimes writing about it can help.
2. Find a location in which to write where you will not be disturbed. The more special this situation is, the better. That is, it is helpful if the place in which you write acts as a situational cue for the type of writing you will do.
3. When you write, do not worry about spelling, grammar, or the quality of your

prose. Just put it down on paper. If you run into a mental block, then repeat what you just wrote. This may help to unblock the process. It may not be necessary to write every day. In order to get the ball rolling, however, you might find it useful to set aside 20 or 30 minutes each day for your writing. Be sure to leave a few minutes after you are finished so that you can compose yourself. Again, to get yourself started, you may want to write for three or four days consecutively.

4. When you write about the event, write about both what happened and your feelings surrounding the event. Explore your deepest emotional reactions to the event. Really let go, and explore your feelings. Include both positive and negative emotions, but make a special effort to find the positive emotions associated with the event. It is often helpful to include why you think you feel that way as well as what it is you feel. In addition, it is usually helpful to really explore the complexity of the issue. How have this event and the emotions affected your life, your relationships, and how you see yourself? Is it related to your childhood experiences? How has it related to your future self? Try to construct a narrative that can serve as an explanation of the events and can put it into context and give it meaning.
5. Generally, it is helpful if you plan to keep what you write private. In fact, you may even wish to destroy what you have written after its finished. Remember that sharing what you have written generally inhibits what you put on paper.
6. Remember that after you are finished, you will probably feel somewhat sad. No one can express difficult issues without generating some negative emotions. However, most people find that the negative feelings fade away with an hour or so. Be prepared, however; for some people, the negative emotions may last a few days. If the negative emotions generated by this exercise are very strong or they persist for days or weeks, then it is best to seek professional counseling.

Those interested in using writing as a method for personal growth and exploration may also want to read the work of Ira Progoff (1983, 1992), who developed a method that systematically uses journal writing as a tool for personal exploration. He called his technique the Intensive Journal Method. Progoff's method of journaling begins by writing the answer to a single question, "Where am I now in my life?" Answers to this question are written in various sections of the journal workbook such as "career," "family," or "spirituality." The intent is to create an on-going dialogue between aspects of the person's inner and outer lives. Progoff's journaling method has been used for personal exploration and the enhancement of meaning in a number of settings such as university classes, alcohol treatment centers, prisons, and divinity schools, and as a tool for business executives (see Gestwicki, 2001).

Applications of Mindfulness

One of the more interesting applications of meditation has been the work of Jon Kabat-Zinn at the University of Massachusetts Medical Center (Kabat-Zinn, 1993). He initially took on the difficult task of treating chronic pain patients—many of whom had not responded well to traditional pain management therapies. Over the years, he expanded into the treatment of many other conditions. His novel approach is to teach the patients a form of meditation called *mindfulness meditation,* which is based on the idea that if we try to ignore or repress unpleasant thoughts or sensations, then we only end up increasing their intensity. In mindfulness meditation, a person is taught to allow thoughts, images, and sensations to occur, observe them nonjudgmentally, and then let them dissipate as other thoughts and sensations naturally replace them. In many ways, this treatment approach seems completely paradoxical—teaching people to deal with pain by helping them to become more aware of their sensations. The trick is to help people also let go of the constant tension that goes along with fighting the pain—a process that actually keeps one's awareness on the pain longer. Kabat-Zinn found good support for his technique to help people deal with stress-related problems and pain (Kabat-Zinn, Lipworth, Burney, & Sellers, 1986; Kabat-Zinn et al., 1992).

Recent studies have found benefits of mindfulness in other areas as well as in pain management. Kirk Brown and Richard Ryan (2003) found that people who were more mindful throughout the day tended to also show enhanced self-awareness, were more able to regulate their behavior, and reported more positive emotional states. Ron Ritchhart and David Perkins (2000) suggest that teaching children to be more mindful may help enhance classroom learning.

Training for Forgiveness

Forgiveness has long been of interest to psychologists, theologians, an others. Because abuses of various kinds can be all too commonplace, Archbishop Desmond Tutu has said that "forgiveness is an absolute necessity for continued human existence" (quoted in Enright & North, 1998, p. xiii). Without the ability to forgive, anger, resentment, and hurt can consume lives and create ever-increasing cycles of hostility and desire for revenge. Michael McCullough (2000) says that forgiveness allows us to move beyond a desire for revenge and to reinstitute social ties.

For a number of years, Robert Enright and his colleagues at the University of Wisconsin–Madison have studied forgiveness. They followed the suggestions of Joanna North and defined forgiveness as "a willingness to abandon one's right to resentment, negative judgment, and indifferent behavior toward one who unjustly injured us, while fostering the underserved qualities of compassion, generosity, and even love toward him or her" (Enright, Freedman, & Rique, 1998, pp. 46–47). They note that this definition includes a number of aspects including emotional (overcoming resentment), cognitive (changing negative judgments), and behavioral (ending indifference). In general, their definition says that forgiveness is getting over the hurt, resentments, and aggressions that go along with being the target of abuse—whether minor or severe. Forgiveness does not require the offending party to either accept or even know about the other's act of forgiveness—it is an individual act. Enright and his colleagues, as well as McCullough (2000), are also quick to note what forgiveness is *not.* According to them, it is not simply tolerating or forgetting an injustice. It is not using denial or suppression to stop being angry toward the person who injured us. True forgiveness is not forgetting, denying, or minimizing the hurt or condoning what was done. It is recognizing and acknowledging that a transgression occurred against us and finding ways to move beyond it. True forgiveness is about breaking free of both the wrong that was done to us and the person who did the wrong.

Some people may ask, why should we even bother? The answer is that in the long run, anger, resentment, and obsessive rumination about an event only serve to hurt us. Other reasons for the act of forgiveness go beyond the fact that it is a gift we give ourselves. Forgiveness is not only something people do to make themselves feel better or to eliminate their own negative feelings. Enright believes that it must also include a sense of shared humanity with the larger community. Forgiveness is an opportunity to use one's painful experiences in order to deepen a connection with others and increase a sense of compassion.

McCullough (2000) notes that the ability to forgive has links to factors that promote well-being, primarily, the maintenance and fostering of healthy and supportive interpersonal relationships. In addition, the ability to forgive can also help a person modulate hostility, which has been linked to poor health outcomes. Recent studies have reported that people who were able to forgive someone from their past subsequently reported better health status; even people who simply imagined forgiving someone showed noticeable decreases in blood pressure and muscle tension (Lawler et al., 2003).

Robert Enright, Suzanne Freedman, and Julio Rique (1998) proposed a four-phase model of the steps involved in the process of forgiving. Phase one is the *uncovering phase.* At this point, people explore how chronically holding onto resentment, anger, or hate has a negative impact on their own lives. The *decision phase* involves making a choice to try and forgive. The *work phase* is when the person tries to forgive by reframing the incident, accepting the hurt, and trying to find an empathic understanding of why the offender acted as he or she did. Phase four is the *deepening phase,* where the person tries to gain a deeper sense of meaning as a result of having gone through the injury. This phase may include a feeling of universality prompted by realizing that many people have experienced many hurts and that one is not alone. Research using this model with incest survivors found that those who completed their forgiveness education program gained in their ability to forgive and to hope and decreased their scores on anxiety and depression (Enright, Freedman, & Rique, 1998).

Comments on Interventions

From the earliest years of psychology as a science, researchers and clinicians have been trying to foster positive well-being, greater adaptability, and build emotional strengths. The success over the years shows that by focusing on positive emotions and behavior, it is possible to enhance quality of life and help people move beyond adapting into flourishing lifestyles. One of the more interesting findings is that a focus on positive emotions, virtues, and strengths may even be helpful in combating more devastating emotional problems, such as depression. Recent contributions to assessment and psychotherapy continue to focus on positive emotions and behaviors and to expand the possibilities of interventions (Lopez & Snyder, 2003; Peterson & Seligman, 2004). One day, perhaps, psychotherapy, counseling, and education will focus just as much on joy, hope, and optimism as on anxiety and helplessness.

Summary

This chapter covered classifications systems for positive mental health and interventions to enhance well-being. The disease model is a poor fit for understanding well-being, and new systems of classifying positive behavior are needed. Initial attempts to classify well-being created by Jahoda, Ryff, Keyes and Lopez, and Peterson and Seligman were mentioned. Positive therapy is a general term for new approaches to counseling and psychotherapy that focus on a client's strengths and competencies. A number of these therapies were discussed, including strategies that focus on children. Other interventions that focus on more specific emotions, such as happiness and forgiveness, were also discussed.

Learning Tools

Key Terms and Ideas

COMPLETE MENTAL HEALTH
DISEASE MODEL
POSITIVE THERAPY
PSYCHOLOGICAL WELL-BEING (RYFF)
VALUES IN ACTION (VIA)

Books

Enright, R. (2001). *Forgiveness is a choice: A step-by-step process for resolving anger and restoring hope.* Washington, DC: American Psychological Association. Enright gives details of his forgiveness program for general audiences.

Jahoda, M. (1958). *Current concepts of positive mental health.* New York: Basic. More than likely this book will be found only in university or college libraries. This is Jahoda's summary of how optimal personality development was defined in Western psychology up to the 1960s. Although the research findings are dated, many of Jahoda's comments on optimal mental health are still relevant (professional/popular).

Lopez, S. J., & Snyder, C. R. (Eds.). (2003). *Positive psychological assessment: A handbook of models and measures.* Washington, DC: American Psychological Association. An examination of the measures that can be used to assess positive functioning (professional).

Research Articles

Bentall, R. (1992). A proposal to classify happiness as a psychiatric disorder. *Journal of Medical Ethics, 18,* 94–98. A satirical piece that shows how being happy meets all the criteria of a mental disorder. Bentall suggests that this disorder be labeled "affective disorder, pleasant type."

Seligman, M. E. P. (2002). Positive psychology, positive prevention, and positive therapy. In C. R. Snyder & S. Lopez (Eds.). *Handbook of Positive Psychology* (2002). New York: Oxford University Press (professional).

On The Web

Fredrickson, B. (2000). Cultivating positive emotions to optimize health and well-being. *Prevention & Treatment, 3* (March). Available on the Web at http://journals.apa.org/prevention/volume3/pre0030001a.html.

http://www.projectresilience.com. This is the Web site for Sybil and Steve Wolin's research on teaching resiliency to at-risk adolescents.

http://psych.upenn.edu/seligman/taxonomy.htm. Web site for the Values in Action (VIA) classification system and the VIA Manual.

http://www.mygoals.com. This Web site helps you create step-by-step procedures to achieve a wide variety of goals.

Personal Explorations

How were you resilient as a child? Either individually or in a group, discuss one to two incidents from your childhood in which you showed resiliency. What did you do? How did you manage to cope well with the situations?

Do an assessment of your strengths. Go to http://www.positivepsychology.org/strengths and take the strengths assessment. How do these results fit with the strengths you see yourself as having? What others would you add?

For this exercise, create a diary. Take at least five minutes every day for the next week and record in your diary the positive things that happened to you or the things you can be grateful for. If any day it is hard to find something positive, think for a moment about how you can see something positive in what happened that day. After a week evaluate how the exercise made you feel.

CHAPTER 10

Religion, Spirituality, and Well-Being

> I think that the very purpose of life is to seek happiness. That is clear. Whether one believes in religion or not . . . we are all seeking something better in life. So, I think, the very motion of our life is toward happiness.
>
> *Tenzin Gyatso, the current Dalai Lama (1998)*

Religiosity and Subjective Well-Being

The term *spirituality* refers to the human tendency to search for meaning in life through self-transcendence or the need to relate to something greater than the individual self. *Religion* refers to a spiritual search that is connected to formal religious institutions, while spirituality does not depend on an institutional context (Zinnbauger, Pargament, & Scott, 1999). Therefore, *spirituality* is the more inclusive term for a search for the sacred, and *religion* refers to a search that is grounded in institutional forms of spirituality.

There now exists a fairly substantial number of studies that have looked at how religiosity and spirituality may have an impact on physical and mental health (Chamberlain & Hall, 2000; Koenig, McCullough, & Larson, 2001). Most of these studies have found that people who are more religious and who engage in more religious activities tend to be healthier, both mentally and physically. Studies have been fairly consistent in finding that greater participation in religious activities is significantly related to higher well-being, lower rates of delinquency, alcoholism, drug abuse, and other social problems (Donahue & Benson, 1995). David Myers (1992) states, "Survey after survey across North American and Europe reveals that religious people more often than non-religious people report feeling happy and satisfied with life" (p. 183). In fact, James Peacock and Margaret Poloma (1999) found that one's perceived closeness to God was the single biggest predictor of life satisfaction across all age ranges. However, while the correlations between subjective well-being and religiosity are significant, the size of the relationships tend to be moderate to small (Argyle, 1999). In addition, studies do not consistently find significant relationships (e.g., Lewis, Lanigan, Joseph, & de Fockert, 1997).

The inconsistent findings do not necessarily negate the relationships between well-being and religion but rather specify situations under which the relationships are strongest. For instance, women tend to show stronger relationships between well-being and religiosity than men. In terms of race, African Americans tend to also show stronger relationships between well-being and religiosity than Caucasians (Argyle, 1999). African Americans also have significantly stronger beliefs in the curative power of prayer than do other ethnic groups (Klonoff & Landrine, 1996).

Age also seems to be a factor. Older persons tend to show a stronger relationships between religiosity and well-being (McFadden, 1995). In fact, Morris Okun and William Stock (1987) found that religiousness and good health were the two strongest predictors of psychological well-being among older people. Among older persons, belief in life after death has been highly correlated with a belief that their current life was exciting (Steinitz, 1980). Looking across the life span, people are motivated to participate in spiritual or religious activities by different needs at different points in life. During the first half of life, people may seek out religion in order to help with identity formation and to build social relationships. During the second half of life, people may need religion to help restructure life priorities and to help confront the reality of approaching death (Peacock & Poloma, 1999). Interestingly, the relationship between religious participation and well being is stronger in the United States than in Europe (Argyle, 1999).

Other qualifying factors are related to which particular aspect of religion is being assessed and how well-being is measured. Stronger and significant correlations are usually based on actual religious behavior rather than religious attitudes (Witter, Stock, Okun, & Haring, 1985). That is, people who participate in activities related to religious faith (e.g., attend church, pray) often report greater well-being than those who simply hold proreligious attitudes. In fact, the biggest predictor in the relationship between religiosity and well-being is "public religious participation" or active involvement in religious activities (George, Larson, Keonig, & McCullough, 2000). However, some have found that religious activities such as church attendance tend to be associated more with self-reported life satisfaction than with self-reported happiness (Witter, Stock, Okun, & Haring, 1985; Chamberlain & Zika, 1988). It also is reasonable that religion should have a significant impact on how a person forms a sense of meaning and purpose in life. Margaret Poloma and Brian Pendleton (1990) found that if well-being is measured as having a sense of meaning and purpose in life, then there is a stronger relationship between well-being and religiosity.

While there are a number of qualifying factors, in general, the research has found that people who are committed to religious beliefs and practices experience higher levels of well-being. Again, the effect, although small, is consistently found and does have an impact on a person's quality of life.

Religiosity and Health

One of the more interesting areas of research in recent years concerns the relationships between religiosity and physical health. In terms of physical health, people who report greater religiosity tend to have fewer illnesses, tend to live longer by having lower rates for cancer and heart attacks, recover more quickly from illness or surgery, and have a greater tolerance for pain (George et al., 2000). Once again, in this context the strongest predictor of illness onset and longevity is active participation—in this case, whether or not people attend religious services. The strongest predictor of how fast a person recovers, or if they recover from serious illness, is the use of religiously oriented coping strategies.

Given these very positive findings, one might ask if religiosity has any negative consequences on physical or mental health. George et al. (2000) state that they found no evidence that religiosity can be harmful when looking at representative samples of people. However, there is evidence that neglecting medical services because of religious beliefs can be harmful. There are higher rates of childhood deaths in families that favor faith healing over standard medical practices (Asser & Swan, 1998). African Americans who hold very strong beliefs in the curative power of prayer also tend to exercise less frequently and are less interested in being actively involved in their own health care (Klonoff & Landrine, 1996). In this last instance, a strong faith in the power of prayer seems to lead people to believe that they need not be as careful about their own health—apparently believing that prayer is so powerful that it can heal in spite of bad health practices.

Prayer and Health

A number of studies have looked at the relationships between prayer and health status (see Koenig et al., 2001). These studies have found that higher frequency of prayer is associated with indices of health such as better postoperative emotional health in cardiac patients, greater vitality and mental health, greater psychological well-being, and decreases in depression after cardiac surgery (Ai, Dunkle, Peterson, & Bolling, 1998; Ai, Bolling, & Peterson, 2000). One six-year longitudinal study of older adults found that private religious activities such as prayer or Bible study predicted survival rates. Those who had more religious participation, such as daily prayer, lived longer. However, this effect held only for people whose daily activity level was not impaired at the beginning of the study. So, prior health status did seem to make a difference in whether prayer had an impact on health. Why might prayer effect health status? Herbert Benson, who developed the Relaxation Response technique (a form of meditation), also investigated prayer and found that prayer seems to help the immune system work better and can aid in healing (Benson, 1983).

The volume of studies on the relationship between prayer and healing prompted one physician to write an article titled, "Should physicians prescribe prayer for health?" (Marwick, 1995). His answer was an unqualified, "Not yet." Similarly, Michael McCullough (1995) reviewed the research on prayer and health and found that most of the studies had relatively serious flaws and that further research still needs to be done. Research efforts in this area are just beginning, and the exact mechanism responsible for this relationship remains quite a mystery at this point. While the scientific evidence is being debated, however, currently nearly two thirds of medical schools in the United States now include course work that focuses on spiritual issues (Sheler, 2001). In terms of the onset of and recovery from mental illness, however, the impact of religiosity on mental health is even greater than the impact on physical health.

Why Is Religiosity Related to Well-Being?

There is a small but significant and consistently reported effect of religiosity on well-being. Why would this be the case? Researchers have hypothesized that religion may influence mental and physical health because of at least six factors (see Pargament, Smith, Koenig and Perez, 1998; Emmons, 1999):

1. Religiosity provides for social support.
2. Religiosity helps support healthy lifestyles.
3. Religiosity helps promote personality integration.
4. Religiosity may increase generativity.
5. Religiosity provides unique coping strategies.
6. Religiosity provides a sense of meaning and purpose.

Religiosity Provides for Social Support

Some authors suggest that the social support factor is one of the most important reasons for the relationships between religion and well-being (Argyle, 1999; Myers, 2000). Social support is one of the strongest predictors of subjective well-being, so it seems logical that participation in church activities within a community of like-minded individuals should be a source of satisfaction. Being with other people who are supportive and helpful in a religious context can be an important factor in physical health. This should not be too surprising given the large impact that social support has on stress and the immune system (see Chapter 6). However, religious dedication can also create interpersonal conflicts if other people in a person's life do not understand or support the new direction that a religious convert has taken (Emmons, 1999).

Unlike other forms of social support, a religion-based sense of social support could extend to what many consider the source of an ultimately supportive relationship—a relationship with God. Melvin Pollner (1989) speculated about why this relationship might be important to well-being. He suggested that people might believe God would intervene at certain times when needed, that one's sense of self-esteem could be enhanced by the belief that God loved him or her, or that a relationship with God was an always available resource in times of trouble.

Religiosity Helps Support Healthy Lifestyles

Studies have found that one of the effects of increased religiosity is a tendency to engage in fewer health-risk behaviors. For example, people who are more religious consume less alcohol and smoke fewer cigarettes (see Myers, 2000). This effect is also seen in denominational differences in health behaviors. Denominations that are more likely to prohibit risky health behaviors (e.g., Mormons, Seventh Day Adventists) tend to be healthier than people in other denominations (George et al., 2000).

Religiosity Helps Promote Personality Integration

Robert Emmons (1999) believes that religion increases a sense of well-being partially because it facilitates personality integration. He reports on a study that looked at fifty Jesuit novices who undertook a "4-week period of secluded meditation." After the experience, they showed increases in personality integration and mental health. Emmons believes that personality integration is fostered because an increase in one's religious dedication or commitment can help resolve internal conflicts. Some researchers have argued that internal conflict is the primary stimulus for seeking religious experiences because conversion and other experiences can resolve those internal conflicts. In addition, deeper spiritual commitment can also help people focus their goals and personal strivings on what is seen as a more significant life quest. Further, because spiritual goals are never fully realized, they offer life-long goals that can be useful at all stages of life.

Religiosity May Increase Generativity

As discussed in Chapter 8, generativity, or expending time and effort for the benefit of others, has been associated with greater well-being, particularly in middle age and later. Somewhat paradoxically, efforts at generativity require both humility and self-sacrifice along with positive self-regard, self-efficacy, and confidence. This balancing of different aspects of personality can also help increase integration. The research on altruism, however, offers one caveat to this idea. Studies of altruism have found that if the person who needs help seems to hold different values or different religious beliefs, then being religious can decrease helping.

Religiosity Provides Unique Coping Strategies

One way to look at the relationships between religiosity and well-being is to view these behaviors as forms of religious coping. Studies of religion-oriented coping strategies have found a wide range of strategies people use to deal with stress and difficulties in life (Pargament, Smith, Koenig, & Perez, 1998). For instance, a religion-based sense of meaning can help in a number of ways, such as providing hope, giving reasons for unexpected and unwanted stressors (e.g., "God gives you difficulties to help make you strong"), or helping people place their lives in a larger framework. Emmons notes that increases in religious commitment also allow a person to create a new identity based on a life narrative focused around connections to a larger, transcendent purpose. This adoption of the "big picture" can help to integrate aspects of personality into a larger personal narrative. Religious forms of coping can also include seeking social support from church members or using religious beliefs to aid the process of forgiveness and suppression of negative emotions.

Religious coping can also include a sense of optimism or hope that is fostered by religious beliefs. Martin E. P. Seligman (2002a) reports on a study, done by one of his students, that looked at religiosity and hope. Sheena Iyengar surveyed a number of religious congregations across the United States and found that increases in hope entirely accounted for the increases in well-being brought about by greater religiosity. Other studies have also found that religiosity is associated with increased optimism (Sethi & Seligman, 1993; Mathews-Treadway, 1996). In fact, the connection between religiosity and optimism is one of the more obvious connections to well-being.

Religious forms of coping can be divided into private forms of coping (e.g., faith, prayer) and social forms (e.g., getting more involved in church activities, discussing problems with one's minister). Harold Koenig, Linda George, and Ilene Siegler (1988) found that in their sample of older persons, the majority of people used private forms of religious coping. In fact, they found that religious forms of coping were the most frequently reported of *all types* of coping used by older people.

Religious coping can also be divided into positive and negative forms (Pargament, Smith, Koenig, and Perez, 1998). Positive forms of coping were those that depended on positive emotions, such as support, compassion, or hope. An example is a belief that "God doesn't give you things in life that you can't endure." Negative forms of coping involve negative emotions, such as guilt or fear of retribution from God. One example is the excessive use of guilt to punish oneself for a wrongdoing and thereby "make amends" to God. Only the positive forms of coping have a beneficial impact on mental and physical health status. In addition, religious forms of coping that view the person and God as working together to solve problems seem to be more beneficial than forms that see all problems as totally in God's hands (Pargament, Smith, Koenig, & Perez, 1998).

Religiosity Provides a Sense of Meaning and Purpose

Recall from earlier chapters that a sense of meaning and purpose is related to subjective well-being and the ability to cope positively with stress and challenge. One of the most obvious reasons why people adopt religious perspectives is to gain a sense of meaning and purpose in their lives. Religion, more than almost any other institution, supplies a larger perspective on human life and gives explanations for why unexpected events may happen. Particularly when life is difficult, religion provides solace through explanations for unexpected events and by providing hope. In fact, Linda George et al. (2000) found that the ability of religion to provide a sense of meaning and purpose or a sense of coherence was the *most important* predictor of improved health status. They suggested that the ability of religious beliefs, faith, and religious activities to buffer the impact of stress may be the primary reason that religiosity is associated with health.

A Sense of Meaning and Purpose in Life

A common theme that runs through the research on religion and spirituality is the idea of finding meaning in life. Someone might reasonably ask what having a sense of meaning and purpose gives to a person. Crystal Park and Susan Folkman (1997) define *meaning* as simply, "perceptions of significance" (p. 116). They argue that meaning gives life significance. In fact, we may have innate needs for meaning.

The Needs for Meaning

Roy Baumeister (1991) suggests that the creation of meaning is a process of finding a way for our lives to make sense and be understandable. Baumeister gives four reasons why people need a sense of meaning. The first reason is to help find a *purpose in life.* For the most part, this refers to having goals in the future. Goals, however, are not necessary simply, because people need to achieve and accomplish tasks. Baumeister believes that goals also serve to place actions in time so that present and past events can be seen as leading to future goals. In other words, purpose comes from knowing that our actions make sense in terms of where we are now, where we have been, and where we are going in relation to our goals. Second, people need meaning because it can provide a *sense of efficacy or control.* Meaning allows us to believe that we are more than pawns tossed about by the events of the world. A sense of purpose is important to a feeling of control as well. Interestingly, the belief that one has some control over events does not have to be accurate for a sense of meaning and purpose to be created (see "positive illusions" in Chapter 2). The third need is that meaning helps *create ways to legitimize or justify actions.* One's sense of meaning can even allow reasons for actions that in some cases appear counterintuitive, such as Jesus' counsel to "turn the other cheek" or not retaliate when someone does us harm. Methods of legitimization and justification also help to create a foundation for values, morality, and ethics. Finally, Baumeister says that people need meaning in their lives because a sense of meaning helps to *foster a sense of self-worth.* Partially, this is because people tend to congregate with others who share their sense of meaning and the sense of community can build a sense of worth. Once again, however, creating a sense of self-worth through group association can also have a negative side to it. On one hand, it can be used to devalue others who are not members of the group. On the other hand, religion can also provide a way to connect with all of humanity through beliefs about the interconnectedness of all life.

Types of Meaning

One of the problems that has plagued research on meaning is that the concept itself is quite broad and has been used in many different ways by different researchers. When people say "a sense of meaning," they are referring to a least two general categories. The first is *cosmic meaning* (Yalom, 1980), or *global meaning* (Park & Folkman, 1997). This refers to inquiries about whether "life in general, or at least human life, fits into some overall coherent pattern" (Yalom, 1980, p. 423). People search for cosmic meaning when they need to believe that some design or order exists in the universe. Another way to look at cosmic meaning is that it is an attempt to find the "grand plan" that moves and shapes the universe. Park and Folkman (1997) see it as the search for enduring beliefs, valued goals, and a sense of order and coherence to existence. According to Park and Folkman, global meaning is composed of a search for both order and purpose. They believe that we find order through our beliefs about the benevolence of the others and the world, about self-worth, about control, and about the value and trustworthiness of intimate relationships. They see our sense of purpose as created from our beliefs that organize, justify, and direct our strivings toward various goals. Therefore, they see global (or cosmic) meaning as a relatively complex amalgam of beliefs about justice, fairness, trustworthiness, self-worth, control, and the types of goals worth pursuing.

The other type of meaning is the search for *personal and secular meaning* in life (Yalom, 1980), or *situational meaning* (Park & Folkman, 1997). This type of meaning is associated with finding one's purpose in life. In addition, while a person can find cosmic meaning by adopting the beliefs of an institutional form of religion, the individual creates his or her own secular meaning. Note that this definition of secular or situational meaning implies that it usually depends upon cosmic meaning. Generally, without a sense of how order and coherence exists in the universe, it is impossible for an individual to find out how she or he fits in.

Finding Meaning in Life

Most researchers who have studied meaning believe that people have to create a sense of meaning in life that is personal and based on their own experience. It is simply not enough to blindly adopt someone else's sense of meaning. In fact, there is a term for a group of people who blindly accept someone else's meaning system—it is called a *cult*. Irwin Yalom (1980) notes that the sense of meaning and purpose usually changes over the course of one's life. So, how do people create and develop a sense of meaning in life? Although meaning can be created in many ways, the following are the more common avenues to greater meaning:

1. Greater harmony, coherence, and congruence among the various aspects of self-identity and goals in life
2. Development of a consistent life scheme
3. Congruency of current situations with overall goals
4. Service to others
5. Dedication to a worthy cause
6. Creativity
7. Life lived as fully and deeply as possible
8. Suffering
9. Spiritual experiences.

Greater Harmony, Coherence, and Congruence among the Various Aspects of Self-Identity and Goals in Life

Brian Little (Little, 1983; McGregor & Little, 1998) has investigated the predictors of meaning and subjective well-being. According to Little, greater meaning is created when there is greater harmony, coherence, and congruence among the various aspects of our self-identity and our goals in life. For instance, if a person's main goals in life all revolve around music, then that person will feel that life is more meaningful if she or he is also playing music, learning about music, spending time with other musicians, and has enough innate musical talents to continue playing music throughout life. The frustrated musician who cannot find the time, the effort, or the talent to actually be involved with music would probably find life less meaningful.

Development of a Consistent Life Scheme

Thompson and Janigian (1988) also argued that greater coherence and congruence result in greater meaning. According to them, however, greater coherence is represented by a consistent *life scheme*—a life story or narrative of who we are, where we are going, problems to be overcome, and basic assumptions about how the world works. A consistent life scheme helps to organize events in the world and fosters the attainment of goals. A significant aspect of our life schemes is the way in which we decide about causes in the world. Many negative events are at least bearable if we can discover a cause or a reason for their occurrence. Therefore, a search for meaning can be seen in part as a search for reasonable causes for the events in the world. Recall from Chapter 6 that Antonovsky's theory of the sense of coherence also says that people cope better with stress when they can find some reason for the events in their lives.

Congruency of Current Situations with Overall Goals

A person can also find meaning and purpose in life through striving to achieve goals (Emmons, 1999). Goals provide guidelines for living that direct our efforts in consistent directions. Park and Folkman (1997) see the process of finding meaning as the process of trying to reduce the discrepancy between our current situational meaning and our global meaning. That is, life is meaningful when we perceive that our current situations are congruent with our overall goals. Similarly, the restoration of lost meaning is the process of decreasing the incongruence between global and situational meaning. Often, this is accomplished by finding a renewed sense of control, predictability, and order as well as by restoring a sense that benevolence, justice, and fairness exist in some way in both people and in the world.

Service to Others or Dedication to a Worthy Cause

People can also create a sense of personal meaning and purpose by being of service to others. By taking time to help others, a person can feel that she or he is contributing to the general welfare and in some ways makes a difference in the world. In fact, this sense that one "makes a difference" is one of the core elements of a sense of meaning and purpose. Feeling that one's life has a purpose means that one feels the world is a different place because he or she is in it. A similar way to create a sense of meaning and purpose is to dedicate oneself to a worthy cause. This dedication allows people to feel that they are involved with issues larger than themselves.

Creativity

Some people can use creativity to discover a purpose in life. In this instance, the creation of something new gives life importance. Creation can help people to experience life in a different way, and in some instances the creation may even outlive the person. Yalom (1980) notes that Beethoven was quite explicit about the fact that music and creativity were the only things that kept him from suicide. Note that creativity in science can also be a source of meaning and purpose as new ideas and concepts are created and given to the world. A person could also view creativity in terms of self-discovery or creating a new sense of self and identity.

Life Lived as Fully and Deeply as Possible

The next strategy for increasing a sense of meaning requires a bit of explanation. For some people, finding a sense of purpose involves efforts to live one's life as fully and deeply as possible (Yalom, 1980). Note that this does not mean obsessive efforts to seek pleasure and avoid pain. That strategy usually results in unhappiness and disillusionment. Instead, a desire to experience life fully can provide a sense of active participation and involvement in life. It is similar to Rogers' (1961) and Maslow's (1968) theories on openness to experience (see Chapter 8) and to Cantor and Sanderson's (1999) theory on active participation in living a full life (see Chapter 2).

Suffering

The existentialist psychotherapist Viktor Frankl (1963) said that our approach to suffering was one of the primary determinants of how we experience meaning in life. This is not, however, an attempt at self-denial or a futile "war against the flesh," as the monasteries of the Middle Ages practiced. Rather, it is recognition that through suffering and difficulties people are forced to reevaluate their lives. Through this reevaluation, there is a possibility for transformation.

Emmons (1999) mentions that most of the world's major religions view suffering as a potential stimulus for spiritual growth. Similarly, Tedeschi and Calhoun (1995) studied the consequences of struggling with difficulties and found three broad categories of benefits: (1) the possibility of increased self-confidence, (2) opportunities for enhanced interpersonal relationships, and (3) avenues for changing one's philosophy of life or how one creates meaning.

Religious Experiences

Another way to increase a sense of meaning in life is through emotional experiences that are given a religious or spiritual interpretation. Often, *religious experiences* are at the heart of religiosity. Most people know that religion and spirituality are more than philosophical and intellectual statements of belief. Generally, religious sentiments must involve an emotional component. Often this component is tied to certain experiences that have been interpreted in a religious or spiritual fashion. That is, many people would argue that the heart of religion and spirituality is found in emotional religious experiences.

Religious experiences may be mild, such as a feeling of comfort and security when entering a religious building, or they may be very intense, such as profound spiritual illuminations. Studies have found that religious conversions can alter attitudes, goals, feelings, behaviors, and life meanings, and can increase positive emotion (McCullough, 1995; Beit-Hallahmi & Argyle, 1997; Paloutzian, Richardson, & Rambo, 1999). For instance, one study reported a correlation of .60 between self-reported happiness and having had a religious experience. In this case, the religious experience was feeling that one was "bathed in light" (Greely, 1975, reported in Argyle, 1999). Similar increases in well-being have been reported as a result of conversion experiences. Whatever the depth and intensity of the experience, they all serve to deepen a person's faith by providing both access to emotions associated with spirituality and apparent evidence of a spiritual reality alive in this world. Of course, what appears to be evidence of a spiritual reality may be nothing of the sort, but the experiences are nonetheless extraordinarily significant for many people. George, Larson, Koenig, and McCullough (2000) have said that, unfortunately, science knows "almost nothing about the spiritual experience itself. . . . [S]piritual experience is the most ignored dimension of spirituality" (pp. 112–113).

Elation and Awe Most people have witnessed unsolicited acts of kindness, charity, or compassion. For many people, just viewing these acts produces a variety of positive emotions. Jonathon Haidt (2000b) has studied experiences of momentary joy that produce a variety of physiological and psychological responses associated with greater well-being—experiences that he terms **elation.** As an example of what Haidt is talking about, when people witness a spontaneous act of compassion or truly selfless giving, most report a warm feeling in their chests, a sense of expanding in their hearts, an increased desire to help, and a sense of connection with others. Interestingly, our reactions to these acts of charity and kindness may be universal responses. In his research, Haidt has used a film about Mother Teresa and found that simply viewing her acts of compassion is enough to produce these feelings of elation (also see description of McClelland's study in Chapter 6). Haidt even found these effects in second-, fourth-, and sixth-grade children, suggesting an innate element to feelings of elation.

Haidt (2000b) quoted a woman's response to seeing a spontaneous act of kindness by a young man, "I felt like jumping out of the car and hugging this guy. I felt like singing and running, or skipping and laughing. Just being active. I felt like saying nice things about people. Writing a beautiful poem or love song. . . .Telling everybody about his deed" (p. 3). As in this narrative, Haidt has found that the most common reactions to seeing compassionate acts are desires to help other people, resolutions to become a better person, increased needs to affiliate with other people, and increases in feelings of love, compassion, and general well-being. Haidt also mentions that these experiences are potentially life-altering events. For some people, these moments of elation are so powerful that they can reorient their lives in significant ways as a result of the feelings produced.

Haidt's (2000a) model for experiences of elation involves three basic dimensions of social cognition. The first two dimensions have been studied for a number of years by other researchers: (1) sociability, or how we perceive connections/social relationships, and (2) hierarchy, or how we perceive social stratification and how we order relationships into "better than us" and "less than us." The new dimension that Haidt proposes is one with "purity" and "elevation" on one end of the continuum and "pollution" and "disgust" on the other end. According to Haidt, we have innate, often visceral, responses to certain acts or experiences that we see as disgusting. At the opposite end of this continuum, we also have innate and visceral reactions to acts of charity, gratitude, compassion, and sacrifice done by others. He refers to them as our responses to "acts of moral beauty."

Similarly, Dacher Keltner (2000) has studied the experience of **awe** or "deep appreciative wonder." Normally, this is thought of as wonder at the immensity, beauty, and complexity of a phenomenon that takes on universal significance. Keltner has found that stimuli for these experiences include nature, art, and observing human excellence. Paradoxically, during this experience, the sense of self may be diminished as a person realizes what a small part of the universe she or he actually occupies while at the same time a sense of connection to it all is increased. In Robert Plutchik's (1980) emotion wheel, the feeling of awe is a combination of surprise and fear. The feeling of awe when contemplating the size of the universe is a combination of surprise at its utter immensity plus fear over the relative insignificance of any single part of the whole.

In Rudolph Otto's book, *The Idea of the Holy* (1977), he refers to awe in a religious context as the *"mysterium tremendum,"* or the trembling before the mystery of God. Awe is the experience we get when touching the inexpressible mystery, majesty, and power of the divine. Otto also states that this emotion is a combination of wonder and mystery along with dread and fear over the immense power of God. He says this feeling is "[a] unique emotional moment in religious experience, a moment whose singular *daunting* and awe inspiring character must be gravely disturbing to those persons who will recognize nothing in the divine nature but goodness, gentleness, love, and a sort of confidential intimacy" (p. 19). That is, in the experience of awe, the emotions of wonder and dread combine to create a unique emotional experience that is usually interpreted as a positive emotion. A positive and a negative emotion combine in a unique way to produce an emotion that seems to transcend both of the emotions that produced it.

Peak Experiences Another association between religious experiences and mental health comes from Maslow's descriptions of **peak experiences.** He saw peak experiences as those brief moments when people experience extreme joy, wonder, appreciation, or connection to a larger spiritual reality. These experiences tend to be more intense than Haidt's descriptions of elation but closer to Keltner's accounts of awe. Maslow's (1954) description of peak experiences may be instructive at this point: "There were the same feelings of limitless horizons opening up to the vision, the feeling of being simultaneously more powerful and also more helpless than one ever was before, the feeling of great ecstasy and wonder and awe, the loss of placing in time and space with, finally, the conviction that something extremely important and valuable had happened, so that the subject is to some extent transformed and strengthened even in his daily life by such experiences" (p. 216).

Peak experiences may be associated with experiences in nature, moving aesthetic experiences, special moments when relationships are particularly intimate and loving, the birth of a child, religious worship, intense moments of intellectual insight or discovery, moments of excellence, or any number of other stimuli (Maslow, 1968, 1976). Maslow (1987) said these experiences can lead to greater psychological health, at least temporarily:

> The main finding relevant to our topic was that an essential aspect of peak experience is integration within the person and therefore between person and the world. In these states of being, the person becomes unified; for the time being, the splits, polarities, and dissociations within him tend to be resolved; the civil war within is neither won nor lost but transcended. In such a state, the person becomes far more open to experience and far more spontaneous and fully functioning (p. 163).

Linda Bourque and Kurt Black (1968) found two basic types of peak experiences: those based on aesthetic and religious stimuli. In a study that looked at aesthetically produced peak experiences, Panzarella (1980) found that the self-reported after-effects of the experience included more positive feelings about self, more positive relationships with other people, vivid and stimulating memories of the experience, enhanced appreciation of aesthetics, and greater optimism. Others report dramatic changes in how they create meaning in life as a consequence of intense peak experiences (Maslow, 1976). The *noetic* or spiritual quality to certain peak experiences is one of the most prominent features of the experience. The poet e. e. cummings (1958) expressed how these experiences can provide a sense of acceptance, joy, and wonder at the simple events of the world:

> out of the lie of no
> rises a truth of yes
> (only herself and who
> illimitably is)
>
> making fools understand
> (like wintry me)that not
> all matterings of mind
> equal one violet*

Toward the end of his life, Maslow mentioned that certain elements of peak experiences could become almost permanent aspects of daily experience. He termed this phenomenon the **plateau experience** (see Krippner, 1972; Maslow, 1976). In the plateau experience, all aspects of the world take on a sacred quality or are seen as manifestations of a divine presence. Maslow referred to this quality as **resacralization,** or restoring a sense of the sacred to the ordinary world. He saw this process as an antidote to a new defense mechanism that he named *desacralization.* This defense mechanism was found when people repressed a sense of the sacred and saw the world as simply objects with no inherent meaning or value.

Maslow also described experiences that had the same intensity and focus of peak experiences, but the emotional tone was negative. He termed these **nadir experiences** (footnote, p. 84, Maslow, 1968). These might involve a deep emotional sense of meaninglessness, loss, or loneliness. Maslow had earlier noted that struggle and difficulties are sometimes necessary for personal growth. Following this reasoning, can people use nadir experiences to enhance personal growth? Ebersole (1970) presented preliminary support for this idea. He found that some people reported using moments of deep despair and meaninglessness to create a new sense of meaning and purpose for their lives. Similarly, Wilson and Spencer (1990) asked people to report their "most intense" positive or negative experience. They found that 60 to 70 percent of people reported using *either* positive *or* negative experiences in some way to change their lives. Nadir experiences may also immediately precede deeply profound and extremely positive religious experiences. In Christianity, references to the "Dark Night of the Soul" describe nadir experiences that are often followed by profound religious illuminations (see Wapnick, 1980).

Near-Death Experiences This section also describes a dramatic example of the creation of meaning through an experience that has religious significance for most people. The phenomenon has been termed the *near-death experience*. The name comes from the situations that were initially thought to precede the experience—a close encounter with death. While it appears that people throughout history have reported near-death experiences (Groth-Marnat & Schumaker, 1989), it is only within the last thirty years that scientists have begun systematic investigations into these phenomena. In 1975, Dr. Raymond Moody Jr. published a collection of reports given by patients who had been declared clinically dead and then revived (Moody, 1975). The patients described visions that were extremely vivid and felt extraordinarily real. Dr. Moody also heard consistent themes and nearly identical experiences from patients who came from various backgrounds and who had quite different incidents as the trigger to the experience. There were recognizable patterns to these experiences that did not depend upon prior learning or the personality structure of the person. Moody termed these experiences *near-death experiences*.

Dr. Kenneth Ring (1980) of the University of Connecticut conducted the first contemporary psychological investigations into near-death experience. His study found that many people who reported a near-death experience also reported fairly dramatic changes in their orientation to life and their sense of meaning as a result of the experience. These changes included a dramatically decreased fear of death, decreased materialism, less concern with seeking social status or social recognition, increased meaningfulness to life, increased desire to be of service to other people, and increased orientation to spirituality—although often this meant less orientation to traditional religion (Ring, 1980). Because the near-death experience happens without warning and lasts only a few seconds of ordinary time, for some people the experience seemed to provide an almost instantaneous leap to greater psychological well-being and increased meaning in life. However, the full integration of the experience can take years (van Lommel, van Wees, Meyers, & Elfferich, 2001). Similarly, Paloutzian (1981) found that fear of death declined immediately after a religious conversion experience and continued to decline for six months after the experience.

Comments on Religious Experiences and the Creation of Meaning

Rapid changes in what constitutes a meaningful life suggests that at least *some* potentials for psychological well-being may lie dormant in individuals and, therefore, could be accessible at any time. In addition, the people who experience those leaps do not need to undergo extensive psychological struggle prior to their experience. However, it may be that the new meaning in life gained during these experiences needs time to be integrated into a person's life, and this is where the psychological work becomes important. For instance, in a longitudinal study, Pim van Lommel and a team of Dutch researchers found that the positive effects of a near-death experience may take up to eight years to be integrated completely into a person's life (van Lommel et al., 2001).

Finally, any discussion of elation, awe, peak, religious, or conversion experiences must also be qualified somewhat. Searching for personal religious experiences simply because they provide temporary feelings of joy or bliss may result in fairly superficial orientations to religion. Developing a lasting sense of meaning and purpose in life is more than having dramatic experiences. As the comparative theologian Houston Smith (1976) put it, "The goal, it cannot be stressed too often, is not religious experiences: it is the religious life" (p. 155).

Psychological Theories of Spiritual Development

While many surveys have found a relationship between religiousness and psychological well-being, psychologists have also been quite right to not accept a simple connection between religion and mental health. It is fairly obvious that religion, like any other behavior or belief, can be used as a defense against anxiety, self-doubt, and honest self-examination. Obviously, some differentiation must be made between a religious orientation that is supportive of mental health and one that is not. In order to get closer to answers about religiousness and psychological well-being, some researchers have developed psychological theories and assessment instruments to measure the variety of ways people can be religious.

Intrinsic and Extrinsic Religiosity

One of the earliest attempts to provide such an assessment instrument was that of Gordon Allport. He was interested in the different ways in which people use religion in their lives. To help understand these differences, he developed the concepts of **intrinsic** and **extrinsic religiousness** and the Religious Orientation Scale (Allport & Ross, 1967) to measure them. According to Allport, persons whose religious practices are extrinsic use their religion as a means to personal and social ends. Extrinsic religiousness "is the religion of comfort and social convention, a self-serving, instrumental approach shaped to suit oneself" (Donahue, 1985, p. 400). For instance, extrinsic persons might attend church in order to be seen by others, to raise their stature in the community, or to fit in with social expectations. Concerning measures of extrinsic religiousness, Michael Donahue (1985) stated that they do "a good job of measuring the sort of religion that gives religion a bad name. [Extrinsic religiosity] is positively correlated with prejudice, dogmatism . . . trait anxiety . . . fear of death . . . and is apparently uncorrelated with altruism" (p. 416). Intrinsic religiousness, however, is a style of religiousness that is used for the sense of meaning and purpose that it affords the person, regardless of the social benefits that might accrue. According to Allport, only intrinsic religiousness should be associated with positive mental health.

Allport originally thought that intrinsic and extrinsic religiousness were opposite ends of a bipolar continuum. That is, he thought a person must be either intrinsic or extrinsic but could never be both. His studies indicated, however, that this was not true. Therefore, Allport and Ross (1967) expanded the theory into a fourfold typology by adding two additional categories: indiscriminately proreligious (i.e., scores high on both intrinsic and extrinsic) and indiscriminately antireligious (i.e., scores low on both intrinsic and extrinsic). Donahue's (1985) analysis of studies investigating intrinsic and extrinsic religiousness concluded that intrinsic, as a single global dimension, correlated only moderately with indicators of psychological well-being. When viewed as part of the fourfold typology, however, intrinsic religiousness was a much more powerful indicator of mental health. That is, when high "intrinsic" and high "indiscriminately proreligious" were separated in the analyses, having an intrinsic religious orientation was associated with mental health. Scoring high on "indiscriminately proreligious" was not associated with better mental health.

Cognitive-Developmental Perspectives on Faith

Other psychologists have looked at the variety of ways people can be religious and have seen consistencies in how religious concepts develop over the course of a lifetime and how challenges to our initial ideas about religion are dealt with and resolved. Cognitive-developmental theorists view this process as involving changes in cognitive skills such as the use of abstract thinking, the ability to understand metaphors, and perspective taking or being able to step outside oneself and view situations from multiple perspectives. As one example, James W. Fowler (1981) developed a stage theory of faith development that speaks to the ways in which a sense of faith can change throughout a person's life. Fowler defines **faith** as a set of assumptions about how we are connected to others and to the world. Faith is the way we find meaning and coherence in our lives. It is the "master story" that people use to answer such basic questions as, What is life about? Who's in charge? and How do I live a good and worthy life? In this way, faith is how we relate to whatever is of transcendent worth and value to us. Even the scientist who constantly doubts any claims to final authority or the validity of timeless religious truths may be enacting a vibrant faith. That is, his or her faith may be one that rests on the certain knowledge that every assumption and every truth must be questioned, examined, tested, and reexamined in an ever-expanding exploration of reality. In other words, for Fowler, the opposite of faith is not doubt but nihilism, or the belief that life has no meaning. Faith is not a static set of beliefs but an activity that is a way of trusting, committing, and relating to the world (Fowler, 1981).

Fowler's stage theory divides faith into six stages and one initial prestage. Approximate age ranges are associated with many of the stages. The first two stages cover childhood up to about 11 years of age. At this point, children have acquired the religious beliefs, stories, and myths of their culture through their families. Children take these stories literally. At this stage, God really is a "Father." Ethics and morality fall into two distinct categories—good/bad, right/wrong, saint/sinner.

Third is the *synthetic-conventional* stage (ages 12 to adulthood). At this stage, the development of a personal identity results in the formation of a personal "myth" of the self, a life narrative, or a story of who we are as a person. It is a stage of conformity to religious authority (Meadows & Kahoe, 1984). However, it is difficult at this stage for the person to view those symbols as abstractions. Often the attitude taken toward other faiths is "If it doesn't fit with my beliefs, then it can't be true." Conflicts within one's own faith are ignored at this stage because any examination of those conflicts might threaten the coherence of beliefs.

Stage four is referred to as *individuating-reflexive* faith (young adulthood). This stage is characterized by the ability to reflect critically on one's religion. The new openness to the complexity of faith, however, increases the person's awareness of the contradictions and conflicts in their faith (e.g., how can a loving all-powerful God allow cruelty in the world?).

Stage five describes *conjunctive* faith (midlife; usually not seen before age 30). It is a stage that is not very common in the population. The conflicts of the previous stage have been resolved by using more complex, dialectical styles of reasoning. Personal desires and feelings no longer automatically lead to belief systems centered on the self. The person also recognizes that any "ultimate truth" must be more multidimensional, more interdependent, and larger than any particular statement of belief could possibly capture.

Stage six, *universalizing* faith, is rarely achieved. The uncommon individuals who operate at this stage almost never find their way to it before age 40. At this stage, the person operates from universal principals of love and justice for all beings. People are seen in terms of a universal community, and the person responds to them with a compassion that transcends divisions of creed and belief. Obviously, people who operate from stage six are usually seen as great religious teachers, humanitarians, or saints.

Psychodynamic Perspectives on Religion

Most psychologists assume that a mature spirituality is associated with greater altruism and tolerance, as well as less self-centeredness.

Psychodynamic theorists have explained the processes that help create a mature spirituality by looking at our relationship to our own unconscious. The basic idea behind these theories is that unresolved psychological conflicts can interfere with a person's awareness of spiritual needs or religious impulses. In essence, people can become so preoccupied with the resolution of personal psychological issues or with self-focused goals that they do not recognize or comprehend the spiritual dimension in life.

Early psychodynamic theorists like Alfred Adler (1964) and Erich Fromm (1955) believed that resolution of unconscious conflicts resulted in increases in compassion, altruism, brotherly love, and a deeper spirituality. Other theorists have said that a deeper level of unconscious processing is present in people and that access to this deeper unconscious inevitably leads to an increase in spirituality. The one psychodynamic psychologist who embraced the spiritual dimension more than most was Carl G. Jung. He believed that religion and spirituality were associated with the innate psychological and emotional needs to find meaning in life, to create a sense of wholeness or completeness, and to connect with something larger than the individual self.

Jung's personality theory continues to be one of the most unusual perspectives in Western psychology. Jung divided the unconscious into the *personal* and the *collective*. The personal unconscious holds memories and conflicts from childhood and repressed experiences of adult life. It is similar to Freud's idea of the unconscious. The **collective unconscious** contains psychological material that is more universal and is shared by all members of the human species. The main contents of the collective unconscious are **archetypes,** which are innate universal tendencies to respond emotionally to certain stimuli from the environment. At one point, Jung referred to the archetypes as "psychological instincts." While some contemporary theories in psychology, such as attachment theory, also postulate innate tendencies to respond emotionally to certain stimuli in the environment, Jung proposed a wide variety of archetypes and gave them a central place in his theory.

Jung believed that both the need for spirituality and the motivation to pursue it are found by gaining access to specific archetypes in the collective unconscious. These archetypes represent the universal psychological and emotional impulses that underlie the religious and spiritual quest for all human beings regardless of culture. For Jung, a mature understanding of spirituality and religion is too complex to be captured by simple statements of belief. The only way to express this understanding is through images, symbols, or rituals that help connect conscious and unconscious experience (see Fowler's stages 5 and 6, discussed earlier).

Comments on the Psychological Perspectives on Religion

All psychological perspectives agree that religion and spirituality can develop from less mature and less sophisticated conceptualizations into more mature and more complex ideas. In addition, all agree that more mature forms involve less use of religion as a simple hedge against existential anxiety or, even worse, as a way to raise one's social status. Many theories, such as Fowler's and Jung's, go even further and propose a specific direction for the maturation of faith. In general, the process of development described by these theorists moves from an egocentric or self-centered orientation to other-centered concerns; from literal and concrete interpretations of spirituality to abstract ones; and from reliance on external authority to reliance on internalized principles and beliefs. They also see a deepening spirituality emerging from an openness to certain aspects of unconscious life, a willingness to wrestle with spiritual paradox and contradictions, and an intellectual flexibility that will allow spiritual beliefs to change over time. Interestingly, these general developmental themes are also seen in a number of perspectives on optimal mental health (see Meadows & Kahoe, 1984, for comparisons).

Eastern Religions: Ideas from Buddhism

It will be helpful at this point to examine a model of spirituality from a different cultural context. We will look at the model of spirituality presented by Eastern religions—in particular, the Buddhist perspective. Eastern religions are the oldest in the world. Some of the ideas from Hinduism go back at least 5,000 years, and ideas from Buddhism and Taoism go back 2,500 years or more.

At their core, all Eastern religions are examples of contemplative religious or spiritual disciplines. The term *contemplative spirituality* describes religious disciplines that seek to find a direct and very personal experience of God or whatever is seen as the ultimate force in the universe (Woods, 1980). Having a direct spiritual experience is said to be an extremely positive emotional experience and can result in a spiritual transformation or spiritual conversion (see Emmons & Paloutzian, 2003). While contemplative spiritual traditions have also existed for many years in Christianity, Judaism, and Islam, the Eastern religious traditions have tended to be more explicit statements of this style of spirituality. Another major difference between Eastern and Western approaches to religion is that Eastern thought has never divided the human experience into separate disciplines for religion, psychology, and philosophy. In the East, all these disciplines are just facets of one field of study that attempts to help people find greater well-being.

The Buddhist Perspective on Happiness

The Reality of Constant Change

Buddhism begins by stating what it considers the one irrefutable truth of life: life is constant change. Despite our wishes or attempts to change it, life always changes; we are born, we age, we die; pain follows pleasure or joy follows heartache as surely as night follows day (Rahula, 1974).

The Desire for Security and Permanence

The second basic truth of Buddhism states that the cause of unhappiness is that in spite of the reality of constant change, we crave security, permanence, stability, and a permanent end to doubt and worry. In this sense, when we find something that appears to provide pleasure and stability, such as a job or a belief system, then we hold on to it for dear life. In Buddhism, this craving for something permanent that will insure permanent satisfaction and well-being is referred to as "attachment" or "grasping." Ultimately, this approach to life means that we suffer when we do not get what we want, and we suffer when we get what we want for fear of losing it. The Buddha said that all our attempts to control and manipulate life so that we experience only the positive and pleasant will be doomed to failure. Further, our attempts to completely control life in this way are, in fact, *the primary cause* of our suffering and discomfort.

Awareness and Detachment

In Buddhism, the cure for these problems and the route to happiness can be found by accepting the reality of change in life. In order to do this, two skills are cultivated and developed: awareness and detachment. Through disciplined meditation, a person learns to increase his or her awareness of everyday experiences and psychological processes. Detachment is the ability to "let go" and allow experiences to change without interference. In a sense, detachment means being open so that we experience each moment, bringing acute awareness to each changing moment and being willing to let each moment of awareness naturally change and flow into the next moment.

Nirvana, Enlightenment, and the Ideal of the Arhat

Meditation allows awareness and interested detachment to develop so that *all* elements of psychological processes are observed in a mindful way without grasping or clinging. When this process develops to a certain point, Buddhists believe it is then possible to experience the extinction of attachment or grasping as the basis for one's life. In Sanskrit, this release is called **nirvana,** or "the extinction of thirst" (Rahula, 1974). That is, to realize nirvana is to be released from all needs and desires based on greed, anger, and delusion . The realization of nirvana is accompanied by profound positive emotions. Buddhist monk and scholar, Walpola Rahula (1974) says, "He who has realized the Truth, Nirvana, is the happiest being in the world. . . . He is joyful . . . free from anxiety, serene and peaceful . . . full of universal love, compassion, kindness, sympathy, understanding and tolerance" (p. 43).

A person who has realized nirvana is said to have experienced **enlightenment.** A person can have numerous enlightenment experiences, each of which may be deeper, with more profound insights. In Buddhism, it is assumed that the person who had the deepest and most profound enlightenment experience possible was the Buddha. In fact, the word "Buddha" is an honorific term that means the "enlightened" or "awakened" one. The path to enlightenment requires the simultaneous cultivation and alignment of eight qualities of mind and behavior. Three of the qualities are concerned with the development of meditation skills (i.e., right effort, concentration, and mindfulness), two are concerned with the development of wisdom (i.e., right thinking, and understanding), and three relate to ethical conduct (i.e., right speech, action, and livelihood).

One of the consequences of an enlightenment experience is that a person's personality is permanently altered. Generally, this means that a portion of a person's negative personality traits are permanently eliminated. In Buddhism, the full development of the eight qualities of enlightenment results in the *total* elimination of the unhealthy mental factors and their replacement by the healthy mental factors (Goleman, 1975) (see Table 10.1).[1] In general, the healthy mental factors represent the two core traits of optimal mental health from the Buddhist perspective: compassion and wisdom.

To Western psychologists, probably the most incredible assumption of Buddhism and other Eastern religions is the idea that all negative emotions, behaviors, and personality traits can be totally eliminated. However, the Buddhist perspective, as well as other Eastern perspectives, is quite serious about this. In Buddhism, the *arhat* is an enlightened person who has achieved this state.[2] Goleman (1975) states, "The arhat embodies the essence of mental health in [Buddhist psychology]. His personality traits are permanently altered; all his motives, perceptions, and actions that he formerly engaged in under the influence of unhealthy factors will have vanished. . . . While the arhat may seem virtuous beyond belief from the perspective of Western psychology, he embodies characteristics common to the ideal type in most every Asian psychology. The arhat is the enlightened being, a prototype notable in the main for its absence in Western personality theory" (pp. 177–178).

In summary, in Eastern religions, a sense of well-being is fostered by accepting all aspects of life with equanimity and by finding a sense of meaning and purpose to life through insights into the nature of human consciousness (de Silva, 1979). All these are achieved through the practice of meditation, which allows for experiencing the world and the self in fundamentally

TABLE 10.1 **HEALTHY AND UNHEALTHY MENTAL FACTORS OF BUDDHISM**

Unhealthy Factors	Healthy Factors
Wisdom Factors	
Delusion	Insight
False View	Mindfulness
Shamelessness	Modesty
Recklessness	Discretion
Egoism	Confidence
Compassion Factors	
Agitation	Composure
Greed	Nonattachment
Aversion	Nonaversion
Envy	Impartiality
Avarice	Buoyancy
Worry	Pliancy
Contraction	Adaptability
Torpor	Proficiency
Perplexity	Rectitude

Source: Adapted from table entitled "Primary Mental Factors in Classical Buddhist Psychology," Daniel Goleman (1975), "Mental health in classical Buddhist psychology," *Journal of Transpersonal Psychology*, 7(2), 176–181.

different ways and diminishes the need for goal attainment as a source of happiness because ultimate happiness is present in each moment.

Stark and Washburn (1977) speculated about what personality traits might be found in someone who had achieved a high level of spiritual realization—either from Eastern or Western contemplative spiritual disciplines. They listed eight traits:

1. An adventuresome sense of life
2. A sense of tranquillity
3. A frequent experience of bliss
4. Nonattachment or the ability to let go of barriers and limitations
5. The ability to bring presence and absorption to all everyday experiences
6. Openness to experience
7. High resilience
8. A sense of spontaneity.

Their model combines a sense of spiritual peace, high subjective well-being, frequent flow or optimal experiencing, an openness to the experiences of life, and high adaptability and spontaneity.

Research on Religious Experiences and Eastern Psychology

Eugene d'Aquili and Andrew Newberg call their approach to the study of religious experiences *neurotheology*, in reference to the use of neurological imaging techniques to study religious experiences (d'Aquili & Newberg, 1999). In one study, they used neuro-imaging technology to record brain activity in very experienced Tibetan Buddhist monks while they were meditating. They found that specific areas of the brain were activated during deep meditative experiences. Interestingly, those were the cortical areas of the brain, which are involved in creating a sense of self in conscious experience. They argued that activation of those areas could lead to a sense that the perceptual boundary between "self" and "other" was temporarily breaking down, and this would result in a feeling of "oneness" with the world. In other words, they believed that they had found preliminary physiological correlates to the experiences reported by meditators for centuries. Similarly, in his book, *Zen and the Brain* (1998), neurologist James Austin reviews a number of physiological studies on meditation. He concludes that profound spiritual experiences do produce consistent physiological effects that can be measured with contemporary techniques of science.

A very recent study by Richard Davidson (2002) recorded brain activity of a Tibetan Buddhist monk who had extensive experience with meditation. The monk said he could voluntarily induce feelings of universal compassion during meditation. In fact, during meditation, each time the monk signaled that he was entering the compassionate meditative state there were significant and consistent changes in his brain wave activity. Davidson also found recognizable patterns of brain activity that are associated with both positive and negative moods (Davidson et al., 2003). Davidson and others have found that for most people, meditation changes brain activity toward the patterns associated with positive moods. Davidson also found that of all the people tested in one study, a Tibetan lama had the most extreme shift toward the brain pattern associated with positive emotions.

Studies have also shown that the practice of meditation and other spiritual disciplines can help increase factors associated with positive mental health such as empathy, creativity, and self-actualization. Further, studies of experienced meditators have found that meditation can induce experiences such as equanimity, bliss, ineffability, and a sense of selflessness (see Murphy & Donovan, 1997). In terms of theoretical perspectives, Buddhist ideas have been explained using psychodynamic concepts (Suzuki, Fromm, & De Martino, 1960; Epstein, 1988), and rather ambitious theories have been developed that seek to integrate Eastern and Western psychological perspectives (e.g., Wilber, 2000; Mikulus, 2002). Although these efforts to translate Eastern concepts into Western theory have been interesting, they are few in number and may be difficult to investigate scientifically. Researchers still know very little about the personality characteristics, behaviors, and emotional experiences of advanced practitioners of meditation or other contemplative disciplines.

Comments on Religion and Well-Being

The wide variety of perspectives discussed in this chapter all agree on the importance of spirituality or religiosity to well-being. One of the major functions of spirituality seems to be in providing a context for the development of global meaning systems. In fact, some have argued that the need for this type of meaning may be innate (see the discussion of Carl Jung in the "Psychodynamic Perspectives on Religion" section earlier in this chapter). In a similar fashion, other, more contemporary researchers have suggested that a need for religiosity is innate and part of the human condition. In fact, d'Aquili and Newberg (1999) go so far as to suggest that the need for spirituality is "hard-wired" into neural pathways of the human brain. Others do not go quite that far, but nonetheless believe that there is an innate need for spirituality or that it is a basic personality factor (Piedmont, 1999; Compton, 2001). From a scientific point of view, one of the difficulties with this topic of study is that the basic assumptions, beliefs, and principles of various religious perspectives are simply not open to scientific testing. However, the *impact* of spiritual and religious beliefs on well-being can be studied from a scientific point of view. One of the problems in this area of research is that more work needs to be done on which specific elements of religiosity or spirituality are required for a mature and healthy sense of well-being. It is all too obvious that religious principles and doctrines have been used throughout history to justify the most horrific acts of violence and cruelty. At the same time, it is also quite obvious that some of the world's most serene, compassionate, and happy people are found in religious environments.

Summary

This chapter has covered a number of issues related to religion and spirituality. First, studies were reviewed that found significant relationships between religious attitudes and behavior and both psychological and physical well-being. It was mentioned, however, that the benefits of religion to well-being may be confined to those who are intrinsically religious. Second, the topic of meaning was reviewed. Global meaning seems to be related to well-being because it provides a sense of coherence, understandability, and the "big picture" on life events. Situational meaning seems related to well-being through number of avenues such as goal attainment. Next, religious experiences were discussed, such as elation, awe, near-death experiences, and peak and nadir experiences. These dramatic experiences are striking in that some people show rapid changes in how they perceive meaning after the experience. Fowler's stage theory of faith was then discussed. He believes that faith (or our "master story") develops over the course of one's lifetime. Next, Jung's psychology and his approach to spirituality were discussed. His unique ideas on the collective unconscious tie the religious impulse to universal symbols, myths, and personality development. Finally, the perspective of Eastern religions, especially Buddhism, was discussed.

Notes

1. It is interesting to compare the unhealthy and healthy mental factors of Buddhism with the seven deadly sins and the seven virtues of Christianity (see Chapter 1) as well as with the list of virtues presented by Peterson & Seligman (see Chapter 8).

2. In Mahayana Buddhism, the idea of the arhat is changed into the ideal of the bodhisattva, who vows not to realize final Nirvana until all other beings are saved from suffering.

Learning Tools

Key Terms and Ideas

ARCHETYPES
AWE
COLLECTIVE UNCONSCIOUS
ELATION
ENLIGHTENMENT
EXTRINSIC RELIGIOUSNESS
FAITH (FOWLER'S DEFINITION)
INTRINSIC RELIGIOUSNESS
NADIR EXPERIENCES
PEAK EXPERIENCES

Books

d'Aquili, E. G., & Newberg, A. B. (1999). *The mystical mind: Probing the biology of religious experiences.* New York: Fortress Press. The authors developed the field of "neurotheology" by using current neuro-imaging technologies to see how the brains of spiritual practitioners process information (popular).

The Dalai Lama with Cutler, H. C. (1998). *The art of happiness: A handbook for living.* Interviews with the current Dalai Lama about happiness from a Buddhist perspective (popular).

Koenig, H. (ed.) (1998). *The handbook of religion and mental health.* New York: Academic Press. A collection of research reviews on many aspects of how religion effects mental health by well-known authors in the field (professional).

Research Articles

Bergin, A. (1991). Values and religious issues in psychotherapy and mental health. *American Psychologist, 46*(4), 394–403.

Emmons, R. A., & Paloutzian, R. F. (2003). The psychology of religion. *Annual Review of Psychology, 54,* 377–402.

George, L. K., Larson, D. B., Koenig, H. G., & McCullough, M. E. (2000). Spirituality and health: What we know, what we need to know. *Journal of Social and Clinical Psychology, 19*(1), 102–116.

On the Web

www.selectsmart.com. This Web site offers a number of "selectors" that will quiz you on your beliefs, personality types, and other qualities. Please note that no claim is made for the validity of these questionnaires. However, they are interesting exercises that will stimulate thought. The selectors most relevant to this chapter are those that focus on religion. Take one or more of the quizzes, and see how your ideas match with the answers. You may wish to change a few of your answers to certain questions and see how the change effects the religion match. You can also do this as a group exercise and discuss your answers with others.

Personal Explorations

Do you see a difference between "spirituality" and "religion" If so, what is the difference(s)?

Return to Fowler's stage theory of faith development. Do you think that a person's spirituality should mature and develop over time? If so, how? Do you think that Fowler's stages capture mature faith?

Many religions say that people should be humble, compassionate, charitable, and should think of other people's well-being first. For instance, part of the St. Francis prayer is, "Lord grant that I may not so much seek to be consoled, as to console; seek to be understood, as to understand; and seek to be loved, as to love. For it is in giving that we receive." Some people might say that research on subjective well-being suggests we should focus on building our self-esteem and fostering our own happiness first. Are these two positions actually different? Do people really have to choose between these two? Why or why not?

PART *iv*

POSITIVE INSTITUTIONS AND A LOOK TOWARD THE FUTURE

CHAPTER 11

Work, Community, Culture, and Well-Being

> No man is an island entire of itself; every man is a piece of the Continent, a part of the main . . . any man's death diminishes me, because I am involved in Mankind; and therefore never send to know for whom the bell tolls; it tolls for thee.
>
> *John Donne (1623)*

Job Satisfaction and Well-Being

One of the most significant areas of most people's lives is the world of work. This world can include both salaried and nonsalaried workers as well as those who are involved in running a household and caring for children. Most research on the impact of work on well-being, however, has looked at the world of professional and paid work. Hopefully, the unfortunate neglect of the work involved in being a stay-at-home mom or dad will be remedied in the near future. For this section of the book, however, the focus will have to be on paid employment. To begin this chapter, it is helpful to define **job satisfaction.** It has been defined as an emotional reaction that "results from perceptions that one's job fulfills or allows the fulfillment of one's important job values" (Locke, 1976, p. 1307). Therefore, job satisfaction is intimately tied to a person's values and needs. Satisfaction is further defined as our emotional reaction to how well those needs are satisfied and our values are supported. However, virtually no research has been done on what specific emotions comprise our overall emotional reaction of what we call job satisfaction (Pinder, 1998). In fact, it is more than likely that the specific emotions that make up each person's sense of satisfaction will be different and will depend on her or his own needs, values, attitudes, and perceptions. Finally, job satisfaction and job morale are generally not seen as identical concepts. Often, the idea of *job morale* is used to describe a person's desire to remain at their job, or it may be used to describe aspects of group behavior at work rather than individual attitudes (Pinder, 1998). Researchers have found that the idea of job satisfaction is fairly complex, and it is now assumed that satisfaction must be measured as a multidimensional construct.

Elements of Job Satisfaction: The Person

Studies have found that dispositions to experience positive emotionality can have a significant impact on job satisfaction. People who tend to score higher on measures of positive emotionality are often described as more enthusiastic, more energetic, and more excited about their jobs. It will probably come as no surprise that they tend to report higher levels of job satisfaction (see Warr, 1999). In fact, positive emotions at work can be partially responsible for a number of processes that enhance both personal fulfillment and even worker productivity. Allison Isen and her colleagues (Isen, 2001, 2002) have studied the impact of positive emotions on a number of basic psychological processes as well as the potential impact in the workplace. They have found that positive emotions will generally enhance problem solving and decision making, and can lead to more flexible, innovative, and creative solutions. Positive emotions may also lead to more favorable evaluations of others and can increase positive behaviors in the workplace, such as helping, generosity, and empathy.

There is also growing evidence that employees who experience more positive emotions at work make greater contributions to organizational effectiveness (Pinder, 1998). When people are in good moods they are more sociable, less aggressive, and better able to recall positive information. More positive moods also contribute to positive *spontaneous behavior* at the workplace (George & Brief, 1992). In other words, without thinking much about it they are more likely to be helpful to others, develop skills that will help the organization, make criticisms that are constructive rather than destructive, spread goodwill, and take actions that will help protect the organization from threats and dangers. Further, workers who experience more positive emotions tend to be injured less on the job.

Barry Staw (2000) also hypothesized that positive emotionality at work may help inoculate people against the impact of various stressors at work. In particular, positive emotionality may help people adjust and adapt when they find that their jobs are not exactly what they expected them to be. Interestingly, he also cautioned that people who exhibit more negative traits at work might also serve a useful purpose in organizations. At times, someone needs to be cautious, worried, or doubtful in order for organizations to function effectively.

While positive emotions seem to have any number of positive benefits to people at work, the question remains whether it is the frequency of positive emotions at work or the intensity that is most important. A similar question was asked in Chapter 3 in terms of overall subjective well-being. Just as in that research, the frequency of positive emotions at work may be more important than their intensity. One example of how this may be important comes from efforts by management to motivate employees. In today's competitive economy, some businesses spend substantial amounts of money to hire motivational consultants. The task of these consultants is to increase employee motivation, self-confidence, commitment to the organization, and build better teamwork. These consultants may give inspiring lectures, lead employees through a series of outdoor adventures similar to military boot camp, or go for more dramatic esteem building exercises such as having employees walk over burning hot coals. Unfortunately, many companies get very little for all the money and effort they put into these motivational exercises. Of course, employees often feel huge bursts of self-confidence, enthusiasm, and camaraderie after attending these seminars, workshops, and personal tests of courage. The problem is that these bursts of positive emotion simply do not last. Research suggests that organizations could do more for their employees and for productivity by creating work environments that fostered less intense levels of positive emotions but fostered them on a more consistent and reliable basis.

"It's Not Just a Job, It's a Calling"

Amy Wrzesniewski and colleagues (Wrzesniewski, McCauly, Rozin, & Schwartz, 1997) found that people in jobs ranging from clerical to professional viewed their occupations in three basic ways. Some people saw them as simply a "job," in that they focused on the financial gains from work and on the necessity of work and earning a living. Others conceptualized their work as a "career." For these people, their jobs were a way to facilitate achievement motivation, stimulate their need for competition, or enhance prestige and satisfaction.

The third way that some people viewed their work was as a "calling." For these people, their work was a source of personal fulfillment. For many, this sense of fulfillment and meaning came from recognizing or simply believing that what they did had a socially useful purpose. In a sense, their jobs were a way to be of service both to themselves and to other people. It would seem that the type of meaning people derive from their work should also be different for these three different ways of conceptualizing one's job. For those who see their work as just a job, the meaning that they gain from work may have more to do with being a provider for their family or from activation of the work ethic. For those who see work as a career, meaning probably comes from accomplishing goals and from a sense of personal pride in achievements. Last, those who see their work as a calling probably derived meaning from a personal sense of fulfillment that was partially based on a sense of community.

Wrzesniewski found that these three ways of conceptualizing work were found across many different types of occupations. Issues such as income, status, and job prestige may have little to do with how people view their reasons and motivations for work, especially when work is a calling. The following quotation from a piano tuner suggests that occupations of all types can be seen as a calling: "Piano tuning is not really business. It's a dedication. . . . I enjoy every second of it. . . . I don't see any possibility of separating my life from my work. . . . There seems something mystic about music, about piano tuning. There's so much beauty comes out of music. There's so much beauty comes out of piano tuning" (Terkel, 1974).

Being in Flow at Work

As discussed in the chapter on flow, some people report experiencing flow at work. Mihaly Csikszentmihalyi has found that people who enjoy their jobs often report being in a state of flow while at work (Csikszentmihalyi & LeFevre, 1989; Csikszentmihalyi, 1990). In fact, Haworth and Hill (1992) found that for most people, their flow experiences—when high skills were matched with high challenges—came primarily from the work environment. However, Csikszentmihalyi (1997) also found that people report positive experiences of flow at work but at the same time may feel less happy at work than in other contexts. Nonetheless, Csikszentmihalyi believes that having more flow experiences may be one key to job satisfaction.

Emotional Intelligence at Work

Another factor that is important to satisfaction at work is a person's emotional intelligence. In fact, some have suggested that a person's level of emotional intelligence may be one of the most important factors in career success as well as job satisfaction (for instance, Goleman, 1995). For instance, one major American company takes this idea so seriously that they have instituted a program to help managers become "emotional coaches" for their employees (see Salovey, Meyers, & Caruso, 2002). Of course, it seems quite obvious that positive social relationships at work should be related to emotional self-control and insight into one's own emotions and those of others. However, current ideas take this idea even further and may be creating new avenues for career success and satisfaction by focusing on our emotional lives.

Improving Job Satisfaction: The Person

So, what can individuals do to help enhance their own career satisfaction? It would also be nice if these efforts resulted in personal growth and greater well-being outside of work. One interesting perspective comes from Marcus Buckingham, Don Clifton, Curt Coffman, Gabriel Gonzalez-Molina, and Paula Nelson at the Gallup Organization (Clifton & Nelson, 1992; Buckingham & Coffman, 1999; Buckingham & Clifton, 2001; Coffman & Gonzalez-Molina, 2002). They recently began emphasizing what they called *personal strengths*—those traits, abilities, interests, and skills that show us at our best and make us unique. They first discussed the myths that they say inhibit us from finding our potential.

1. The first myth is that fixing our weaknesses is a better strategy than fostering and building our strengths. This myth says that we improve ourselves by "fixing" what is wrong with us. Of course, people must try to improve their weaknesses and must try to change what is less adaptive or even counterproductive. However, the problem with this myth is that many people believe that fixing what is wrong is the most efficient way to fulfill potentials. In many ways, this myth is identical to the idea that the best way to become happier is to eliminate negative emotions. Instead, as discussed earlier, people must use different strategies to eliminate negative emotions and to foster positive emotions.
2. The second myth says that anyone can do anything they put their mind to. Clifton and colleagues mentioned two common aphorisms that express this myth: "If at first you don't succeed, try, try again," and "If you can conceive it, you can achieve it." These little sayings are often heard in motivational seminars. Many people even have sayings like this on their desk calendars or on motivational posters around the office. These sayings represent a myth because for most people, they are completely unworkable. They represent impossible goals. The idea that anyone can do anything is ridiculous. There are real limits to what we can accomplish in life. A better strategy is to know what those limits are and work with them. For instance, for most people in the world, even attending countless self-motivation seminars or endless self-improvement courses will never turn them into the next Mozart, Einstein, or Bill Gates. On a smaller scale, within professions, some people are a better fit with certain jobs than with other jobs. Part of this has to do with which jobs are intrinsically motivating for us. Part of it also has to do with personality traits. Because personality traits tend to be relatively stable throughout life, it makes very little sense to focus large amounts of energy on trying to change basic innate personality characteristics. Note that the second myth dovetails with the first myth. If certain jobs seem to be a poor fit with one's basic personality traits, then it makes very little sense to spend a majority of one's time trying to fix the "weakness" that is presented by that trait.

Clifton and colleagues suggest instead that people should focus on their strengths. People should focus on what they do right. They suggest that we should find out what we do very well and do more of it. So, what about the weaknesses? They suggest that weaknesses should be managed. That is, we should recognize those areas in which we do not do all that well and find ways to compensate for them, such as by delegating those responsibilities to others. They also suggest that in our search for strengths we should focus on just one strength at first; as that strength develops, then others will present themselves. Because many people are in the habit of looking for weaknesses, one might ask how does a person recognize one of his or her strengths.

Recognize Your Strengths

Clifton and colleagues suggest there are five characteristics of the strength we can use to help recognize them. First they *represent "yearnings"*—strong psychological pulls that we have toward certain interests, goals, or directions. They are the internal compasses that can point out our direction if we listen. Of course, there are such things as "*mis*yearnings." Often, these are desires for goals that other people have told us we "should" have. Some examples are misyearnings for status, power, glamour, and wealth. The second characteristic of a strength is that when we use it, it *gives us intrinsic satisfactions.* When we activate a strength, we feel good about ourselves and about the activity. Activating a true strength makes us feel better about ourselves. The third characteristic of a strength is that when we are using it in certain contexts, *learning comes easier.* It is easier to absorb information and integrate it in ways that seem more satisfying. The fourth characteristic of a strength is that in moments when we activate that strength *we perform extraordinarily well.* At those times, we glimpse excellence. Sometimes, we may find ourselves in a flow state at these moments. The fifth characteristic combines many of the previous ones, for it says that when we activate a strength, performance seems to *take less effort,* we are *interested in the activity,* we *are involved,* we *learn quicker,* and there seems to be *a deeper sense of satisfaction.*

The Development of Strengths

Clifton and colleagues also mentioned that strengths develop best *in relation to another person.* They believe that interpersonal support, understanding, empathy, and commitment to relationships help create the crucible in which strengths can grow. Strengths also develop when we *place positive expectations on others and ourselves.* What they are referring to is our positive expectations for achievement. Note that this is not the old "you can do anything" type of expectation. Rather, it is a realistic trust in potential that is already there and that can be actualized.

Finally, Clifton and colleagues also believe that strengths develop best within the framework of *a mission.* They believe that if we can find a deep commitment for the future or even a passion for life, then it is easier to find our strengths in this context. The mission provides an overall direction or purpose for our life and may state in relatively simple terms the basic foundations of our life. Clifton and colleagues caution that a mission is not the same thing as a goal. Goals can be associated with filling a mission, but they need not be the same. Note that part of what they are saying is that a mission can give us direction in life even if we fail to reach some of the goals that are part of that mission. That is, if we have a mission, then the failure of any single goal does not derail us from the mission.

Elements of Job Satisfaction: The Work Environment

Characteristics of the job itself and the work environment are also important to satisfaction. After all, just having a cheerful personality is not enough to create high satisfaction in *absolutely any* job situation! Once questions about job satisfaction turn to elements of the work environment, the findings begin to get more complicated. Primarily, this is because there are so many different factors that create the environments in which people do their jobs. Consider that the work environment is composed of factors such as multiple social relationships, the amount of time that one is expected to put into the job, the type of organizational structure, opportunities for advancement or recognition, ability to use one's learned skills or learn new skills, and numerous elements that involve the issues of pay and equity.

Job Characteristics and Well-Being

In 1964, Fred Emery proposed that there are six intrinsic factors of the work environment that make work satisfying (Emery, 1964, quoted in Weisbord, 1987). He said that workers needed:

1. Variety and challenge
2. Elbow room for decision making
3. Good feedback to enhance learning
4. Mutual support and respect
5. Wholeness and meaning to work
6. Room to grow, or an optimistic and bright future.

Emery said that optimal satisfaction comes from a certain balance in each of these areas. The first three should be moderated—not too much or too little. The last three are more open-ended. That is, no one can have too much of them.

Almost thirty years later, a 1991 Gallup poll asked people how important certain aspects of work were to their job satisfaction. The most important aspect of work was having good health insurance. Other aspects that were important to more than 50 percent of the respondents were interesting work, job security, chances to learn new skills, adequate vacation time, freedom to work independently, and recognition from coworkers (Hugick & Leonard, 1991).

Ten Qualities of Positive Work Environments

Recently, Peter Warr (1999) reviewed the research on job satisfaction and classified the major elements of the work environment that determined well-being at work. His list obviously overlaps with the factors described in the previous section. His list includes the following categories, given with examples of a few factors that fall under that heading.

1. *Opportunity for personal control.* A number of studies have found that people enjoy a certain degree of freedom, autonomy, participation in decision making, and self-determination on their jobs. The chance to make decisions about how one reaches goals and a chance to have input to various aspects of one's job helps create a sense of competence.
2. *Opportunity for skill use.* Recall that at least one theory believes that the need for competence is one of the three basic human needs (see Deci & Ryan in Chapter 2). Meeting this need is also related to having opportunities for using one's skills and talents on the job. Just imagine the frustration a person might feel on the job if he or she was a skilled and creative graphic artist who was stuck designing boring industrial labels for boxes of rubber bands.
3. *Reasonable externally generated goals.* Satisfaction is associated with having moderately strong and clear goals that stimulate challenging work conditions. If those goals are such that they create unnecessary demands that result in feelings of being overloaded, then satisfaction goes down. One of the more consistently reported examples of this phenomenon is that lower job satisfaction tends to be associated with jobs that require very high demands with very low opportunities for personal control.
4. *Variety.* The 1991 Gallop poll found that "interesting work" and "chances to learn new skills" were ranked second and fourth in importance to job satisfaction. People like to learn new skills, to challenge themselves, and to use certain aspects of work to stimulate curiosity and even personal growth. In fact, some people have said that those who are more satisfied with their jobs have the ability to change tasks that might seem boring into small personal challenges.

5. *Environmental clarity.* One element is the clarity of feedback, or how well people communicate tasks, assignments, concerns, and goals within the organization. Job security is related to this issue. In the 1991 Gallop poll, "job security" was ranked third in importance to job satisfaction. Fears that one's job could be eliminated at any moment generally cause people to be less satisfied at work.
6. *Availability of money.* First, some amount of job satisfaction is associated with a person's absolute level of pay. However, studies have also shown that a substantial portion of satisfaction with income can be explained by looking at how people compare their own income to the income that other people are making for doing the same job. Clark and Oswald (1996) found that it is possible to calculate an average rate of pay for different jobs, or what is called the "going rate." They found that the more people believed that their pay was less than this rate, the less their overall job satisfaction. We saw earlier that people engage in certain self-evaluations by using social comparison processes. It appears that similar processes occur when people evaluate their satisfaction with their rate of pay. People use an absolute standard to some degree, but more frequently they compare their pay to others who are doing the same job. If they come out below what others are paid, then they tend to feel less satisfied with their pay. Note that people seem to accept the fact that some amount of discrepancy in income is fair. The fact that surgeons make more money than day-care workers seems acceptable to most people. Dissatisfaction comes in, for instance, when day-care workers compare their salaries to those of other day-care workers.
7. *Physical security.* This refers to good working conditions, safety on the job, and ergonomically adequate equipment.
8. *Supportive supervision.* Supportive management and effective leadership.
9. *Opportunity for interpersonal contact.* The eight and ninth items refer to one of the most important aspects of job satisfaction—the satisfaction with social relationships at work. Because coworkers can be a source of support, recognition, validation, and other forms of social rewards, when those relationships are positive, satisfaction with work tends to be positive. One early study (Van Zelst, 1951) found that acceptance by coworkers or social popularity showed an extremely high correlation of .82 with job satisfaction! In fact, the loss of social relationships at work is one of the reasons that retirement can be stressful and can lead to initial decreases in well-being. It also seems to be one reason why lottery winners who quit their jobs can feel a sense of loss, loneliness, and boredom.
10. *Valued social position.* This element takes into account more than just the prestige or social status that one's job may hold. While these can be a factor in satisfaction, many people also need to feel that what they do is important in some way. People can derive a sense of meaning and purpose from their jobs. For many people, a sense of meaning and purpose comes from feeling that what they do makes a real difference in the lives of other people (London & Strumpf, 1986). In a 1987 Harris poll, it was found that 48 percent of respondents listed "my job gives a feeling of real accomplishment" as the most important aspect of their work. A related issue may be a concern for members of minority groups. Studies have found that perceptions of racial or ethnic discrimination decrease job satisfaction (Lewis, 2002). However, when members of minority groups had high collective esteem, or positive evaluations of their ethnic group, then job satisfaction increased.

Comments on the Ten Qualities

While high satisfaction with all ten categories is not necessary for high job satisfaction, there is evidence that the more of these areas a person feels satisfied with, the higher his or her overall job satisfaction. It is also important to note that for many of the ten areas, a person's satisfaction depends on relative judgments. While the absolute level counts for a portion of satisfaction, in some cases it is the person's *perception* of that area that has the greatest impact on satisfaction. The case of income is one of the best examples. Finally, note the strong similarity between Emery's 1964 list of positive work environments and the list created by Warr thirty-five years later. It appears that the qualities that make a job satisfying may be fairly stable despite social changes (see also Frey, Jonas, & Greitemeyer, 2003).

Improving Job Satisfaction: Healthy Work Environments

Nick Turner, Julian Barling, and Anthea Zacharatos (2002) have suggested that work environments can be changed, even in the face of new demands, so that people feel a sense of satisfaction, and even support, in their jobs. Their analysis focuses on three major points: (1) work redesign, (2) teams and work groups, and (3) transformational leadership. The basic assumption behind their suggestions for redesigning work is that people should be encouraged to be actively engaged with tasks of their job and the work environment. They say that people need a certain degree of autonomy, challenge, and opportunities for positive social interactions at work.

Work Redesign

Turner et al. (2002) believe that when skill variety, task identity, and task difficulty are structured to provide a healthy working environment, then three psychological states are fostered: work seems more meaningful, there is more felt responsibility for job outcomes, and there is greater knowledge of results and of work outcomes. They cite research evidence supporting the idea that changing jobs in this way leads to more positive personal and work outcomes such as greater motivation, satisfaction, and performance as well as lower absenteeism and turnover.

One central assumption of this model is that high task control, along with adequate and supportive feedback, is crucial for satisfying job characteristics. Other aspects of redesigning work in positive ways include having clear lines of communication, knowing whom one reports to when there are difficulties, and finding a good fit between one's personality and the role one fills at work. Finally, the need for appropriate workloads is becoming increasingly important in today's job environments. Studies have found that having inappropriate workloads is positively related to both poorer physical health and more negative mood (see Turner et al., 2002).

Teams and Work Groups

The second major area in Turner et al.'s analysis concerns teams and work groups. They believe that the positive impact of team building and productive work groups has been thoroughly demonstrated through both research and practical applications on the job (also see Pfeffer, 2001). One of the more obvious advantages of teams is that they can provide the social networks, they provide for companionship, and they give people readily available sources for help and practical assistance. In fact, in almost any group the members feel more positive benefits when a sense of cohesion exists among the members. Groups also operate better when there is a sense of group purpose.

New Models of Leadership

The third element mentioned by Turner et al. concerns an unfamiliar concept: an organizational factor termed **transformational leadership** (also see Turner, Barling, & Epitropaki,

2002). This refers to a style of leadership in which supervisors, managers, and others help establish a sense of mission or vision for the future. Transformational leaders, in a sense, help to make the workplace more meaningful for employees. Rather than being seen as authority figures, they may be more akin to coaches who can motivate, inspire, and provide a sense of direction. These types of leaders tend to stimulate internal drives toward achievement and self-actualization. Those who are truly transformational leaders also bring to the workplace a strong sense of justice, ethics, and fairness. As we will see later, they are the type of leaders who "put people first." Transformational leaders challenge employees to do their very best, convince people they can perform beyond expectations, encourage workers to think for themselves, and help employees to challenge assumptions and think in new ways—or "outside the box." Although the idea of transformational leadership is new, research evidence supports it as a factor in higher employee morale, greater job satisfaction, more positive perceptions of supervisors, and greater commitment to the organization. However, transformational leadership may have its impact by facilitating other elements of the working environment rather than as a direct cause of satisfaction.

Wayne Baker (2003) created the idea of **breakthrough leadership.** He sees these types of leaders as men and women who seize the opportunities that come from extraordinary incidents or events. Breakthrough leaders seize these moments and help others explore the possibilities these events open up. Baker believes that people need to belong, need to contribute, and need a sense of meaning. He also believes that people seek transcendence, which means that people must find ways to rise above the temporary and immediate difficulties of life. People who can do so often place difficulties in a larger framework, can find a higher purpose to their lives, or can see life as a universal quest. Breakthrough leaders have the ability to help facilitate the development of these transformations in other people, especially in difficult times. They know that difficult times call for openness, honesty, fostering a sense of connection between people, dialogue, giving immediate events a sense of meaning, and providing a worthy goal or mission that can serve as a guide toward a better future.

"Putting People First" in Organizations

Jeffrey Pfeffer (1998) has strongly argued that organizations actually are more successful when they "put people first." This includes providing employment security even when economic times are tough. He reports on a review of more than 130 field studies of organizational change in which 75 percent of the studies found increases in economic performance for companies that put people first. Note that his review found increases in economic performance, not just job satisfaction. Some of the organizational changes that he suggests include: more focus on extensive training of employees, guarantees of job security, increased wages, simplification of job classification hierarchies, simplified systems of job compensation, placing emphasis on self-managed teams that hold a good deal of decision-making power, and more sharing of information among employees. Pfeffer argues that the company "bottom line" is actually helped by focusing on creating satisfying and healthy work environments.

Is This the Best Company in the World to Work For?

There is a real company that utilizes many of these principles in the work environment. The company is SAS, a software company in North Carolina. One employee said of her job, "I'm never going to leave SAS, just bury me here. I'm just gonna stay here forever." This employee is not the only one who feels this way about his or her job. This company has regularly been voted one of the best companies, and sometimes *the best* company, to work for. One of the reasons that people love working for this company is the level of benefits it provides to employees. The first big benefit is that every employee gets free medical care. Of course, many companies offer similar benefits for their employees. However, here is just a partial list of the rest of the perks and benefits of working for SAS: swimming pool, weight room, aerobics classes, basketball court, playing fields for Frisbee or soccer, tennis courts, reduced-cost on-site day care, washing and dry-cleaning services, a subsidized cafeteria with a pianist to set the mood, car washing facilities, and an on-site masseuse. One employee said that he has turned down other job offers that pay $30,000 more per year because working for SAS provides such a positive work environment. He said, "But to me and my wife there are some things more important than money. And I have peace of mind." As might be expected, all of this results in extraordinarily high job morale at SAS. It also results in very low turnover rates. Because turnover can be costly to a company, does that mean that these amenities and perks are actually cost effective? A business professor at Stanford studied SAS and estimated that the low turnover and high morale actually contribute to savings of about $75 million dollars a year. It may be that you can have your cake and eat it too! (CBS News, "Another Extraordinary Day On the Job," February 8, 2001).

Comments on Job Satisfaction

In general, people are more satisfied with jobs where stress is manageable, where they are provided with challenges and opportunities to learn new skills, and where they have freedom to reach their own solutions to problems. A good fit between the person's personality style and the demands of the organization is also related to satisfaction. The old idea that everyone wants a job that pays tremendous amounts of money for doing little work is simply a myth. People have a need to feel competent and to believe that their efforts contribute in some way to the society.

In the end, however, a definitive summary of job satisfaction is difficult to find. Despite volumes of research studies, researchers still do not agree precisely on what job satisfaction really is, how it is influenced by factors such as work organizations, or just what its consequences are for running organizations or managing people (Pinder, 1998). Everyone seems to agree that it is important, but like many other areas of human behavior the complexities of the relationships involved have proved to be quite challenging.

Social Well-Being

Corey Lee M. Keys and Shane Lopez argue that a complete classification system for mental health should include three general components: emotional well-being, psychological well-being, and social well-being (Keys & Lopez, 2002). In their model, emotional well-being refers to both immediate and long-term emotional and cognitive reactions to events in life. The research on subjective well-being (see Chapter 3) has focused on this aspect of mental health. The second component, psychological well-being, represents the basic behavioral and emotional dimensions for evaluating one's life. Carol Ryff's model of psychological well-being illustrates this component (see Chapter 9). Keys developed the third component, which consists of five dimensions of social well-being (Keys, 1998).

The first of the five dimensions of social well-being is *social acceptance,* or the degree to which people generally hold positive attitudes toward other people. The second dimension is *social actualization,* or the degree to which people believe that society has the capacity to develop and grow toward being a better place. *Social contribution,* the third dimension, refers to how much people believe their daily activities contribute to the society and how much those activities are valued by their community. The fourth dimension is *social coherence,* or the degree to which the society seems to be understandable, predictable, and logical. The last dimension is *social integration,* which refers to how much a person feels a part of their own community as well as how much support and commonality they feel with others in their social world.

Keys (1998) found that the dimensions of social well-being correlated positively with measures of happiness, life satisfaction, generativity, optimism, feelings of neighborhood trust and safety, as well as subjective perceptions of people's own physical health and degree of community involvement in the past. The social dimensions correlated negatively with measures of depression, meaninglessness, and perceived constraints and obstacles in life. Keys also found that social well-being tended to increase with education level and age. He also found that the new measure of social well-being was similar to other measures of mental health but not identical. Social well-being is a distinct way in which people judge their own sense of well-being, and it is important for overall mental health and well-being. We turn next to how psychologists have investigated social well-being.

Positive Communities and Community Psychology

In the past, psychological studies tended to ignore the impact that social contexts have on our behavior and our emotions. Often, this means that conclusions from research may wrongly attribute responsibility for behavior completely to individual personality traits. Marybeth Shinn and Siobhan Toohey (2003) refer to this problem as the **context minimization error.** They present examples of how presumed "facts" about human behavior, such as the best parenting style or the role of parent-child attachment in well-being, can actually be dependent on community contexts. One of the ways that psychology has moved outside the emphasis on the individual or the study of our immediate small-group social relationships is through the specialty area of community psychology. **Community psychology** emphasizes the role of the environment and the social world in both the creation of problems and through an emphasis on how to intervene to solve problems. Community psychology studies the person-in-social-context (Rappaport & Seidman, 2000). While social psychology also studies people in social context, it is in the second role of community psychology, the alleviation of problems, that this discipline partially distinguishes itself from studies in social psychology. Julian Rappaport (1977) said that community psychology should be thought of as a perspective that is built on three general foundations: cultural relativity, diversity, and ecology. These three aspects of community psychology imply a few basic assumptions about working with many different types of people in their social and cultural environments.

First, *cultural relativity* suggests an acknowledgment of the fact that social rules, mores, and standards may differ for different cultural groups. This is increasingly true in a world where travel between countries is relatively easy and immigration is fairly widespread in certain countries of the world.

Second, the idea of *diversity* acknowledges that fact that in many societies, the reality of cultural diversity presents the necessity of recognizing that differences between subgroups in a community will continue to exist. In the past, the ideal model for immigration in the United States was that it would be a great "melting pot" for people from all over the world. The image implied that after a short period of time all differences between immigrants would vanish as everyone became "American." Over the years, however, it has become fairly obvious that cultural heritage is a valuable resource that people use to create a sense of identity. An acceptance of diversity changes the image of the melting pot to the idea of the great "American quilt."

Community psychologists tend to reject the idea that a single social norm should be used as the standard for all behavior for all people in a society. This does not, however, lead to the idea that anything goes. Tensions between competing social norms inevitably will become part of this mix. However, these tensions and their solutions add immeasurably to the growth of the society.

Finally, the notion of *ecology* is here applied not just to the natural environment but also to the reality of a human ecology. The community psychology perspective then recognizes that people exist not in isolation but in a constant variety of intricate relationships with their environment. Community psychology, therefore, studies the full multidimensional complexities of people in various social systems and cultural settings that create a sense of community. Usually, it is assumed that these multileveled relationship structures are part of reciprocal relationships between people and their social worlds.

These perspectives of community psychology imply several principles (Phares & Trull, 1997). One of the primary implications is that one cannot be exclusively concerned with either the individual or the environment in isolation. Instead, what is most important is the *person-environment fit.* When the fit between the individual and the environment is poor, then problems can occur. When the fit is good, then the probability of human flourishing increases. Another implication is that community psychology should *focus on competencies.* Change happens by identifying the strengths, resources, and efficiencies of people and environments. In addition to this, under certain circumstances community psychology is also involved with *political activism.* This direct participation in political activities makes community psychology somewhat unusual among the specialty areas of psychology. Finally, community psychology tends to be more heavily involved in prevention than other applied areas of psychology.

Empowerment

One of the key ideas in community psychology is that of **empowerment** (Rappaport & Seidman, 2000). Empowerment refers to the process of enabling people who are marginalized or underprivileged to gain a measure of personal and political power. To be empowered is to take charge of one's life and feel a sense of efficacy, competence, and self-determination. If there is one common theme that runs through community psychology, it is the idea of empowerment. Community psychology interventions are designed to help people take control of their own environments and to master their own problems.

As a real-world example of empowerment, some of the findings relevant to community crime prevention will be discussed next. One of the factors that criminologists discuss concerning crime prevention is called the "broken window" theory of crime (Sampson, 2001a, 2001b). At first glance, this theory seems naive and simpleminded. However, many police departments across the country use this idea to combat criminal activity. The theory predicts that if a criminal walks into a neighborhood and sees litter, broken windows, unoccupied buildings, graffiti, unkempt lawns and parks, abandoned cars, and other signs of neglect, then he or she assumes that the neighborhood is a place where people do not care about what goes on around them. If that neighborhood also has no one sitting on front porches, no children playing in the parks, no one out for a casual walk, or no one working outside on gardens and lawns, then the criminal assumes that the neighborhood is a place where no one really cares to know what is going on around them. Therefore, it is a safe place to commit crimes because the neighbors just are not paying attention.

Former vice-president Al Gore Jr. believes that environments like this can create a sense of *learned powerlessness* (Gore, 2001). This idea is similar to Seligman's idea that learned helplessness can lead to depression. That is, if a person's efforts to solve problems in their own neighborhood are consistently unsuccessful, then the person begins to believe that they have no real impact on changing conditions in their community for the better. People lose hope, optimism, and a sense of self-efficacy in their abilities to implement meaningful changes in their lives and their immediate environments. The opposite of learned powerlessness, however, may be a sense of **learned empowerment** (Gore, 2001). Through community activity that has real results, people can learn to take a measure of control over their communities.

Robert Sampson (2001a, 2001b) believes that one form of learned empowerment is a sense of **collective efficacy.** In general, collective efficacy is a sense of social cohesion in a community that creates local friendship networks and a sense of agency or a willingness to intervene in making the neighborhood a better place to live. When collective efficacy is high in a neighborhood, then criminal activity is lowered. A sense of cohesion and informal social ties with one's neighbors buffers a sense of community fear and mistrust (Ross & Jang, 2000). A sense of trust can be partially built by a willingness to intervene. Intervention can take the form of participation in neighborhood organizations such as crime watch or voluntary community cleanups, or voluntary associations such as the PTA that have an impact on the neighborhood by paying attention to the quality of the schools. A sense of agency or a willingness to intervene can also come from the little things like watching for neighbor's children at the park, paying attention to unusual activity going on at neighbors' homes, or keeping one's lawn mowed. Neighborhoods that are high in coordination of available social services also contribute to more positive outcomes—especially for women in those neighborhoods. In general, research has found that high social organization, the presence of social capital (i.e., positive social networks and norms that facilitate trust, coordination, and cooperation), and a sense of community contribute to better neighborhood quality of life (Shinn & Toohey, 2003).

Community Interventions

One of the unique aspects of community psychology is the emphasis on positive interventions at a community level. Obviously, if intervention strategies work well, they can be highly effective ways to have an impact on large groups of people and help improve both their personal lives and the lives of the communities they live in. A few examples of community intervention strategies will be described next.

Community Strengths

The first example of how to build successful community interventions comes from John and Susan Blood, who seem to have taken the advice of positive psychologists because they help focus community activists on their strengths (Holland, 2001). The Bloods run a nonprofit organization that helps people work together and share their resources, talents, and skills to improve their neighborhoods and build stronger, more self-reliant communities. They begin by asking people to engage in the processes of "asset-mapping" and "appreciative inquiry" by listing their internal assets. These are not the material assets but rather what they have to contribute right now in terms of strengths, relationships, partnerships, goals, and dedication. An essential next step is often to focus on goals for the community or what people want to accomplish. Of critical importance to these goals is the requirement that they be stated in positive terms and not as "problems." For instance, they believe that a goal stated as "fighting crime" often results only in stimulating old stereotypes or negative images that may undermine the process. This old image, for instance, implies that residents should give the responsibility to the police because they are the people designated to "fight" crime. Instead, the goal should be to form a "healthy and safe neighborhood." The residents need to take responsibility and create their own solution. Of course, this solution will also form a partnership with the police, but the people of the neighborhood need to find and utilize their own unique strengths and skills to reach their collective goal. The Bloods have seen their efforts pay off in successful projects such as a Spanish language radio station that was created by teenagers in Texas, the creation of economic opportunities and a healing arts program for the community in Pueblo, New Mexico, and a successful community opera company (Holland, 2001).

In another example of building community strengths that included a recognition of cultural values in the program, Bragg (1997) reported on a program aimed at improving individual and community self-esteem in a Native American community. Residents of the community helped to design and implement activities that promoted traditional Native American values and included traditional stories, myths, and legends. The community residents wrote and performed a series of plays that focused on healthy community behavior prior to the European invasion. These plays focused on the qualities that enabled their ancestors to survive and flourish and presented positive culturally relevant alternatives to negative attitudes and behaviors that might foster lower self-esteem and poor health outcomes.

The next example involves an unusual program in a community called Hope Meadows, which focuses on a healthy alternative for children in foster care (W. Smith, 2001; Gurwitt, 2002). Brenda Ehart, a sociology professor at the University of Illinois at Champaign-Urbana, founded this community in 1994. She was concerned with the overburdened foster care system and decided to create a small alternative for some of the children. She and her colleagues wanted to create a real community that could provide stability, love, and acceptance for the children and a supportive environment for the families who cared for the foster children. The children presented difficult challenges because of histories of neglect or abuse. Ehart and colleagues contracted with the Pentagon to sign over to the project eighty-four abandoned housing units at the Chanute Air Force Base. Into this ready-made housing development they moved a small number of families who were willing to adopt children out of foster care. However, they did not have eighty-four families for the homes. In a brilliant solution, they rented the remaining houses to retired persons at a very low rent. The retirees and the foster parents would work together as a community to provide support, nurturance, and guidance for the children. What they created was a neighborhood, a community for the children, a sense of renewal and purpose for the retirees, and a source of emotional and practical support for the foster parents. This melding of needs happened almost by accident at Hope Meadows, but "In this neighborhood, three of the groups often disregarded by American society—children caught in the child welfare system, families who adopt kids with special emotional and medical needs, and retirees—have made a home for one another" (Gurwitt, 2002, p. 89).

Volunteerism

Earlier, we saw that people tend to report feeling happier when they pursued goals that had meaning for them personally (Oishi, Diener, Suh, & Lucas, 1999). They also found that if one of those goals was to be more involved in their communities, then people also tended to feel greater well-being. One of the ways in which people can become involved with their communities is by being volunteers.

Every day millions of people around the world donate their time, efforts, and emotional support to the welfare of other people who are more often than not complete strangers. Gil Clary and Mark Snyder (1999, 2002) reported that every day over 100 million people donate their time to volunteer organizations and causes. On average, people donate 3.5 hours per week to a huge variety of organizations and causes. Why would anyone do this? According to some theories of motivation in psychology, there are no immediate and tangible rewards for volunteering. In some volunteer situations, of course, this is not the case. If one is helping another person in some direct and "hands-on" fashion, then rewards can be immediate because the person being helped is, of course, present. But what about volunteering for a political cause, working on environmental issues, or other causes that are oriented toward future hopes and dreams—why do people volunteer for these causes?

Mark Snyder, Gil Clary, and their colleagues have studied the processes that lie behind volunteerism (Clary & Snyder, 1999, 2002; Snyder, Clary, & Stukas, 2000). They found that about 80 percent of volunteers are women and that volunteerism is more common in the 30- to 50-year-old age range. They also found that rather than being a single motive behind volunteerism, people volunteer for a number of different reasons, including altruism, a wish to gain knowledge and understanding, as a result of social pressures, and from a wish to enhance self-esteem. They also found that only a few of those motives relate to long-term volunteerism. Interestingly, the strength of a person's altruistic motives is not associated with long-term volunteerism. People who volunteer over extended periods of time tend to be motivated by a desire for knowledge or greater understanding and by a desire to enhance their self-esteem. In some ways, they view their efforts as contributing to their own personal growth.

One interesting program used volunteerism as a way to intervene with at-risk teenagers. The Teen Outreach program involved seventh- to twelfth-grade children in volunteer community service activities. The adolescents did not just take part in activities such as answering the phones, but instead they took on active, meaningful roles as positive help-givers (Allen et al., 1990, cited in Shinn & Toohey, 2003). Teens who participated showed reduced risk for pregnancy and school failure. Success was related to a growing sense of autonomy and relatedness in the volunteers, as well as to both the intensity and the quality of the volunteer experiences.

Comments on Healthy Communities

Often, students of psychology are unfamiliar with the substantial work done by community psychologists. This is unfortunate because many different studies have shown the impact of social contexts on behavior to be significant. Community interventions and organizations can also be quite successful methods to foster positive community and individual changes. In their review of studies on community interventions, Marybeth Shinn and Siobhan Toohey (2003) found that these changes can include "reducing physical deterioration and crime, promoting social services, enhancing informal neighboring, and influencing individual attitudes such as trust, confidence, experience of personal and political efficacy, and a sense of community" (Shinn & Toohey, 2003, p. 445).

Subjective Well-Being in Different Cultures

It could be argued that one of the least-explored influences on subjective well-being is the influence that our culture has on how we think about self, others, and even the fabric of reality itself (Berger & Luckman, 1966). One definition of *culture* is "the set of attitudes, values, beliefs, and behaviors shared by a group of people, communicated from one generation to the next via language or some other means of communication" (Barnouw, 1985, quoted in Matsumoto, 1994, p. 4). If we define happiness as the most generic and unqualified emotional state of feeling good, then studies have found that people in all cultures have some notion of this generic,

TABLE 11.1 **SUBJECTIVE WELL-BEING VALUES OF NATION**

Nation	Life Satisfaction	Hedonic Balance	Positive Affect	Negative Affect
Bulgaria	5.03	.91	1.93	1.01
Russia	5.37	.29	1.69	1.41
Belarus	5.52	.77	2.12	1.35
Latvia	5.70	.92	2.00	1.08
Romania	5.88	.71	2.34	1.63
Estonia	6.00	.76	2.05	1.28
Lithuania	6.01	.60	1.86	1.26
Hungary	6.03	.85	1.96	1.11
India	6.21	.33	1.41	1.09
South Africa	6.22	1.15	2.59	1.44
Slovenia	6.29	1.53	2.33	.80
Czech Republic	6.30	.76	1.84	1.08
Nigeria	6.40	1.56	2.92	1.36
Turkey	6.41	.59	3.09	2.50
Japan	6.53	.39	1.12	.72
Poland	6.64	1.24	2.45	1.21
South Korea	6.69	—	—	—
East Germany	6.72	1.25	3.05	1.80
France	6.76	1.33	2.34	1.01
China	7.05	1.26	2.34	1.08
Portugal	7.10	1.33	2.27	.94
Spain	7.13	.70	1.59	.89
West Germany	7.22	1.43	3.23	1.79
Italy	7.24	1.21	2.04	.84
Argentina	7.25	1.26	2.45	1.19
Brazil	7.39	1.18	2.85	1.68
Mexico	7.41	1.38	2.68	1.30
Britain	7.48	1.64	2.89	1.25
Chile	7.55	1.03	2.78	1.75
Belgium	7.67	1.54	2.46	.93
Finland	7.68	1.18	2.33	1.15
Norway	7.68	1.59	2.54	.95
United States	7.71	2.21	3.49	1.27
Austria	7.74	1.77	2.90	1.13
Netherlands	7.84	1.81	2.91	1.10
Ireland	7.87	1.99	2.89	.90
Canada	7.88	2.31	3.47	1.15
Sweden	7.97	2.90	3.63	.73
Iceland	8.02	2.50	3.29	.78
Denmark	8.16	1.90	2.83	.93
Switzerland	8.39	1.14	1.39	.24

Source: Table 22.1, "Subjective Well-Being Values of Nation," in *Well-Being: Foundations of Hedonic Psychology*, D. Kahneman, E. Diener, and N. Schwartz (Eds.).

Note: Values are weighted to achieve probability samples of nations, and respondents with apparent data errors were dropped before analyses.

positive emotional state (Wierzbicka, 1986). Although all cultures have some conceptualization for the emotion of happiness, there are also substantial differences in how this general feeling is understood, expressed, and experienced.

Studies that have looked at national levels of well-being have found rather substantial differences between countries (see Diener & Suh, 1999, for a review). Table 11.1 shows the results of one such survey.

As the table indicates, ratings of life satisfaction go from lows of 5.03 for Bulgaria and 5.37 for Russia to highs of 8.16 for Denmark and 8.39 for Switzerland. Results of more recent studies vary from this table somewhat, but in each case the Danes, the Dutch, or Icelanders are ranked as the happiest people in the world. Studies have also found that national differences in happiness and satisfaction are fairly stable over time (see Inglehart & Rabier, 1986; Diener & Suh, 1999).

The first thing to note about Table 11.1 is that most of the average life satisfaction values are above the neutral point on the 10-point scale. Most countries report above-average satisfaction levels. Second, notice the column for "Hedonic Balance." This column represents the difference between the frequency of self-reported positive emotions and negative emotions. Therefore, values above 1.0 represent more self-reported positive emotions than negative emotions—people report being more happy than sad. As you can see, the lower values tend to be associated with lower life satisfaction ratings. Note that the relationship between life satisfaction and hedonic balance is not perfect. Some interesting variations include the fairly low life satisfaction rating of 6.40 from Nigeria along with a moderately high hedonic balance ration of 1.56. Nigerians are relatively less satisfied, but they report frequent positive emotions. Looking at an opposite relationship, the satisfaction rating of Switzerland is at the top of the chart, and yet the hedonic balance rating of 1.14 is toward the low end of the rating scale. The Swiss are very satisfied, but they report only slightly more positive than negative emotions.

The next questions obviously are concerned with why these differences exist between nations.

Money, Wealth, and Income

The first big difference (discussed in Chapter 3) relates to money and wealth. A casual glance at the chart shows that the countries with higher life satisfaction ratings also tend to be countries with higher average incomes and gross national products (GNPs). In fact, correlations between level of subjective well-being and national wealth vary from .61 to .84 (see Diener et al., 1999). However, in a manner that is similar to the impact of individual income and well-being, the impact of national wealth on happiness and life satisfaction may be greatest when nations are less wealthy. That is, once a nation gains a moderate level of prosperity, then further increases may have less effect on well-being (Diener & Oishi, 2000). However, the jury is still out on this question, because some researchers have found a rather direct linear relationship such that the greater the economic prosperity, the greater the reported level of happiness (Schyns, 1998; see Diener & Suh, 1999).

The relationship between national wealth and subjective well-being is in part because virtually every social indicator measured in these studies is related to the prosperity and wealth of nations (Diener & Diener, 1996). For example, more prosperous nations also tend to have a more adequate food supply, better drinking water, better schools, better medical care, increased longevity, better human rights, and more income equity, as well as a number of other indicators of a higher quality of life (Diener & Suh, 1999). Because wealthier nations also tend to have better human rights records, more gender equity, and more individual freedoms, it is possible that these social factors are also related to increased satisfaction.

In spite of these significant relationships, even in wealthier nations, self-reported well-being has not risen dramatically over the years while income levels have risen (Diener & Suh, 1999). Again, this pattern is similar to the one found for well-being within individuals where disposable income has risen with virtually no changes in happiness over the same period of time (see Figure 3.2). Robert Lane (2000) suggested that as income and other indicators of higher quality of life increase, then the value people place on "happiness" decreases because people realize that they "want more out of life" than just personal happiness. He believes that well-being ultimately depends on happiness plus personal development, virtuous behavior, and justice.

Finally, an unusual proposal on an international level to promote happiness needs to be mentioned. The most frequently seen cross-cultural measure of well-being or the "health" of countries is their GNP, an index based on economic indicators. However, it should be obvious by now that individual well-being is not simply a matter of economic factors. Therefore, the king of Bhutan, a small Buddhist nation in the foothills of the Himalayas, proposed the creation of a Gross National Happiness, or GNH, index to measure psychological well-being in countries. The king further proposed to launch the Gross International Happiness Project, which would connect efforts in many nations to develop new indices of national well-being (retrieved: positive psychology listserver, December 2, 2003; also see Diener, 2000a).

Democracy and Social Norms

A few other factors of cultural differences have also been studied. One such factor is the amount of cultural unrest in a country. Studies have found that, as might be expected, political instability in a country is related to lower levels of subjective well-being (Inglehart, 1990). Frey and Stutzer (2000) looked at the relationship between subjective well-being and opportunities to participate in the democratic process. Based on an analysis of people in Switzerland, they found that the more developed were the institutions of democracy, the more well-being people reported. People who were able to use the democratic process more easily to effect changes tended to be more satisfied with their lives. People also seemed to be more satisfied simply by engaging in the democratic process itself. Processes such as discussion, debate, and other processes of democracy were related to greater well-being. This aspect of nations is related to collective levels of interpersonal trust. Nations in which people tend to be more distrustful of others or the government show lower levels of overall subjective well-being in spite of income levels (Inglehart & Rabier, 1986).

Finally, the significant predictors of subjective well-being may not be identical in every nation and culture. Studies have found, for instance, that satisfaction with government is a relatively small predictor of life satisfaction in the United States but a rather larger predictor in Cuba. Diener and Suh (1999) suggest that satisfaction depends to some degree on a person's values and goals, and these can be related to aspects of culture such as social norms, expectations, roles, and attitudes. Other research suggests that self-esteem is more important in individualistic countries.

Cultural Conceptualization of Emotion

Most people in Western cultures assume that "emotions" are individually experienced internal states or reactions to events and are either positive or negative. Many Westerners do not realize that people in other cultures differ in how they define, label, express, and give meaning to emotions (Matsumoto, 1994).

Many people recognize that certain words used to describe emotion in other cultures may have no exact equivalent in English. For instance, the Japanese word *amae* is a core idea in their culture. A rough translation is "a desire or expectation for other's indulgence, benevolence, or favor" (Matsumoto, 1994, p. 27). Emotions such as *amae* that are unique to specific cultures are called *indigenous emotions.* Even though there is no precise English equivalent, English speakers can still get a sense of what this emotion describes. Nonetheless, differences among cultural understanding of emotion can go much deeper than this. As an initial example, consider that in the West, we understand emotions to be inner, subjective experiences that have personal meaning. Emotions inform people about themselves. In contrast, some cultures view emotions as statements about the relationships among people and their environments. In these cultures, emotions are shared experiences that are created by people and their environments. Emotions are, therefore, social constructions rather than individual reactions.

People in different cultures also experience emotions in different ways. For instance, Americans and Europeans tend to experience their emotions more intensely and for longer periods of time than do the Japanese. In addition, on one hand, Americans and Europeans tend to report basic physiological sensations associated with feeling emotions more often than the Japanese. On the other hand, the Japanese report feeling all emotions more often than Americans and Europeans (see Matsumoto, 1994). Events that trigger emotions may also differ. Problems with relationships tend to trigger sadness for the Japanese but are more associated with anger for Americans.

The cultural rules for how emotions should be expressed are called *cultural display rules,* and they also show interesting cultural variations. The classic studies of Paul Ekman (1993) and Carroll Izard (1971) found that people from most cultures recognize some basic facial expressions of emotion. Interestingly, studies also looked at how emotions were expressed in different social situations. In these studies, Americans and Japanese were observed either alone or with others while they watched films that were nonstressful or stressful (e.g., a film of eye surgery). When viewing the stressful film alone, there were no differences in how emotional reactions were expressed. When viewing the stressful film with other people, however, the Japanese tended to inhibit the expression of their emotion and even smiled more frequently more often than the Americans. Display rules in Japanese culture emphasize both the inhibition of certain emotions as well as the expression of a more positive front to others (see Friesen, 1972).

Other cultural differences can be more extreme than these. The people who live on the Micronesian atoll of Ifaluk have an indigenous emotion called *ker,* which is roughly a combination of happiness and excitement. In many cultures, this emotion would be seen as positive and desirable. However, for those who live on Ifaluk, *ker* is perceived as dangerous and socially disruptive. To take contrasts even further, some cultures, such as the Tahitians, do not even have a specific word for "emotion" (see Matsumoto, 1994).

Cultural Conceptualizations of Self and Well-Being

Recently, interest has increased in how Western ideas of individualism and the self have influenced ideas about happiness, well-being, and social relationships (Kitayama, Markus, Matsumoto, & Norasakkunkit, 1997; Diener & Suh, 1999). One of the major findings in subjective well-being research is that a positive self-concept is highly related to a greater sense of well-being. However, while the general desire for happiness and positive emotions is universal, the meaning attached to positive emotions and happiness is partially connected with how the self is construed in one's culture (Diener & Suh, 1999). Obviously, when we define the self, or who we are inside, we simultaneously define what aspects of the world will not be part of our self-identity. In fact, cultures differ in how they define the boundaries of self-identity. In turn, this boundary of self is related to how we define roles, expectations, and responsibilities for ourselves and others.

The Self in Individualistic and Collectivist Cultures

In cross-cultural studies, one difference among cultures is the dimension of individualism-collectivism. Very **individualistic cultures** tend to place greater emphasis on individualism, autonomy, freedom of expression, and on each person's internal thoughts, emotions, and experiences. These societies place a greater emphasis on self-sufficiency or self-reliance, expressing oneself, and on "actualizing the inner self." Individualistic cultures tend to highlight socially disengaged emotions or emotions that encourage the independence of the self, such as self-satisfaction or self-righteous anger. The United States and most western European countries are very individualistic.

In contrast, **collectivist cultures,** such as East Asian countries like China and Japan, tend to be more socially oriented and place emphasis on a person's immediate group and on the significant relationships between members of the group. In general, a greater emphasis is placed on the welfare of a person's extended family; the individual's needs and desires are secondary to those of the group. Autonomy and independence are often de-emphasized in order to focus on the welfare of the group. Feelings of self-worth in collectivist societies may depend on how well a person can respect authority and fit in with his or her important and significant relationships (Matsumoto, 1994; Price & Crapo, 2002). This is particularly true for women in collectivist cultures (Lu, Shih, Lin, & Ju, 1997). Collectivist cultures tend to emphasize socially engaged emotions or those that highlight communal relationships such as humility or indebtedness.

Well-Being in Individualistic and Collectivist Cultures

Studies have found that this very broad cultural variable is an important factor in how people experience subjective well-being. For instance, the relationship between high life satisfaction and high self-esteem is stronger in individualistic cultures than in collectivist ones (Diener & Diener, 1995). Similarly, in the United States, it is important to see oneself as acting consistently across various situations and in accord with the self. Such consistency implies a person who is fairly autonomous of the social situations he or she encounters on a daily basis. In South Korea, however, self-consistency across situations is not a strong predictor of well-being. In fact, high self-consistency regardless of the social situation was negatively associated with ratings of likability by friends and family (Suh, 1999). Enkook Suh, Ed Diener, Shigehiro Oishi, and Harry Triandis (1998) looked at cultural differences in hedonic balance or the degree to which pleasant emotions are experienced more than unpleasant emotions (see Table 11.1). They found that self-ratings of how much positive or negative emotion one feels were more important to self-reports of subjective well-being in individualistic cultures. That is, paying attention to one's inner self was very important to how a person rated their own well-being. In contrast, in collectivist cultures, the important information used to make a subjective well-being judgment concerned social norms about how good or acceptable it was to feel satisfied. Similarly, satisfactions with self, freedom, and recreation were important predictors of life satisfaction in individualistic countries but less important in collectivist countries (Diener, Oishi, & Lucas, 2003).

The distinction mentioned earlier between socially engaged and disengaged emotions is also relevant to how people experience well-being in different cultures. A study of American and Japanese college students by Shinobu Kitayama, Hazel Markus, Hisaya Matsumoto, and Vinai Norasakkunit (1997) found that for American students, more general positive emotions were associated with socially disengaged emotions, while the Japanese students felt generally more positive when experiencing socially engaged emotions. The impact of social roles and expectations can have an effect on other aspects of self-evaluation. The self-serving bias, or the tendency to interpret events in a way that is more flattering to the self than might be justified by the situation, is more common in individualistic countries. This is also true for the fundamental attribution error, or the tendency to infer an internal, personality-based cause for other's behavior in spite of obvious situation constraints (Matsumoto, 1994). In general, self-reports of high subjective well-being from people in individualistic countries tend to be based on awareness of one's emotional state, experiencing many positive emotions, success at achieving goals relevant to the self, inferring internal causality for positive outcomes, and pursuing immediate hedonic goals for fun, enjoyment, or self-enhancement. In contrast, self-reports of high subjective well-being from people in collectivist countries tend to be based on an awareness of and alignment with social norms, success at achieving goals that make others happy, and sacrifice of positive emotions in order to engage in activities that are related to future goals (Diener, Oishi, & Lucas, 2003).

Because individualism-collectivism is such an important factor in cultural reports of subjective well-being, the next questions concern the reason for this. In a very general sense, in cultures where the individual self is more valued and is the focus of one's attention, it is a more significant factor in self-reported well-being. People in individualistic cultures pay more attention to their own inner lives than do people in collectivist cultures. Therefore, questionnaires that ask about one's personal happiness are focusing on a topic that is of more relevance to people in individualistic cultures. People in collectivist cultures tend to emphasize interpersonal relationships and gauge their well-being by looking at how those relationships are functioning. In addition, people in collectivist cultures are also accustomed to social norms that emphasize and respect humility and self-deferential behaviors. In collectivist cultures, giving oneself very high ratings on "happiness" indicates arrogance. In contrast, in individualistic cultures, a very high self-rating on "happiness" is considered to be healthy self-confidence or as giving oneself a well-deserved "pat on the back." These differences have an effect on how people interpret the wording of questionnaires used to measure subjective well-being. Samuel Ho (2003) found that when the Satisfaction with Life Scale was translated into more collectivist language so that it reflected Chinese values, then levels of life satisfaction among Chinese respondents were comparable to those found in Westerners.

Comments on Culture and Well-Being

There is little doubt that the social context of our lives can have a major impact on how we perceive ourselves, our relationships, and our responsibilities. It is also increasingly clear that broad social contexts can have an impact on how we view the nature of the self and what goals we pursue in order to achieve greater happiness, satisfaction, or well-being. Although social psychology investigates the impact of small groups on individual behavior, psychology has often neglected the impact of broad social contexts on behavior. Too often, this results in definitive statements being made about "human behavior" that actually apply only to people living in specific cultural situations. However, cross-cultural research on subjective well-being has very quickly become part of the standard research literature in positive psychology, and this change signals an appreciation of the role of social contexts in how people experience well being and the good life.

Summary

This chapter covered the search for well-being in the larger community and in cultures. The first topic was well-being at work. Job satisfaction is an important element of overall well-being, and positive emotions at work enhance job performance and satisfaction. Important aspects of higher job satisfaction include dispositional positive emotionality, task variety, job control, and equitable pay. Focusing on personal strengths and talents increases job satisfaction. The communities and societies in which we live can also have an impact on well-being. Some examples from community psychology illustrated how positive community change can influence people's lives for the better. The final aspect of well-being concerns the cultural traditions, expectations, and norms. A short review illustrated how individualistic and collectivist cultures have different ideas about well-being.

LEARNING TOOLS

Key Terms and Ideas

COLLECTIVE EFFICACY
COLLECTIVIST CULTURES
CONTEXT MINIMIZATION ERROR
EMPOWERMENT
INDIVIDUALISTIC CULTURES
JOB SATISFACTION
TRANSFORMATIONAL LEADERSHIP

Books

Buckingham, M., & Clifton, D. (2001). *Now, discover your strengths.* New York: Free Press. The program developed by the Gallup organization to foster your personal strengths and talents in the world of work (popular).

Guzman, S. (2002). *The Latina's bible: The nueva Latina's guide to love, spirituality, family, and la vida.* New York: Three Rivers Press. A handbook for contemporary Latina women that covers love, careers, family relationships, and living in the Western world. A number of other books are also available that cover the challenges of other cultures (e.g., Asian, African American) in a pluralistic society (popular).

Homan, M. (1999). *Promoting community change: Making it happen in the real world.* Pacific Grove, CA.: Brooks/Cole. A book designed as a practical aid for those who want to change their communities and make them better (popular/professional).

Matsumoto, D. (1994). *People: Psychology from a cultural perspective.* Pacific Grove, CA: Brooks/Cole. A very readable survey of cross-cultural findings on human behavior, emotion, attitudes, and memory.

Pfeffer, J. (1998). *The human equation: Building profits by putting people first.* Boston, MA: Harvard Business School Press.

Rappaport, J., & Seidman, E. (Eds.) (2000). *Handbook of community psychology.* New York: Kluwer/Plenum. A collection of articles on the fascinating specialty area of community psychology (professional).

Research

Diener, E., Oishi, S., & Lucas, R. (2003). Personality, culture, and subjective well-being: Emotional and cognitive evaluations of life. *Annual Review of Psychology, 54,* 403–425.

Shinn, M., & Toohey, S. (2003). Community contexts of human welfare. *Annual Review of Psychology, 54,* 427–459.

Web Sites

http://www.sosig.ac.uk/roads/subject-listing/World-cat/persat.html. The social Science Information Gateway with information on personnel attitudes and job satisfaction.

http://www.networkforgood.org/volunteer/. Looking for a way to volunteer in your community? This Web site lists volunteer opportunities in many cities in the United States. Just go to the site, put in information about where you live, and it lists opportunities in your area.

http://worldvolunteerweb.org. Information about volunteering all over the world.

http://wvs.isr.umich.edu/papers/genes.htm. A paper by Ronald Inglehart and Hans-Dieter Klingemann at the University of Michigan that argues culture is just as important to well-being as genetics.

Personal Explorations

Which brings you more fulfillment: pleasures or philanthropy (see www.positivepsychology.org/teaching resources.htm, by Martin E. P. Seligman)? Write down all activities you did last week that were either pleasurable or philanthropic. How does each of these kinds of activities make you feel? For the next week, experiment with philanthropic activities by increasing the frequency of things you do for other people. How did it change how you feel?

CHAPTER 12

A Look toward the Future of Positive Psychology

> We must take care to live not merely a long life, but a full one; for living a long life requires only good fortune, but living a full life requires character. Long is the life that is fully lived; it is fulfilled only when the mind supplies its own good qualities and empowers itself from within.
>
> *Seneca, the Younger (first century AD)*

Although positive psychology was founded only in 1998, the focus area is establishing a firm footing in the field of psychology. The number of books, research articles, scholarly conferences, and related Web sites on positive psychology are increasing at a fairly rapid rate. On a personal note, I have noticed that many undergraduate and graduate students express a very high level of interest in positive psychology. Interest is so strong that often students ask me how they can make a career out of studying positive psychology. The area is attracting eager students and enthusiastic professionals.

As any interest area evolves, however, it must change to meet the growing demand for increased scholarship, research, and practical applications. In order for any scientific endeavor to remain relevant, it must create new knowledge, adjust to the new knowledge base being created, and utilize that knowledge to help people make their lives better. Of course, if any interest area in psychology could be expected to not only adjust but to also thrive as it meets the challenges of change, that area should be positive psychology. Therefore, this chapter will briefly discuss some directions in which positive psychology will probably move in the future.

How Do We Recognize a Life Lived Well, a Life Worthy of Admiration and Respect?

So far, many of the research studies in positive psychology have investigated well-being by assuming that happiness and life satisfaction are the best criteria for defining the good life. While feeling happy and satisfied with one's life are worthy goals, these are also not the only criteria to define a life lived well. In fact, much of this book has explored other criteria that can be used to measure positive outcomes in life. These have included experiencing flow states, feeling love and affection for others, being deeply involved in creative activities, realizing one's potentials, and increasing a sense of meaning by experiencing a spiritual dimension in life. Of course, one could argue that all of these experiences simply lead to different types of happiness and satisfaction. But this argument ignores the real complexities of a full and rich life. For instance, love can be a thrilling and beautiful emotion, but it is also directly tied to the risk of rejection, struggle, sacrifice, or conflict. In fact, love becomes more meaningful when it has withstood difficult and uncomfortable challenges and threats that might have destroyed it.

Having happiness as a goal in life is actually quite a new belief. It was not until the mid-1900s that the majority of people in industrialized countries believed they should actively seek happiness as a major goal in life. Prior to that, life was often toil and struggle. Most people simply tried to remain physically healthy, safe from harm, and hoped for a few moments of joy in life. From a historical perspective, does an exclusive focus on happiness negate or minimize those people's struggles? Although they were not happy, many had dignity, courage, perseverance, and dedication to their families and friends. Should not those qualities also count toward a judgment that life has been lived well?

Expanding the Criteria for the Good Life

Most positive psychologists have recognized that any adequate definition of the good life cannot be based solely on how much positive emotion a person feels each day. Recent articles on positive psychology have begun to debate how to define a full, rich, and fulfilling life. Of course, positive emotions will always be part of how people define well-being. As was seen throughout this book, there are numerous scientific studies that support the benefits of positive emotions. New criteria for the good life must include positive emotions but must also expand definitions to fit the complexity of human life (Aspinwall & Staudinger, 2003). The following is a very brief discussion of a few perspectives on defining the good life.

Happiness as a By-Product, Not a Goal, in Life

Given the complexities of human emotions, some psychologists have proposed that happiness should not be a goal in life but rather a by-product of how a person lives. According to Gordon Allport, one of the "fathers" of personality psychology, happiness and life satisfaction are not goals but possible consequences of full involvement in life. Allport considered immediate concerns about positive emotions to be less than secondary (Allport 1955). He said, "Nor does the hedonistic conception of the pursuit of 'happiness' help us. . . . The state of happiness is not itself a motivating force but a by-product of otherwise motivated activity. Happiness is far too incidental and contingent a thing to be considered a goal in itself" (p. 68). Allport believed that well-being was found through willingness and eagerness to experience all that life has to offer plus a drive to expand the sense of self (note the similarity to Carl Rogers's approach, discussed in Chapter 8). Nancy Cantor and Catherine Sanderson (1999) expressed similar ideas by saying that well-being is found through active involvement in life activities. From their perspective, people should first become participants in life and the well-being will follow. Albert Einstein (1932) provided another perspective when he said, "Only a life lived for others is a life worthwhile" (in Calaprice, 2000, p. 147). Einstein suggested that altruism and a focus on the welfare of others, rather than our own happiness, are the best path to well-being.

We Should Seek Meaning Rather than Happiness

In a similar fashion, the existentialist psychologist Viktor Frankl believed that the creation of meaning—not happiness—must be the major criterion for the good life. He was extremely forthright in his belief that the creation of meaning cannot be tied to happiness, joy, or any other specific emotional experience. Frankl (1978) said, "The more one's search for meaning is frustrated, the more intensively he devotes himself to . . . the pursuit of happiness." When this pursuit originates in a frustrated search for meaning . . . it is self-defeating, for happiness can arise only as a result of living out one's self-transcendence, one's devotion to a cause to be served, or a person to be loved" (pp. 82–83). Frankl was also quite clear that the creation of meaning has little to do with finding a comfortable belief system that sustains self-esteem. According to him, mental health is associated with a deep commitment to self-awareness, honesty, courage, responsibility, and active involvement in whatever was presented by life. According to Frankl, the meaning of life must be found in each moment as a person confronts the challenges and choices of his or her life.

Robert Emmons (1999) provides a similar perspective on the creation of meaning by pointing out one difference between the pursuit of happiness and the pursuit of meaning. He notes that while happiness is centered on finding positive emotions in life, meaning often involves recognizing and accepting both positive and negative emotions. He suggests that meaning is found by accepting and integrating all emotions into a life that is filled with rich and varied experiences. Emmons (1999) quotes Rozick, who said, "It is not clear that we want these moments [of happiness] constantly or want our lives to consist wholly and only of them. We want other experiences too . . . we want experiences, fitting ones, of profound connection with others, of deep understanding of natural phenomena, of love, of being profoundly moved by music or tragedy. . . . What we want, in short, is a life and a self that happiness is a fitting response to—and then give it that response" (p. 138).

Maturity and Positive Personality Development

Another factor that can influence well-being is an individual's level of psychological development or maturity. Cowen and Kilmer (2002) suggested that positive psychology should pay more attention to the developmental paths that people take as they move through life. The nature of well-being and the good life may be quite different at different points in life or for different life goals that people pursue. We know, for instance, that people define and create a sense of well-being differently between age groups (Ryff & Heidrich, 1997). Somewhat more theoretically, a wide variety of theories exist that hypothesize developmental stages or age-related challenges that can have an impact on how people foster their own sense of happiness and satisfaction. These perspectives include ideas about psychosocial development (Erikson, 1950), maturity (Heath, 1991), ego development (Loevinger, 1976), moral development (Gilligan, 1982; Kohlberg, 1984), the evolution of the self (Kegan, 1982), the use of healthy defense mechanisms (Vaillant, 2000), as well as a number of others. Unfortunately, a number of these theories are developmental stage theories and suffer from problems common to stage theories, such as difficulties finding pure invariant sequences of stages. Nonetheless, many of the ideas about positive personality development in these theories have been supported by research, and it seems quite clear that some people possess more psychological maturity than others. For instance, it is fairly reasonable to assume that someone who scores very high on measures of wisdom will create their sense of well-being in a somewhat different fashion than other people who may not have the perspective and empathy born of deep and rich life experiences. Longitudinal and developmental perspectives on well-being attempt to describe those factors that allow people to develop well-being and thrive as they confront the challenges of living life over time.

Beyond Happiness and Life Satisfaction
Therefore, it seems that well-being and the nature of the good life can be found through any number of different avenues. Most of the current research, however, has focused on the hedonic outcomes of happiness and life satisfaction. The leading researchers in subjective well-being have said that happiness may be "necessary" to the good life but not "sufficient" (Diener, Oishi, & Lucas, 2003). They have said that positive emotionality needs to be part of a whole life package that also includes factors such as prosocial values, good health, and working toward socially desirable goals.

In addition, all people sense that they possess unrealized potentials. In fact, all of us know that we could be realizing more of our potentials and be better persons. The philosopher Soren Kierkegaard (1843/1987) said, "If I were to wish for anything, I should not wish for wealth or power, but for the passionate sense of the potential, for the eye which, ever young and ardent, sees the possible. Pleasure disappoints, possibility never. And what wine is so sparkling, what so fragrant, what so intoxicating, as possibility!"

For those interested in positive psychology, a substantial variety of other avenues exist for the definition of well-being. Researchers in positive psychology will be kept busy for some time to come exploring personality, lived environments, and the interpretation of life events and how these relate to the various criteria for well-being and the good life.

People Need Both Positive and Negative Emotions

One potential problem with well-being studies is that they may implicitly assume that people are always motivated to feel positive emotions. This assumption is basically the hedonistic perspective on human motivation. However, we know that violations of hedonism are common (Parrott, 1993). People often do things that increase stress or challenges in life while pursuing their goals.

One of the most frequently found comments about the future of positive psychology concerns the necessity of integrating positive and negative emotions into a broader conceptualization of well-being and the good life (see Aspinwall & Staudinger, 2003). Researchers have pointed out that in order to experience certain positive outcomes in life it is necessary to balance positive and negative emotions rather than eliminate the negative ones. As discussed in Chapter 9, James Pennebaker studied the use of writing about trauma as a way to resolve emotional issues associated with it. He found that the use of both positive and negative emotions in the narratives helps people to release the trauma and move past it (also see King, 2001). A number of theories of optimal mental health also postulate that a truly healthy self-regard is possible only through recognition and integration of both positive and negative attributes (e.g., Jung, 1964; Maslow, 1968). In a similar fashion, a few recent studies have looked at the phenomenon of "growth through adversity" or how people need challenges and difficulties to prompt new coping strategies and new ways of adapting to life events (see Ryff & Singer, 2003). In fact, Allport believed that it was possible to exhibit optimal mental health and *not* be happy! Similarly, some of Maslow's exemplars of self-actualization had troubled and difficult lives (e.g., Abraham Lincoln in his last years). In other words, some exposure to unwelcome life events may be needed in order to cultivate personal strengths (Stokols, 2003).

Remember from Chapter 10 that one of the ways we can find meaning is through our relationship with suffering. Frankl (1963) believes that suffering offers us a way to "actualize the highest value, to fulfill the deepest meaning. . . . For what matters above all is the attitude we take toward suffering" (p. 178). Therefore, he views our attitude toward unavoidable suffering as one of the primary ways in which we can reject resentment, depression, and anger over "our" suffering and transcend this self-focused orientation to create meaning that embraces *both* the joy and the pain of life. The discussion of Robert Enright's work on forgiveness in Chapter 9 is also relevant here. Recall that his forgiveness therapy requires a person to feel both positive and negative emotions in order to move beyond a wrong that was done to them.

The studies of Sharon Shapela and her colleagues (Shapela et al., 1999) on courageous resistance illustrate the idea that certain positive outcomes demand a blend of both positive and negative emotions. They studied people who risked their own lives in order to help Jews in Nazi Germany and resist oppression. Usually, courageous resistors were ordinary people who found themselves faced with a choice to ignore injustice or to do something to help. It was difficult to know who would become a courageous resistor until they were faced with a choice. The following story of "the cellist of Sarajevo" illustrates how a host of various emotions, including hope, courage, grief, and anger, combined and turned an unknown musician into a hero, even if only for a few weeks.

The story takes place in 1992 in Sarajevo during the Bosnian War. The city had suffered mass shelling, and few bakeries were still open. One afternoon, twenty-two people were in line waiting for bread outside one of the open bakeries when a mortar shell struck the bakery, killing all twenty-two people. Vedran Smajlovic, who had been the principal cellist of the National Theater Philharmonic Orchestra, heard about the tragedy. The very next day, he put on his work clothes—a black tuxedo—took his cello to the bomb crater, and began playing music in memory of the victims. He returned for the next twenty-one days, playing one day for each of the victims. After this, Smajlovic began to play his cello at bomb craters throughout Sarajevo. He continued to make music, playing his cello in his tuxedo, while bombs and mortars exploded around the city. People said it was "unreal" to see him playing in the bomb craters. He seemed to be "protected" from the destruction around him. Smajlovic's fame spread, and he became a hero in Bosnia. A physician who was in Sarajevo at the time said, "He seemed connected to some sky that was nicer than the one we lived under. We were all trying to find our own spiritual way to survive that hell. It meant a lot to see that kind of spiritual courage. For some people [his action] was a kind of stupidity, for me it was a perfect example of how the soul can carry you beyond that kind of horror." Smajlovic continued to play until his cello was destroyed and he was forced to leave his homeland (Scott, 1999).

The Need for New Research Methods

When psychologists begin to reflect on what direction their own discipline is heading, often the call is heard for newer and better research strategies (e.g., Slife, 1999). In positive psychology, as well, a number of researchers have proposed strategies to help enhance scientists' abilities to answer questions about well-being and the good life. Diener, Suh, Lucas, and Smith (1999) proposed that well-being needs to be studied with multiple measurement strategies. For example, Jules Seeman (1983) tested his theory of personality integration by using self-report measures, collateral reports from others, behavioral measures, and physiological assessments. Others, such as Douglas Heath (1991) and George Vaillant (2000), looked at people in longitudinal studies to see how well-being develops over the lifetime. Kevin Rathunde (2001) suggested that positive psychology could benefit from the examples of early psychologists such as William James, John Dewey, and Abraham Maslow. These early theorists of positive mental health used subjective experience to help develop their theories and saw introspective reports of personal experience as valuable tools to be used in conjunction with other research strategies. Gergen and Gergen (2001) believe that positive psychologists should make research a more collaborative process between scientists and their research participants. In general, many scientists agree that the use of multiple research strategies will be more necessary in the future. After all, people are complex, and an adequate understanding may require equally complex tools of investigation. Sometimes, however, the complexity of human behavior tends to push the limits of the tools that science has to work with.

Systems Theory

At many points in this text, suggestions have been made that psychology needs to begin looking at human beings as integrated systems of mind, body, emotions, and spirit. This was especially true in the discussion of wellness and health psychology (see Chapter 6). A number of researchers also say that positive psychology needs to view people in a more holistic fashion than has been done in the past (Magnusson & Mahoney, 2003). In order to illustrate this idea, a brief example of a holistic systems view will be presented next.

One of the more fascinating recent changes in psychological theory is the conceptualization of human beings as integrated organisms that can be described by various subsystems—physical, emotional, intellectual, behavioral, and spiritual. Any definition of well-being must include healthy functioning in all the subsystems as well as healthy integration between subsystems. In many ways, this idea revived the ancient Greek concept of the ideal person, which held that a healthy body, a rational mind, and a sense of social obligation were the hallmarks of the good life. With this perspective, researchers began to see persons as integrated systems, the different elements of which complemented each other and should not be looked at in isolation from each other.

"Billiard Ball" Model of Causality

Systems theory is a way to describe complex causal relationships among a number of different factors. Many of the earlier approaches to causality in science assumed the so-called "billiard ball" model of causality: one object moves and hits another object, causing the second to move. This was transformed into psychological models that explain human behavior as a series of stimuli that influence people and then cause certain responses to occur. Although the stimulus-response model is simple and easily applied to many situations, it rather quickly becomes problematic under certain conditions.

In order to illustrate this idea, let us follow the causal pathways of this model. Start with someone who increases his or her exercise routine. This results in enhanced mood. The enhanced mood leads to greater willingness to be involved socially, which leads to positive feedback from others, which enhances self-esteem and mood even further. The exercise also decreases stress, which also results in more positive social relations, less tension, and more optimism about the future. All of this would also lead to a greater sense of well-being.

Beyond the Billiard Ball

So far, this model could fit with "billiard ball" models of causality. However, a complete understanding of these processes must acknowledge that the enhanced mood, self-esteem, and well-being could also increase the probability that exercise will continue as part of the person's life. In fact, the process does not have to start with exercise. It is also true that a cognitive commitment to better health could enhance the person's optimism and mood that allows an exercise routine to begin, which would stimulate the process from a different starting point. Once this process begins, it is also difficult to know what part of the process actually causes another part to occur. Does exercise cause better mood or does better mood cause more frequent exercise? The answer is that *both* are true. If both are true, then the "billiard ball" model of causality that says a specific "A" must cause a specific "B" does not fit the phenomena under observation. Lines of causal influence are distributed throughout the model, and causality is no longer unidirectional (i.e., A only causes B) but bidirectional (i.e., A and B cause each other) and possibly transactional (i.e., causality is a function of the on-going relationship patterns between A and B).

Further, in this more complex model, the individual causal connection between A and B may be less important to behavior than the total organization of the system. That is, how all of the parts work together may be more important than any one element of the system. For example, Jules Seeman (1983, 1989) developed his theory of personality integration around systems theory. He commented on how the organizations of the parts are essential to this perspective. Seeman (1983) wrote, "Holism in a system means that a system cannot be understood adequately by examining its parts as entities, for the parts take their meaning not as entities at all but as sub-organizations in the *unitas* [unity]. . . . What is fundamental about the components of a system is not relationship but organization" (p. 215).

Systems theory was designed as a way to describe these more complex models in ways that do not distort the world by using overly simplistic models of causality. The idea of *holism*—in which the whole is greater than the sum of its parts—was adopted into this perspective. This particular development is, in many ways, one of the potentially most significant changes in theoretical perspectives on psychological well-being.

While the idea that people are integrated and complex systems of biological, emotional, intellectual, and even spiritual systems is undoubtedly true, what does this mean for the study of well-being? Limitations with current research methodologies make the implications of this idea somewhat difficult. Current research methods are often not able to describe the multiple lines of influence in holistic models. So, while we know that people are integrated systems, it is hard to study them in that way. One avenue may be to look at how environmental scientists study complex biological and ecological systems. While there are some suggestions for newer research strategies (e.g., Magnusson & Mahoney, 2003), the holistic study of well-being still remains a challenge for the future of positive psychology and the science of psychology in general.

Future Applications of Positive Psychology

All scientific endeavors must eventually show that they can have an impact on the world in some way. Good theory is interesting, but science must show results in the real world as well. Researchers hope the impact brings a better world for all people. Positive psychology must also show that the theories and research findings that fuel academic and scientific progress can be translated into positive changes in the world. As we saw in Chapter 9, this translation of research into real-world changes is already underway and is meeting quite a bit of success. Interventions have already succeeded in helping build resilience, hope, optimism, happiness, states of flow, healthier relationships, and better health. People are also looking at how to help improve education, use new models of transformational leadership in business, and create stronger communities. Application of ideas found in positive psychology has also begun to influence how psychotherapy and counseling are delivered.

New Intervention Strategies

As ideas from positive psychology spread, people are also beginning to create new avenues for careers that are based on positive emotionality and positive assumptions about human beings. One of those newer career paths is that of life coaching. The idea of life coaching is that many people who are well adjusted and functioning satisfactorily may find themselves stuck at some point in life. They may need a consultant to help them reach a major decision, nurture a new direction in life, or to find better ways to find fulfillment in life. These people are not suffering from any major psychological problem, they only need a few suggestions, a new perspective, or a little encouragement to get moving again. Therefore, the idea of a life coach was created to fill this need. Currently, thousands of life coaches are working in the United States alone. Unfortunately, there are no consistent standards for certification or training in life coaching. It is to be hoped that as positive psychologists become interested in life coaching, they will bring pressure on organizations to standardize training and certification.

Some philosophers have adopted an idea similar to life coaching. The American Philosophical Practitioners Association (www.appa.edu) is an organization for philosophers who bring their skills out into the world to help people grapple with philosophical issues. At first glance, this may seem a bit silly. After all, how many people really care if Socrates was correct about the source of valid knowledge? However, a number of people do care about how issues of assisted suicide should influence medical decisions, or how a corporation should implement high ethical standards and still remain competitive in a business environment that can be quite unethical. Even more people are concerned at times about the proper basis for an intelligent sense of meaning and purpose in life. Similarly, the Society for Philosophical Inquiry has created "Socrates Cafes" or informal philosophical discussions in coffee houses, libraries, hospices, or any number of informal spaces. These groups get together to talk about significant issues in people's lives, believing that asking questions is often more important than finding answers (www.philosopher.org). These people may be seeking a return of the Greek "Golden Age" when ideas, debate, and discussion were real tools for deciding about the nature of the good life.

New Methods of Assessment

In addition to these new models of positive intervention, some psychologists are continuing to develop methods of personality and behavioral assessment based on ideas from positive psychology. Christopher Peterson and Martin Seligman have recently published their handbook on the classification of strengths and virtues (Peterson & Seligman, 2004). As we saw in Chapter 9, their Values in Action project seeks to identify the core strengths and virtues that are important to well-being. Shane Lopez and C. R. Snyder have also recently published a book that examines a number of assessment instruments used to measure constructs associated with positive psychology (Lopez & Snyder, 2003). Their book looks at measures of hope, optimism, gratitude, and quality of life, to name a few. These efforts point to the day when the assessment of positive emotions and virtues will present an alternative to the deficit-based assessment of the current medical model. Therefore, in the future, people can be evaluated on both their current emotional problems and existent strengths that might be cultivated as they emerge from despair into positive well-being.

Toward the Future with Optimism

This chapter explored the ways that positive psychologists are creating future directions for positive psychology. New models of well-being and the good life were discussed that expand the criteria for the good life and take into account both positive and negative emotions. In addition, new models of research were discussed that involve multiple measurement strategies or wrestle with the complexities of human behavior. Finally, new forms of positive intervention and assessment were covered

Positive psychology has touched a chord in many professionals and students. Every year the area draws more attention. Many people seem enthusiastic about an approach to the study of human beings that emphasizes the positive, the adaptive, the healthy, and the admirable qualities of humanity. Applications of the findings are beginning to show that by focusing on human strengths and virtues it is possible to increase success in many areas of life such as education, job satisfaction, romantic relationships, health, and general well-being. The future looks optimistic for positive psychology and for the people it may serve in the future.

LEARNING TOOLS

Books

Aspinwall, L. G., & Staudinger, U. M. (Eds.). (2003). *A psychology of human strengths: Fundamental questions and future directions for a positive psychology.* Washington, DC: American Psychological Association (professional).

References

Ackerman, S., Zuroff, D. C., & Moskowitz, D. S. (2000). Generativity in midlife and young adults: Links to agency, communion, and subjective well-being. *International Journal of Aging & Human Development, 50*(1), 17–41.

Adams, J. (2001). *Conceptual blockbusting: A guide to better ideas.* Reading, MA: Perseus.

Ader, R., & Cohen, N. (1975). Behaviorally conditioned immunosuppression. *Psychosomatic Medicine, 37,* 333–340.

Ader, R., & Cohen, N. (1993). Psychoneuroimmunology: Conditioning stress. *Annual Review of Psychology, 44,* 53–85.

Adler, A. (1964). *Social interest: A challenge to mankind.* New York: Capricorn. (Original work published 1938)

Ai, A. L., Bolling, S. F., & Peterson, C. (2000). The use of prayer by coronary artery bypass patients. *International Journal for the Psychology of Religion, 10*(4), 205–220.

Ai, A. L., Dunkle, R. E., Peterson, C., & Bolling, S. F. (1998). The role of private prayer in psychological recovery among midlife and aged patients following cardiac surgery. *Gerontologist, 38*(5), 591–601.

Alfermann, D., & Stoll, O. (2000). Effects of physical exercise on self-concept and well-being. *International Journal of Sport Psychology, 31*(1), 47–65.

Allen, L., & Beattie, R. (1984). The role of leisure as an indicator of overall satisfaction with community life. *Journal of Leisure Research, 16*(2), 99–109.

Allison, M. T., & Duncan, M. C. (1987). Women, work, and leisure: The days of our lives. *Leisure Sciences, 9,* 143–162.

Allport, G. W. (1955). *Becoming.* New Haven: Yale University Press.

Allport, G., & Ross, J. M. (1967). Personal religious orientation and prejudice. *Journal of Personality and Social Psychology, 5,* 432–443.

Amabile, T. M. (1983). *The social psychology of creativity.* New York: SpringerVerlag.

American Psychiatric Association (2000). Diagnostic and statistical manual of mental disorders (4th ed., text version). Washington, DC: Author.

Anderson, R. (1996). Nine psycho-spiritual characteristics of spontaneous and involuntary weeping. *Journal of Transpersonal Psychology, 28*(2), 167–173.

Andreasen, N. C. (1987). Creativity and mental illness: Prevalence rates in writers and their first-degree relatives. *American Journal of Psychiatry, 144,* 1288–1292.

Andrews, F. M., & Withey, S. B. (1976). *Social indicators of well-being: Americans' perceptions of life quality.* New York: Plenum.

Ansbacher, H. L. (1992). Alfred Adler's concepts of community feeling and of social interest and relevance of community feeling for old age. *Individual Psychology, 48*(4), 402–412.

Anshel, M. H. (1993). Drug abuse in sports: Causes and cures. In J. M. Williams (Ed.). *Applied sport psychology: Personal growth to peak performance* (pp. 310–327). Mountain View, CA.: Mayfield.

Anthony, E. J. (1987). Children at risk for psychosis growing up successfully. In E. J. Anthony & B. J. Cohler (Eds.), *The invulnerable child.* New York: Guildford.

Anthony, E. J., & Cohler, B. J. (Eds.). (1987). *The invulnerable child.* New York: Guilford.

Antonovsky, A. (1979). *Health, stress, and coping: New perspectives on mental and physical well-being.* San Francisco: Jossey-Bass.

Antonovsky, A. (1987). *Unraveling the mystery of health.* San Francisco: Jossey-Bass.

Ardelt, M. (1997). Wisdom and life satisfaction in old age. *Journal of Gerontology, 52,* 15–27.

Argyle, M. (1987). *The psychology of happiness.* London: Methuen.

Argyle, M. (1999). Causes and correlates of happiness. In D. Kahneman, E. Diener, & N. Schwartz (Eds.), *Well-being: The foundation of hedonic psychology.* New York: Russell Sage Foundation.

Arieti, S. (1976). *Creativity: The magic synthesis.* New York: Basic Books.

Aristotle. (trans. 1908). Nicomachean ethics. In W. D. Ross (Ed.), *The works of Aristotle, Vol. 9.* Oxford: Clarendon Press.

Asendorpf, J. B., & Ostendorf, F. (1998). Is self-enhancement healthy? Conceptual, psychometric, and empirical analysis. *Journal of Personality & Social Psychology, 74*(4), 955–966.

Ashby, F. G., Isen, A. M., & Turken, A. U. (1999). A neuropsychological theory of positive affect and its influence on cognition. *Psychological Review, 106,* 529–550.

Aspinwall, L. G., & Brunhart, S. M. (2000). What I do know won't hurt me: Optimism, attention to negative information, coping, and health. In J. E. Gillham (Ed.), *Laws of Life Symposia Series. The science of optimism and hope: Research essays in honor of Martin E. P. Seligman* (pp. 163–200). Philadelphia, PA: John Templeton Foundation Press.

Aspinwall, L. G., & Staudinger, U. M. (Eds.). (2003). *A psychology of human strengths: Fundamental questions and future directions for a positive psychology.* Washington, DC: American Psychological Association.

Aspinwall, L. G., & Taylor, S. E. (1992). Modeling cognitive adaptation: A longitudinal investigation of the impact of individual differences and coping on college adjustment and performance. *Journal of Personality & Social Psychology, 63*(6), 989–1003.

Asser, S. M., & Swan, R. (1998). Child fatalities from religion-motivated medical neglect. *Pediatrics, 101,* 625–629.

Austin, J. H. (1998). *Zen and the brain: Toward an understanding of meditation and consciousness.* Cambridge, MA: MIT Press.

Averill, J. R. (2002). Emotional creativity: Toward "spiritualizing the passions." In C. R. Snyder & S. J. Lopez (Eds.), *Handbook of positive psychology* (pp. 172–188). New York: Oxford University Press.

Baker, W. *Breakthrough leadership: Believe, belong, contribute, transcend.* Retrieved January 2, 2003, from University of Michigan Business School, Leading in Trying Times Web site: wysiwyg://3/http://www.bus.umich.edu/leading/Breakthrough_Leadership.htm.

Baltes, P. B. (1993). The aging mind: Potential and limits. *Gerontologist, 33*(5), 580–594.

Baltes, P., & Staudinger, U. (2000). Wisdom: A metaheuristic (pragmatic) to orchestrate mind and virtue toward excellence. *American Psychologist, 55*(1), 122–136.

Bammel, G., & Burrus-Bammel, L. L. (1996). *Leisure and human behavior.* Dubuque, IA: Brown & Benchmark.

Bandura, A. (1977). Self-efficacy: Toward a unifying theory of behavioral change. *Psychological Review, 84,* 191–215.

Bandura, A. (1986). *Social foundations of thought and action.* Englewood Cliffs, NJ: Prentice-Hall.

Barnes, M. L., & Sternberg, R. J. (1997). A hierarchical model of love and its prediction of satisfaction in close relationships. In R. J. Sternberg & M. Hojjatt (Eds.), *Satisfaction in close relationships* (pp. 79–101). New York: Guilford Press.

Barrett, W. (1962). *Irrational man: A study of existential philosophy.* New York: Doubleday Anchor.

Barron., F. (1963). *Creativity and psychological health.* Princeton, NJ: Van Nostrand.

Barron, F. (1988). Putting creativity to work. In R. L. Sternberg (Ed.), *The nature of creativity: Contemporary psychological perspectives* (pp. 76–98). Cambridge: Cambridge University Press.

Barron, F., & Harrington, D. M. (1981). Creativity, intelligence, and personality. *Annual Review of Psychology, 32,* 439–476.

Baumeister, R. F. (1987). How the self became a problem: A psychological review of the historical research. *Journal of Personality and Social Psychology, 52,* 163–176.

Baumeister, R. F. (1989). The optimal margin of illusion. *Journal of Social and Clinical Psychology, 8,* 176–189.

Baumeister, R. F. (1991). *Meanings of life.* New York: Guilford Press.

Baumeister, R. F., Heatherton, T. F., & Tice, D. M. (1993). When ego threats lead to self regulation failure: Negative consequences of high self-esteem. *Journal of Personality and Social Psychology, 64,* 141–156.

Bedard, J., & Chi, M. T. (1992). Expertise. *Current Directions in Psychological Science, 1*(4), 135–139.

Beer, J. S., & Robbins, R. W. (2000, February). *Positive illusions about the self: Their correlates and consequences.* Paper presented at the 1st Annual Meeting of the Society for Personality and Social Psychology, Nashville, TN.

Beit-Hallahmi, B., & Argyle, M. (1997). *The psychology of religious behaviour, belief, and experience.* London: Routledge.

Belsky, J. (1997). *The adult experience.* St. Paul, MN: West Publishing.

Benson, H. (1975). *The relaxation response.* New York: Morrow.

Benson, H. (1983). The relaxation response and norepinephrine: A new study illuminates mechanisms. *Integrative-Psychiatry, 1*(1), 15–18.

Benson, H., & Stark, M. (1996). *Timeless healing: The power and biology of belief.* London: Simon & Schuster.

Bentall, R. (1992). A proposal to classify happiness as a psychiatric disorder. *Journal of Medical Ethics, 18,* 94–98.

Berg, I. K. (1994). *Family-based services: A solution-focused approach.* New York: W. W. Norton.

Berger, P. L., & Luckman, T. (1966). *The social construction of reality: A treatise on the sociology of knowledge.* Garden City, NY: Doubleday.

Bergin, A. E. (1991). Values and religious issues in psychotherapy and mental health. *American Psychologist, 46*(4), 394–403.

Berkman, L. F., & Syme, S. L. (1979). Social networks, host resistance, and mortality: A nine-year follow-up study of Alameda County residents. *American Journal of Epidemiology, 109,* 186–204.

Berlyne, D. E. (1960). *Conflict, arousal and curiosity.* New York: McGraw Hill.

Berscheid, E., & Lopes, J. (1997). A temporal model of relationship satisfaction and stability. In R. Sternberg & M. Hojjat (Eds), *Satisfaction in close relationships* (pp. 129–159). New York: Guildford Press.

Bohart, A. C., & Greenberg, L. S. (Eds.) (1997). *Empathy reconsidered: New directions in psychotherapy.* Washington, DC: American Psychological Association.

Bond, M. H. (1986). *The psychology of the Chinese people.* New York: Oxford University Press.

Borque, L. B. , & Back, K. W. (1968). Values and transcendental experience. *Social Forces, 47*(1), 34–38.

Bowker, J. (Ed.). (1997). *The Oxford dictionary of world religions.* Oxford: Oxford University Press.

Bradburn, N. (1969). *The structure of psychological well-being.* Chicago: Adine.

Bradbury, T. N., & Fincham, F. D. (1990). Attributions in marriage: Review and critique. *Psychological Bulletin, 107,* 3–33.

Bragg, M. (1997). An empowerment approach to community health education. In B. W. Spradley & J. A. Alexander (Eds.), *Readings in community health nursing* (5th ed., pp. 504–510). Philadelphia: J. B. Lippincott.

Brannon, L., & Feist, J. (2000). *Health psychology: An introduction to behavior and health* (4th ed.). Belmont, CA: Wadsworth.

Brickman, P., & Campbell, D. T. (1971). Hedonic relativism and planning the good society. In M. H. Appley (Ed.),

Adaptation level theory: A symposium (pp. 287–304). NY: Academic Press.

Brickman, P., Coates, D., & Janoff-Bulman, R. (1978). Lottery winners and accident victims: Is happiness relative? *Journal of Personality and Social Psychology, 36,* 917–927.

Brinthaupt, T. M., & Shin, C. M. (2001). The relationship of academic cramming to the flow experience. *College Student Journal, 35*(3), 457–471.

Brockway, W., & Weinstock, H. (1958). *Men of music: their lives, times, and achievements.* New York: Simon & Schuster.

Brown, K. W., & Ryan, R. M. (2003). The benefits of being present: mindfulness and its role in psychological well-being. *Journal of Personality and Social Psychology, 84*(4), 822–848.

Brunstein, J. C. (1993). Personal goals and subjective well-being: A longitudinal study. *Journal of Personality and Social Psychology, 65*(5), 1061–1070.

Brunstein, J. C., Schulthesis, O. C., & Graessman, R. (1998). Personal goals and emotional well-being: The moderating role of motive dispositions. *Journal of Personality and Social Psychology, 75*(2), 494–508.

Bryant, F. B. (1989). A four-factor model of perceived control: Avoiding, coping, obtaining, and savoring. *Journal of Personality,* 57, 773–797.

Bryant, F. B., & Veroff, J. (2004). *Savoring: Towards a process model for positive psychology.* Unpublished manuscript, Loyola University Chicago, Chicago, IL.

Buckingham, M., & Clifton, D. (2001). *Now, discover your strengths.* New York: Free Press.

Buckingham, M., & Coffman, C. (1999). *First, break all the rules: What the world's greatest managers do differently.* New York: Simon & Schuster.

Burg, M., Blumenthal, J., Barefoot, J., Williams, R., & Haney, T. (1986, July). *Social support as a buffer against the development of coronary artery disease.* Paper presented at the Society of Behavioral Medicine Meeting, San Francisco, CA.

Burman, B., & Margolin, G. (1992). Analysis of the association between marital relationships and health problems: An interactional perspective. *Psychological Bulletin, 112,* 39–63.

Buss, D. M. (2000). The evolution of happiness. *American Psychologist, 55*(1), 15–23.

Cain, D. J., & Seeman, J. (Eds.) (2002). *Humanistic psychotherapies: Handbook of research and practice.* Washington, DC: American Psychological Association.

Calaprice, A. (Ed.). (2000). *The expanded quotable Einstein.* Princeton, NJ: Princeton University Press.

Campbell, A. (1981). *The sense of well-being in America.* New York: McGraw-Hill.

Campbell, A., Converse, P. E., & Rodgers, W. L. (1976). *The quality of American life.* New York: Russell Sage Foundation.

Campbell, W. K., Reeder, G. D., Sedikides, C., & Elliot, A. (2000). Narcissism and comparative self-enhancement strategies. *Journal of Research in Personality, 34,* 329–347.

Cantor, N., & Sanderson, C. A. (1999). Life task participation and well-being: The importance of taking part in daily life. In D. Kahneman, E. Diener, & N. Schwarz (Eds.), *Well-being: The foundation of hedonic psychology* (pp. 230–243). New York: Russell Sage Foundation.

Carstensen, L. L. (1992). Social and emotional patterns in adulthood: Support for socioemotional selectivity theory. *Psychology and Aging, 7,* 331–338.

Carstensen, L. L. (1995). Evidence for a life-span theory of socioemotional selectivity. *American Psychological Society, 4*(5), 151–156.

Carstensen, L. L., Mayr, U., Nesselroade, J. R., & Pasupathi, M. (2000). Emotional experience in everyday life across the adult life span. *Journal of Personality and Social Psychology, 79*(4), 644–655.

Caspi, A., & Herbener, E. S. (1990). Continuity and change: Assortative marriage and the consistency of personality in adulthood. *Journal of Personality and Social Psychology, 58*(2), 250–258.

Caspi, A., Herbener, E. S., & Ozer, D. J. (1992). Shared experiences and the similarity of personalities: A longitudinal study of married couples. *Journal of Personality and Social Psychology, 62*(2), 281–291.

CBS News (2001, February 8). Another extraordinary day on the job.

Chamberlain, K., & Zika, S. (1988). Religiosity, life meaning, and well-being. *Journal for the Scientific Study of Religion, 27,* 411–420.

Chamberlain, T. J., & Hall, C. A. (2000). *Realized religion: Research on the relationship between religion and health.* Philadelphia, PA: Templeton Foundation.

Chang, E. C. (2001). A look at the coping strategies and styles of Asian Americans: Similar and different? In C. R. Snyder (Ed.) *Coping with stress: Effective people and processes* (pp. 222–239). London: Oxford University Press.

Charnetski, C. J., Brennan, F. X., Jr., & Harrison, J. F. (1998). Effect of music and auditory stimuli on secretory immunoglobulin A (IgA). *Perceptual and Motor Skills, 87*(3, pt. 2), 1163–1170.

Clark, A. E., & Oswald, A. J. (1996). Satisfaction and comparison income. *Journal of Public Economics, 61,* 359–81.

Clark, M. S., & Bennett, M. E. (1992). Research on relationships: Implications for mental health. In D. N. Ruble, & P. R. Costanzo (Eds.). *Social psychology of mental health: Basic mechanisms and applications* (pp. 166–198). New York: Guilford Press.

Clarke, S. G., & Haworth, J. T. (1994). "Flow" experience in the lives of sixth-form college students. *British Journal of Psychology, 85,* 511–523.

Clary, E. G., & Snyder, M. (1999). The motivations to volunteer: Theoretical and practical considerations. *Current Directions in Psychological Science, 8*(5), 156–159.

Clary, E. G., & Snyder, M. (2002). Community involvement: Opportunities and challenges in socializing adults to participate in society. *Journal of Social Issues, 58*(3), 581–591.

Clayton, V. (1982). Wisdom and intelligence: The nature and function of knowledge in the later years. *International Journal of Aging and Human Development, 15*(4), 315–321.

Clifton, D., & Nelson, P. (1992). *Soar with your strengths.* New York: Dell.

Cloninger, R., Svrakic, D. M., & Przybeck, T. R. (1993). A psychobiological model of temperament and character. *Archives of General Psychiatry, 50,* 975–990.

Coan, R. W. (1974). *The optimal personality.* New York: Columbia University Press.

Coan, R. W. (1977). *Hero, artist, sage, or saint.* New York: Columbia University Press.

Coffman, C., & Gonzales-Molina, G. (2002). *Follow this path: How the world's greatest organizations drive growth by unleashing human potential.* New York: Warner.

Cohen, S., Doyle, W. J., Skoner, D. P., Rabin, B. S., & Gwaltney, J. M., Jr. (1998). Types of stressors that increase susceptibility *to* the common cold in healthy adults. *Health psychology, 17,* 214–233.

Cohen, S., & Syme, S. L. (1985). *Social support and health.* San Diego, CA: Academic Press.

Cohen, S., Tyrrell, D. A. J., & Smith, A. P. (1991). Psychological stress and susceptibility to the common cold. *New England Journal of Medicine, 325,* 606–612.

Cohen, S., Tyrrell, D. A. J., & Smith, A. P. (1993). Negative life events, perceived stress, negative affect, and susceptibility to the common cold. *Journal of Personality and Social Psychology, 64,* 131–140.

Coleman, L. J. (1994). "Being a teacher": Emotions and optimal experience while teaching gifted children. *Gifted Child Quarterly, 38*(3), 146–152.

Colvin, C. R., & Block, J. (1994). Do positive illusions foster mental health? An examination of the Taylor and Brown formulation. *Psychological Bulletin, 116,* 3–20.

Compas, B. E. (1987). Coping with stress during childhood and adolescence. *Psychological Bulletin, 101*(3), 393–403.

Compton, W. C. (1992). Are positive illusions necessary for self-esteem: A research note. *Personality and Individual Differences, 13*(12), 1343–1344.

Compton, W. C. (2000). Meaningfulness as a moderator of subjective well-being. *Psychological Reports, 87,* 156–160.

Compton, W. C. (2001). Toward a tripartite factor structure of mental health: Subjective well-being, personal growth, and religiosity. *Journal of Psychology, 135*(5), 486–500.

Compton, W. C., Seeman, J., & Norris, R. C. (1991). Predicting hardiness: A search for the parameters of deep cognitive structures, *Medical Psychotherapy, 4,* 121–130.

Compton, W., Smith, M., Cornish, K., & Qualls, D. (1996). Factor structure of mental health measures. *Journal of Personality and Social Psychology, 71*(2), 406–413.

Cooper, A. (1998). *Playing in the zone: Exploring the spiritual dimensions of sports.* Boston: Shambala.

Cosma, J. B. (1999). Flow in teams. *Dissertation Abstracts International.60*(6–A), 1901.

Costa, P., & McCrae, R. (1984). Personality as a lifelong determinant of well-being. In C. Malatesta & C. Izard (Eds.), *Affective processes in adult development and aging* (pp. 141–157). Beverly Hills, CA: Sage Publications.

Costa, P. T., & McCrae, R. R. (1986). Personality stability and its implications for clinical psychology. *Clinical Psychology Review, 6,* 407–423.

Costa, P. T., & McCrae, R. R. (1988). Personality in adulthood: A six-year longitudinal study of self-reports and spouse ratings on the NEO Personality Inventory. *Journal of Personality & Social Psychology, 54*(5), 853–863.

Cousins, N. (1981). *Anatomy of an illness.* New York: Norton.

Cowen, E. L., & Kilmer, R. P. (2002). Positive psychology: some plusses and some open issues. *Journal of Community Psychology, 30*(4), 449–460.

Cramer, P., & Davidson, K. (Eds.). (1998). Defense mechanisms in contemporary personality research. [Special issue]. *Journal of Personality, 66*(6).

Crandall, R., Nolan, M., & Morgan, L. (1980). Leisure and social interaction. In S. Iso-Ahola (Ed.), *Social-psychological perspectives on leisure and recreation* (pp. 285–306). Springfield, IL: Charles C. Thomas.

Crooker, K. J., & Near, J. P. (1998). Happiness and satisfaction: Measures of affect and cognition? *Social Indicators Research, 44*(2), 195–224.

Csikszentmihalyi, M. (1975). Play and intrinsic rewards. *Journal of Humanistic Psychology, 15*(3), 41–63.

Csikszentmihalyi, M. (1988). *Society, culture, and person: A systems view of creativity.* New York: Cambridge University Press, 323–339.

Csikszentmihalyi, M. (1990). *Flow: The psychology of optimal experience.* New York: Harper & Row.

Csikszentmihalyi, M. (1997). *Finding flow: The psychology of engagement with everyday life.* New York: Basic Books.

Csikszentmihalyi, M., & Csikszentmihalyi, I. S. (1988). *Optimal experience: Psychological studies of flow in consciousness.* New York: Cambridge University Press.

Csikszentmihalyi, M., & LeFevre, J. (1989). Optimal experience in work and leisure. *Journal of Personality and Social Psychology, 56*(5), 815–822.

Csikszentmihalyi, M., & Rathunde, K. (1993). The measurement of flow in everyday life. *Nebraska Symposium on Motivation, 40,* 57–97.

cummings, e. e. (1958). *95 poems by e. e. cummings.* New York: Harcourt, Brace & World.

Cummins, R. A. (1996). The domains of life satisfaction: An attempt to order chaos. *Social Indicators Research, 38*(3), 303–328.

Dalai Lama with Cutler, H. C. (1998). *The art of happiness: A handbook for living.* New York: Riverhead.

d'Aquili, E. G., & Newberg, A. B. (1999). *The mystical mind: Probing the biology of religious experiences.* Minneapolis, MN: Fortress Press.

Danner, D, Snowdon, D., & Friesen, W. (2001). Positive emotions in early life and longevity: Findings from the nun study. *Journal of Personality and Social Psychology, 80,* 804–813.

Davidson, R. J. (2002, October). *Positive affective styles: Perspectives from affective neuroscience.* Paper presented at the First International Positive Psychology Summit. Washington, DC.

Davidson, R. J., Kabat-Zinn, J., Schumacher, J., Rosenkranz, M., Muller, D., Santorelli, S. F., et al. (2003). Alternations in brain and immune function produced by mindfulness meditation. *Psychosomatic Medicine, 65*(4), 564–570.

Deci, E. L. (1975). *Intrinsic motivation.* New York: Plenum.

Deci, E. L., & Flaste, R. (1996). *Why we do what we do.* New York: Penguin.

Deci, E. L., & Ryan, R. M. (1985). *Intrinsic motivation and self-determination in human behavior.* New York: Plenum.

De Fruyt, F. (1997). Gender and individual differences in adult crying. *Personality and Individual differences, 22*(6), 937–940.

deGroot, A. D. (1965). *Thought and choice in chess.* The Hague: Mouton. (Original work published 1946.)

DeNeve, K. M., & Cooper, H. (1998). The happy personality: A meta-analysis of 137 personality traits and subjective well-being. *Psychological Bulletin, 124*(2), 197–229.

de Shazer, S. (1985). *Keys to solution in brief therapy.* New York: Norton.

de Silva, P. (1979). *An introduction to Buddhist psychology.* London: McMillan.

Dewey, J. (1934). *Art as experience.* Oxford, UK: Minton, Balch.

Diener, E. (1984). Subjective well-being. *Psychological Bulletin, 93*(3), 542–575.

Diener, E. (1994). Assessing subjective well-being: Progress and opportunities. *Social Indicators Research, 31,* 103–157.

Diener, E. (2000a). Subjective well-being: The science of happiness and a proposal for a national index. *American Psychologist, 55*(1), 34–43.

Diener, E. (2000b). *Is happiness a virtue?* Paper presented at the Positive Psychology Summit 2000, October. Washington, DC.

Diener, E., & Biswas-Diener, R. (2002). Will money increase subjective well-being? A literature review and guide to needed research. *Social Indicators Research, 57,* 119–169.

Diener, E., & Diener, C. (1996). The wealth of nations revisited: Income and quality of life. *Social Indicators Research, 36,* 275–86.

Diener, E., Diener, M., & Diener, C. (1995). Factors predicting the subjective well-being of nations. *Journal of Personality & Social Psychology, 69,* 653–663.

Diener, E., Emmons, R., Larsen, R., & Griffin, S. (1985). The satisfaction with life scale, *Journal of Personality Assessment, 49*(l), 71–75.

Diener, E., Horwitz, J., & Emmons, R. A. (1985). Happiness of the very wealthy. *Social Indicators, 16,* 263–274.

Diener, E., & Larsen, R. J. (1984). Temporal stability and cross-situational consistency of affective, behavioral, and cognitive responses. *Journal of Personality and Social Psychology, 47,* 871–883.

Diener, E., Larsen, R. J., & Emmons, R. A. (1984). Person X situation interactions: Choice of situations and congruence response models. *Journal of Personality and Social Psychology, 47,* 580–592.

Diener, E., Larsen, R. J., Levine, S., & Emmons, R. (1985). Intensity and frequency: Dimensions underlying positive and negative affect. *Journal of Personality & Social Psychology, 48*(5), 1253–1265.

Diener, E., & Lucas, R. (1999). Personality and subjective well-being. In D. Kahneman, E. Diener, & N. Schwarz (Eds.), *Well-being: The foundation of hedonic psychology* (pp. 213–229). New York: Russell Sage Foundation.

Diener, E., & Lucas, R. E. (2000). Explaining differences in societal levels of happiness: Relative standards, need fulfillment, culture, and evaluation theory. *Journal of Happiness Studies, 1,* 41–78.

Diener, E., Oishi, S., & Lucas, R. E. (2003). Personality, culture, and subjective well-being: Emotional and cognitive evaluations of life. *Annual Review of Psychology, 54,* 403–425.

Diener, E., Sandvik, E., Seidlitz, L., & Diener, M. (1993). The relationship between income and subjective well-being: Relative or absolute? *Social Indicators Research, 28,* 195–223.

Diener, E., & Seligman, M. E. P. (2002). Very happy people. *Psychological Science, 13*(1), 81–84.

Diener, E., & Suh, E. M. (2000). *Culture and subjective well-being.* Cambridge, MA: MIT Press.

Diener, E., Suh, E. M., Lucas, R. E., & Smith, H. L. (1999). Subjective well-being: Three decades of progress. *Psychological Bulletin, 125*(2), 276–302.

Diener, E., Wolsic, B., & Fujita F. (1995). Physical attractiveness and subjective well-being. *Journal of Personality and Social Psychology, 69,* 120–129.

Dillon, K., Minchoff, B., & Baker, K. (1985–1986). Positive emotional states and enhancement of the immune system. *International Journal of Psychiatry in Medicine, 15,* 13–18.

Doi, K. (1985). The relation between the two dimensions of achievement motivation and personality of male university students. *Japanese Journal of Psychology, 56,* 107–110.

Donahue, E. M., Robins, R. W., Roberts, B. W., & John, O. P. (1993). The divided self: Concurrent and longitudinal effects of psychological adjustment and social roles on self-concept differentiation. *Journal of Personality and Social Psychology, 64,* 834–46.

Donahue, M. J. (1985). Intrinsic and extrinsic religiousness: Review and meta-analysis. *Journal of Personality and Social Psychology, 48*(2), 400–419.

Donahue, M. J., & Benson, P. L. (1995). Religion and the well-being of adolescents. *Journal of Social Issues, 51*(2), 145–160.

Dunn, H. (1961). *High-level wellness.* Arlington, VA: Beatty

Durrant, M., & Kowalski, K. (1993). Enhancing views of competence. In S. Friedman (Ed.), *The new language of change* (pp. 107–137), Adelaide, Australia: Dulwich Centre Publications.

Ebersole, P. (1970). Effects of nadir experiences. *Psychological Reports, 27*(1), 207–209.

Edlin. G., & Golantry, E. (1992). *Health and wellness: A holistic approach.* Boston, MA: Jones & Bartlett.

Edwards, B. (1999). *The new drawing on the right side of your brain.* Los Angeles: J. P. Tarcher.

Ekman, P. (1993). Facial expression and emotion. *American psychologist, 48,* 384–392.

Ekman, P., Friesen, W. V., & O'Sullivan, M. (1988). Smiles when lying. *Journal of Personality and Social Psychology, 54,* 414–420.

Emmons, R. A. (1986). Personal strivings: An approach to personality and subjective well-being. *Journal of Personality and Social Psychology, 51*(5), 1058–1068.

Emmons, R. A. (1992). Abstract versus concrete goals: Personal striving level, physical illness, and psychological well-being. *Journal of Personality and Social Psychology, 62*(2), 292–300.

Emmons, R. A. (1999). *The psychology of ultimate concerns: Motivation and spirituality in personality.* New York: Guilford.

Emmons, R. A., & Crumpler, C. A. (1999). Religion and spirituality? The roles of sanctification and the concept of God. *The International Journal for the Psychology of Religion, 9*(1), 17–24.

Emmons, R. A., & King, L. A. (1988). Conflict among personal strivings: Immediate and long-term implications for psychological and physical well-being. *Journal of Personality and Social Psychology, 54*(6), 1040–1048.

Emmons, R. A., & Paloutzian, R. F. (2003). The psychology of religion. *Annual Review of Psychology, 54,* 377–402.

Enright, R. F. (2001). *Forgiveness is a choice: A step-by-step process for resolving anger and restoring hope.* Washington, DC: American Psychological Association.

Enright, R. D., & North, J. (1998). *Exploring forgiveness.* Madison, WI: University of Wisconsin Press.

Enright, R. D., Freedman, S., & Rique, J. (1998). The psychology of interpersonal forgiveness. In R. D. Enright & J. North (Eds.), *Exploring forgiveness* (pp. 46–62). Madison, WI: University of Wisconsin Press.

Epel, E. S., McEwen, B. S., & Ickovics, J. R. (1998). Embodying psychological thriving: Physical thriving in response to stress. *Journal of Social Issues, 53*(2), 301–322.

Epstein, M. (1988). The deconstruction of the self: Ego and "egolessness" in Buddhist insight meditation. *Journal of Transpersonal Psychology, 20*(1), 61–69.

Ericsson, K. A. (Ed.). (1996). *The road to excellence.* Mahwah, NJ. Lawrence Erlbaum Associates.

Ericsson, K. A., & Charness, N. (1994). Expert performance. *American Psychologist, 49*(8), 725–747.

Ericsson, K. A., Krampe, R. T., & Tesch-Roemer, C. (1993). The role of deliberate practice in the acquisition of expert performance. *Psychological Review, 100*(3), 363–406.

Erikson, E. (1950). *Childhood and society.* New York: Norton.

Erikson, E., Erikson, J. M., & Kivnick, H. Q. (1986). *Vital involvement in old age.* New York: Norton.

Fackelman, K. A. (1993). Marijuana and the brain. Scientists discover the brain's own THC. *Science, 143,* 88–94.

Fadiman, J., & Frager, R. (1994). *Personality and personal growth* (3rd ed.). New York: Harper-Collins.

Farrell, P. A., Gustafson, A. B., Morgan, W. P., & Pert, C. B. (1987). Enkephalins, catecholamines, and psychological mood alterations: Effects of prolonged exercise. *Medicine and Science in Sports and Exercise, 19*(4), 347–353.

Fava, G. A. (1999). Well-being therapy: Conceptual and technical issues. *Psychotherapy and Psychosomatics, 68,* 171–179.

Fava, G., Rafanelli, C., & Cazzaro, M. (1998). Well-being therapy: A novel psychotherapeutic approach for residual symptoms of affective disorders. *Psychological Medicine, 28*(2), 475–480.

Fehr, B., & Russell, J. A. (1991). Concept of love viewed from a prototype perspective. *Journal of Personality and Social Psychology, 60,* 425–438.

Fenchel, G. H. (1985). Time as self and ego experience. *Issues in Psychoanalytic Psychology, 8*(1 & 2), 73–81.

Feshbach, N. (1984). Empathy, empathy training, and the regulation of aggression in elementary school children. In R. M. Kaplan, V., Konccni, & R. Novaco (Eds.), *Aggression in children and youth* (pp. 192–208). The Hague: Martinus Nijhoff.

Firestone, R. W., Firestone, L. A., & Catlett, J. (2003). *Creating a life of meaning and compassion: The wisdom of psychotherapy.* Washington, DC: American Psychological Association.

Fitzpatrick, S. M. (2001, October 1). Choose Beauty. *The Scientist, 64,* 4.

Fordyce, M. W. (1977). Development of a program to increase personal happiness. *Journal of Counseling Psychology, 24*(6), 511–521.

Fordyce, M. W. (1981). *The psychology of happiness: A brief version of the fourteen fundamentals.* Ft. Myers, FL: Cypress Lake Media

Fordyce, M. W. (1983). A program to increase happiness: Further studies. *Journal of Counseling Psychology, 30*(4), 483–498.

Fordyce, M. W. (1988). A review of research on the happiness measures: A sixty second index of happiness and mental health, *Social Indicators Research, 20,* 355–381.

Fowers, B. J. (2000). *Beyond the myth of marital happiness: How embracing the virtues of loyalty, generosity, justice, and courage can strengthen your relationship.* San Francisco: Jossey-Bass.

Fowers, B. J. (2001). The limits of a technical concept of a good marriage; Exploring the role of virtue in communication skills. *Journal of Marital and Family Therapy, 27*(3), 327–340.

Fowler, J. W. (1981). *Stages of faith: The psychology of human development and the quest for meaning.* San Francisco: Harper & Row.

Frank, J. D., & Frank, J. B. (1991). *Persuasion and healing: A comparative study of psychotherapy* (3rd Ed.). Baltimore, MD: Johns Hopkins University Press.

Frankl, V. E. (1963). *Man's search for meaning.* New York: Pocket Books.

Frankl, V. E. (1978). *The unheard cry for meaning: Psychotherapy and humanism.* New York: Simon & Schuster.

Franklin, M. B., & Kaplan, B. (Eds.). (1994). *Development and the arts: Critical perspectives.* Hillsdale, NJ: Lawrence Erlbaum Associates.

Fredrickson, B. L. (1998). What good are positive emotions? *Review of General Psychology, 2*(3), 300–319.

Fredrickson, B. L. (2001). The role of positive emotions in positive psychology: The broaden-and-build theory of positive emotions. *Journal of American Psychological Association, 54*(3), 218–226.

Frederickson, B. L. (2002). Positive emotions. In C. R. Snyder & S. J. Lopez (Eds.), *Handbook of positive psychology (pp.* 120–134). New York: Oxford University Press.

Fredrickson, B., & Joiner, T. (2002). Positive emotions trigger upward spirals toward emotional well-being. *Psychological Science,* 13, 172–175.

Fredrickson, B., & Levenson, R. (1998). Positive emotions speed recovery from the cardiovascular sequelae of negative emotions. *Cognition and Emotion, 12,* 191–220.

Frenz, A. W., Carey, M. P., & Jorgensen, R. S. (1993). Psychometric evaluation of Antonovsky's Sense of Coherence Scale. *Psychological Assessment, 5*(2), 145–153.

Freud, S. (1952). Group psychology and the analysis of the ego. In *The major works of Sigmund Freud* (pp. 664–696). Chicago: Encyclopedia Britannica. (Original work published 1921)

Freud, S. (1960). *The Interpretation of Dreams.* New York: Basic Books. (Original work published 1901)

Frey, B. S., & Stutzer, A. (2000). Happiness prospers in democracy. *Journal of Happiness Studies, 1,* 79–102.

Frey, D., Jonas, E., & Greitemeyer, T. (2003). Intervention as a major tool of a psychology of human strengths: Examples from organizational change and innovation. In L. G. Aspinwall & U. M. Staudinger (Eds.), *A psychology of human strengths: Fundamental questions and future directions for a positive psychology* (pp. 149–164). Washington, DC: American Psychological Association.

Friesen, W. V. (1972). *Cultural differences in facial expression in a social situation: An experimental test of the concept of display rules.* Unpublished doctoral dissertation, University of California, San Francisco.

Frijda, N. (1986). *The emotions.* Cambridge, UK: Cambridge University Press.

Fromm, E. (1941). *Escape from freedom.* New York: Holt, Rinehart, & Winston.

Fromm, E. (1955). *The sane society.* New York: Holt, Rinehart, & Winston.

Fuchs, E., & Havinghurst, R. (1973). *To live on this earth: American Indian education.* New York: Anchor Books.

Fujita, F. (1991). *An investigation of the relation between extroversion, neuroticism, positive affect, and negative affect.* Unpublished masters thesis, University of Illinois at Urbana-Champaign.

Fujita, F., Diener, E., & Sandvik, E. (1991). Gender differences in negative affect and well-being: The case for emotional intensity. *Journal of Personality and Social Psychology, 61,* 427–434.

Funder, D. C. (1997). *The personality puzzle.* New York: Norton.

Galway, W. T. (1974). *The inner game of tennis.* New York: Random House.

Gardner, H. (1993). *Creating minds, An anatomy of creativity seen through the lives of Freud, Einstein, Picasso, Stravinsky, Eliot, Graham, and Gandhi.* New York: Basic Books.

Garfield, C. A., & Bennett, H. Z. (1984). *Peak performance: Mental training techniques of the world's greatest athletes.* Los Angeles: Tarcher.

Garmezy, N., Masten, A. S., & Tellegren, A. (1984). The study of stress and competence in children: A building block for developmental psychopathology. *Child Development, 55,* 97–111.

Gay, V. P. (2001). *Joy and the objects of psychoanalysis.* Buffalo, New York: State University of New York Press.

Gaynor, M. P. (2002). *The healing power of sound.* Boulder, CO: Shambhala.

Gentry, W. D., & Ouellette-Kobash, S. C. (1984). Social and psychological resources mediating stress-illness relationships in humans. In W. D. Gentry (Ed.), *Handbook of behavioral medicine* (pp. 87–116). New York: Guilford.

George, J. M., & Brief, A. P. (1992). Feeling good-doing good: A conceptual analysis of the mood at work-organizational spontaneity relationship. *Psychological Bulletin, 112,* 310–329.

George, L. K., Larson, D. B., Koenig, H. G., & McCullough, M. E. (2000). Spirituality and health: What we know, what we need to know. *Journal of Social and Clinical Psychology, 19*(1), 102–116.

Gergen, K., & Gergen, M. (2001, November 28). Collaborative caring as a research goal. *The Positive Aging Newsletter.*

Gestwicki, R. (2001). Ira Progoff (1921–1998): The creator of the intensive journal method and a new profession. *Journal of Humanistic Psychology, 41*(3), 53–74.

Getting better all the time: Face to face with Paul McCartney. (2001, November). *Readers Digest.* 78–87, 157–160.

Ghani, J. A., & Deshpande, S. P. (1994). Task characteristics and the experience of optimal flow in human-computer interaction. *The Journal of Psychology, 128*(4), 381–391.

Gilbert, D. T., & Malone, P. S. (1995). The correspondence bias. *Psychological Bulletin, 117,* 21–38.

Gilligan, C. (1982). *In a different voice: Psychological theory and women's development.* Cambridge, MA: Harvard University Press.

Glancy, M., Willits, F. W., & Farrell, P. (1986). Adolescent activities and adult success and happiness. *Sociology and Social Research, 70,* 242–270.

Glenn, N. D., & Weaver, C. N. (1988). The changing relationship of marital status to reported happiness. *Journal of Marriage and the Family, 50,* 317–324.

Goldberg, N., & Guest, J. (1986). *Writing down the bones: Freeing the writer within.* Boulder, CO: Shambhala.

Goleman, D. (1975). Mental health in classical Buddhist psychology. *Journal of Transpersonal Psychology, 7,* 176–181.

Goleman, D. J. (1995). *Emotional intelligence.* New York: Bantam Books.

Goleman, D. J. (1989). What is negative about positive illusions? When benefits for the individual harm the collective. *Journal of Social and Clinical Psychology, 8*(2), 190–197.

Goleman, D. J. (1995). *Emotional intelligence.* New York: Bantam Books.

Goleman, D. (1996). *Vital lies and simple truths.* New York: Touchstone.

Goodwin, F. K., & Jamison, K. R. (1990). *Manic-depressive illness.* London: Oxford University Press.

Gore, Al, Jr. (2001, November 8). Building healthy communities. Speech at Middle Tennessee State University.

Gorman, M. O. (1998, March). Do you love him? *Prevention,* 92.

Gottman, J. M. (1998). Psychology and the study of the marital processes. *Annual Review of Psychology, 49,* 169–297.

Gottman, J., & Declaire, J. (2001). *The relationship cure: A five-step guide for building better connections with family, friends, and lovers.* New York: Crown.

Gottman, J. M., & Gottman, J. S. (1999). The marriage survival kit: A research-based marital therapy. In R. Berger & M. T. Hannah (Eds.), *Preventive approaches in couples therapy* (pp. 304–330). Philadelphia, PA.: Brunner/Mazel.

Gottman, J. M., & Levenson, R. W. (2000). The timing of divorce: Predicting when a couple will divorce over a 14-year period. *Journal of Marriage and the Family, 63*(3), 737–745.

Gottman, J. M., & Notarius, C. I. (2000). Decade review: Observing marital interaction. *Journal of Marriage and the Family, 62*(4), 927–947.

Gottman, J., & Silver, N. (1999). *The seven principles for making marriage work.* New York: Crown.

Green, J., & Shellenberger, R. (1991). *The dynamics of health and wellness: A biopsychosocial approach.* Fort Worth, TX: Holt, Rinehart, & Winston.

Greenberg, J. Pyszczynski, T., & Soloman, S. (1986). The causes and consequences of the need for self-esteem: A terror management theory. In R. F. Baumeistser (Ed.), *Public self and private self* (pp. 189–207). New York: Springer-Verlag.

Greenberg, L. S., & Rice, L. N. (1997). Humanistic approaches to psychotherapy. In P. L. Wachtel & S. B. Messer (Eds.), *Theories of psychotherapy: Origins and evolution* (pp. 97–129). Washington, DC: American Psychological Association.

Greenspan, M. J., & Feltz, D. E. (1989). Psychological interventions with athletes in competitive situations: A review. *The Sport Psychologist, 3,* 219–236.

Groth-Marnat. G., & Schumaker, J. F. (1989). The near-death experience: A review and critique. *Journal of Humanistic Psychology, 29*(1), 109–133.

Grubin, D. (Producer). (1993). *Healing and the mind with Bill Moyers, 2: The Mind Body Connection* [video recording]. New York: David Grubin Productions.

Guilford, J. P. (1950) Creativity. *American Psychologist, 5,* 444–54.

Gurwitt, R. (2002, March/April). Fostering hope. *Mother Jones,* 65–67.

Guzman, S. (2002). *The Latina's bible: The nueva Latina's guide to love, spirituality, family, and la vida.* New York: Three Rivers Press.

Haggerty, M. R. (1999). Testing Maslow's hierarchy of needs: National quality-of-life across time. *Social Indicators Research, 46,* 249–271.

Haidt, J. (2000a, October). *Elevation and the positive moral emotions.* Paper presented at the Positive Psychology Summit, October 2000.

Haidt, J. (2000b). The positive emotion of elevation. *Prevention and Treatment, 3*(3).

Halpern, S., & Savary, L. (1985). *The music and sounds that make us whole.* San Francisco: Harper & Row.

Hamilton-Holcomb, J. A. (1976/1977). Attention and intrinsic rewards in the control of psychophysiologic states. *Psychotherapy and Psychosomatics, 27,* 54–61.

Hamilton, J. A., Haier, R. J., & Buchsbaum, M. S. (1984). Intrinsic enjoyment and boredom coping scales: Validation with personality, evoked potential and attention measures. *Personality & Individual Differences, 5*(2), 183–193.

Han, S. (1988). The relationship between life satisfaction and flow in elderly Korean immigrants. In M. Csikszentmihalyi & I. S. Csikszentmihalyi (Eds.), *Optimal experience: Psychological studies of flow in consciousness* (pp. 138–149). New York: Cambridge University Press.

Harker, L., & Keltner, D. (2001). Expressions of positive emotion in women's college yearbook pictures and their relationship to personality and life outcomes across adulthood. *Journal of Personality and Social Psychology, 80*(1), 112–124.

Hart, G. M. (1978). *Values clarification for counselors.* Springfield, IL: Charles C. Thomas.

Harter, Susan. (2002). Authenticity. In C. R. Snyder, & S. J. Lopez (Eds.). *Handbook of positive psychology* (pp. 382–394). New York: Oxford University Press.

Hatfield, E. (1988). Passionate and companionate love. In R. J. Sternberg & M. L. Barnes (Eds.), *The psychology of love* (pp. 191–217). New Haven, CT: Yale University Press.

Haworth, J. T., & Hill, S. (1992). Work, leisure, and psychological well-being in a sample of young adults. *Journal of Community & Applied Social Psychology, 2*(2), 147–160.

Hayes, K. F., & Brown, C. H, Jr. (2004). *You're on! Consulting for peak performance.* Washington, DC: American Psychological Association.

Headey, B., Veenhoven, R., & Wearing, A. (1991). Top-down versus bottom-up theories of subjective well-being. *Social Indicators Research, 24,* 81–100.

Heath, D. H. (1991). *Fulfilling lives: Paths to maturity and success.* San Francisco: Jossey-Bass.

Helson, H. (1947). Adaptation-level as frame of reference for prediction of psychophysical data. *American Journal of Psychology, 60,* 1–29.

Hendrick, S. S., & Hendrick, C. (1992). *Romantic love.* Newbury Park, CA: Sage Publications.

Hendrick, S. S., Hendrick C., & Adler, N. L. (1988). Romantic relationships: Love, satisfaction, and staying together. *Journal of Personality and Social Psychology, 54,* 980–988.

Hernstein, R. J., Nickerson, R. S., de Sanchez, M. & Swets, J. A. (1986). Teaching thinking skills. *American Psychologist, 41,* 1279–1289.

Herrigel, E. (1971). *Zen in the art of archery.* New York: Vintage.

Hertsgaard, M. (1995). *A day in the life: The music and artistry of the Beatles.* New York: Delacorte Press.

Herzog, A. R., Rodgers, W. L., & Woodworth, J. (1982). Age and satisfaction: Data from several large surveys. *Research on Aging,* 3, 142–165.

Hewitt, J. P. (2002). The social construction of self-esteem. In C. R. Snyder, & S. J. Lopez (Eds.), *Handbook of positive psychology* (pp. 135–147). London: Oxford University Press.

Higgins, E. T. (1987). Self-discrepancy: A theory relating self and affect. *Psychological Review, 94*(3), 319–340.

Ho, S. M. Y. (2003, August). *Indigenous positive psychology: Do we need it?* Paper presented at the Positive Psychology Summer Institute 2003, Monchanin, Delaware.

Hojjat, M. (1997). Philosophy of life as a model of relationship satisfaction. In R. J. Sternberg & M. Hojjatt (Eds.),

Satisfaction in close relationships (pp. 102–128). New York: Guilford Press.

Holland, G. B. (2001, November). Connecting inner assets. *Noetic Sciences Review: Institute for Noetic Sciences,* 31–33.

Homan, M. (1999). *Promoting community change: Making it happen in the real world.* Pacific Grove, CA.: Brooks/Cole.

Honderich, T. (Ed.) (1995). *The Oxford companion to philosophy.* New York, NY: Oxford University Press.

Hoyle, R., Kernis, M., Leary, M., & Baldwin, M. (1999). *Selfhood: Identity, esteem, & regulation.* Boulder, CO: Westview Press.

Hsee, C. K., & Abelson, R. P. (1991). Velocity relation: Satisfaction as a function of the first derivative of outcome over time. *Journal of Personality and Social Psychology, 60,* 341–347.

Hughes, R. (1980). *The shock of the new.* New York: Knopf.

Hugick, L., & Leonard, J. (2001, September). Job dissatisfaction grows. *Gallup Poll Monthly,* 2–15.

Hunt, M. (1959). *The natural history of love.* New York: Alfred Knopf.

Inglehart, R. (1990). *Culture's shift in advanced industrial society.* Princeton, NJ: Princeton University Press.

Inglehart, R., & Rabier, J. R. (1986). Aspirations adapt to situations—but why are the Belgians so much happier than the French? In F. M. Andrews (Ed.), *Research on the quality of life* (pp. 1–56). Ann Arbor: Institute for Social Research, University of Michigan.

Irving, L. M., Snyder, C. R., & Crowson, J. J., Jr. (1998). Hope and coping with cancer by college women. *Journal of Personality, 66*(2), 195–214.

Isen, A. M. (2001). An influence of positive affect on decision making in complex situations: Theoretical issues with practical implications. *Journal of Consumer Psychology, 11*(2), 75–85.

Isen, A. M. (2002). A role for neuropsychology in understanding the facilitating influence of positive affect on social behavior and cognitive processes. In C. R. Snyder & S. J. Lopez (Eds.), *Handbook of positive psychology* (pp. 528–540). New York: Oxford University Press.

Izard, C. E. (1971).*The face of emotion.* New York: Appleton-Century-Crofts.

Jackson, S. A., & Csikszentmihalyi, M. (1999). *Flow in Sports.* Champaign, IL: Human Kinetics.

Jackson, S. A., Kimiecik, J. C., & Ford, S. K. (1998). Psychological correlates of flow in sport. *Journal of Sport & Exercise Psychology, 20*(4), 358–378.

Jacob, J. C., & Brinkerhoff, M. B. (1999). Mindfulness and subjective well-being in the sustainability movement: A further elaboration of multiple discrepancies theory. *Social Indicators Research, 46,* 641–368.

Jahoda, M. (1958). *Current concepts of positive mental health.* New York: Basic Books.

James, W. (1958). *The varieties of religious experience.* New York: Mentor (Original work published 1902.)

Johnson, D. J., & Rusbult, C. E. (1989). Resisting temptation: Devaluation of alternative partners as a means of maintaining commitment in close relationships. *Journal of Personality and Social Psychology, 57,* 967–980.

Jones, A., & Crandall, R. (Eds.). (1991). Handbook of Self-actualization. [Special issue]. *Journal of Social Behavior and Personality, 6*(5).

Jung, C. G. (Ed.). (1964). *Man and his symbols.* New York: Doubleday.

Jung, C. G. (1965). *Memories, dreams, and reflections.* New York: Vintage.

Kabat-Zinn, J. (1993). Mindfulness meditation: Health benefits of an ancient Buddhist practice. In D. Goleman & J. Gurin (Eds.), *Mind/body medicine: How to use your mind for better health* (pp. 259–275). Yonkers, NY: Consumer Reports Books.

Kabat-Zinn, J., Lipworth, L., Burney, R., & Sellers, W. (1986). Four year follow-up of a meditation-based program for the self-regulation of chronic pain: Treatment outcomes and compliance. *Clinical Journal of Pain, 2,* 159–173.

Kagan, J., & Snidman, N. (1991). Temperamental factors in human development. *American Psychologist, 46*(8), 856–862.

Kahneman, D., Diener, E., & Schwarz, N. (Eds.). (1999). *Well-being: The foundations of hedonic psychology.* New York: Russell Sage Foundation.

Karney, B. R., & Bradbury, T. N. (1995). The longitudinal course of marital quality and stability: A review of theory, method, and research. *Psychological Bulletin, 118,* 3–34.

Kasser, T., & Ryan, R. M. (1993). A dark side of the American dream: Correlates of financial success as a life aspiration. *Journal of Personality and Social Psychology,* 65, 410–422.

Kegan, R. (1982). *The evolving self.* Cambridge, MA: Harvard University Press.

Keil, C. P. (1998). Loneliness, stress, and human-animal attachment among older adults. In C. C. Wilson & D. C. Turner (Eds.), *Companion animals in human health* (pp. 123–134). Thousand Oaks, CA: Sage Publications.

Kelly, E. L., & Conley, J. J. (1987). Personality and compatibility: A prospective analysis of marital stability and marital satisfaction. *Journal of Personality and Social Psychology, 52,* 27–40.

Kelly, H. H., & Thibaut, J. W. (1978). *Interpersonal relations: A theory of interdependence.* New York: Wiley.

Kelly, J. R., & Ross, J. E. (1989). Later-life leisure: Beginning a new agenda. *Leisure Sciences, 11*(1), 47–59.

Keltner, D. (2000, October). *Laughter, smiling, and the sublime.* Paper presented at the Positive Psychology Summit. Washington, DC.

Kemp, S. (1989). "Ravished of a fiend": Demonology and medieval madness. In C. A. Ward (Ed.), *Altered states of consciousness and mental health: A cross-cultural perspective.* Newbury Park, CA: Sage Publications.

Keyes, C. L. M. (1998). Social well-being. *Social Psychology Quarterly, 61*(2), 121–140.

Keyes, C. L. M., & Lopez, S. J. (2002). Toward a science of mental health: Positive directions in diagnosis and interventions. In C. R. Snyder, & S. J. Lopez (Eds.), *Handbook of positive psychology* (pp. 45–59). London: Oxford University Press.

Kiecolt-Glaser, J. K., Fisher, L., Ogrocki, P., Stout, J. C., Speicher, C. E., & Glaser, R. (1987). Marital quality, marital disruption, and immune function. *Psychosomatic Medicine, 49,* 13–35.

Kiecolt-Glaser, J. K., Garner, W., Speicher, C., Penn, G. M., Holliday, J., & Glaser, R. (1984). Psychosocial modifiers of immunocompetence in medical students. *Psychosomatic Medicine, 46,* 7–14.

Kiecolt-Glaser, J. K., Newton, T., Cacioppo, J. T., MacCallum, R. C., Glaser, R., & Malarkey, W. B. (1997). Marital conflict and endocrine function: Are men really more physiologically affected than women? *Journal of Consulting and Clinical Psychology, 64,* 324–332.

Kiefer, C. S. (1988). *The mantle of maturity: A history of ideas about character development.* Albany, New York: State University of New York Press.

Kierkegaard, S. (1843, trans. 1987). *Diapsalmata* (Vol. 1), *Either/Or.* Retrieved March 1, 2004, from http://www.barleby.com/66/62/32562.html.

Kimiecik, J. C., & Stein, G. L. (1992). Examining flow in sports contexts: Conceptual issues and methodological concerns. *Journal of Applied Sport Psychology, 4,* 144–160.

King, L. A. (2001). The health benefits of writing about life goals. *Personality and Social Psychology Bulletin, 27*(7), 798–807.

King, L. A., & Miner, K. N. (2000). Writing about the perceived benefits of traumatic events: Implications for physical health. *Personality and Social Psychology Bulletin, 26*(2), 220–230.

King, L. A., & Napa, C. K. (1998). What makes life good? *Journal of Personality and Social Psychology, 75*(1), 156–165.

Kitayma, S., Markus, H., Matsumoto, H., & Norasakkunkit, V. (1997). Individual and collective processes in the construction of the self: Self-enhancement in the United States and self-criticism in Japan. *Journal of Personality and Social Psychology, 72*(6), 1245–1267.

Klonoff, E. A, & Landrine, H. (1996). Belief in the healing power of prayer: Prevalence and health correlates for African-Americans. *Western Journal of Black Studies 20*(4), 204–210.

Knapp, R. R. (1990). *Handbook for the personal orientation inventory* (2nd Ed.). San Diego, CA: EDITS.

Knee, C. R., & Zuckerman, M. (1996). Causality orientations and the disappearance of the self-serving bias. *Journal of Research in Personality, 30*(1), 76–87.

Knee, C. R., & Zuckerman, M. (1998). A nondefensive personality: Autonomy and control as moderators of defensive coping and self-handicapping. *Journal of Research in Personality, 32*(2), 115–130.

Kobasa, S. C. (1979). Stressful life events, personality, and health: An inquiry into hardiness. *Journal of Personality and Social Psychology,* 37, 1–11.

Kobasa, S. C., Maddi, S. R., & Courington, S. (1981). Personality and constitution as mediators in the stress-illness relationship. *Journal of Health and Social Behavior, 22,* 368–378.

Kobasa, S. C., Maddi, S. R., & Kahn, S. (1982). Hardiness and health: A prospective study. *Journal of Personality and Social Psychology,* 42, 168–177.

Kobasa, S. C., Maddi, S. R., Puccetti, M. C., & Zola, M. A. (1994). Effectiveness of hardiness, exercise and social support as resources against illness. In A. Steptoe & J. Wardle (Eds.), *Psychosocial Processes and Health: A Reader* (pp. 247–260). Cambridge: Cambridge University Press.

Koenig, H. G., George, L. K., & Siegler, I. C. (1988). The use of religion and other emotion-regulating coping strategies among older adults. *Gerontologist, 28*(3), 303–310.

Koenig, H. G., McCullough, M. E., & Larson, D. B. (2001). *Handbook of religion and health.* London: Oxford University Press.

Kohlberg, L. (1984). *Essays on moral development, Vol.2: The nature and validity of moral stages.* San Francisco: Harper & Row.

Kolt, L., Slawsby, E. A., & Domar, A. D. (1999). Infertility: Clinical, treatment, and practice development issues. In L. VandeCreek & T. L. Jackson (Eds.), *Innovations in clinical practice: A sourcebook, Vol. 17* (pp. 185–203). Sarasota, FL: Professional Resource Press/Professional Resource Exchange.

Kramer, D. A. (2000). Wisdom as a classical source of human strength: Conceptualization and empirical inquiry. *Journal of Social & Clinical Psychology, 19*(1), 83–101.

Krippner, S. (Ed.). (1972). The plateau experience: A. H. Maslow and others. *Journal of Transpersonal Psychology, 4*(2), 107–120.

Kris, E. (1952). *Psychoanalytic Explorations in Art.* New York: International Universities.

Kubie, L. S. (1958). *Neurotic distortion of the creative process.* Lawrence: University of Kansas Press.

Kwan, V. S. Y., John, O. P., Robins, R. W., Bond, M. H., & Kenny, D. A. (2000, February). *Conceptualization and measurement of individual differences in self-enhancement.* Paper presented at the First Annual Meeting of the Society for Personality and Social Psychology, Nashville, TN.

Labouvie-Vief, G. (1990). Wisdom as integrated thought: Historical and developmental perspectives. In R. J. Sternberg (Ed.), *Wisdom: Its nature, origins, and development* (pp. 52–86). Cambridge, NY: Cambridge University Press.

Lambert, M. J. (1992). Psychotherapy outcome research. In J. C. Norcross & M. R. Golfried (Eds.), *Handbook of psychotherapy integration* (pp. 94–129). New York: Basic Books.

Landers, D. M., Han, M., Salazar, W., & Petruzzello, S. J. (1994). Effects of learning on electroencephalographic and electrocardiographic patterns in novice archers. *International Journal of Sport Psychology, 25*(3); 313–330.

Lane, R. E. (2000). Diminishing returns to income, companionship and happiness. *Journal of Happiness Studies, 1*(3), 103–119.

Langer, E. J. (1989). *Mindfulness.* Reading MA: Perseus.

Langer, E. J., & Rodin, J. (1976). The effects of choice and enhanced personal responsibility for the aged: A field experiment in an institutional setting. *Journal of Personality & Social Psychology, 34*(2), 191–198.

Larsen, R. J., & Kasimatis, M. (1990). Individual differences in entrainment of mood to the weekly calendar. *Journal of Personality and Social Psychology, 58*(1), 164–171.

Larsen, R. J., & Ketelaar, T. (1991). Personality and susceptibility to positive and negative emotional states. *Journal of Personality and Social Psychology, 61,* 132–140.

Lauer, R. H., Lauer, J. C., & Kerr, S. T. (1990). The long-term marriage: Perceptions of stability and satisfaction. *International Journal of Aging and Human Development, 31*(3), 189–195.

Lawler, K. A., Younger, J. W., Piferi, R. L., Billington, E., Jobe, R., Edmondson, K., Jones, W. H. (2003). A change of heart: Cardiovascular correlates of forgiveness in response to interpersonal conflict. *Journal of Behavioral Medicine, 26*(5), 373–393.

Lazarus, R. S., & Folkman, S. (1984). Coping and adaptation. In W. D. Gentry (Ed.), *Handbook of behavioral medicine.* New York: Guilford Press.

Lee, G. R., Seccombe, K., & Shehan, C. L. (1991). Marital status and personal happiness: An analysis of trend data. *Journal of Marriage and the Family, 53,* 839–844.

Lefcourt, H. M. (1981). *Research with the locus of control construct.* New York: Academic Press.

Lefcourt, H. M. (2002). Humor. In C. R. Snyder, & S. J. Lopez (Eds.), *Handbook of positive psychology* (pp. 619–631). New York.: Oxford University Press.

LeFevre, J. (1988). Flow and the quality of experience during work and leisure. In M. Csikszentmihalyi & I. Csikszentmihalyi (Eds.), *Optimal experience* (pp. 307–318). Cambridge: Cambridge University Press.

Leitner, M. J., & Leitner, S. F. (1996). *Leisure in later life* (2nd ed.). New York: Haworth Press.

Lemonick, M. D. (reported by S. Steptoe). (2004). Do gay couples have an edge? *Time,* January 19, p. 96.

Leonard, H. S. (1997). The many faces of character. *Consulting Psychology Journal, 49*(4), 235–245.

Leonardi, F., Spazzafumo, L, Marcellini, F., & Gagliardi, C. (1999). The top-down/bottom-up controversy from a constructionist approach: A method for measuring top-down effects applied to a sample of older people. *Social Indicators Research, 48,* 187–216.

Lepper, M., & Greene, D. (1978). *The hidden costs of reward.* Hillsdale, NJ: Lawrence Erlbaum Associates.

Lepper M., Greene, D., & Nisbett, R. (1973). Undermining children's intrinsic interest with extrinsic rewards: A test of the "overjustification" hypothesis. *Journal of Personality and Social Psychology, 28,* 129–137.

Levenson, R. W., Carstensen, L. L., & Gottman, J. M. (1994). Influences of age and gender on affect, physiology, and their interrelations: A study of long-term marriages. *Journal of Personality and Social Psychology, 67*(1), 56–68.

Lewinsohn, P. M.; Sullivan, J. M., & Grosscup, S. J. (1980). Changing reinforcing events: An approach to the treatment of depression. *Psychotherapy: Theory, Research & Practice, 17*(3), 322–334.

Lewis, C. A., Lanigan, C., Joseph, S., & deFockert, J. (1997). Religiosity and happiness: No evidence for an association among undergraduates. *Personality and Individual Differences, 22*(1), 119–121.

Lewis, M. L. (2002). *Multicultural health psychology: Special topics acknowledging diversity.* Boston: Allyn & Bacon.

Lichter, S., Haye, K., & Kammann, R. (1980). Increasing happiness through cognitive training. *New Zealand Psychologist, 9,* 57–64.

Little, B. R. (1983). Personal projects: A rationale and method for investigation. *Environment and Behavior, 15,* 273–309.

Little, B. R. (1989). Personal projects analysis: Trivial pursuits, magnificent obsessions, and the search for coherence. In D. Buss & N. Cantor (Eds.), *Personality psychology: Recent trends and emerging directions* (pp. 15–31). New York: Springer-Verlag.

Locke, E. A. (1976). The nature and causes of job satisfaction. In M. D. Dunnette (Ed.), *Handbook of industrial and organizational psychology* (pp. 1297–1350). Chicago: Rand McNally.

Locke, S., & Colligan, D. (1986). *The healer within.* New York: Dutton.

Loevinger, J. (1976). *Ego development.* San Francisco: Jossey-Bass.

Logan, R. D. (1985). The "flow experience" in solitary ordeals. *Journal of Humanistic Psychology, 25*(4), 79–89.

London, E. C. J., & Strumpf, S. A. (1986). Individual and organizational career development in changing times. In D. T. Hall & Associates (Eds.). *Career development in organizations.* San Francisco, CA: Jossey-Bass.

Lopez, S. J., Bouwkamp, J., Edwards, L. M., & Teramoto-Pedrotti, J. (2002, October). *Making hope happen via brief interventions.* Paper presented at the Second Positive Psychology Summit, Washington, DC.

Lopez, S. J., Floyd, R. K., Ulven, J. C., & Snyder, C. R. (2000). Hope therapy: Building a house of hope. In C. R. Snyder (Ed.), *The handbook of hope: Theory, measures, and applications* (pp. 123–148). New York: Academic Press.

Lopez, S. J., & Snyder, C. R. (Eds.). (2003). *Positive psychological assessment: A handbook of models and* measures. Washington DC: American Psychological Association

Lowry, R. (1982). *The evolution of psychological theory.* New York: Aldine.

Lu, L., Shih, J. B., Lin, Y. Y., & Ju, L. S. (1997). Personal and environmental correlates of happiness. *Personality and Individual Differences, 23*(3), 453–462.

Lucas, R. E., Diener, E., Grob, A., Suh, E. M., & Shao, L. (2000). Cross-cultural evidence for the fundamental features of extroversion. *Journal of Personality and Social Psychology, 79,* 452–468.

Lykken, D. (2000). *Happiness: The nature and nurture of joy and contentment.* New York: St. Martin's Griffin.

Lykken, D., & Tellegen, A. (1996). Happiness is a stochastic phenomenon. *Psychological Science, 7*(3), 186–189.

Lyubomirsky, S. (2001). Why are some people happier than others? The role of cognitive and motivational processes in well-being. *American Psychologist, 54*(3), 239– 249.

Lyubomirsky, S., & Lepper, H. S. (1999). A measure of subjective happiness: Preliminary reliability and construct validation. *Social Indicators Research, 46,* 137–155.

Lyubomirsky, S., & Ross, L. (1997). Hedonic consequences of social comparison: A contrast of happy and unhappy people. *Journal of Personality and Social Psychology, 73,* 1141–1157.

Maddi, S. R (1972). *Personality theories: A comparative analysis.* Homewood, IL: Dorsey.

Maddux, J. E. (2002). Stopping the "madness": Positive psychology and the deconstruction of the illness ideology and the *DSM.* In C. R. Snyder, & S. J. Lopez (Eds.), *Handbook of positive psychology* (pp. 13–25). New York: Oxford University Press.

Magnusson, D., & Mahoney, J. L. (2003). A holistic person approach for research on positive development. In L. G. Aspinall & U. M. Staudinger (Eds.), *A psychology of human strengths: fundamental questions and future directions for a positive psychology* (pp. 227–244). Washington, DC: American Psychological Association.

Mann, J. H. (1979). Human potential. In R. J. Corsini (Ed.) *Current psychotherapies* (2nd ed.) (pp. 500–535). Itasca, IL: F. E. Peacock.

Mannes, E. (Producer). (1990). *Amazing Grace with Bill Moyers* [video recording]. Beverly Hills, CA: PBS Video.

Mansfield, E. D., & McAdams, D. P. (1996). Generativity and themes of agency and communion in adult autobiography. *Personality & Social Psychology Bulletin, 22*(7), 721–731.

Marwick, C. (1995). Should physicians prescribe prayer for health? Spiritual aspects of well-being considered. *Journal of the American Medical Association, 273*(20), 1561–1562.

Maslow, A. H. (1954). *Motivation & personality.* New York: Harper & Row.

Maslow, A. H. (1968). *Toward a psychology of being.* New York: John Wiley & Sons.

Maslow, A. H. (1971). *The farther reaches of human nature.* New York: Viking.

Maslow, A. H. (1976). *Religions, values, and peak experiences.* New York: Penguin.

Maslow, A. H. (1987). *Motivation and personality* (3rd ed. rev.). New York: Harper Collins.

Masten, A. S., & Reed, M. G. J. (2002). Resilience in development. In C. R. Snyder, & S. J. Lopez (Eds.), *Handbook of positive psychology* (pp. 74–88). London: Oxford University Press.

Mathews-Treadway, K. (1996, July). Religion and optimism: Models of the relationship. *Der Zeitgeist: The Student Journal of Psychology,* 1–13.

Matsumoto, D. (1994). *People: Psychology from a cultural perspective.* Pacific Grove, CA: Brooks/Cole.

Matt, G. E., Vazquez, C., & Campbell, W. K. (1992). Mood-congruent recall of affectively toned stimuli: A meta-analytic review. *Clinical Psychology Review, 12,* 227–55.

Mayer, J. D., Caruso, D. R., & Salovey, P. (2000). Emotional intelligence meets traditional standards for an intelligence. *Intelligence, 27*(4), 267–298.

McAdams, D. P., & de St. Aubin, E. (Ed). (1998). *Generativity and adult development: How and why we care for the next generation.* Washington, DC: American Psychological Association.

McAdams, D. P., Diamond, A., de St. Aubin, E., & Mansfield, E. (1997). Stories of commitment: The psychosocial construction of generative lives. *Journal of Personality & Social Psychology, 72*(3), 678–694.

McCafferty, D. (2003, March 7–9). The happiest guy. *USA Weekend,* 6–9.

McCaffrey, N., & Orlick, T. (1989). Mental factors related to excellence among top professional golfers. *International Journal of Sport Psychology, 20*(4),256–278.

McClelland, D. C. (1985). *Human motivation.* Glenview, IL: Scott, Foresman.

McClelland, D. C., & Kirshnit, D. (1982). *Effects of motivational arousal on immune functions.* Unpublished manuscript, Harvard University, Department of Psychology and Social Relations.

McCrae, R., & John, O. (1992). An introduction to the five-factor model and its applications. *Journal of Personality, 60,* 175–210.

McCullough, M. E. (1995). Prayer and health: Conceptual issues, research review, and research agenda. *Journal of Psychology and Theology, 23*(1), 15–29.

McCullough, M. E. (2000). Forgiveness as human strength: Theory, measurement, and links to well-being. *Journal of Social & Clinical Psychology, 19*(1), 43–55.

McCullough, M. E., & Snyder, C. R. (2000). Classical source of human strength: Revisiting an old home and building a new one. *Journal of Social & Clinical Psychology, 19*(1), 1–10.

McFadden, S. H. (1995). Religion and well-being in aging persons in an aging society. *Journal of Social Issues, 51*(2), 161–175.

McGregor, I., & Little, B. R. (1998). Personal projects, happiness, and meaning. On doing well and being yourself. *Journal of Personality and Social Psychology, 74,* 494–512.

McQuillan, J., & Conde, G. (1996). The conditions of flow in reading: Two studies of optimal experience. *Reading Psychology: An International Quarterly, 17,* 109–135.

Meadows, M. J., & Kahoe, R. D. (1984). *The psychology of religion: Religion in individual lives.* New York: Harper & Row.

Medalie, J. H., & Goldbourt, U. (1976). Angina pectoris among 10,000 men, II: Psychosocial and other risk factors. *American Journal of Medicine, 60,* 910–921.

Medalie, J. H., Strange, K. C., Zyzanski, S. J., & Goldbourt, U. (1992). The importance of biopsychosocial factors in the development of duodenal ulcer in a cohort of middle-aged men. *American Journal of Epidemiology, 10,* 1280–1287.

Menard, V. (2003). *Latinas in love: A modern guide to love and relationships.* New York: Marlowe.

Middlebrook, P. N. (1980). *Social psychology and modern life.* New York: Alfred Knopf.

Mikulus, W. L. (2002). *The integrative helper: Convergence of Eastern and Western traditions.* Pacific Grove, CA: Brooks/Cole.

Moody, R. (1975). *Life after life.* Covington, CA: Mockingbird.

Morretti, M. M., & Higgins, E. T. (1990). Relating self-discrepancy to self-esteem: The contribution of discrepancies beyond actual-self ratings. *Journal of Experimental Social Psychology, 26,* 108–123.

Morris, W. N. (1999). The mood system. In D. Kahneman, E. Diener, & N. Schwarz (Eds.). *Well-being: The foundations of hedonic psychology* (169–189). New York: Russell Sage Foundation.

Moskowitz, D. S., & Cote, S. (1995). Do interpersonal traits predict affect? A comparison of three models. *Journal of Personality and Social Psychology, 69,* 915–924.

Mroczek, D. K., & Kolarz, C. M. (1998). The effect of age on a positive and negative affect: A development perspective on happiness. *Journal of Personality and Social Psychology, 75,* 1333–1349.

Murphy, M., & Donovan, S. (1997). *The physical and psychological effects of meditation: A review of contemporary research with a comprehensive bibliography.* Sausalito, CA: Institute of Noetic Sciences.

Murphy, M. M. (1998). *Character education in America's blue ribbon schools: Best practices for meeting the challenge.* Joliet, IL: College of St. Francis.

Murray, S. L., & Holmes, J. G. (1997). A leap of faith? Positive illusions in romantic relationships. *Personality and Social Psychology Bulletin, 23*(6), 586–604.

Murray, S., Holmes, J., Dolderman, D., & Griffin, D. (2000). What the motivated mind sees: Comparing friends' perspectives to married partners' views of each other. *Journal of Experimental Social Psychology,* 36, 600–620.

Myers, D. G. (1992). *The pursuit of happiness.* New York: Avon Books.

Myers, D. G. (2000). The funds, friends, and faith of happy people. *American Psychologist, 55*(1), 56–67.

Myers, D. G., & Diener, E. (1995). Who is happy? *Psychological Science, 6,* 10–19.

Nakamura, J., & Csikszentmihalyi, M. (2002). The concept of flow. In C. R. Snyder & S J. Lopez (Eds.), *Handbook of Positive Psychology* (pp. 89–105). New York: Oxford University Press.

Nauta, A., Brooks, J. D., Johnson, J. R., Kahana, E., & Kahana, B. (1996). Egocentric and nonegocentric life events: Effects on the health and subjective well-being of the aged. *Journal of Clinical Geropsychology, 2*(1), 3–21.

Neulinger, J. (1974). *The psychology of leisure.* Springfield, IL.: Charles C. Thomas.

Newburg, D., Kimieck, J., Durand-Bush, N., & Doell, K. (2002). The role of resonance in performance excellence and life engagement. *Journal of Applied Sport Psychology, 14,* 249–267.

Nicholls, J. G. (1972). Creativity in the person who will never produce anything original and useful: The concept of creativity as a normally distributed trait. *American Psychologist,* 27(8), 717–727.

Nolen-Hoeksema, S. (1991). Responses to depression and their effects on the duration of depressive episodes. *Journal of Abnormal Psychology, 100*(4), 569–582.

Nolen-Hoeksema, S., & Rusting, C. L. (1999). Gender differences in well-being. In D. Kahneman, E. Diener, & N. Schwarz (Eds.), *Well-being: The foundations of hedonic psychology* (pp. 330–352). New York: Russell Sage Foundation.

Norwich, J. J. (Ed.). (1975). *Great architecture of the world.* New York: Random House.

Nuckolls, K., Cassel, J., & Kaplan, B. (1972). Psychosocial assets, life crisis and the prognosis of pregnancy. *American Journal of Epidemiology, 95,* 431–441.

O'Connell, B., & Palmer, S. (Eds.) (2003). *Handbook of solution-focused therapy.* Newbury Park, CA: Sage Publications.

Ogilvie, D. M. (1987). Life satisfaction and identity structure in late middle-aged men and women. *Psychology & Aging, 2*(3), 217–224.

Oishi, S., & Diener, E. (2001). Re-examining the general positivity model of subjective well-being: The discrepancy between specific and global domain satisfaction. *Journal of Personality, 69*(4), 641–666.

Oishi, S., Diener, E., & Lucas, R. E. (1999). Cross-cultural variations in predictors of life satisfaction: Perspectives from needs and values. *Personality & Social Psychology Bulletin, 25*(8), 980–990.

Oishi, S., Diener, E., & Suh, E. (1999). Value as a moderator in subjective well-being. *Journal of Personality, 67*(1), 157–184.

Oishi, S., Diener, E., Suh, E., & Lucas, R. E. (1999). Value as a moderator in subjective well-being. *Journal of Personality, 67*(1), 157–184.

Okun, M. A., & Stock, W. A. (1987). Correlates and components of subjective well-being among the elderly. *Journal of Applied Gerontology, 6,* 95–112.

Okun, M. A., Stock, W. A., Haring, M. J., & Witter, R. A. (1984). Health and subjective well-being: A meta-analysis, *International Journal of Aging and Human Development, 19,* 111–132.

O'Leary, V., & Ickovics, J. (1995). Resilience and thriving in response to challenge: An opportunity for a paradigm shift in women's health. *Women's Health: Research on Gender, Behavior, and Policy, 1,* 121–142.

Ostir, G., Markides, K., Black, S., & Goodwin, J. (2000). Emotional well-being predicts subsequent functional independence and survival. *Journal of the American Geriatric Society, 48,* 473–478.

Otto, R. (1958). *The idea of the holy.* New York: Oxford Press.

Ouellette, S. C. (1993). Inquiries into hardiness. In L. Goldberger & S. Breznitz (Eds.), *Handbook of stress: Theoretical and clinical aspects* (2nd ed.) (pp. 77–100). New York: Free Press.

Pajares, F. (2001). Toward a positive psychology of academic motivation. *Journal of Educational Research, 95*(1), 27–35.

Paloutzian, R. (1981). Purpose in life and value changes following conversion. *Journal of Personality and Social Psychology, 41*(6), 1153–1160.

Paloutzian, R. F., Richardson, J. T., & Rambo, L. R. (1999). Religious conversion and personality change. *Journal of Personality, 67,* 1047–1079.

Panzarella, R. (1980). Aesthetic peak experiences. *Journal of Humanistic Psychology, 20,* 69–85.

Pargament, K. I., Smith, B. W., Koenig, H. G., & Perez, L. M. (1998). Patterns of positive and negative religious coping with major life stressors. *Journal for the Scientific Study of Religion, 37*(4), 710–724.

Park, C. L., & Folkman, S. (1997). Meaning in the context of stress and coping. *Review of General Psychology, 1*(2), 115–144.

Parlee, M. B. (1979, October). The friendship bond. *Psychology Today,* p.53.

Parrott, W. G. (1993). Beyond hedonism: Motives for inhibiting good moods and for maintaining bad moods. In D. M. Wegner & J. W. Pennebaker (Eds.). *Century Psychology Series. Handbook of mental control* (pp. 278–305). Upper Saddle River, NJ: Prentice-Hall.

Pascual-Leone, J. (1990). An essay on wisdom: Toward organismic processes that make it possible. In R. J. Sternberg (Ed.). *Wisdom: Its nature, origins, and development* (pp. 244–278). Cambridge, NY: Cambridge University Press.

Paulhus, D. L., Heine, S. J., & Lehman, D. R. (2000, February). *Variants of self-enhancement.* Paper presented at the First annual meeting of the Society for Personality and Social Psychology, Nashville, TN.

Pavot, W., Diener, E., & Fujita, F. (1990). Extraversion and happiness. *Personality and Individual Differences, 11,* 1299–1306.

Paykel, E. S. (1979). Recent life events in the development of the depressive disorders. In R. A. Depu (Ed.), *The psychology of the depressive disorders: Implications for the effects of stress* (pp. 245–262). New York: Academic Press.

Peacock, J. R., & Poloma, M. M. (1999). Religiosity and life satisfaction across the life course. *Social Indicators Research 48,* 321–345.

Peng, C. K., Havlin, S., Stanley, H. E., & Goldberger, A. L. (1995). Quantification of scaling exponents and crossover phenomena in nonstationary heartbeat time series. *Chaos* (5)582–87.

Peng, C. K., Mietus, J., Hausdorff, J. M., Havlin, S., Stanley, H. E., & Goldberger, A. L. (1993). Long-range anticorrelations and non-Gaussian behavior of the heartbeat. *Physicians Review Letters* (70)1343–1346.

Pennebaker, J. W. (1993). Putting stress into words: Health, linguistic, and therapeutic implications. *Behavior Research and Therapy, 31,* 539–548.

Pennebaker, J. W. (1997). *Opening up: The healing power of expressing emotions* (rev. ed). New York, Guilford Press.

Pennebaker, J. W., Kiecolt-Glaser, J. K., & Glaser, R. (1988). Disclosure of trauma and immune function: Health implications for psychotherapy. *Journal of Consulting and Clinical Psychology, 56,* 239–245.

Pert, C. B. (1997). *Molecules of emotion: Why you feel the way you feel.* New York: Scribner.

Pesechkian, N. (1997). *Positive psychotherapy: Theory and practice of a new method.* Berlin: Springer-Verlag.

Pesechkian, N., & Tritt, K. (1998). Positive psychotherapy: Effectiveness study and quality assurance. *European Journal of Psychotherapy, Counseling, and Health, 1,* 93–104.

Peterson, C. (1999). Personal control and well-being. In D. Kahneman, D. Diener, & Schwarz (Eds.). *Well-being: The foundations of hedonic psychology* (288–301). New York: Russell Sage Foundation.

Peterson, C. (2000). The future of optimism. *American Psychologist, 55*(1), 44–55.

Peterson, C., & Seligman, M. E. P. (2004). *Character strengths and virtues: A handbook and classification.* New York: Oxford University Press/Washington, DC: American Psychological Association.

Peterson, C., & Steen, T. A. (2002). Optimistic explanatory style. In C. R. Snyder & S. J. Lopez (Eds.), *Handbook of positive psychology* (pp. 244–256). New York: Oxford University Press.

Peterson, C., & Stunkard, A. J. (1989). Personal control and health promotion. *Social Science and Medicine, 28,* 819–828.

Peterson, C., Seligman, M. E., & Vaillant, G. E. (1988). Pessimistic explanatory style is a risk factor for physical illness: A thirty-five-year longitudinal study. *Journal of Personality & Social Psychology, 55*(1), 23–27.

Pfeffer, J. (1998). *The human equation: Building profits by putting people first.* Boston, MA: Harvard Business School Press.

Phares, E. J., & Trull, T. J. (1997). *Clinical psychology: Concepts, methods, and profession* (5th ed.). Monterey, CA.: Wadsworth.

Piedmont, R. I. (1999). Does spirituality represent a sixth factor of personality? Spiritual transcendence and the five-factor model. *Journal of Personality, 67*(6), 985–1014.

Pinder, C. C. (1998). *Work motivation in organizational behavior.* Upper Saddle River, NJ: Prentice-Hall.

Plutchik, R. (1980). *Emotion: A psychoevolutionary synthesis.* New York: Harper & Row.

Pollner, M. (1989). Divine relations, social relations, and well-being. *Journal of Health and Social Behavior, 30*(1), 92–104.

Poloma, M. M., & Pendeleton, B. F. (1990). Religious domains and general well-being. *Social Indicators Research, 22,* 255–276.

Pratt, M. W., Norris, J. E., Arnold, M. L., & Filyer, R. (1999). Generativity and moral development as predictors of value-socialization narratives for young persons across the adult life span: From lessons learned to stories shared. *Psychology & Aging, 14*(3), 414–426.

Price, W. F., & Crapo, R. H. (2002). *Cross-cultural perspectives in introductory psychology* (4th ed.). Pacific Grove, CA: Wadsworth.

Privette, G. (1965, May). Transcendent functioning. *Teachers College Record,* 733–739.

Privette, G. (1981). Dynamics of peak performance. *J. Humanistic Psychology, 21*(1), 57–67.

Privette, G. (1983). Peak experience, peak performance, and flow: A comparative analysis of positive human experiences. *Journal of Personality and Social Psychology, 45*(6), 1361–1368.

Privette, G., & Landsman, T. (1983). Factor analysis of peak performance: The full use of potential. *Journal of Personality and Social Psychology, 44*(1), 195–200.

Progoff, I. (1983). *Life-study: Experiencing creative lives by the intensive journal method.* New York: Dialogue House.
Progoff, I. (1992). *At a journal workshop* (Rev. Ed.). Los Angeles: J. P. Tarcher.
Rahula, W. (1974). *What the Buddha taught.* New York: Grove Press.
Rappaport, J. (1977). *Community psychology: Values, research, and action.* New York: Holt, Rinehart, & Winston.
Rappaport, J., & Seidman, E. (Eds.) (2000). *Handbook of Community Psychology.* New York: Kluwer/Plenum.
Rathunde, K. (1988). Optimal experience and the family context. In M. Csikszentmihalyi & I. S. Csikszentmihalyi (Eds.), *Optimal Experience* (pp. 342–363). Cambridge: Cambridge University Press.
Rathunde, K. (2001). Toward a psychology of optimal human functioning: What positive psychology can learn from the "experiential turns" of James, Dewey, and Maslow. *Journal of Humanistic Psychology, 41*(1), 135–153.
Rich, G. J. (2002). *Massage therapy: The evidence for practice.* New York: Mosby Harcourt Health Sciences.
Richards, R., Kinney, D. K., Lunde, I., & Benet, M. (1988). Creativity in manic-depressives, cyclothymes, their normal relatives, and control subjects. *Journal of Abnormal Psychology, 97*(3), 281–288.
Ring, K. (1980). *Life at death: A scientific investigation of the near-death experience.* New York: Coward, McCann, & Georghegan.
Ritchart, R., & Perkins, D. N. (2002). Life in the mindful classroom: Nurturing the disposition of mindfulness. *Journal of Social Issues, 56*(1), 27–47.
Robinson, D. N. (1990). Wisdom through the ages. In R. J. Sternberg (Ed.), *Wisdom: Its nature, origins, and development* (pp. 13–24). Cambridge, UK: Cambridge University Press.
Robinson, D., & Groves, J. (1998). *Introducing philosophy.* New York: Totem Books.
Robinson, M. D., & Ryff, C. D. (1999). The role of self-deception in perceptions of past, present, and future happiness. *Personality & Social Psychology Bulletin, 25*(5), 595–606.
Robitschek, C. (1998). Personal growth initiative: The construct and its measure. *Measurement & Evaluation in Counseling & Development, 30*(4), 183–198.
Robitschek, C., & Cook, S. W. (1999). The influence of personal growth initiative and coping styles on career exploration and vocational identity. *Journal of Vocational Behavior, 54*(1), 127–141.
Robitschek, C., & Kashubeck, S. (1999). A structural model of parental alcoholism, family functioning, and psychological health: The mediating effects of hardiness and personal growth orientation. *Journal of Counseling Psychology, 46,* 159–172.
Rogers, C. R. (1959). A theory of therapy, personality, and interpersonal relationships as developed in the client-centered framework. In S. Koch (Ed.), *Psychology: A study of a science* (p. 3) New York: McGraw-Hill.
Rogers, C. R. (1961). *On becoming a person.* Boston: Houghton Mifflin.
Rogers, S. J., & Amato, P. R. (1997). Is marital quality declining? The evidence from two generations [Electronic Version]. *Social Forces, 75*(3), 1089–1101.
Rogers, S. J., & Amato, P. R. (2000). Have changes in gender relations affected marital quality? [Electronic Version]. *Social Forces, 79*(2), 731.
Rollins, B. C., & Cannon, R. L. (1974). Marital satisfaction over the family life cycle. *Journal of Marriage and the Family, 36,* 271–282.
Ross, C. E., & Jang, S. J. (2000). Neighborhood disorder, fear, and mistrust: The buffering role of social ties with neighbors. *American Journal of Community Psychology, 28,* 401–420.
Rostad, F. G., & Long, B. C. (1996). Exercise as a coping strategy for stress: A review. *International Journal of Sports Psychology, 27,* 197–222.
Rothbaum, F., Weisz, J. R., & Snyder, S. S. (1982). Changing the world and changing the self: A two-process model of perceived control. *Journal of Personality and Social Psychology, 42,* 5–27.
Rothenberg, A. (1990). *Creativity and madness: New findings and old stereotypes.* Baltimore, MD: Johns Hopkins University Press.
Rotter, J. B. (1966). Generalized expectancies for internal versus external control of reinforcement. *Psychological Monographs: General and Applied, 81*(1), 1–28.
Ruch, W. (2001, October). *The sense of humor: Issues in the definition and assessment of a highly valued human strength.* Paper presented at the 2001 Positive Psychology Summit. Washington, DC.
Rusbult, C. E. (1991). Commentary on Johnson's "Commitment to personal relationships": What's interesting, and what's new? In W. H. Jones & D. Perlman (Eds.), *Advances in personal relationships* (Vol. 3, pp. 151–169). London: Jessica Kingsley.
Russek, L G., Schwartz, G. E . (1997). Perceptions of parental caring predict health status in midlife: A 35-year follow-up of the Harvard Mastery of Stress Study. *Psychosomatic Medicine, 59*(2), 144–149.
Rusting, C. L., & Larsen, R. J. (1998). Personality and cognitive processing of affective information. *Personality and Social Psychology Bulletin, 24*(2), 200–213.
Ryan, R. M., & Deci, E. L. (2000). Self-determination theory and the facilitation of intrinsic motivation, social development, and well-being. *American Psychologist, 55*(1), 68–78.
Ryan, R. M., & Deci, E. L. (2001). On happiness and human potentials: A review of research on hedonic and eudaimonic well-being. *Annual Review of Psychology, 52,* 141–166.
Ryff, C. D. (1985). Adult personality development and the motivation for personal growth. In D. Kleimer & M. Maehr (Eds.), *Advances in motivation and achievement: Motivation and adulthood. Vol. 4* (pp. 55–92). Greenwich, CT: JAI Press.
Ryff, C. D. (1989a). Beyond Ponce de Leon and life satisfaction: New directions in quest of successful ageing. *International Journal of Behavioral Development, 12*(1), 35–55.
Ryff, C. D. (1989b). Happiness is everything, or is it? Explorations on the meaning of psychological well-being,

Journal of Personality & Social Psychology, 57(6), 1069–1081.
Ryff, C. D. (1995). Psychological well-being in adult life. *Current Direction in Psychological Science, 4*(4), 99–104.
Ryff, C. D., & Heidrich, S. M. (1997). Experience and well-being: Explorations on domains of life and how they matter. *International Journal of Behavioral Development, 20*(2), 193–206.
Ryff, C. D., & Keyes, C. L. M. (1995). The structure of psychological well-being revised. *Journal of Personality and Social Psychology, 69*(4), 719–727.
Ryff, C. D., & Singer, B. (1998). The contours of positive human health. *Psychological Inquiry, 9*(1), 1–28.
Salovey, P. & Mayer, J. D. (1990). Emotional intelligence. *Imagination, Cognition and Personality, 9,* 185–211.
Salovey, P., Mayer, J. D., & Caruso, D. (2002). The positive psychology of emotional intelligence. In C. R. Snyder and S. J. Lopez (Eds.), *Handbook of positive psychology* (pp. 159–171). New York: Oxford University Press.
Salovey, P., Rothman, A., Detweiller, J., & Steward, W. (2000). Emotional states and physical health. *American Psychologist, 55*(1), 110–121.
Sampson, R. J. (2001a). How do communities undergird or undermine human development? Relevant contexts and social mechanisms. In A. Booth, & A. C. Crouter (Eds.), *Does it take a village?: Community effects on children, adolescents, and families* (pp. 3–30). Mahwah, NJ: Lawrence Erlbaum Associates.
Sampson, R. J. (2001b). Crime and public safety: Insights from community on social capital. In S. Saegert & J. P. Thompson (Eds.). *Social capital and poor communities* (89–114). New York: Russell Sage Foundation.
Sandage, S. J., & Hill, P. C. (2001). The virtues of positive psychology: The rapprochement and challenges of an affirmative postmodern perspective. *Journal of the Theory of Social Behavior, 31,* 241–260.
Sandvik, E., Diener, E., & Seidlitz, L. (1993). Subjective well-being: The convergence and stability of self-report and non-self-report measures. *Journal of Personality, 61,* 317–342.
Sarason, B. R., Sarason, I. G., & Pierce, G. R. (Eds.). (1990). *Social support: An interactional view.* New York: Wiley.
Sarason, S. B. (1990). *The challenge of art to psychology*. New Haven, CT: Yale University Press.
Sattler, D. N., & Shabatay, V. (1997). *Psychology in context: Voices and perspectives.* New York: Houghton-Mifflin.
Scheier, M., & Carver, C. (1985). Optimism, coping, and health: Assessment and implications of generalized outcome expectancies. *Health Psychology, 4*(3), 219–247.
Scheier, M., & Carver, C. (1987). Dispositional optimism and physical well-being: The influence of generalized outcome expectancies on health,. *Journal of Personality, 55*(2), 169–210.
Scheier, M. F., & Carver, C. S. (1992). Effects of optimism on psychological and physical well-being: Theoretical overview and empirical update. *Cognitive Therapy and Research, 16,* 201–228.
Schimmel, S. (1997). *The seven deadly sins: Jewish, Christian, and classical reflections on human psychology.* Oxford: Oxford University Press.
Schimmel, S. (2000). Vices, virtues and sources of human strength in historical perspective. *Journal of Social and Clinical Psychology, 19*(1), 137–150.
Schlaug, G (2001). The brain of musicians: A model for functional and structural adaptation. In R. J. Zatorre, & I. Peretz (Eds.), The biological foundations of music. *Annals of the New York Academy Sciences, Vol. 930* (pp. 281–299). New York: New York Academy of Science.
Schneider, K. J., Bugental, J. F. T., & Pierson, J. F. (Eds.). *The handbook of humanistic psychology: Leading edges in theory, research, and practice.* Thousand Oaks, CA: Sage Publications.
Schneider, S. (2001). In search of realistic optimism: meaning, knowledge, and warm fuzziness. *Journal of American Psychologist, 54*(3), 250–263.
Schultz, D. (1977). *Growth psychology: Models of the healthy personality.* Pacific Grove, CA: Brooks Cole.
Schwarz, N., & Clore, G. L. (1996). Feelings and phenomenal experiences. In E. T. Higgins & A. W. Kruglanski (Eds.). *Social psychology: Handbook of basic principles* (pp. 433–465). New York: Guilford.
Schyns, P. (1998). Cross-national differences in happiness: Economic and cultural factors explored. *Social Indicators Research, 43*(1–2), 3–26.
Scott, C. (Executive Producer). (1999, June 10). The cellist of Sarajevo. *All things considered* [radio broadcast]. New York and Washington, DC: National Public Radio.
Sedikides, C. (1992). Attentional effects on mood are moderated by self-conception valence. *Personality and Social Psychology Bulletin 18,* 580–584.
Sedikides, C. (1993). Assessment, enhancement, and verification determinants of the self-evaluation process. *Journal of Personality and Social Psychology 65,* 317–338.
Seeman, J. (1983). *Personality integration: Studies and reflections.* New York: Human Sciences Press.
Seeman, J. (1989). Toward a model of positive health. *American Psychologist, 44*(8), 1099–1109.
Seidlitz, L., & Diener, E. (1993). Memory for positive versus negative events: Theories for the differences between happy and unhappy persons. *Journal of Personality and Social Psychology, 64,* 654–664.
Seiffge-Krenke, L., & Schulman, S. (1990). Coping style in adolescence: A cross-cultural study. *Journal of Cross-Cultural Psychology, 21,* 351–377.
Seligman, M. E. P. (1975). *Helplessness: On depression, development, and death.* San Francisco. Freeman.
Seligman, M. E. P. (1990). *Learned optimism.* New York: Simon & Schuster.
Seligman, M. E. P. (1994). *What you can change and what you can't.* New York: Knopf.
Seligman, M. E. P. (1995). The effectiveness of psychotherapy: The Consumers Reports study. *American Psychologist, 50,* 965–974.
Seligman, M. E. P. (2000, October). *Positive psychology: A progress report.* Paper presented at the Positive Psychology Summit 2000. Washington, DC.
Seligman, M. E. P. (2002a). *Authentic happiness.* New York: Free Press.

Seligman, M. E. P. (2002b). Positive psychology, positive prevention, and positive therapy. In C. R. Snyder, & S. J. Lopez (Eds.), *Handbook of positive psychology* (pp. 3–13). New York: Oxford University Press.

Seligman, M. E. P., & Csikszentmihalyi, M. (2000). Positive psychology: An introduction. *American Psychologist, 55*(1), 5–14.

Seligman M. E. P., Reivich, K., Jaycox, L., & Gillham, J. (1995). *The optimistic child.* New York: Houghton Mifflin.

Seligman, M. E. P., Schulman, P., DeRubeis, R. J., & Hollon, S. D. (1999). *The prevention of depression and anxiety. Prevention and Treatment,* 2 [*http://journals.apa.org/prevention/].*

Sethi, S., & Seligman, M. E. P. (1993). Optimism and fundamentalism. *Psychological Science 4*(4), 256–259.

Shackelford, T. K., & Buss, D. M. (1997). Satisfaction in evolutionary psychological perspective. In. R. J. Sternberg & M. Hojjatt (Eds) (pp. 7–25). *Satisfaction in close relationships.* New York: Guilford Press.

Shapela, S. T. (with Cook, J., Horlitz, E., Leal, R., Luciano, S., Lutfy, E., et al.). (1999). Courageous resistance: A special case of altruism. *Theory & Psychology, 9*(6), 787–805.

Shapiro, A. F., Gottman, J. M., & Carrere, S. (2000). The baby and the marriage: Identifying factors that buffer against decline in marital satisfaction after the first baby arrives. *Journal of Family Psychology, 14*(1), 59–70.

Shedler, J., Mayman, M., & Manis, M. (1993). The illusion of mental health. *American Psychologist, 48*(11), 1117–1131.

Sheldon, K. M, Fredrickson, B., Rathunde, K., Csikszentmihalyi, M., & Haidt, J. (2000). *A positive psychology manifesto.* Retrieved October 1, 2002, from http://www.positive psychology.org/akumalmanifesto.htm.

Sheldon, K. M., & Kasser, T. (1998). Pursuing personal goals: Skills enable progress, but not all progress is beneficial. *Personality and Social Psychology Bulletin, 24*(12), 1319–1331.

Sheldon, K. M., & King, L. (2001). Why positive psychology is necessary. *American Psychologist, 54*(3), 216–217.

Sheldon, K. M., Ryan, R. M., Rawsthorne, L. J.& Ilardi, B. (1997). Trait self and true self: Cross-role variation in the big-five personality traits and its relations with psychological authenticity and subjective well-being. *Journal of Personality and Social Psychology, 73,* 1380–1393.

Sheler, J. L. (2001, July 2). Drugs, scalpel . . . and faith? Doctors are noticing the power of prayer. *U.S. News and World Report,* 46–47.

Shinn, M., & Toohey, S. M. (2003). Community contexts of human welfare. *Annual Review of Psychology, 54,* 427–459.

Siegal, J. M. (1990). Stressful life events and use of physician services among the elderly: The moderating role of pet ownership. *Journal of Personality and Social Psychology, 58,* 1081–1086.

Simon, S. B., Howe, L. W., & Kirschenbaum, H. (1972). *Values clarification: A handbook of practical strategies for teachers and students.* New York: Hart.

Simonton, D. K. (1988). Age and outstanding achievement: What do we know after a century of research? *Psychological Bulletin, 104,* 251–267.

Simonton, D. K. (1999). *Origins of genius: Darwinian perspectives on creativity.* New York: Oxford University Press.

Simonton, D. K. (2000). Creativity: Cognitive, personal, developmental, and social aspects. *American Psychologist, 55*(1), 151–158.

Simonton, D. K. (2002). Creativity. In C. R. Snyder, & S. J. Lopez (Eds.), *Handbook of positive psychology* (pp. 189–201). New York: Oxford University Press.

Simpson, J. A., Ickes, W., & Blackstone, T. (1995). When the head protects the heart: Empathic accuracy in dating relationships. *Journal of Personality and social Psychology, 69*(4), 629–641.

Singer, I. (1987). *The nature of love: The modern world* (vol. 3). Chicago, IL: University of Chicago Press.

Sirgy, M. J. (1998). Materialism and quality of life. *Social Indicators Research, 43,* 227–260.

Skolnick, A. (1981). Married lives: Longitudinal perspectives on marriage. In D. H. Eichorn, J. A. Clausen, N. Haan, M. P. Honzik, & P. H. Mussen (Eds.), *Present and past in middle life: Married life* (pp. 270–300). New York: Academic Press.

Slife, B. D. (1999). Methodological pluralism: A framework for psychotherapy research. *Journal of Clinical Psychology, 55*(12), 1453–1465.

Smith, H. (1976). *The forgotten truth: The primordial tradition.* New York: Harper & Row.

Smith, M. B. (1969). *Social psychology and human values.* Chicago, IL: Aldine.

Smith, W. (2001). *Hope Meadows: Real-life stories of healing and caring from an inspiring community.* New York: Berkley.

Smith, W., Compton, W., & West, B. (1995). Meditation as an adjunct to a happiness enhancement program. *Journal of Clinical Psychology, 51*(2), 269–273.

Smyth, J. M., & Pennebaker, J. W. (1999). Sharing one's story: Translating emotional experiences into words as a coping tool. In C. R. Snyder (Ed.), *Coping: The psychology of what works* (pp. 70–89). New York: Oxford Press.

Snyder, C. R. (1994). *The psychology of hope: You can get there from here.* New York: Free Press.

Snyder, C. R. (Ed.). (1999). *Coping: The psychology of what works.* New York: Oxford University Press.

Snyder, C. R., & Dinoff, B. L. (1999). Coping: Where have you been? In C. R. Snyder (Ed.). *Coping: The psychology of what works* (pp. 3–19). New York: Oxford University Press.

Snyder, C. R., & Lopez, S. J. (Eds.). (2002). *Handbook of positive psychology.* New York: Oxford University Press.

Snyder, C. R., McDermott, D., Cook, W., & Rapoff, M. (1997). *Hope for the journey: Helping children through the good times and the bad.* San Francisco: Harper Collins.

Snyder, C. R., Rand, K. L., & Sigmon, D. R. (2002). Hope theory: A member of the positive psychology family. In C. R. Snyder, & S. J. Lopez (Eds.), *Handbook of positive psychology* (pp. 257–276). London: Oxford University Press.

Snyder, M., Clary, E. G., & Stukas, A. A. (2000). The functional approach to volunteerism. In G. R. Maio & J. M. Olson (Eds.). *Why we evaluate: Functions of attitudes* (pp. 365–393). Mahwah, NJ: Lawrence Erlbaum Associates.

Sosa, R., Kennell, J., Klaus, M., Robertson, S., & Urrutia, J. (1980). The effect of a supportive companion on perinatal problems, length of labor and mother-infant interaction. *New England Journal of Medicine, 303,* 597–600.

Spiegel, D., Kraemer, H. C., Bloom, J. R., & Gottheil, E. (1989, October 14). Effect of psychosocial treatment on survival of patients with metastatic breast cancer. *Lancet,* 2(8668), pp. 888–891.

Stanton, A. L., Parsa, A., & Austenfield, J. L. (2002).The adaptive potential of coping through emotional approach. In C. R. Snyder & S. J. Lopez (Eds.), *Handbook of positive psychology* (pp. 148–158). Oxford: Oxford University Press.

Stark, M. J., & Washburn, M. C. (1977). Beyond the norm: A speculative model of self-realization. *Journal of Religion and Health, 16*(1).

Staw, B. (2000, October). *The role of dispositional affect in job satisfaction and performance.* Paper presented at the Positive Psychology Summit. Washington, DC.

Steinitz, L. Y. (1980). Religiosity, well-being and weltanschauung among the elderly. *Journal for the Scientific Study of Religion, 19,* 60–67

Sternberg, R. J. (1986). A triangular theory of love. *Psychological Review, 93,* 119–135.

Sternberg, R. J. (Ed.). (1990). *Wisdom: Its nature, origins, and development.* Cambridge: Cambridge University Press.

Sternberg, R. J. (Ed.). (1999). *Handbook of creativity.* New York, NY. Cambridge University Press.

Sternberg, R. J. (2000). Images of mindfulness. *Journal of Social Issues, 56*(1), 11–26.

Sternberg, R. J. (2004, April). *Culture and intelligence.* Paper presented at the Fiftieth annual meeting of the Southwestern Psychological Association, San Antonio, TX.

Sternberg, R. J., & Hojjat, M. (1997). *Satisfaction in close relationships.* New York: Guilford Press.

Sternberg, R. J., & Lubart, T. I. (1995). Defying the crowd: Cultivating creativity in a culture of conformity. New York : Free Press.

Stirling, D., Archibald, G., McKay, L., & Berg, S. (2000). *Character education Connections: For School, home and community.* St. Louis, MO: Cooperating School Districts.

Stokols, D. (2003). The ecology of human strengths. In L. G. Aspinall & U. M. Staudinger (Eds.), *A psychology of human strengths: Fundamental questions and future directions for a positive psychology* (pp. 311–344). Washington, DC: American Psychological Association.

Stone-McCown, K., Jensen, A. L., Freedman, J. M., & Rideout, M. C. (1998). *Self-science: The emotional intelligence curriculum* (2nd ed.). San Mateo, CA: Six Seconds.

Stossel, J. (Producer). (1997, September 4). "The mystery of happiness: Who has it and how to get it" [television broadcast]. New York: 20/20 ABC News Special.

Strack, F., Argyle, M., & Schwarz., N. (1991). *Subjective well-being.* Oxford: Pergamon Press.

Strickland, B. R. (1978). Internal-external expectancies and health-related behaviors. *Journal of Consulting & Clinical Psychology, 46*(6), 1192–1211.

Suh, E. M. (1999). Culture, identity, consistency, and subjective well-being. *Dissertation Abstracts International, 60-09* (Sect B): 4950.

Suh, E. M., Diener, E., & Fujita, F. (1996). Events and subjective well-being: Only recent events matter. *Journal of Personality and Social Psychology, 70,* 1091–1102.

Suh, E. M., Diener, E., Oishi, S., & Triandis, H. (1998). The shifting basis of life satisfaction judgments across cultures: Emotions versus norms. *Journal of Personality and Social Psychology, 74*(2), 482–493.

Suzuki, D. T., Fromm, E., & De Martino, R. (1960). *Zen Buddhism and psychoanalysis.* New York: Harper & Row.

Swann, W. B., Jr., Hixon, J. G., & De La Ronde, C. (1992). Embracing the "bitter truth": Negative self-concepts and marital commitment, *Psychological Science, 3,* 118–121.

Tardif, T. Z., & Sternberg, R. J. (1988). What do we know about creativity? In R. J. Sternberg (Ed.), *The nature of creativity* (pp. 429–440) New York: Cambridge University Press.

Tarnas, R. (1991). *The passion of the western mind: Understanding the ideas that have shaped our world view.* New York: Ballantine.

Tashiro, T., Frazier, P., Humbert, R., & Smith, J. (2001, October). *Personal growth following romantic relationship breakups.* Poster presented at the 2001 Positive Psychology Summit, Washington, DC.

Tatarkiewicz, W. (1976). *Analysis of happiness.* The Hague: Martinus Nijhoff.

Taylor, C. (1989). *Sources of the self: The making of the modern identity.* Cambridge, MA: Harvard University Press.

Taylor, S. (1989). *Positive illusions: Creative self-deception and the healthy mind.* New York: Basic Books.

Taylor, S., & Brown, J. (1988). Illusion and well-being: A social psychological perspective on mental health. *Psychological Bulletin, 103*(2), 193–210.

Taylor, S., Kemeny, M., Reed, G., Bower, J., & Gruenewald, T. (2000). Psychological resources, positive illusions, and health. *American Psychologist, 55*(1), 99–109.

Tedeschi, R. G., & Calhoun, L. G. (1995). *Trauma and transformation: Growing in the aftermath of suffering.* Thousand Oaks, CA: Sage Publications.

Telfer, E. (1980), *Happiness.* New York: St. Martin's Press.

Tellegen, A., Lykken, D. T., Bouchard, T. J., Wilcox, K. J., Segal, N. L., & Rich, S. (1988). Personality similarity in twins reared apart and together. *Journal of Personality and Social Psychology, 54,* 1031–1039.

Terkel, S. (1974). *Working: People talk about what they do all day and how they feel about what they do.* New York: Pantheon.

Terman, L. M., Buttenweiser, P., Ferguson, L. W., Johnson, W. B., & Wilson, D. P. (1938). *Psychological factors in marital happiness.* New York: McGraw-Hill.

Tharp, T. (2003). *The creative habit.* New York: Simon & Schuster.

Thayer, R. E., Newman, J. R., & McClain, T. M. (1994). Self-regulation of mood: Strategies for changing in a bad mood, raising energy, and reducing tension. *Journal of Personality and Social Psychology, 67,* 910–25.

Thompson, S. C., & Janigian, A. S. (1988). Life schemes: A framework for understanding the search for meaning. *Journal of Social and Clinical Psychology,* 7(2/3), 260–280.

Thoreau, H. D. (1980). *Walden or, life in the woods and On the duty of civil disobedience.* New York: New American Library. (Original work published in 1854.)

Thorson, J. A., Powell, F. C., Sarmany-Schuller, I., & Hampes, W. P. (1997). Psychological health and sense of humor. *Journal of Clinical Psychology 53*(6), 605–619.

Tice, D. M., Butler, J. L., Muraven, M. B., & Stillwell, A. M. (1995). When modesty prevails: Differential favorability of self-presentation to friends and strangers. *Journal of Personality and Social Psychology, 69*(6), 1120–1138.

Trope, I., Rozin, P., Nelson, D. K., & Gur, R. C. (1986). Information processing in separated hemispheres of the callosotomy patients. Does the analytic-holistic dichotomy hold? *Brain and Cognition, 19,* 123–147.

Trotter, R. J. (1986, July). The mystery of mastery. *Psychology Today,* 32–38.

Trull, T. J., & Phares, E. J. (2001). *Clinical psychology: Concepts, methods, and profession* (6th Ed.). Monterey, CA: Wadsworth/Thomson Learning.

Turner, N., Barling, J., & Epitropaki, O. (2002). Transformational leadership and moral reasoning. *Journal of Applied Psychology, 87*(2), 304–311.

Turner, N., Barling, J., & Zacharatos, A. (2002). Positive psychology at work. In C. R. Snyder, S. J., & Lopez (Eds.), *Handbook of positive psychology* (pp. 715–728). London: Oxford University Press.

U.S. Department of Health and Human Services. (2000). *Healthy people 2000: National health promotion and disease prevention objectives.* DHHS Publication No. (PHS) 91–50213. Washington, DC: U.S. Government Printing Office.

United Way of America. (1992). *What lies ahead: A decade of decision.* Alexandria, VA: United Way Strategic Institute.

Vaillant, G. E. (1977). *Adaptation to life.* Boston: Little Brown.

Vaillant, G. E. (2000). Adaptive mental mechanisms: Their role in a positive psychology. *American Psychologist, 55*(1), 89–98.

van Lommel, P. V., van Wees, R. V., Meyers, V., & Elfferich, I. (2001). Near-death experience in survivors of cardiac arrest: A prospective study in the Netherlands. *The Lancet, 358,* 2039–2045.

Van Zelst, R. (1951). Worker popularity and job satisfaction. *Personnel Psychology, 4,* 405–412.

Veehoven, R. (1999). World Database of Happiness. Erasmus University, Rotterdam, Netherlands. Web site: *http://www.eur.nl/fsw/research/happiness.*

Viney, W., & King, D. B. (1998). *A history of psychology: Ideas and context* (2nd. ed.). Boston: Allyn & Bacon.

Vingerhoets, A. J. J. M., Cornelius, R. R., Van Heck, G. L., & Becht, M. C. (2000). Adult crying: A model and review of the literature. *Review of General Psychology 4*(4), 354–377.

Wahba, M. A., & Bridwell, L. G. (1976). Maslow reconsidered: A review of research on the need hierarchy theory. *Organizational Behavior and Human Performance, 15,* 212–240.

Walker, C. (1977). Some variations in marital satisfaction. In R. Chester & J. Peel (Eds.), *Equalities and inequalities in family life* (pp. 127–139). London: Academic Press.

Wallas, G. (1926). *The Art of Thought.* New York: Harcourt, Brace.

Wapnick, K. (1980). Mysticism and schizophrenia. In R. Woods (Ed.), *Understanding mysticism.* Garden City, NY: Image Books.

Warr, P. (1990). The measurement of well-being and other aspects of mental health. *Journal of Occupational Psychology,* 63, 193–210.

Warr, P. (1999). Well-being and the workplace. In D. Kahneman, E. Diener, & N. Schwarz (Eds.). *Well-being: The foundations of hedonic psychology* (392–412). New York: Russell Sage.

Waterman, A. S. (1993). Two concepts of happiness: Contrasts of personal expressiveness (Eudaimonia) and hedonic enjoyment. *Journal of Personality and Social Psychology, 64*(4), 678–691.

Watson, D. (2002). Positive affectivity: The disposition to experience pleasurable emotional states. In C. R. Snyder & S. J. Lopez (Eds.), *Handbook of positive psychology* (pp. 106–119). New York: Oxford University Press.

Watson, D., & Clark, L. A. (1984). Negative affectivity: The disposition to experience aversive emotional states. *Psychological Bulletin,* 96, 465–490.

Watson, D., & Pennebaker, J. W. (1989). Health complaints, stress, and distress: Exploring the central role of negative affectivity. *Psychological Review, 96,* 234–254.

Webster, J. D. (2003). An exploratory analysis of a self-assessed wisdom scale. *Journal of Adult Development, 10*(1), 13–22.

Webster, J., Trevino, L. K., & Ryan, L. (1993). The dimensionality and correlates of flow in human computer interactions. *Computers in Human Behavior* 9(4), 411–426.

Wehmeyer, M. L. (1996). Self-determination as an educational outcome: Why is it important to children, youth and adults with disabilities? In D. J. Sands & M. L. Wehmeyer (Eds.), *Self-determination across the life span: Independence and choice for people with disabilities* (pp. 15–34). Baltimore: Paul H. Brookes.

Weinstein, N. D. (1980). Unrealistic optimism about future life events. *Journal of Personality and Social Psychology, 39*(5), 806–820.

Weisbord, M. R. (1987). *Productive workplaces: Organizing and managing for dignity, meaning, and community.* San Francisco: Jossey-Bass.

Welch, I. D., Tate, G. A., & Medeiros, D. C. (1987). *Self-actualization: An annotated bibliography of theory and research.* New York: Garland Publishing.

Wells, A. (1988). Self-esteem and optimal experience. In M. Csikszentmihalyi & I. Csikszentmihalyi (Eds.), *Optimal experience* (pp. 327–341). Cambridge: Cambridge University Press.

Welwood, J. (1997). *Love and awakening: Discovering the sacred path of intimate relationship.* New York: Harper Collins.

Werner, E. E. (1995). Resilience in development. *Current Directions in Psychological Science, 4*(3), 81–85.

Werner, E. E., & Smith, R. S. (1992). *Overcoming the odds: High risk children from birth to adulthood.* Ithaca, NY: Cornell University Press,

White, R. (1959). Motivation reconsidered: The concept of competence. *Psychological Review, 66,* 297–323.

Whitfield, K., Markham, H., Stanley, S., & Blumberg, S. (2001). *Fighting for your African American marriage.* San Francisco: Jossey-Bass.

Whittaker, A. E., & Robitschek, C. (2001). Multidimensional family functioning: Predicting personal growth initiative. *Journal of Counseling Psychology, 48*(4), 420–427.

Wierzbicka, A. (1986). Human emotions: Universal or culture-specific? *American Anthropologist, 88,* 584–594.

Wilbur, K. (2000). *Integral psychology.* Boston: Shambhala.

Williams, D., Spencer, M., Jackson, J., & Ashmore, R. (1999). Race, stress, and physical health: The role of group identity. In R. Contrada & R. Ashmore (Eds.). *Self, social identity and physical health* (pp. 71–100). New York: Oxford University Press.

Williams, J. M. (Ed.). (1993). *Applied sport psychology: personal growth to peak performance.* Mountain View, CA: Mayfield.

Williams, J. M., & Krane, V. (1993) Psychological characteristics of peak performance. In J. M Williams (Ed.), *Applied sport psychology: Personal growth to peak performance* (pp. 137–147). Mountain View, CA: Mayfield.

Williamson, G. M. (2002). Aging well: Outlook for the 21st century. . In C. R. Snyder & S. J. Lopez (Eds.), *Handbook of positive psychology* (pp. 676–686). New York: Oxford University Press.

Wilson, S. R., & Spenser, R. C. (1990). Intense personal experiences: Subjective effects, interpretations, and after-effects. *Journal of Clinical Psychology, 46*(5), 565–573.

Wilson, W. (1967). Correlates of avowed happiness. *Psychological Bulletin, 67*(4), 294–306.

Wink, P., & Helson, R. (1997). Practical and transcendental wisdom: Their nature and some longitudinal findings. *Journal of Adult Development, 4,* 1–15.

Winner, E. (2000). The origins and ends of giftedness. *American Psychologist, 55*(1), 159–169.

Witter, R., Stock, W. A., Okun, M. A., & Haring, M. J. (1985). Religion and subjective well-being in adulthood: A quantitative synthesis. *Review of Religious Research, 26,* 332–42.

Wolin, S., & Wolin. S. (2000, October). *The struggle to be strong: Resilience as process.* Paper presented at the Positive Psychology Summit 2000. Washington, DC.

Women's Own (1974). A questionaire. October 12, 1974.

Wood, W., Rhodes, N., & Whelan, M. (1989). Sex differences in positive well-being. A consideration of emotional style and marital status. *Psychological Bulletin,* 106, 249–264.

Woods, R. (1980). *Understanding mysticism.* New York: Image Books.

Woolfolk, R. L. (2002). The power of negative thinking: Truth, melancholia, and the tragic sense of life. *Journal of Theoretical & Philosophical Psychology, 22*(1), 19–27.

World Health Organization. (1948). *Constitution of the World Health Organization.* Geneva, Switzerland: Author.

World Values Study Group (1994). World Values Survey 1981–1984 and 1990–1993. Inter-University Consortium for Political and Social Research (ICPSR) version (computer file). Ann Arbor: Institute for Social Research, University of Michigan.

Wright, B. A., & Lopez, S. J. Widening the diagnostic focus: A case for including human strengths and environmental resources. In C. R. Snyder & S. J. Lopez (Eds.), *Handbook of positive psychology* (pp. 26–62). New York: Oxford Press.

Wright, S. S. (2000). Looking at the self in a rose-colored mirror: Unrealistically positive self-views and academic performance. *Journal of Social & Clinical Psychology, 19*(4), 451–462.

Wrzesniewski, A., McCauley, C., Rozin, P., & Schwartz, B. (1997). Jobs, careers, and callings: People's relations to their work. *Journal of Research in Personality, 31*(1), 21–33.

Yalom, I. D. (1980). *Existential psychotherapy.* New York: Basic Books.

Yang, K. S. (1982). Causal attributions of academic success and failure and their affective consequences. *Chinese Journal of Psychology (Taiwan), 24,* 65–83. (Abstract only in English.)

Zatorre, R. J., & Peretz, I. (Eds.). (2001). *The biological foundations of music.* New York: New York Academy of Science.

Zautra, A. J., & Reich, J. W. (1981). Positive events and quality of life. *Evaluation and Program Planning, 4,* 355–361.

Zimmerman, M. A. (1990). Toward a theory of learned hopefulness: A structural model analysis of participation and empowerment. *Journal of Research in Personality, 24,* 71–86.

Zinnbauger, B. J., Pargament, K. I., & Scott, A. B. (1999). The emerging meanings of religiousness and spirituality: Problems and prospects. *Journal of Personality, 67*(6), 889–920.

Name Index

Subject Index